The Earliest English Kings

The Earliest English Kings

D. P. KIRBY

London
UNWIN HYMAN
Boston   Sydney   Wellington

Published by the Academic Division of
Unwin Hyman Ltd
15/17 Broadwick Street, London W1V 1FP, UK

Unwin Hyman Inc.,
955 Massachusetts Avenue, Cambridge, Mass., 02139, USA

Allen & Unwin (Australia) Ltd,
8 Napier Street, North Sydney, NSW 2060, Australia

Allen & Unwin (New Zealand) Ltd in association with the
Port Nicholson Press Ltd,
Compusales Building, 75 Ghuznee Street, Wellington 1, New Zealand

First published in 1991

British Library Cataloguing in Publication Data

Kirby, D. P. (David Peter) *1936–*
    The earliest English kings: studies in the political
history of the Anglo–Saxon heptarchy, c.575–875.
    1.   England. Kings, to 1154
    I. Title
    940.12

ISBN 0–04–445691–3
ISBN 0–04–445692–1 pbk

Library of Congress Cataloging in Publication Data

Available on request from the Library of Congress

Typeset in 10/12 Bembo
Printed by The University Press, Cambridge

Contents

Abbreviations

AC *Annales Cambriae*, ed. E. Phillimore, 'The *Annales Cambriae* and the old Welsh genealogies from Harleian MS 3859', *Y Cymmrodor*, vol. 9 (1888), pp. 141–83, and *Annales Cambriae*, ed. J. W. ab Ithel (Rolls series: London, 1860), the Harleian annals translated by J. Morris, *Nennius* (Chichester, 1980)

ASC *Anglo-Saxon Chronicle*, ed. B. Thorpe, 2 vols (Rolls series: London, 1861), currently being re-edited by D. Dumville and S. Keynes, *The Anglo-Saxon Chronicle: A Collaborative Edition* (Cambridge, 1983-), and translated *The Anglo-Saxon Chronicle*, ed. D. Whitelock, D. C. Douglas and S. I. Tucker (London, 1961)

AT *Annals of Tigernach*, ed. W. Stokes, *Revue Celtique*, vol. 17 (1896)

AU *Annals of Ulster (to A.D. 1131)*, Part I, ed. S. Mac Airt and G. Mac Niocaill (Dublin Institute of Advanced Studies, 1983)

BAR British Archaeological Reports

ByT *Brut y Tywysogion or Chronicle of the Princes*, ed. and trans. T. Jones, 4 vols (Board of Celtic Studies, University of Wales History and Law Series, nos VI, XI, XVI, XXV: Cardiff, 1941–71)

CA K. Gabrowski and D. Dumville, *Chronicles and Annals of Mediaeval Ireland and Wales* (Woodbridge, Suffolk, 1984)

CBA Council for British Archaeology

CS *Cartularium Saxonicum*, ed. W. de Gray Birch, 3 vols (London, 1885–93)

EHD *English Historical Documents*, Vol. I, *c. 550–1042*, ed. D. Whitelock (2nd edn, 1979)

HB *Historia Brittonum*, ed. T. Mommsen, *Chronica Minora*, Vol. III, *MGH Auctores Antiq.*, Vol. XIII (Berlin, 1894), currently being re-edited by D. N. Dumville, *The Historia Brittonum* (Cambridge, 1985-), and translated J. Morris, *Nennius* (London and Chichester, 1980)

HE *Historia Ecclesiastica*, ed. C. Plummer, *Venerabilis Baedae Opera Historica*, 2 vols (Oxford, 1892, 1896) and ed. and trans. B. Colgrave and R. A. B. Mynors, *Bede's Ecclesiastical History of the English People* (Oxford, 1969)

MGH *Monumenta Germaniae Historica*

S P. H. Sawyer, *Anglo-Saxon Charters: An Annotated List and Bibliography* (Royal Historical Society Guides and Handbooks, no. 8: London, 1968)

List of figures

x

*Dedicated to the memory of
Martin Kirby*

Preface

This book has drawn principally upon the evidence of the written texts of pre-Viking England – charters, king-lists, genealogies, annals (in particular the *Anglo-Saxon Chronicle*), saints' *Lives* and Bede's *Ecclesiastical History of the English People* – to illuminate political and military activity among the rulers of the several kingdoms of the Anglo-Saxon 'heptarchy' from the end of Roman Britain until the Scandinavian invasions of the second half of the ninth century when the heptarchy collapsed in the face of Viking attack. Ecclesiastical matters are dealt with only in so far as they involve political action.

The source-record is rich and varied but it is fragmentary and incomplete. It does not tell the historian everything that he would wish to know, nor does it answer all his many questions. Rather, it illuminates fitfully and for short periods only what are really often little more than local developments in early England. The *Anglo-Saxon Chronicle*, for example, is not a national history but a sequence of irregularly sustained, generally quite cryptic annals relating almost entirely to the kings of Wessex, and Bede's natural preoccupation in his *Ecclesiastical History* with spiritual and religious experience meant that for him the secular activities of kings and the aspirations of princes were largely peripheral. It is often impossible for us, therefore, to be at all certain about quite essential matters of detail concerning what happened and when. Royal and ecclesiastical interests profoundly shaped how traditions about the past were preserved. Narrative sources are only infrequently even approximately contemporary with the events they record. A hundred years, for example, separated Bede when he wrote the *Ecclesiastical History* from the conversion of the first Christian Northumbrian king. The *Anglo-Saxon Chronicle* presents a view of West Saxon history in the sixth and seventh centuries but it was not compiled until the end of the ninth century. Not surprisingly, therefore, the chronology of events so long in the past presented problems at the time these works were written, so that, for example, if matters chronological figure prominently in this study now it is because they still do present problems and an attempt to resolve them is necessarily an integral part of the historical process. There are other difficulties. The evidence is so slight, for example, that it is impossible for us to establish exactly how individual Anglo-Saxon kingdoms evolved or quite why, with the exception of Wessex, they ultimately proved so vulnerable to Viking attack. The significance of the great overlord called *brytenwealda* or *bretwalda* remains enigmatic. Nor can an examination of the political pretensions of even a dominant and long-reigning king like Offa of Mercia in the second half of the eighth century guarantee definitive results. All that can be offered are possibilities, occasionally probabilities, rarely certainties. For many, of course, this is part of the attraction and fascination of early medieval history.

I have allowed the chapters of this book to assume their own shape and length at the dictates of the variable quality and quantity of the available evidence for successive phases of development. I am extremely grateful to Dr Alfred Smyth for his encouraging comments on an earlier draft and to Mr James Campbell whose patient and careful reading of the text saved me from a number of errors and whose discerning advice to restrain my enthusiasm for over-emphasis has, I know, induced a more circumspect approach. I would also like to thank Dr John Davidson of the Department of History, University College of Wales, Aberystwyth, whose help in the final stages of preparation of this book has been invaluable. For any errors or infelicities of style and presentation which remain I alone am responsible.

D. P. Kirby
Department of History
University College of Wales
Aberystwyth

Figure 1 Pre-Viking England

xiv

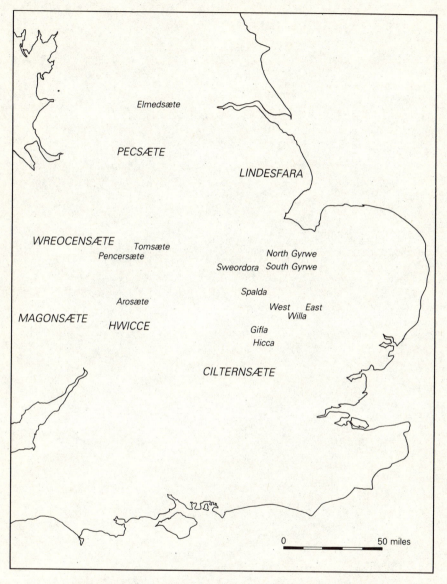

Figure 2 Identifiable folk-groups of midland England

xv

1 The peoples and kingdoms of pre-Viking England

The 'Heptarchy'

In 865, following over half a century of Viking raiding activity, what contemporaries came to call the 'great heathen army' landed in East Anglia. Across the next decade these Scandinavian warriors shattered the political map of England. In 867 they defeated Aella, king of the Northumbrians, and put him to death at York, dismembering his kingdom. In 869 they slew Eadmund, king of the East Angles, and annexed East Anglia. In 873–4 they drove out Burgred, king of the Mercians, and in 877 divided Mercia. Only Wessex avoided conquest and partition at this time under King Alfred and by 886, when all the *Anglecyn*, in the words of the *Anglo-Saxon Chronicle* A (*s.a.* 886),[1] not under subjection to the Danes submitted to him, the West Saxon ruling family would seem to have been the only native dynasty still holding royal power.

These Anglo-Saxon kingdoms (see Map 1) which disintegrated in the face of Viking attack, together with the surviving West Saxon kingdom (with its by now dependent territories in Essex, Sussex and Kent), had roots deep in earlier history. The fifth and early sixth centuries AD witnessed the collapse of the Roman Empire in the west and the emergence in a sub-Roman, though still largely Catholic, world of Germanic barbarian 'successor-states' in Italy, Gaul and Spain. The Anglo-Saxon kingdoms similarly had their origins in the post-Roman period of the conquest and settlement of much of Britain by pagan Germanic peoples from Denmark and north Germany under leaders for whom later generations claimed royal status and descent from ancient Germanic gods. Poets such as Widsith – 'the ideal wandering minstrel'[2] – sang their praises and long regaled the kings of their day with heroic tales (of which the epic *Beowulf* is a fine surviving example),[3] set in the age of the migration. The rulers of the Anglo-Saxon kingdoms of early England regarded themselves as the successors and descendants of the heroic figures of the migration period and are so represented in their king-lists and royal genealogies.[4]

At a time when royal power was rooted in lordship over an armed following, Germanic leaders attracted to themselves warriors (not infrequently young men in their mid-teens) who joined their retinues and hoped to be rewarded with treasure and eventually with landed estates. Bede says that noble youths came from almost every kingdom to serve Oswine, king

1

of the Deirans in Northumbria, in the mid-seventh century (*HE* III, 14). Such young men were a landed aristocracy in the making. In later life they served as royal officials (ealdormen) and acted as the king's principal counsellors, constituting his *witan* or wise men and advising him on the conduct of affairs, the dispensing of justice, the raising of taxes and the resolution of internal disputes and feuds. They were expected to uphold the law and to guarantee with the king a perpetuation of a right order in society.

Anglo-Saxon society was clearly graded, though probably more so in legal theory than in actual practice. The bulk of the population was composed of wholly dependent slaves and of peasants who normally lived in varying degrees of personal and economic bondage. Though merchants were probably often prosperous individuals, the urban population was small. Wealthy peasants and successful merchants might aspire to improve their social standing though the process took generations. The aristocracy constituted a dominant élite. Whereas the life of a peasant, expressed in terms of his *wergild* (man-price), was valued at 200 West Saxon or Mercian shillings (or their equivalent), even a member of lesser class among the nobility had a value placed on his life of 600 shillings and the standard value of the life of a nobleman or thegn was 1200 shillings, so that a nobleman of this rank was worth, literally, six peasants. A bishop's life and an ealdorman's was valued at twice as much as this. The pinnacle of society was the royal family. The life of an aetheling or prince was valued at six times that of a 1200 shilling nobleman, that of a king at as much again, half of which sum belonged to the royal kindred and half to the king's subjects.[5] Nothing encapsulates so concisely the paramount position of the king in Anglo-Saxon society.

The coming of Christianity brought the earliest English kings into contact with the Latin culture of Catholic Europe and introduced bishops, abbots and priests into the deliberative processes of the *witan*. Wihtred, king of Kent, for example, in 695 legislated with the consent of his leading men in the presence of Church dignitaries and so did Ine, king of the West Saxons, at about the same time, with his bishops, ealdormen and councillors. Kings founded churches and monasteries and made generous grants of land in return for ecclesiastical blessing and support. Across the seventh century the helmet-crowned warrior rulers of the Anglo-Saxons emerged as patrons and protectors of a Church which validated their actions, not as descendants of pagan deities but as kings by the divine grace of the Almighty, their pre-eminence and transcendent royal authority sanctified further from the late eighth century at the latest by the ecclesiastical rite of anointing with holy oil.[6]

The kingdoms of early England enjoyed in the main a lively cultural and artistic life. The Christian Church saw them as poor transitory creations by comparison with the fair kingdom of the high King of Heaven over which angels kept watch and Christ guarded, but in the heroic imagery of vernacular prose and verse their strongholds were repositories of wealth and riches which wide-ruling, gold-bestowing, ring-giving kings and their spear-warriors protected. Such kingdoms were perceived as peoples (Northumbrians, East Angles, Mercians) but were rather units of government, in which royal power was exercised over territories[7] on which were imposed fiscal[8] and military[9] obligations. Moreover, resources were finite. Bede expressed concern in 734 in a letter to Ecgberht, bishop of York, that so lavish had been the endowment of monasteries in Northumbria that there was no longer enough available land in the kingdom to reward young warriors.[10] In socio-economic terms these kingdoms can be characterized less as states than as chiefdoms, that is, they were not so much centralized regimes, the economic base of which was a thriving market economy, as noncentralized communities with a relatively weak market economy and fissiparous (separatist) tendencies which precluded any overlord, however powerful, from establishing anything other than a merely personal hegemony in the absence of a sound enough economic base.[11]

This is not to say that their economy was so primitive that kings had no choice but to embark on a ceaseless peregrination around the territories of their kingdoms to sustain themselves by living off local dues and food renders.[12] Large estates were probably already characteristic of Anglo-Saxon England by the seventh century as was the collection of local dues organized through royal *tuns* upon which whole districts were dependent and which were administered by royal reeves.[13] By the last quarter of the seventh century the more widely spread silver *sceattas* had replaced an earlier gold coinage of limited duration and circulation. They testify to the re-emergence of a money-using economy and possibly to a 'gradual expansion of commercial exchanges'.[14] Centralized places of exchange during the seventh and eighth centuries acted as stimuli to urban growth. London is described by Bede in the early eighth century as an emporium for many nations (*HE* II, 2). Trading emporia on the European mainland at Quentovic, south of Boulogne, and Dorestad, near Utrecht, disseminated manufactured goods and luxuries through Anglo-Saxon trading portals in Kent, London, Ipswich and *Hamwic*, near Southampton.[15] Offa, king of the Mercians (758–96), is thought to have constructed a series of relatively large *burhs* or forts (for example, at Bedford, Hereford, Northampton, Nottingham, Oxford and Stamford), which served both as defensive and administrative centres and as regional markets and mark an intermediate stage in the process of change from chiefdom to state.[16] They paved the way for the Alfredian *burhs* of the late ninth century and the Anglo-Saxon market system of the early tenth century onwards when 'a new form of government was created, administratively much more exacting, and the market . . . integral to its operation'.[17]

3

The collapse of these intermediate-stage kingdoms in the ten years or so following 865 is to be attributed in all probability more to the strength of the Viking military challenge than to internal or inherent weakness, but it is also the case that the pre-Viking political map had never been static for very long and the Viking attack itself was really only one, albeit dramatic, phase in a long process of assimilation of smaller by larger units and the termination of the independent existence of weaker kingdoms by external military action.[18]

The pre-Viking Anglo-Saxon kingdoms have been known to historians since the sixteenth century as the 'heptarchy', signifying that there were seven of them: those of the Northumbrians, the Mercians, the East Angles, the East Saxons, the West Saxons, the South Saxons and the men of Kent (sometimes referred to as Northumbria, Mercia, East Anglia, Essex, Wessex, Sussex and Kent). This heptarchic scheme is one which was deployed by Henry of Huntingdon in his *Historia Anglorum* in the first half of the twelfth century.[19] At the same time William of Malmesbury in his *De Gestis Regum Anglorum*[20] adopted much the same approach, except that he regarded the kingdoms of the Northumbrians, Mercians, West Saxons and the men of Kent as the important ones with East Anglia and the kingdom of the East Saxons as less significant and ignored the South Saxons as of virtually no significance at all. Yet historians have been expressing increasing reservations about the use of the term heptarchy in this context. C. R. Hart in 1971 thought it 'high time it was given a decent burial'.[21] Why is this? It is because there probably never was a time when Anglo-Saxon territory was divided simply into seven kingdoms, each ruled by only one king. Not only did more than one king reign at once in some of these territories at certain times but there were other important kingdoms which do not appear in the heptarchic scheme. The early twelfth-century compiler of the Worcester *Chronicon ex Chronicis*[22] is unusual in his awareness of smaller principalities which tended to be excluded from contemporary reviews of the early Anglo-Saxon polity. The multiplicity of kingdoms in early England, therefore, must not be obscured by too generalized a use of the term heptarchy. On the other hand, the process of assimilation meant that in 865 there were only four remaining independent kingdoms – Northumbria, Mercia, East Anglia and Wessex – so that the Anglo-Saxon kingdoms then constituted a tetrarchy.[23]

So the political situation was fluid. One difficulty is a paucity of contemporary descriptions of these kingdoms. The *Anglo-Saxon Chronicle*, first put together at the court of Alfred, king of Wessex, *c.* 890, was recalling tradition about the pre-Viking world within the general framework of a pentarchy, dominated by Northumbria, Mercia, East Anglia, Wessex and Kent but with detailed reference only to the dynastic tradition of the West Saxons. The *Anglo-Saxon Chronicle*, therefore, presents a very narrowly based view of the pre-Alfredian past. Fortunately, a hundred and fifty years or so earlier, Bede, a monk of the monastery of Wearmouth and Jarrow in Northumbria, published an ecclesiastical history of the Anglo-Saxons in Britain which, though concerned primarily to witness to their evangelization by Christian missionaries and transformation into a Christian people, acknowledged the crucial supporting role of the ruling dynasties within the political framework of the several kingdoms of early England. Reviewing the 'state of the whole of Britain' in 731 in the penultimate chapter of his *Historia Ecclesiastica Gentis Anglorum*,[24] he concluded, appropriately enough for a writer of ecclesiastical history, with an account of those who currently held episcopal office among the kingdoms of the Anglo-Saxons. Though he did not include a comparable review of the secular rulers of the Anglo-Saxon kingdoms, Bede does make a number of references to contemporary kings and throughout the *History* provides so much incidental information about the various kingdoms of his day that the political map of the country can be reconstructed in some detail for the first time since the end of Roman Britain. This information can be brought together as follows:

(i)   The kingdom of Kent
      The people of Kent, the Cantware, were separated from the territory of the East Saxons to the north by the Thames, while to the south and west of Kent was the territory of the South Saxons (*HE* II, 3). The archbishop of Canterbury, together with the bishop of Rochester, presided over the churches of Kent, and the archbishop directed the affairs of the whole Anglo-Saxon Church.

(ii) The kingdom of the East Saxons
      The kingdom of the East Saxons lay to the north of the Thames and the bishop of the East Saxons normally had his see at London (*HE* III, 7). The River Stour seems to have separated the East Saxons from the East Angles.

(iii) The kingdom of the South Saxons
      Bede describes the kingdom of the South Saxons as stretching south and west from Kent as far as the land of the West Saxons (*HE* V, 23), the boundary separating the South from the West Saxons being opposite the Isle of Wight (*HE* IV, 16). The site of the South Saxon bishopric was at Selsey (*HE* V, 23).

(iv) The kingdom of the West Saxons
      If part of West Saxon territory bordered on the land of the South Saxons, another part bordered on the Hwicce (*HE* II, 2), a people of the south-west midlands. By 731 there was a bishop at Winchester in east Wessex and another in west Wessex beyond Selwood (*HE* V, 18), known independently of Bede to have been at Sherborne.

(v)   The kingdom of the East Angles
      North of the Stour, the East Anglian kingdom had two bishoprics (*HE* V, 23), one at *Dommoc* (*HE* II, 15), possibly Dunwich in

Suffolk, the other generally thought to have been at North Elmham in Norfolk; and Ely fell within the kingdom (*HE* IV, 19).

(vi) The kingdom of the Mercians

Bede says that the kingdom of the Mercians was divided into northern and southern Mercia by the River Trent (*HE* III, 24), and its bishopric was at Lichfield (*HE* V, 23).

(vii) The kingdom of the Northumbrians

Bede saw its location north of the Humber as the distinguishing feature of the Northumbrian kingdom (*HE* II, 9), and regarded it as composed of two peoples, the Deirans between the Humber and the Tees and, north of the Tees, the Bernicians (*HE* III, 1).[25] By 731 there were Northumbrian bishoprics at York, Lindisfarne, Hexham and Whithorn (*HE* V, 23).

These are the seven kingdoms to which the term heptarchy is normally understood to refer, but in addition it is important to include in any survey of Anglo-Saxon kingdoms the following peoples with their territories which, although in the process of being absorbed into larger political creations by *c.* 731, had earlier seemingly enjoyed an independent existence:

(viii) The Wihtware

The inhabitants of the Isle of Wight were under West Saxon domination and subject in ecclesiastical matters to the bishop of Winchester by 731 (*HE* V, 23), but they certainly had had a royal dynasty of their own as late as the 680s to which Bede refers (*HE* IV, 16).

(ix) The Hwicce

The Hwicce, falling increasingly into dependence on the Mercians, were the north-western neighbours of the West Saxons (*HE* II, 2) (in Warwickshire, Worcestershire and Gloucestershire) with their own royal dynasty and a bishopric (*HE* V, 23), known independently of Bede to have been at Worcester.[26]

(x) The Middle Angles

Bede refers to the Middle Angles as the Angles of the midlands (*HE* III, 21), by which the east midlands is meant, and describes them as subject to Mercian control. They had their own bishopric (*HE* IV, 23) and in 737 it was re-established at Leicester. Bede regarded the territory of the Middle Angles as a former kingdom (*HE* III, 21).

(xi) The Lindesfara

Bede describes the territory of the men of Lindsey, dominated at first by the Northumbrians and then by the Mercians, as the first land south of the Humber towards the sea (*HE* II, 61), where it lay between the Humber and the Lincolnshire Witham.[27] They had their own bishopric (*HE* V, 23), known independently of Bede to have been at *Syddensis*, and their own royal dynasty.[28]

(xii)   The Magonsaete

Though the Magonsaete, also called the western Hecani, are first mentioned by name in an early ninth-century royal charter or diploma (*CS* 322: S 1264),[29] Bede knew them as 'the people who dwell west of the River Severn' (*HE* V, 23) in Herefordshire. They fell within a Mercian sphere of influence but had their own bishop by 731 and are said in later sources to have had their own royal dynasty.[30]

A number of territories, therefore, need to be added to the names of the heptarchic kingdoms if our vision of the political realities of the seventh and early eighth centuries is to be improved. Moreover, kingdoms were formed from what had earlier been two or more units and long remained re-divisible. It was practicable, for example, for the northern king, Oswiu, in the mid-seventh century to give only south Mercian territory to Peada, son and successor of King Penda (*HE* III, 24). Divisibility was also possible in kingdoms which seemed to have attained a certain unity and stability at an early stage. Kent appears on the surface as a united realm from the time of the first Christian king, Aethelberht, at the end of the sixth century at the latest, but when Wihtred, king of Kent, died in 725 he left as his royal heirs, according to Bede, his three sons, Aethelberht, Eadberht and Ealric (*HE* V, 23), and, though the implication is not necessarily that all three together succeeded to the kingship, certainly two did. Similarly, at the beginning of the seventh century, Bede says that Saeberht, king of the East Saxons, was succeeded by his three sons. Whether such arrangements meant simply power-sharing or the actual partition of territory has been a subject of debate, but kingdoms were certainly capable of territorial partition. In the early 760s, Sigered, a king of Kent, is styled 'king of half Kent' (*CS* 194: S 33) and his grants of land are known only from the records of Rochester, the diocesan centre of west Kent.[31] Moreover, though royal power-sharing has been seen as a distinct possibility among the East Saxons, the kingship of whom was held by two men on a number of occasions, Bede says of one recorded instance with reference to the 660s that part of the kingdom lapsed from the Christian faith under its apostate king, Sigehere, while Sigehere's co-ruler, Saebbi, remained a Christian (*HE* III, 30). A territorial division seems implied here. The East Saxon kingdom embraced, first, the modern county of Essex, second, part of Hertfordshire and Middlesex, where a people described as Middle Saxons first appear in a document from the late eighth century recording a grant of land in 704 (*CS* 111: S 65), and, third, in all probability part at least of Surrey, south of the Thames.[32] East Saxon territory was certainly extensive enough, therefore, to permit subdivision between the heartland and its peripheries.[33] North of the Humber, in the kingdom of the Northumbrians, when royal power was shared, as on occasion in the second half of the seventh century it was, one of two rulers appears to have been given the former territory of the Deirans to govern. Formerly an independent kingdom until its annexation by the Bernicians in the early seventh century, Deira re-emerged in the course of the mid-seventh century, first under a prince of the native Deiran line, Oswine (*HE* III, 14), and then under the reigning king's nephew, Oethelwald, who appears to have opposed his uncle, Oswiu (*HE* III, 23). Thereafter, Oswiu entrusted it to his sons, first Ealhfrith, and then (if later tradition is to be believed) Ecgfrith, who in turn gave it to his brother, Aelfwine.[34] If Deira could re-surface as a political entity in this way, it is likely that other similarly submerged kingdoms could do the same, and that when Anglo-Saxon kingdoms were partitioned they were often subdivided territorially into their earlier components. West Kent, where Sigered evidently reigned in the 760s, may once have existed as a kingdom separate and independent from east Kent.[35]

H. M. Chadwick thought that the later shires of Wessex – Berkshire, Hampshire, Dorset, Wiltshire, Somerset and Devon – were sub-kingdoms carved out of the kingdom of the West Saxons,[36] but it is more likely that they represent to some extent at least originally independent territories which only in the course of time coalesced into the single kingdom of Wessex. Devon was formerly part of the British kingdom of Dumnonia, and Hampshire (or at least part of it)[37] certainly represented a distinct territory over which the mid-eighth-century king of the West Saxons, Sigeberht, following his deposition as king of the West Saxons by his rival, Cynewulf, could continue to reign (*ASC* A, *s.a.* 755).

Some of the important early groups within the Mercian kingdom are known. In the heartland of southern Mercia were the Tomsaete, along the River Thame, extending westwards into Warwickshire from perhaps as far eastwards as Breedon on the Hill in Leicestershire and including the later principal Mercian centres of Lichfield and Tamworth.[38] Their neighbours to the west were the Pencersaete in the valley of the River Penk and embracing Wolverhampton and Stafford,[39] and to the north possibly the Hrepingas of Repton.[40] Such territories were probably originally ruled by their own royal families. The same is probably true of territories bordering on the Mercians and absorbed by them into their kingdom. The suggestion that Middle Anglia was a royal administrative unit carved out by the seventh-century Mercian king, Penda, for his son Peada[41] is impossible to substantiate, nor is there good reason to suppose that the kingdoms of the Hwicce, the Magonsaete and the Lindesfara were Mercian administrative creations.[42] They are more likely to represent originally independent principalities which were coming in varying degrees but progressively under the control of the Mercian king in the course of the seventh and eighth centuries. They also were divisible, judging from the example of the Hwicce, over whom two or three kings could reign simultaneously, and comprised a number of separate elements; among the Hwicce, for example, there is evidence for groups called the Weorgoran, Stoppingas and Husmerae.[43] The more closely an Anglo-Saxon kingdom is examined, therefore, the more it tends to dissolve into its constituents.

The Tribal Hidage

Some further idea of the mosaic of territories in pre-Viking England can be gained from the document known as the Tribal Hidage (*CS* 297).[44] This is a list of total assessments in terms of hides (units of taxation) for a number of territories south of the Humber, which has been variously dated from the mid-seventh to the second half of the eighth century.[45] It includes a number of middle-sized groups with their assessments, such as the Hwinca – generally regarded as the Hwicce, the Westerna – generally regarded (but not certainly so)[46] as the Magonsaete, and the Wocensaete at 7,000 hides. The meaning of 'Hwicce' is obscure, but the Magonsaete were the settlers in the region of *Magnis* (now Kenchester) in Herefordshire, and the Wocensaete took their name from the Wrekin in Shropshire. Their identity, therefore, appears to derive wholly from the territory they occupied. Also assessed at 7,000 hides were the Lindesfara (with *Heathfeld land*, that is Hatfield Chase in south Yorkshire). Lesser groups range from the Cilternsaete in the Chilterns at 4,000 hides, down to much smaller territories such as that of the Sweordora in the vicinity of Sword Point, Whittlesey Mere, Huntingdonshire, or the Hicca, whose territory probably centred on Hitchin, Hertfordshire, both assessed at a mere 300 hides.[47] The Sweordora are typical of a cluster of smaller population groups in the east midlands in the territory of the Middle Angles whose hidages are recorded in the Tribal Hidage, including, for example, the North and South Gyrwe in the vicinity of Peterborough (*HE* IV, 6) and Crowland at 600 hides each, the Spalda in the vicinity of Spaldwick, Huntingdonshire, also at 600 hides, and the Gifla in the Ivel valley in Bedfordshire at 300 hides (see Map 2).

Over half a dozen of these groups or units can be located in Middle Anglian territory, possibly more, which has led to the speculation that whenever the Tribal Hidage was compiled, the Middle Angles had not then been welded into a single territory.[48] What is more likely, however, is simply that a major element in the Tribal Hidage is a Middle Anglian survey. That it was not the only such survey to be included or drawn on is clear because the Hidage includes among its small groups some who belong elsewhere than in Middle Anglia. The Pecsaete (dwellers in the Peak), assessed at 1,200 hides, were not Middle Angles. The Arosaete, assessed at 600 hides, probably dwelt along the River Arrow in Warwickshire.

9

The Elmedsaete, also assessed at 600 hides, dwelt in Elmet in the former West Riding of Yorkshire. Unfortunately, the Tribal Hidage includes no group north of the Elmedsaete so that the territories which made up the Northumbrian kingdom cannot be reconstructed with its help, nor those to the south which made up the West Saxon. Not all groups can be identified with certainty, however, and some of these unidentified units were large – the Noxgaga, assessed at 5,000 hides, with the Ohtgaga at 2,000, the Hendrica at 3,500 and the Unecungga at 1,200. Other locations may not be as certain as sometimes thought. The Wihtgara, assessed at 600 hides, cannot certainly be identified as the Wihtgara or Wihtware of the Isle of Wight, to whom Bede assigns 1,200 hides not 600 (*HE* IV, 16). Some of these unidentified groups may be derived from another survey which has been included wholly or in part in the Tribal Hidage. It must not be assumed that only the groups or territories which made up the Middle Angles were still capable of being listed in this way. Such units probably survived everywhere in England down to the Viking invasions and beyond. In documents of the late 840s references occur to the boundary of the Tomsaete (*CS* 455(1): S 1272) and to an ealdorman of the Tomsaete (*CS* 454: S 197), and the Wocensaete appear as the Wreocensaete in a charter of 855 (*CS* 487: S 206). In his *Life of King Alfred*,[49] written in the late ninth century, Asser records that in 868 Alfred married the daughter of the ealdorman of the Gaini (ch. 29), whose location has not yet been determined but who were somewhere in Mercia. These groups had not ceased to exist by the end of the seventh century. Amazingly, unless they have been subdivided by some administrative act, even some of the smaller groups still show signs of possibly having once been two separate communities; the North and South Gyrwe, for instance, the East and West Wixna and the East and West Willa, possibly relics of an earlier 'dual classificatory system' of 'symbolically paired settlements'.[50]

The Tribal Hidage is undoubtedly a most valuable record. Its potential value has been described as 'unique' in the absence of any similar continental document. It was not, however, unique in its time. Hidage figures were clearly known and widely circulated. Bede gives a number of such assessments. He knew that the Isle of Man was assessed at 300 hides and Môn (Anglesey) at 960; both islands were at one time in the seventh century under Northumbrian domination. The suggestion has been made, therefore, that Bede took these figures from a list of assessments drawn up for one of the seventh-century Northumbrian overlords.[51] But Bede also knew that the island of Thanet was assessed at 600 hides, the island of Iona at about 5, the Isle of Wight at 1,200, and Selsey, the site of the South Saxon bishopric and at this time nearly an island, at 87 hides; it rather looks as if hidage assessments were part of the general knowledge of the time. Bede even gives total hidages for some of the larger kingdoms of his day, assessing the South Saxons at 7,000 hides (*HE* IV, 13) and recording that it was said that in the mid-seventh century the northern Mercians were assessed at 7,000 hides and the southern at 5,000 (*HE* III, 24), so that the figure for the northern and southern Mercians together was 12,000 hides, far more than for the South Saxons.

The Tribal Hidage includes assessments of the major kingdoms mixed in with Middle Anglian and other figures, almost certainly representing a separate and probably later stratum of calculations. Mercia is assessed, for example, not at 12,000 hides but at 30,000. For this reason alone the Tribal Hidage is not likely to be of mid-seventh century date. Mercia had evidently expanded to include what C. R. Hart called 'Outer Mercia', extending across Northamptonshire, Leicestershire and southern Lincolnshire, Hart leaving this area blank in his map of the Tribal Hidage groups.[52] It may be, however, that it is in this area of Outer Mercia that some at least of the unidentified groups of the Tribal Hidage should be located. Mercia's assessment at 30,000 hides need not be mutually exclusive of all the other units listed. It is possible that the Wreocensaete and the Pecsaete should be included among the groups which brought the total hidage for Mercia to 30,000. The East Angles are also assessed at 30,000 hides, but the men of Lindsey (with Hatfield) and the East Saxons at only 7,000, and the South Saxons also at Bede's figure of 7,000 hides. The South Saxon kingdom had evidently not expanded. It is clear from these figures that kingdoms like Mercia and East Anglia emerged far superior in resources to those of the East and South Saxons, but it is also apparent that many of the groups listed in the Tribal Hidage - the Wreocensaete, the Westerna and the Hwicce (or the Hwinca if they are not the Hwicce) – were the equals of the East and South Saxon kingdoms or the kingdom of Lindsey. The men of Kent are assessed in the Tribal Hidage at 15,000 hides, so Kent would seem to emerge as an appreciably wealthier kingdom than its immediate East and South Saxon neighbours. On the other hand, because the Kentish *sulung* was regarded as the equivalent of two hides the figure of 15,000 may simply represent an approximate doubling of an original 7,000, and there is a possibility that some South Saxon territory has also been included in this Kentish total.[53] To the West Saxon kingdom is assigned the grand total of 100,000 hides. The most likely explanation of this figure is that it reflects a quite late stage in the development of Wessex, which would suggest that the Tribal Hidage in its present form, as P. H. Sawyer observes, 'was compiled in the ninth or tenth century by a West Saxon'.[54]

Contemporaries could refer to any one of these territories as a *provincia* or a *regnum*, and for Bede the words province and kingdom were interchangeable. So also could local rulers be described in different contexts as *rex*, *subregulus*, *princeps*, *dux*, *praefectus* and *comes*.[55] The rulers of the Hwicce provide a valuable illustration of this. The earliest known rulers, the brothers Eanfrith and Eanhere, were clearly already in a dependent relationship before the mid-670s with Wulfhere, king of the Mercians, for Eanfrith's daughter, Eafe, was married to Aethelwealh, king of the South Saxons, probably at Wulfhere's court (*HE* IV, 13), and Oshere, king of the Hwicce, as he designated himself in 693 (*CS* 85: S 53), was subsequently referred to as *subregulus* (sub-king) and *comes* (companion) of Aethelred, king of the Mercians (*CS* 156: S 1429) (cf., Oshere's son, Aethelric, who witnessed a grant of land in the territory of the Hwicce as the sub-king and companion of the *princeps*, Aethelbald (of Mercia) (*CS* 154: S 89)). The Hwiccian princes, Eanberht, Uhtred and Ealdred each appear as *regulus* (petty king or kinglet) in a grant of land in their territory in 759 (*CS* 187: S 56), and in 778 Offa, king of the Mercians, granted land to Ealdred styled 'subregulus, dux, that is, of his own people, the Hwicce' (*CS* 223: S 113), that is, sub-king, and 'military leader'. For the term *dux* the vernacular 'ealdorman' came in the course of time to be increasingly regarded as the equivalent, the general use of *dux* and ealdorman obscuring an older hierarchy of finer distinctions among local provincial governors and royal representatives.[56] It was of course in their relationship to the Mercian king that the Hwiccian rulers were being defined as sub-kings, kinglets or *duces*; in their relationship to their own subjects they remained kings.[57] This is a fundamental feature of the political scene in early England which has been obscured by too great a preoccupation with the dependent aspect of the relationship between a less powerful king and a more powerful one.[58] Nevertheless, a long-term consequence of a dependent relationship could be not only a loss of royal status by a local dynasty but even the extinction of that dynasty.[59]

Some of the Tribal Hidage territories may always have been the administrative subdivisions of a larger kingdom but others will undoubtedly have been originally independent kingdoms, their ruling families retaining royal status in some cases into the seventh and even eighth century – the Magonsaete, for example, and the Hwicce. When Bede, who calls Peada, king of the Middle Angles, *princeps* (*HE* III, 21), also refers to Tondberht, ruler of the Middle Anglian province of the South Gyrwe, as a *princeps* (*HE* IV, 19), he is almost certainly reflecting the royal status of Tondberht's family.[60] Similar principalities, originally under their own ruling families, such as the Elmedsaete, must also have existed in Northumbria.

Angles or Saxons?

In a famous passage Bede writes about the peoples (*gentes*) who invaded Britain at the end of the Roman period - the Angles, Saxons and Jutes from Denmark and north Germany (*HE* I, 15). According to Bede, the people of Kent and the inhabitants of the Isle of Wight and the mainland immediately opposite the Isle of Wight were of Jutish origin; the East Saxons, South Saxons and West Saxons of Saxon; and the East Angles, Middle Angles, Mercians and Northumbrians of Anglian.[61] When Bede located the Saxons in the south of England and the Angles in the north, he was at variance with Pope Gregory the Great who addressed Aethelberht, king of Kent, as 'king of the Angles', and Pope Vitalian, who addressed the northern king, Oswiu, as 'king of the Saxons'. This reversal of the papal order, however, is either an inference from or is corroborated by the nomenclature of the southern kingdoms. That the principal southern kingdoms had become known by the time of Bede as East, South and West Saxon is confirmation of a Saxon sense of identity in these areas which is in striking contrast to the Anglian consciousness of the peoples to the north and east. But we should not imagine that the distinction between Angles and Saxons was absolutely clear-cut; it was not only Pope Vitalian who thought there were Saxons in the north. The early eighth-century *Life of Wilfrid*[62] describes Wilfrid, bishop of York, as bishop of the Saxons (*Vita Wilfridi*, ch. 21), and the Picts as resenting their subjection to the Saxons, meaning the northern Angles (*Vita Wilfridi*, ch. 19). Boniface, West Saxon missionary to the continental Germans, called his homeland Saxonia but referred to himself as of the race of the Angles, while regarding the Northumbrian Willibord as a Saxon.[63] The Irish and Welsh annalists habitually referred to all the Germanic peoples in Britain as Saxons. Though he located both *Angli* and *Saxones* in Britain and could refer to the *gens Saxonum* (*HE* I, 15) and the *natio Saxonum* (*HE* IV, 14), for Bede Pope Gregory the Great's word-play on Angles as 'angels' had a very special significance as foreshadowing the conversion and 'predestined grace of the Anglo-Saxons',[64] so that he conceived of the Church in England as 'the holy Church of the Anglian people' (*gentis Anglorum*) (*HE* III, 29) and used the term Angle in the title of the *Historia Ecclesiastica Gentis Anglorum* to denote not only Angles but Saxons as well.[65] It is not surprising that continental writers began to refer to the Angles and Saxons in Britain as Anglo-Saxons by the late eighth century.[66]

How much significance the division of the invaders into Angles, Saxons and Jutes really possessed may be questioned. It is true that similarities in the archaeological record link Kent with elements in the culture of early Jutland, southern Saxon England with Old Saxony in north Germany, and the more northerly and easterly Anglian territories with Denmark, but it is not certain whether this artefactual evidence bears directly on the ethnic composition of the Anglo-Saxon invaders in different areas of Britain or reflects rather secondary commercial enterprise, the exchange of gifts and related cultural connections. Moreover, other groups may also have been involved in the settlement of Britain. In a less well-known passage Bede appears to number Huns, Danes and Frisians among the Germanic peoples from whom the Germanic inhabitants of Britain took their origins (*HE* V, 9), and the Byzantine historian Procopius also includes the Frisians among the peoples of Britain. In addition Bede mentions the Frankish Boructuari (or Bructeri) (*HE* V, 9), so that archaeologists have probably been right to suspect the presence of Franks among the invaders, rendering still more complicated the Anglo-Saxon-Jutish mix.[67] It cannot be regarded as at all certain, therefore, that all the Germanic inhabitants of Wessex were Saxons, or those of Mercia exclusively Anglian.[68] The bulk of the population in any case will have been of indigenous British extraction and intermarriage a regular feature of post-Roman society. The ruling families and the nobility, on the other hand, may well have regarded themselves as specifically of Anglian or Saxon descent. It may be significant that the later kings of the East Saxons traced their ancestry back to the god, Woden, through the Saxon god, Saxnot, an indication of a powerful identification on their part with Old Saxony,[69] while the later kings of the Mercians included among their reputed ancestors Offa of Angeln, a fifth-century figure of Danish heroic legend.[70] For Susan Reynolds, the Anglo-Saxons were those inhabitants of Britain 'who, wherever their ancestors came from or whatever the mixture of genes in each, were the subjects of kings who apparently thought of themselves or their ancestors as Angles, Saxons and may be Jutes'.[71]

Hierarchies of command: the Brytenwealda

The process by which the Anglo-Saxon kingdoms were formed in Romano-Celtic Britain was protracted and continued well into the seventh century. Doubts remain about the total number of Germanic immigrants,[72] but a Saxon invasion in 410[73] led to a forceful enough Germanic presence by 441–2 for a mid-fifth-century Gallic chronicle to record that in that year the British provinces were subjected to Saxon domination.[74] In his *Ruin of Britain* (*De Excidio Britanniae*),[75] probably written in the early sixth century, Gildas was concerned primarily to condemn contemporary British secular and religious society, but he leaves no doubt that the Britons experienced severe trauma at the hands of Germanic peoples settled in Britain.[76] His account of how a 'proud tyrant' (*tyrannus superbus*), presumably a particularly powerful British leader, attempted to deploy Anglo-Saxon mercenaries against the threatened attacks of Picts and Scots but lost control of the situation when the Germanic troops rebelled (*De Excidio*, ch. 23) may be based on a tradition about the circumstances which led up to the events of 441–2. Though Gildas lived at a time of relative peace, he agonized over what he saw as a continuing military threat to the Britons from their Germanic neighbours, and he pays tribute to those Britons who gained some military success against them under the leadership of Ambrosius Aurelianus, naming specifically a victory at Mount *Badon*, fought in the year of Gildas' birth, forty-three years before (*De Excidio*, chs 25–6); the early ninth-century *History of the Britons* (*Historia Brittonum*)[77] numbered *Badon* among Arthur's battles (ch. 56), but so obscured by

14

inadequate source-material is this 'age of Arthur' that it may never be possible adequately to reconstruct its detail.[78]

How long late Roman military commands and the Romano-British oligarchies of the *civitates* (the principal cities and their dependent territories) survived is unknown. It could be that the first Germanic rulers in Britain were the new governors of fractured parts of the provinces of late Roman Britain. The extent of their territorial power however loosely exercised was probably defined, at least at first, by the configuration of the dismantled Romano-British administrative areas over which they acquired control. Kent derived its name from Cantium, a probably pre-Roman designation of the region which subsequently became the *civitas Cantiacorum* (*civitas* of the Cantiaci), centred on Canterbury.[79] It is possible that the first kings of Kent were military commanders who took control of this Romano-British *civitas*. Similarly, the kingdom of Lindsey, the territory of the Lindesfara, derives its name from that of the Roman *colonia Lindum* (Lincoln). The kingdom of the South Saxons may represent the *civitas Regnensium* and that of the East Saxons the *civitas* of the Trinovantes.[80]

The apparently increasingly centralized accumulation of wealth in the course of the sixth and seventh centuries and the emergence in the archaeological record of a clearly defined hierarchical structure in society[81] need not mean that in the fifth and early sixth centuries the Anglo-Saxons were unfamiliar with uneven access to resources, on the one hand, or social stratification, on the other.[82] The men who directed the invasion of Britain or who responded to opportunities created thereby are likely to have been very powerful individuals indeed, but they are, unfortunately, barely known to us. Early eighth-century dynastic and genealogical tradition remembered Oisc, reputed son of Hengest and father of Ochta, as the first of the Oiscingas kings ('descendants of Oisc') to rule in Kent (*HE* II, 5), Wuffa as the first of the Wuffingas kings to rule in East Anglia (*HE* II, 15), and Icel as the first of the Icelingas who, according to the early eighth-century *Life of Guthlac*,[83] came to dominate Mercia (*Vita Guthlaci*, ch. 2), but details for the period before *c.* 550–75 (and sometimes much later) are too uncertain for these men to be placed in very precise genealogical or historical contexts.[84] Oisc, perhaps originally a mythological figure, may have become famous as the leader of the Anglo-Saxon invasion of Britain before he entered Kentish history, for it is the name Oisc which probably lies behind the *Ansehis* of the Ravenna cosmographer of *c.* 700, according to whom the Saxons who inhabited Britain had come from Old Saxony under their chieftain, Ansehis.[85] By the second half of the eighth century, when royal genealogies were being collected and transcribed first in Northumbria and then in Mercia,[86] Oisc was being represented not as the son of Hengest and father of Ochta but as the grandson of Hengest and son of Ochta[87] – who is portrayed in the *History of the Britons* as leaving north Britain to succeed his father, Hengest, in Kent (*HB* ch. 56). Tradition could clearly be recast.[88] According to the

History of the Britons it was not Wuffa, but his father, Weahha, who was the first to rule over the eastern Angles (*HB* ch. 59). Such conflicts in the evidence mean that the tradition itself was changing. It could also become garbled. It is not at all clear what is the meaning of the statement, also in the *History of the Britons*, that Soemil, regarded as an ancestor of the Deiran prince, Eadwine, was 'the first to separate Deira from Bernicia' (*HB* ch. 61). Presumably Soemil was the first Germanic leader known to have ruled in Deira.

It need not have been the case, of course, that every leader who emerged in this period was a Germanic immigrant. The British name of Cerdic, alleged founder of the West Saxon dynasty, has often been remarked upon,[89] and it may be that in the veins of the ruling dynasties of early Anglo-Saxon England British blood flowed in some quantity. Nor can archaeology necessarily clarify a question of origins; it is far from certain, for example, that the dynasty of the Wuffingas originated in Sweden, as the evidence of the East Anglian Sutton Hoo ship-burial from the early seventh century at one time seemed to suggest.[90] Even Sutton Hoo, it has been said, might be explained 'as the expression of newly claimed power by an aspiring aristocracy, which could have risen from the ranks of the native population'.[91] Nevertheless, it is likely that it was a fairly complex military society which initiated the appropriation of so much British territory by the Anglo-Saxons in the late fifth and sixth centuries. First, the ninth-century *Life* of the eighth-century missionary to the continental Germans, Leofwine, describes how local rulers of the pagan Old Saxons used to gather together to offer prayers to the gods and to pray for guidance, confirming laws and giving judgements, and drawing up plans for the coming year on which they could act in peace or war,[92] and such gatherings may have been a regular feature of the conquest of Britain. Second, among early Germanic leaders there are likely to have been kings of many types. Tacitus' distinction, for example, between peace-time rulers of noble blood (*reges*) and warleaders (*duces*), chosen for their prowess in battle, may still have retained some validity,[93] and in the circumstances of the time *duces* must have been well placed to secure coercive powers to endow their temporary positions of authority with a new-found permanence. Later Anglo-Saxon dynasties would probably have numbered both types among their reputed ancestors.[94] Third, Ammianus Marcellinus records how in the year 357 the Alemanni on the continent were led into battle by ten petty kings, under the command of five kings, under the direction of two commanders.[95] So structured a hierarchy will surely not have been without parallels during the complexities of a transmaritime military operation in Britain.

The major kingdoms of pre-Viking England and the multi-tiered layers of royal power which emerged among the kings of the Anglo-Saxons may well have derived from and evolved out of chains of command at the time of the Anglo-Saxon Conquest. The local rulers of some of the quite tiny groups in the Tribal Hidage are likely to have been always in a dependent position. At the level of divided royal power within a kingdom one king could exercise greater authority than his co-ruler. Eadberht, king of Kent, in 738, for example, declared himself at fault for not seeking confirmation sooner of a grant of land to the bishop of Rochester from his brother, King Aethelberht (*CS* 159: S 27). More powerful kings could place themselves at the head of larger confederacies and wield a wider supremacy, imposing and taking tribute from their dependants (cf., *Vita Wilfridi*, ch. 20). In the mid-seventh century Penda, king of the Mercians, marched against his enemies at the head of an army commanded by himself and led by thirty royal or most noble leaders (*duces regii, ducibus nobilissimis*) (*HE* III, 24), and within Northumbria also the king had his *subreguli* (*Vita Wilfridi*, chs 17, 19) and his *duces regii* (*HE* V, 24).

Such command-structures probably helped to produce the succession of those powerful overlords among the Anglo-Saxons whom historians have come to know as *bretwaldas* and whose existence is so arresting a feature of the political and military history of the pre-Viking period. Hanna Vollrath argued that the position of some of the early Anglo-Saxon overlords depended to a significant degree on acceptance by their royal contemporaries that supreme military leadership (*ducatus*) be invested in them as commanders-in-chief.[96] Bede says of Aethelberht, king of Kent in the early sixth century and described as overlord of all the Anglo-Saxon kingdoms south of the Humber, that even while he lived, Raedwald, king of the East Angles, 'was providing the military leadership (*ducatum*) for his own people ' (*HE* II, 5) - that is, the East Angles.[97] This crucial piece of evidence suggests that an overlord (in this case Aethelberht) would normally exercise military leadership over kings who acknowledged his authority to the extent of directing their military resources. It also reveals, however, that recognition of these powers could be denied (as in this case by Raedwald). There is nothing to show that such agreements were anything other than temporary or that the use of force to coerce and take tribute from those who proved defiant was precluded. But overlordship was only 'one form of relationship' between kings,[98] and powerful rulers must also have profited at times from the establishment of friendly relations with other rulers, seeking the benefits of alliance rather than the repercussions of conquest. Even between overlord and royal dependant, if mutual benefit derived from the relationship, diplomatic harmony is likely to have prevailed.

Bede tended to use *imperium* (overlordship) as opposed to *regnum* (royal power) to describe the type of domination exercised by overkings or overlords who wielded authority in two or more *regna* (kingdoms); it is clear, for example, that the Mercian, West Saxon and Northumbrian kings were thought of as exercising a local *imperium* over their immediately dependent territories.[99] The Anglo-Saxons both during the Anglo-Saxon conquest and after were also capable of producing leaders whose power went beyond such a local *imperium* and who overshadowed their contemporaries as the most powerful rulers of their day. In a well-known passage, Bede lists seven kings who are said to have held in succession an *imperium* over all the Anglo-Saxon kingdoms south of the Humber: Aelle, king of the South Saxons, Ceawlin, king of the West Saxons, Aethelberht, king of Kent, Raedwald, king of the East Angles, Eadwine, king of the Northumbrians, Oswald, also king of the Northumbrians, and Oswiu, likewise king of the Northumbrians (*HE* II, 5). David Dumville has suggested that after Oswiu there may have been others whom Bede did not name.[100] Wulfhere, king of the Mercians, Penda's son and successor in the second half of the seventh century, is an obvious example. He is said to have stirred up all the southern peoples to make war on and impose tribute upon the northern king, Ecgfrith (*Vita Wilfridi*, ch. 20). Aethelbald, king of the Mercians, who, as Bede wrote, dominated all the southern kingdoms (*HE* V, 23), is another. The *Anglo-Saxon Chronicle* A (*s.a.* 827) adds Ecgberht, king of the West Saxons in the early ninth century, and it is the *Chronicle* which describes each of these rulers as *bretwalda* ('ruler of Britain') (A) or *brytenwealda* ('wide-ruler') (BCDE). There is no doubt that the original word was *brytenwealda* and that *bretwalda* is a scribal error,[101] though *brytenwealda* came in the tenth century to acquire the meaning ruler of Britain.[102] King of Britain is the title which Aethelbald, king of the Mercians, is known to have been accorded in the early eighth century. In an original charter of 736 he is actually styled *rex Britanniae* (*CS* 154: S 89). This is also how Offa's hegemony is thought of in a charter of Coenwulf dated 799 in which Offa is referred to as *rex Brittaniae* (*CS* 293: S 155).

Without question the concept of 'Britain' exercised a powerful influence on the imagination of the Anglo-Saxons. Bede transmitted to his audience an image of Roman Britain as a single realm conquered by Claudius and inherited by Constantine, the Romans occupying north to Hadrian's Wall and establishing their domination of the further parts of Britain as well as over the adjacent islands (*HE* I, 11). In addition, Patrick Wormald has suggested that Anglo-Saxon kings were the heirs to the spiritual ambitions of the church of Canterbury, inspired by a papal vision of a single *ecclesia* for a single *gens Anglorum*;[103] and certainly Theodore (668–90) and Beorhtwald (692–731), successive archbishops of Canterbury, cultivated the concept of an archbishop or primate of the island of Britain.[104] Nor was it among the Anglo-Saxons alone or exclusively at Canterbury that ideas about a single ruler for a single people were promulgated. Writing his *Life of Columba c.* 700, Adomnán, abbot of Iona,[105] refers to the northern king, Oswald, the sixth of Bede's seven overlords, as 'emperor of the whole of Britain' (*totius Brittanniae imperator*)[106] paralleling his description of Diarmait, son of Cerbhal, king of Tara in the mid-sixth century, as *totius Scotiae regnatorem*,[107] a statement 'of desire not of fact'.[108] Aethelbald was certainly not in reality 'king of Britain', and nor was Offa. The reality was far more circumscribed. Bede, Aethelbald's older contemporary, describes the extent of Aethelbald's power when he records in 731 that all the kingdoms south of the Humber, together with their rulers, were subject to him (*HE* V, 23). The probability is that Bede's world was profoundly influenced by Aethelbald's southern *imperium*, which must have been a decisive factor in contemporary political and ecclesiastical life, and it cannot be without significance that the geographical extent of the earlier hegemonies of Bede's seven overlords of the southern kingdoms - all the Anglo-Saxon kingdoms south of the Humber - is defined essentially in terms of the contours of Mercian political domination under Aethelbald. Consequently, Aelle, Ceawlin, Aethelberht and Raedwald were all seen as prototypes of Aethelbald, and if the Northumbrian kings had exercised power over kings south of the Humber their position had to be delineated in the same way. In other words, these earlier hegemonies have been largely cast in the mould of the situation current in the early eighth century. Hence, perhaps, the apparent 'double meaning' of *bretwalda* which Patrick Wormald detected – 'at once southumbrian and pan-British'.[109] Two concepts have been fused together, the image of a king of Britain and the actuality of military and political containment south of the Humber. Aethelbald might be styled king of Britain but 'wide-ruler' better characterizes his position, and there can be no doubt that he should have been numbered among the *brytenwealdas*.

It is reasonable to suppose that what Aelle, Ceawlin, Aethelberht and Raedwald acquired as 'wide-rulers' were regional hegemonies, subsequently magnified to embrace all the southern kingdoms. As they stand, Bede's details must contain a substantial element of anachronism. That Aelle was identified by his contemporaries specifically as South Saxon and Ceawlin specifically as West Saxon is questionable – as opposed to being regarded as such by later generations of princes among the South and West Saxons respectively who claimed descent from them. The territorial complexes which spawned Aelle and Ceawlin predate the historic kingdoms of the Anglo-Saxon heptarchy. Archaeological evidence (bearing on craft-specialization, prestige luxury trade, the emergence of rich graves, the centralization of wealth and patronage, and hoarding) indicates that the kingdoms of the Anglo-Saxon heptarchy, as they appear in the seventh century with ports, royal centres and rural settlements, are unlikely to have begun to form before the second half of the sixth century in respect of the more economically advanced areas (such as Kent) and across the seventh in the less advanced.[110] Nor initially was the Humber the political barrier it later became after Northumbria had been defined as north-humbrian in part by virtue of the loss in the course of the seventh century of the bulk of south-humbrian territories.[111] The kingdoms of Bede's England had evolved over a long period and continued to do so. The geography of power was in an almost continuous state of flux as more powerful principalities assimilated weaker neighbours. Offa may conceivably have modelled himself on Aethelbald,[112] but it cannot be assumed that even he was able to create his *imperium* absolutely in the image of Aethelbald's. The political circumstances and interests of the second half of the eighth century seem to have necessitated a new creation in Offa's supremacy in southumbrian England. Nor did new movements terminate with Offa's death. The kingdoms of pre-Viking England were still evolving and shape-changing when the great Viking army intervened in the second half of the ninth century.

The problem of nomenclature

Bede, perhaps inadvertently, conveys the impression that clearly delineated territories of West Saxons or Northumbrians, East Angles or Mercians, actually emerged in the course of the Anglo-Saxon settlement in Britain. In the context of events *c.* 600 or before he refers to the kings and kingdoms of the men of Kent, the East, South and West Saxons, and the Northumbrians. Subsequently, the Alfredian chronicler clearly regarded Wessex as always having existed as the West Saxon kingdom under a consecutive succession of kings of the West Saxons. The chronicler simply conceived of Wessex in its ninth-century form as having sprung into being in the fifth and early sixth centuries, since when nothing had changed. Bede was doing much the same in the early eighth century. In the past historians have tended to follow suit and have regarded the heptarchic kingdom as securely established by the sixth century, if not earlier in some cases. An inflexible and somewhat anachronistic pattern has thereby been imposed on the historical development of these pre-Viking kingdoms.

The only Anglo-Saxon kingdom which is attested in a contemporary sixth-century record is Kent. Gregory of Tours in his Frankish *Histories*, written in the late sixth century, twice refers simply to Kent and once to Kent as a kingdom.[113] Documentation otherwise allows the existence of Bede's principal kingdoms to be traced back in general only into the later part of the second half of the seventh century. The East Saxons are first mentioned by name in the extant records in a grant of land by Oethelred, kinsman of Saebbi, king of the East Saxons (*CS* 81: S 1171), in a late eighth-century text, the original of which probably belongs to 686–8.[114] Their northern neighbours were known as the East Angles by 704–13 when the Whitby *Life* of Pope Gregory,[115] which refers to them as such (ch. 16), was written. The regnal style 'king of the West Saxons' is not found before *c.* 760,[116] but 'West Saxon' appears in an original text of a letter of Wealdhere, bishop of London, to Beorhtwald, archbishop of Canterbury in 704–5.[117] Similarly, the earliest charter to contain a reference to South

Saxons is a grant by Nothhelm, king of the South Saxons in the period 688–705, in 692 according to the text of the charter itself (in what may, however, be a later addition) (*CS* 78: S 45). These names were certainly in use, therefore, by the late seventh or early eighth century; the question is whether they are very much earlier.

Bede includes in the *Historia Ecclesiastica* two conciliar documents from the second half of the seventh century, relating to the councils of Hertford in 672 (*HE* IV, 5) and Hatfield in 679 or 680 (*HE* IV, 17). Both are transcripts of the proceedings of the two councils and – unless Bede has modernized their wording[118] – of great relevance to the study of the nomenclature of the Anglo-Saxon kingdoms. The preamble to the council of Hertford records the presence among others of Leutherius, 'bishop of the West Saxons', and Bisi, 'bishop of the East Angles', and records that proctors represented Wilfrid, 'bishop of the Northumbrian people'. The record of the council of Hatfield is dated by the regnal year of Ealdwulf, 'king of the East Angles'. In the earliest records, however, kings are not given a geographical designation at all. Individual rulers were addressed in papal correspondence as 'king of the Angles', or as 'king of the Saxons'. In the 680s, Sigehere, whom Bede subsequently identified as a king of the East Saxons (*HE* III, 30: IV, 6), was only described in an admittedly suspect Kentish charter as 'king of the Saxons' (*CS* 89: S 233).[119] Ine, king of the West Saxons, is styled 'king of the Saxons' in 701 (*CS* 103: S 243) and before him King Centwine in 682 likewise (*CS* 62: S 237), to whom Aldhelm of Malmesbury also referred as 'king of the Saxons' *c.* 690.[120] On the inscription on his tomb in Rome, where he died in 688, Caedwalla was simply 'king of the Saxons' (*HE* V, 7). This evidence would suggest that terms like 'East' and 'West' Saxons may not long have been in commmon use before they appear in the late seventh or early eighth century. The failure of Bede to mention the Middle Saxons at all could indicate that the name Middle Saxon was not then of long-standing. Bede says that the West Saxons were formerly known as the Gewisse (*HE* III, 7) and it is likely that earlier names among the East, Middle and South Saxons and the East and Middle Angles were similarly discarded when they adopted geographically oriented ones. There is, however, an exception. Among more powerful rulers, the kings of the Mercians avoided similar categorization. They remained kings of the Mercians, the name signifying 'boundary people' or 'people of the border', and their bishops continued to be identified as bishops of the Mercians. It is curious that the Mercians never became the West Angles; it was the Magonsaete who were called West Angles.[121]

What little evidence there is could suggest that it was a Canterbury terminology which imposed on the Anglo-Saxons the territorial designations 'East', 'West', 'South' and 'Middle'. The records of the councils of Hertford and Hatfield, convened under Theodore, archbishop of Canterbury, are Canterbury records, and reveal that such territorial designations

21

may already have been in use in Canterbury circles in the 670s. In the first decade of the conversion of the Anglo-Saxons to Christianity bishoprics were established near the power-bases of the local kings - at Canterbury, London, York, Dorchester-on-Thames - and their diocesan boundaries, vague and ill-defined in the beginning, fluctuated as the political circumstances of the local dynasties waxed and waned. Bede says of Bishop Wilfrid that he administered the see of York as far as the power of King Oswiu extended (*HE* IV, 3). There may have been a need, therefore, to try to define more specifically than was native practice the territory over which a bishop had jurisdiction. The council of Hertford was concerned to declare against any bishop who intruded into the diocese of another. Bishops were to be content with the government of the people committed to their charge. The problem was to define such a people when the secular rulers were simply addressed as kings of the Angles or Saxons without distinction. For some reason, the native names must generally have proved inadequate for the Church's purpose, perhaps because they failed to signify changing political realities. It may be that the earliest bishops of Dorchester were known as bishops of the Gewisse, but the area around Dorchester was lost to the Mercians in the 660s and in 672 at Hertford the title of the bishop of Winchester appears to have been 'bishop of the West Saxons'. Why 'West' specifically? Viewed from Winchester, these Saxons could have been South Saxons, the South Saxons the East Saxons and the East Saxons the North Saxons. From Canterbury's perspective, however, they were West, those of their neighbours towards Kent South, the Saxons to the north of the Thames East, those between the West and the East eventually Middle. The symmetry of it indicates a common Canterbury viewpoint.

The next stage would be to define the kingdoms in the same ecclesiastical terms. This stage had already been reached at Hatfield with the description of Ealdwulf, for example, as king of the East Angles. If this reconstruction is correct, Ealdwulf's kingdom was being defined for him in terms of the diocese of his bishop as perceived by the metropolitan church of Canterbury. Other kingdoms were also so defined across the later years of the seventh century until by the early eighth these probably relatively new designations – West Saxon, East Saxon, South Saxon, East Anglian, Northumbrian – were being universally popularized by Bede and firmly established in the political vocabulary of the heptarchy. Northumbria provides a good illustration of this. The northern ruler, Ecgfrith, king – in the *Ecclesiastical History* – of the Northumbrians (*HE* V, 26), had been styled 'king of the Humbrians' (*rex Humbronensium*) by those who drew up the record of the council of Hatfield (*HE* IV, 17), implying rule over a collection of territories astride the Humber (see below, pp. 64–5). Bede called him king of the transhumbrian regions in his *History of the Abbots*.[122] As early as the council of Hertford in 672, however, Wilfrid, whose episcopal jurisdiction at that time was probably confined north of the Humber (see below, p. 114), was evidently styled 'bishop of the Northumbrian people' (*HE* IV, 5), and this was how the northern kingdom came to be finally defined. By the time of the writing of the *Ecclesiastical History* Bede was consistently referring to it as Northumbria throughout its history.

To avoid too anachronistic a portrayal of early English history, therefore, for the period before *c.* 700, rather than the familiar territorial names, the less specific eastern, southern and western Saxons, and eastern and northern Angles have much to commend them as sufficiently adequate for purposes of identification without the precision which the more familiar names impose.

Notes

1 The *Anglo-Saxon Chronicle* (hereafter abbreviated as *ASC*) was edited by B. Thorpe, 2 vols (Rolls series: London, 1861) and is currently being re-edited by D. Dumville and S. Keynes, *The Anglo-Saxon Chronicle: A Collaborative Edition* (Cambridge, 1983–). A translation is to be found in *English Historical Documents* (hereafter abbreviated as *EHD*), Vol. I: *500–1042*, ed. D. Whitelock (2nd edn, London, 1979) and *EHD* Vol. II: *1042–1189*, ed. D. C. Douglas and G. W. Greenaway (London, 1953), and separately in *The Anglo-Saxon Chronicle*, ed. D. Whitelock, D. C. Douglas and S. I. Tucker (London, 1961). The A text, to which primary reference is made in these chapters, is edited by J. M. Bately as Vol. 3 of the *Collaborative Edition*, ed. D. Dumville and S. Keynes (1986), the B text by S. Taylor as Vol. 4 (1983) and the *Annals of St Neot* by D. Dumville and M. Lapidge as Vol. 17 (1985); the C text was edited by H. A. Rositze, *Beiträge zur englischen Philologie.*, vol. 34 (1940), the D by E. Classen and F. E. Harmer, *An Anglo-Saxon Chronicle from British Museum Cotton MS. Tiberius B.IV* (Manchester, 1926), the E (with A) by C. Plummer (on the basis of an edition by J. Earle), *Two of the Saxon Chronicles Parallel*, 2 vols (Oxford, 1892, 1899; reprinted 1952), and the F by F. P. Magoun, 'Annales Domitiani Latini', *Medieval Studies of the Pontifical Institute of Medieval Studies*, vol. IX (1947), pp. 235–95; G (a copy of A) must still be consulted in A. Whitlock, *Venerabilis Bedae Historia Ecclesiastica* (Cambridge, 1664). References in the text to the *Chronicle* are by annal, according to the *Chronicle's* own dates, and the translation where cited that in *EHD* Vol. I.

2 R. W. Chambers, *Widsith: A Study in Old English Heroic Legend* (Cambridge, 1912), p. 4.

3 On the date of *Beowulf*, see *The Dating of Beowulf*, ed. C. Chase (Toronto and London, 1981).

4 D. N. Dumville, 'Kingship, genealogies and regnal lists', in P. H. Sawyer and I. N. Wood (eds), *Early Medieval Kingship* (Leeds, 1977), pp. 72–104.

5 For these values see 'The Compilation on Status', edited by B. Thorpe, *Ancient Laws and Institutes of England*, 2 vols (London, 1840), Vol. I, pp. 456–69 (*EHD* Vol. I, no. 52). Some of the values given in the 'Compilation' for 'The North People's Law' present difficulties but the relationship between social groups in Wessex and Mercia appears to have been as outlined and was probably the same for all the Anglo-Saxon kingdoms (see also for a West Saxon atheling's *wergild*, below p. 124).

6 See further on kingship in this period, W. A. Chaney, *The Cult of Kingship in Anglo-Saxon England* (Manchester, 1970) and J. M. Wallace-Hadrill, *Early Germanic Kingship in England and on the Continent* (Oxford, 1971); on the ideological impact of Catholic Europe, R. Hodges and J. Moreland, 'Power and exchange in Middle Saxon England', in S. T. Driscoll and M. R. Nieke (eds), *Power and Politics in Early Medieval Britain and Ireland* (Edinburgh, 1988), pp. 79–95; and on anointing, J. L.

Nelson, 'Inauguration Rituals', in Sawyer and Wood (eds), *Early Medieval Kingship*, pp. 50–71 (reprinted in Nelson, *Politics and Ritual in Early Medieval Europe* (London and Ronceverte, 1986), pp. 283–308), and 'The earliest surviving royal *Ordo*: some liturgical and historical aspects', in B. Tierney and P. Lineham (eds), *Authority and Power: Studies in Medieval Law and Government* (Cambridge, 1980), pp. 341–60 (pp. 352–3) (reprinted in Nelson, *Politics and Ritual*, pp. 341–60).

7 S. Reynolds, *Kingdoms and Communities in Western Europe 900–1300* (Oxford, 1984), p. 331. Cf., E. James, 'The origins of barbarian kingdoms: the continental evidence', in S. Bassett (ed.), *The Origins of Anglo-Saxon Kingdoms* (Leicester, 1989), pp. 40–52 (p. 47).

8 F. M. Stenton, *Anglo-Saxon England* (3rd edn, Oxford, 1971), pp. 287–9; P. H. Sawyer, *From Roman Britain to Norman England* (London, 1978), pp. 144, 181.

9 N. Brooks, 'The development of military obligations in eighth- and ninth-century England', in P. Clemoes and K. Hughes (eds), *England before the Conquest* (Cambridge, 1971), pp. 69–84. Cf., also R. P. Abels, *Lordship and Military Obligation in Anglo-Saxon England* (London, 1988). On warfare in early England see S. C. Hawkes (ed.), *Weapons and Warfare in Anglo-Saxon England (Oxford, 1989)*.

10 Bede's letter to Ecgberht is edited by C. Plummer, *Venerabilis Baedae Opera Historica*, 2 vols (Oxford, 1892, 1896), Vol. I, pp. 405 ff. (*EHD* Vol. I, no. 170).

11 Of the now quite extensive literature on chiefdoms and states, see in general H. J. M. Claessen and P. Skalnik (eds), *The Early State* (The Hague, 1978), and on Anglo-Saxon England, R. Hodges, 'State formation and the role of trade in Middle Saxon England', *Social Organization and Settlement*, vol. ii, ed. D. Green, C. Haselgrove and M. Spriggs (BAR International Series (Supplementary) 47 (ii), 1978), pp. 439–53, and C. J. Arnold, 'Social evolution in post-Roman western Europe', in J. Bintliff (ed.), *European Social Evolution: Archaeological Perspectives* (Bradford, 1984), pp. 277–83. For a geographer's approach, see R. A. Dodgshon, *The European Past: Social Evolution and Spatial Order* (London, 1987).

12 Cf., T. M. Charles-Edwards, 'Early medieval kingships in the British Isles', in Bassett, *The Origins of Anglo-Saxon Kingdoms*, pp. 28–39 (p. 32).

13 Sawyer, *From Roman Britain to Norman England*, pp. 164, 181.

14 G. Duby, *The Early Growth of the European Economy*, trans. H. B. Clarke (London, 1974), p. 69. On the Anglo-Saxon coins, see P. Grierson and M. Blackburn, *Medieval European Coinage*, Vol. I: *The Early Middle Ages* (Cambridge, 1986), pp. 155 ff., and *Sceattas in England and on the Continent*, ed. D. Hill and D. M. Metcalf (BAR British Series 128, 1984).

15 R. Hodges, *Dark Age Economics: The Origins of Towns and Trade AD 600–1000* (London, 1982), pp. 66 ff., R. Hodges and D. Whitehouse, *Mohammed, Charlemagne and the Origins of Europe* (London, 1983), pp. 92 ff., and R. Hodges, *The Anglo-Saxon Achievement: Archaeology and the Beginnings of English Society* (London, 1989), pp. 55–6, 69 ff.

16 J. Haslam, 'Market and fortress in England in the reign of Offa', *World Archaeology*, vol. 19 (1987), pp. 76–93 (p. 90). See also for comments Hodges, *The Anglo-Saxon Achievement*, p. 143.

17 Hodges, *Dark Age Economics*, p. 192.

18 For an important new study of the Anglo-Saxon kingdoms see B. E. A. Yorke, *Kings and Kingdoms in Early Anglo-Saxon England* (London, forthcoming). I am grateful to Dr Yorke for allowing me to read her book before publication.

19 *Henrici Archidiaconi Huntendunensis Historia Anglorum*, ed. T. Arnold (Rolls series: London, 1879) (trans. T. Forester, *The Chronicle of Henry of Huntingdon* (London, 1853)); see the comments of J. Campbell, 'Some twelfth-century views of the Anglo-Saxon past', *Peritia*, vol. 3 (1984), pp. 131–50 (pp. 134 ff.) (reprinted in Campbell, *Essays in Anglo-Saxon History* (London and Ronceverte, 1986), pp. 209–28).

20 *Willelmi Malmesbiriensis monachi De Gestis Regum Anglorum*, ed. W. Stubbs, 2 vols (Rolls series: London, 1887, 1889) (trans. J. A. Giles, *William of Malmesbury's Chronicle* (London, 1847)).

21 C. R. Hart, 'The Tribal Hidage', *Transactions of the Royal Historical Society*, vol. 21 (1971), pp. 133–57 (p. 133).

22 *Florentii Wigorniensis monachi Chronicon ex Chronicis*, ed. B. Thorpe, 2 vols (London, 1848) (trans. J. Stevenson, *The Church Historians of England*, Vol. II, Part I (London, 1853)).

23 Cf., D. Dumville, 'Essex, Middle Anglia and the expansion of Mercia', in Bassett, *The Origins of Anglo-Saxon Kingdoms*, pp. 123–40 (p. 126).

24 Bede's *Historia Ecclesiastica* (hereafter cited as *HE*) was edited by C. Plummer, *Venerabilis Baedae Opera Historica*, 2 vols (Oxford, 1892, 1896), and more recently with translation by B. Colgrave and R. A. B. Mynors, *Bede's Ecclesiastical History of the English People* (Oxford, 1969), with a commentary by J. M. Wallace-Hadrill, *Bede's Ecclesiastical History of the English People* (Oxford, 1988). References in the text are by book and chapter.

25 P. Hunter Blair, 'The boundary between Bernicia and Deira', *Archaeologia Aeliana*, vol. 27 (1949), pp. 46–59 (reprinted in Blair, *Anglo-Saxon Northumbria*, ed. M. Lapidge and P. H. Blair (London, 1984)).

26 H. P. R. Finberg, 'The princes of the Hwicce', in H. P. R. Finberg (ed.), *The Early Charters of the West Midlands* (Leicester, 1961), pp. 167–80. Cf., D. Hooke, *The Anglo-Saxon Landscape: The Kingdom of the Hwicce* (Manchester, 1985) and now also S. Bassett, 'In search of the origins of Anglo-Saxon kingdoms', in his *The Origins of Anglo-Saxon Kingdoms*, pp. 3–27 (pp. 6 ff.).

27 Cf., D. Hill, *An Atlas of Anglo-Saxon England* (Oxford, 1978), p. 38.

28 F. M. Stenton, 'Lindsey and its kings', in D. M. Stenton (ed.), *Preparatory to Anglo-Saxon England* (Oxford, 1970), pp. 127–35. See also B. Eagles, 'Lindsey', in Bassett, *The Origins of Anglo-Saxon Kingdoms*, pp. 202–12; S. Bassett, 'Lincoln and the Anglo-Saxon see of Lindsey' (with an appendix, 'The name Lindsey' by M. Gelling), *Anglo-Saxon England*, vol. 18 (1989), pp. 1–32; and R. A. Hall, 'The Five Boroughs of the Danelaw: a review of present knowledge', *Anglo-Saxon England*, pp. 149–206.

29 The standard edition of Anglo-Saxon charters is *Cartularium Saxonicum*, ed. W. de Gray Birch, 3 vols (London, 1885–93) (hereafter abbreviated as *CS* and documents cited by number) and the principal guide to them is P. H. Sawyer, *Anglo-Saxon Charters: An Annotated List and Bibliography* (Royal Historical Society Guides and Handbooks, 8; London, 1968) (hereafter abbreviated as S and documents cited by number).

30 H. P. R. Finberg, 'The princes of the Magonsaete', in his *The Early Charters of the West Midlands*, pp. 217–24. See now also K. Pretty, 'Defining the Magonsaete', in Bassett, *The Origins of Anglo-Saxon Kingdoms*, pp. 171–83.

31 For the charters of Rochester, see now the British Academy edition: *Anglo-Saxon Charters, I: Charters of Rochester*, ed. A. Campbell (London, 1973).

32 B. E. A. Yorke, 'The kingdom of the East Saxons', *Anglo-Saxon England*, vol. 14 (1985), pp. 1–36 (pp. 27–8). On the extent of the *regio* of Surrey (*HE* IV, 6), see J. Blair, 'Frithuwold's kingdom and the origins of Surrey' in Bassett, *The Origins of Anglo-Saxon Kingdoms*, pp. 97–107.

33 K. Bailey, 'The Middle Saxons', in Bassett, *The Origins of Anglo-Saxon Kingdoms*, pp. 108–22. Bailey considers that the eastern Saxons had absorbed the Middle Saxon groups by the end of the sixth century (p. 113).

34 Cf., Plummer, *Venerabilis Baedae Opera Historica*, Vol. II, p. 120.

35 N. Brooks, 'The creation and early structure of the kingdom of Kent', in Bassett, *The Origins of Anglo-Saxon Kingdoms*, pp. 55–74 (pp. 68–9).

36 H. M. Chadwick, *Studies on Anglo-Saxon Institutions* (Cambridge, 1905), pp. 286–8 (cf., pp. 296, 300).

37 B. E. A. Yorke, 'The Jutes of Hampshire and Wight and the origins of Wessex', in Bassett, *The Origins of Anglo-Saxon Kingdoms*, pp. 84–96 (p. 96).

38 *Place-Names of Warwickshire*, ed. A. Mawer and F. M. Stenton (English Place-Name Society, vol. xiii; Cambridge, 1936), pp. xvii–xviii; D. Hooke, *Anglo-Saxon Staffordshire: The Charter Evidence* (Keele, 1983), pp. 19 ff.

39 C. R. Hart, 'The kingdom of Mercia', in A. Dornier (ed.), *Mercian Studies* (Leicester, 1977), pp. 43–61 (pp. 12, 18–19).

40 A. Rumble, '"Hrepingas" reconsidered', in Dornier, *Mercian Studies*, pp. 169–71.

41 W. Davies, 'Middle Anglia and the Middle Angles', *Midland History*, vol. 2 (1973), pp. 18–20.

42 See D. Dumville, 'The terminology of overkingship in early Anglo-Saxon England' (forthcoming). I am grateful to Dr Dumville for allowing me to consult this paper before publication. On the Hwicce, see also Bassett, 'The search for the origins of Anglo-Saxon kingdoms', p. 6. David Dumville is prepared to accept Middle Anglia as a Mercian creation but Professor Davies's arguments against an earlier politically independent existence for the Middle Angles are essentially *ex silentio* (cf., Campbell, 'Bede's *Reges* and *Principes*', *Essays in Anglo-Saxon History*, pp. 85–98 (p. 90)). What the evidence suggests is that Middle Anglia had become an administrative dependency by the mid-seventh century.

43 Hooke, *The Anglo-Saxon Landscape: The Kingdom of the Hwicce*, pp. 78 ff., and see also Bassett, 'In search of the origins of Anglo-Saxon kingdoms', pp. 18–19.

44 See also now D. Dumville, 'The Tribal Hidage: an introduction to the texts and their history', in Bassett, *The Origins of Anglo-Saxon Kingdoms*, pp. 225–30.

45 Hart, 'The Tribal Hidage', pp. 135, 157, proposed the second half of the eighth century and the reign of Offa (cf., Hart, 'The kingdom of Mercia', in Dornier, *Mercian Studies*, pp. 43–61); W. Davies and H. Vierck, 'The contexts of *Tribal Hidage*: social aggregates and settlement patterns', *Frühmittelalterliche Studien*, vol. 8 (1974), pp. 223–93, prefer the second half of the seventh century. Dumville, 'Essex, Middle Anglia and the expansion of Mercia in the South-East Midlands', p. 133, also favours the 670s.

46 M. Gelling, 'The early history of western Mercia', in Bassett, *The Origins of Anglo-Saxon Kingdoms*, pp. 184–201 (p. 192).

47 For attempts to map all the Tribal Hidage groups, see Hart, 'The Tribal Hidage', p. 137, Davies and Vierck, 'The contexts of *Tribal Hidage*', p. 235, and Hill, *An Atlas of Anglo-Saxon England*, p. 76.

48 Dumville, 'Essex, Middle Anglia and the expansion of Mercia', pp. 131–2.

49 *Asser's Life of King Alfred*, ed. W. H. Stevenson (rev. edn, Oxford, 1953). For a translation see S. Keynes and M. Lapidge, *Alfred the Great, Asser's Life of King Alfred and Other Contemporary Sources* (Harmondsworth, 1983). References in the text are by chapter.

50 See Dodgshon, *The European Past*, pp. 51 ff., 159.

51 Hart, 'The Tribal Hidage', p. 147.

52 ibid., p. 137.

53 ibid., p. 155. M. G. Welch, *Early Anglo-Saxon Sussex*, vol. i (BAR British series 112 (i), 1983), pp. 274 ff.

54 Sawyer, *From Roman Britain to Norman England*, p. 111.

55 Campbell, 'Bede's *Reges* and *Principes*', pp. 85–98.

56 A. T. Thacker, 'Some terms for noblemen in Anglo-Saxon England, *c.* 650–900', *Anglo-Saxon Studies in Archaeology and History*, 2, ed. D. Brown, J. Campbell and S. C. Hawkes (BAR British Series 92, 1981), pp. 201–36; cf., H. R. Loyn, 'The term ealdorman in the translations prepared at the time of King Alfred', *English Historical Review*, vol. 68 (1953), pp. 513–25.

57 A. Scharer, *Die angelsächsische Königsurkunde im 7. und 8. Jahrhundert* (Vienna, 1982), p. 215 comments favourably on Offa's treatment of the Hwiccian rulers (which, however, he considers became more oppressive as time went by (see pp. 231 ff.)).

58 Cf., D. Dumville, 'The terminology of overkingship in early Anglo-Saxon England' (forthcoming).

59 ibid.

60 Cf., Dumville, 'Essex, Middle Anglia and the expansion of Mercia', p. 131.

61 Cf., J. N. L. Myres, 'The Angles, the Saxons and the Jutes', *Proceedings of the British Academy*, vol. 56 (1970), pp. 145–74. See also now N. Howe, *Migration and Mythmaking in Anglo-Saxon England* (New Haven and London, 1989).

62 *The Life of Bishop Wilfrid by Eddius Stephanus*, ed. and trans. B. Colgrave (Cambridge, 1927). References in the text are by chapter.

63 W. Levison, *England and the Continent in the Eighth Century* (Oxford, 1946), p. 92 (and n. 1).

64 F. C. Robinson, 'Names in Old English literature', *Anglia* vol. 86 (1968), pp. 14–58 (p.38).

65   Cf., H. M. Chadwick, *The Origin of the English Nation* (Cambridge, 1907), pp. 54 ff. For some further thoughts on Bede's use of 'Saxon' and 'Angle', see N. Jacobs, 'Anglo-Danish relations, poetic archaism and the date of Beowulf', *Poetica*, vol. 8 (1977), pp. 23–43 (pp. 30 ff.); M. Richter, 'Bede's *Angli*: Angles or English?', *Peritia*, vol. 3 (1984), pp. 99–114; and S. Reynolds, 'What do we mean by "Anglo-Saxon" and "Anglo-Saxons"?', *Journal of British Studies*, vol. 24 (1985), pp. 395–414. Cf., also P. Wormald, 'Bede, the *Bretwaldas* and the origins of the *Gens Anglorum*', in P. Wormald, D. Bullough and R. Collins (eds), *Ideal and Reality in Frankish and Anglo-Saxon Society* (Oxford, 1983), pp. 99–129 (pp.120–5).

66   See for example, *MGH Scriptores rer. Langobardicarum*, ed. L. Bethmann and G. Waitz (Hanover, 1878), pp. 124, 169.

67   Cf., A. Russchen, *New Light on Dark Age Frisia* (Drachten, 1967), pp. 29–33; R. H. Bremmer, 'Frisians in Anglo-Saxon England: a historical and toponymical investigation', *Frijske Nammen*, vol. 3 (1981), pp. 45–94. Wallace-Hadrill, *Early Germanic Kingship in England and on the Continent*, pp. 23–4 comments on the debated topic of a Frankish presence in England, and J. M. Whittock, *The Origins of England 400–600* (London, 1986), pp. 223 ff., reviews recent discussion. See also E. James, *The Franks* (London, 1988), pp. 116–17.

68   Cf., Dumville, 'Essex, Middle Anglia and the expansion of Mercia', pp. 127–8.

69   Yorke, 'The kingdom of the East Saxons', p. 14.

70   R. W. Chambers, *Beowulf* (3rd edn, Cambridge, 1959), pp. 31–40.

71   Reynolds, 'What do we mean by "Anglo-Saxon" and "Anglo-Saxons"?', p. 405. See, however, the comments of Charles-Edwards, 'Early medieval kingships in the British Isles', p. 34.

72   For a recent minimalist view of the numbers involved in the Anglo-Saxon invasion of Britain in the post-Roman period, see Hodges, *The Anglo-Saxon Achievement*, pp. 10 ff., 186 ff. Contrast C. Hills, 'The archaeology of Anglo-Saxon England in the pagan period', *Anglo-Saxon England*, vol.8 (1979). pp. 297–329 (p. 313).

73   *Chronica Minora*, Vol. 1, ed. T. Mommsen, *MGH Auctores Antiq.*, Vol. IX (Berlin, 1892), p. 654. Cf., now, M. E. Jones and J. Casey, 'The Gallic Chronicle restored: a chronology for the Anglo-Saxon invasions and the end of Roman Britain', *Britannia*, vol. 19 (1988), pp. 367–98 (pp. 379 ff.).

74   *Chronica Minora*, Vol. 1, p. 660; Jones and Casey, 'The Gallic Chronicle restored', pp. 393 ff.

75   *Gildas*, ed. and trans. H. Williams, 2 vols (Cymmrodorion Record Series, no. 3; London, 1899, 1901). References in the text are by chapter.

76   On Gildas, see *Gildas: New Approaches*, ed. M. Lapidge and D. N. Dumville (Woodbridge, 1984).

77   The *Historia Brittonum* (hereafter abbreviated as *HB*) was edited by T. Mommsen, *Chronica Minora*, Vol. III, *MGH Auctores Antiq.*, Vol. XIII (Berlin, 1894), and is currently being re-edited by D. Dumville, beginning with *The Historia Brittonum*, Vol.3: *The 'Vatican' Recension* (Cambridge, 1985). For a translation, see J. Morris, *Nennius* (London and Chichester, 1980). References in the text are to Mommsen's chapters.

78   Cf., D. N. Dumville, 'Sub-Roman Britain: history and legend', *History*, vol. 62 (1977), pp. 173–92.

79   Cf., Brooks, 'The creation and early structure of the kingdom of Kent', p. 577.

80   On the *civitas Regnensium*, see M. G. Welsh, *Early Anglo-Saxon Sussex*, vol. i, pp. 10–14, and on the *civitas* of the Trinovantes, Bassett, 'In search of the origins of Anglo-Saxon kingdoms', p. 24.

81   See Arnold, 'Social evolution in post-Roman western Europe', pp. 279 ff., and idem, *An Archaeology of the Early Anglo-Saxon Kingdoms*, (London and New York, 1988), pp. 142 ff.

82   M. Carver, 'Kingship and material culture in early Anglo-Saxon East Anglia', in Bassett, *The Origins of Anglo-Saxon Kingdoms*, pp. 141–58 (pp. 149, 150); cf., M. Poston, *The Medieval Economy and Society: An Economic History of Britain in the Middle Ages* (London, 1972), p. 76.

83 *Felix's Life of St Guthlac*, ed. and trans. B. Colgrave (Cambridge, 1956). References in the text are by chapter.

84 Dumville, 'Kingship, genealogies and regnal lists', pp. 91 ff.; H. Moisl, 'Anglo-Saxon royal genealogies and Germanic oral tradition', *Journal of Medieval History*, vol. 7 (1981), pp. 215–48; Sawyer, *From Roman Britain to Norman England*, p. 13.

85 Dumville, 'Kingship, genealogies and regnal lists', p. 91 (n. 105); P. Sims-Williams, 'The settlement of England in Bede and the "Chronicle"', *Anglo-Saxon England*, vol. 12 (1983), pp. 1–41 (pp. 22–3); and Brooks, 'The creation and early structure of the kingdom of Kent', pp. 60–1.

86 D. N. Dumville, 'The Anglian collection of royal genealogies and regnal lists', *Anglo-Saxon England*, vol. 5 (1976), pp. 23–50.

87 ibid., pp. 31, 33, 37.

88 D. P. Kirby, 'Vortigern', *Bulletin of the Board of Celtic Studies*, vol. 23 (1968), pp. 37–59 (pp. 46–8); Brooks, 'The creation and early structure of the kingdom of Kent', pp. 63–4.

89 Cf., K. H. Jackson, *Language and History in Early Britain* (Edinburgh, 1953), pp. 613, 689.

90 See D. M. Wilson, 'Sweden-England', *Vendel Period Studies*, ed. J. P. Lamm and H.-A. Nordstrom (Stockholm, 1983), pp. 163–6, to which R. L. S. Bruce-Mitford replies, 'The Sutton Hoo ship-burial: some continental connections', *Angli e sassoni al di qua e al di là del mare* (Settimane di Studio del centro Italiano di studi sull'alto medioevo, no. 32 (1984): 2 vols, Spoleto, 1986), Vol. I, pp. 143–210 (pp. 195 ff.).

91 M. O. H. Carver, 'Sutton Hoo in context', *Angli e sassoni*, vol. 1, pp. 77–117 (p. 100).

92 *MGH Scriptores*, Vol. XXX (ii), ed. A. Hofmeister (Hanover, 1934), p. 793.

93 Wallace-Hadrill, *Early Germanic Kingship*, p. 21.

94 Cf., James, 'The origins of barbarian kingdoms: the continental evidence', pp. 43 ff.

95 E. A. Thompson, *The Early Germans* (Oxford, 1965), p. 40.

96 H. Vollrath-Reichelt, *Königsgedanke und Königtum bei den Angelsachsen* (Cologne, 1971). For some recent observations, see A. Angenendt, *Kaiserherrschaft und Königstaufe: Kaiser, Könige und Päpste als geistliche Patrone in der abendländischen Missionsgeschichte* (Berlin and New York, 1984), pp. 176 ff.

97 Cf., Plummer, *Venerabilis Baedae Opera Historica*, Vol. II, p. 86. The meaning of this passage has been debated in recent years; see Vollrath-Reichelt, *Königsgedanke und Königtum*, pp. 80 ff., Wormald, 'Bede, the *bretwaldas* and the origins of *Gens Anglorum*', p. 106 (and n. 30), and now Wallace-Hadrill, *Bede's Ecclesiastical History of the English People*, pp. 220–2.

98 Sawyer, *From Roman Britain to Norman England*, p. 55.

99 Levison, *England and the Continent in the Eighth Century*, pp. 123–5; Dumville, 'The terminology of overkingship' (forthcoming). See also B. E. A. Yorke, 'The vocabulary of Anglo-Saxon overlordship', *Anglo-Saxon Studies in Archaeology and History*, 2, ed. D. Brown *et al.*, pp. 171–200.

100 Dumville, 'The terminology of overkingship' (forthcoming).

101 ibid., (forthcoming).

102 E. John, *Orbis Britanniae* (Leicester, 1966), p. 7.

103 Wormald, 'Bede, the *bretwaldas* and the origins of the *Gens Anglorum*', pp. 123 ff.

104 N. Brooks, *The Early History of the Church of Canterbury* (Leicester, 1984), pp. 76, 78, 343 (n. 48).

105 *Adomnan's Life of Columba*, ed. and trans. A. O. and M. O. Anderson (Edinburgh and London, 1961).

106 ibid., I, 1.

107 ibid., I, 36 (and cf., I, 14).

108 Dumville, 'The terminology of overkingship' (forthcoming).

109 Wormald, 'Bede, the *bretwaldas* and the origins of the *Gens Anglorum*', p. 127.

110 Arnold, *An Archaeology of the Early Anglo-Saxon Kingdoms*, pp. 51, 157, 163 ff., 194 ff; cf., idem, 'Wealth and social structure: a matter of life and death', *Anglo-Saxon*

Cemeteries, ed. P. Rahtz, T. Dickinson and L. Watts (BAR British Series 82, 1980), pp. 81–142, and 'Territories and leadership: frameworks for the study of emergent polities in early Anglo-Saxon southern England', in Driscoll and Nieke (eds), *Power and Politics in Early Medieval Britain and Ireland*, pp. 111–27.

111 Sawyer, *From Roman Britain to Norman England*, p. 37.

112 Scharer, *Die angelsächsische Königsurkunde*, p. 216.

113 H. Omout and G. Collon, *Histoire des Francs*, ed. R. Poupardin (Paris, 1913), IV, 19 (26): IX, 26.

114 Cf., Yorke, 'The kingdom of the East Saxons', pp. 5, 33, and P. Wormald, *Bede and the Conversion of England: The Charter Evidence* (Jarrow Lecture 1984), p. 9; see also Scharer, *Die angelsächsische Königsurkunde*, pp. 130 ff.

115 *The Earliest Life of Gregory the Great by an anonymous monk of Whitby*, ed. and trans. B. Colgrave (Lawrence, 1968). References in the text are by chapter.

116 H. Edwards, *The Charters of the Early West Saxon Kingdom* (BAR British series 198, 1988), p. 309.

117 *Councils and Ecclesiastical Documents relating to Great Britain and Ireland*, ed. A. W. Haddan and W. Stubbs, 3 vols (Oxford, 1869–71), Vol. III (Oxford, 1871), pp. 274–5.

118 Cf., Wallace-Hadrill, *Bede's Ecclesiastical History of the English People*, p. 226.

119 Cf., Scharer, *Die angelsächsische Königsurkunde*, pp. 84 ff.

120 *Aldhelmi Opera Omnia*, ed. R. Ehwald, *MGH Auctores Antiq.*, Vol. XV (Berlin, 1919), p. 14; trans. M. Lapidge and J. L. Rosier, *Aldhelm, The Poetic Works* (Woodbridge, 1985), p. 48. S 433 is discussed by Edwards, *The Charters of the Early West Saxon Kingdom*, pp. 105–7.

121 *Florentii Wigorniensis monachi Chronicon ex Chronicis*, Vol. I, p. 259. Aethelweard also referred to the West Saxons as West Angles: *The Chronicle of Aethelweard*, ed. and trans. A. Campbell (Edinburgh and London, 1962), pp. 30, 47, 52.

122 C. Plummer, *Venerabilis Baedae Opera Historica*, Vol. I, p. 367 (and trans. in J. Stevens, revised L. C. Jane, *The Ecclesiastical History of the English Nation* (London, 1951)).

2 Early Kent

In the spring of 597 a company of nearly forty monks from Pope Gregory I's monastic foundation in the city of Rome led by their provost, Augustine, landed on the isle of Thanet in the territory of Aethelberht, king of Kent. Though they were approaching a once Christian land, formerly an integral part of the Roman Empire, and a land in which Christianity still flourished in the west among Celtic-speaking peoples, large tracts of Britain were now dominated by pagan Germanic barbarians from the continent, about whom very little was known in Rome. On their arrival in Britain, Augustine and his companions entered a post-Roman world which compared unfavourably with sub-Roman Gaul and Italy. So much disruption seems to have attended the last phase of Roman Britain and the subsequent invasion and settlement of the Angles, Saxons and Jutes that many of the principal features of the cultural and economic life of Roman Britain exercised no continuing influence. A villa agrarian system and an urban economy had disappeared; so had the diocesan structure of the Romano-British Church. In the areas of Germanic settlement the dominant religious beliefs and practices were non-Christian and there is no evidence for the survival of a class of educated Romano-Britons. There was no surviving literate tradition. There was no currency. All these factors conspired to place the Anglo-Saxons in Britain on the outer fringe of contemporary European civilization..

The preservation of later traditions about the events of the conquest of Britain by the Anglo-Saxons in the fifth and sixth centuries in the *Anglo-Saxon Chronicle*, first compiled at the court of Alfred, king of the West Saxons, in the 890s, and even more the wealth of information concerning the conversion of the Anglo-Saxons to Christianity in the seventh century in Bede's *Historia Ecclesiastica Gentis Anglorum*, completed *c.* 731, can easily obscure the lack of contemporary evidence for much of the history of the Germanic regions of Britain during these post-Roman centuries. It is more appreciated now than ever before that just as the *Chronicle* preserves essentially a late ninth-century view of the Anglo-Saxon Conquest, so the *Ecclesiastical History* provides an early eighth-century view of the conversion of the Anglo-Saxons. Both are some distance removed in time from the events in question, and their materials have been shaped by the interests of their own age. In the absence of any considerable body of earlier evidence it is generally difficult to verify or qualify these later accounts.

Writing his *Histories* in the later decades of the sixth century, however, Gregory, bishop of Tours, makes the earliest extant reference to an

Anglo-Saxon kingdom, namely Kent. Moreover, the survival of copies of papal letters relating to the progress of the Gregorian mission to the Anglo-Saxons in the late sixth century and early seventh, some of them only in Bede's *Historia Ecclesiastica*, creates opportunities for testing Bede's historical narrative concerning events at this time in Kent, which was based essentially on oral tradition, against the evidence of contemporary documentation. It becomes possible, therefore, at this point to analyze conflicts between the historical tradition in the *Historia Ecclesiastica* and the evidence of the contemporary documents with a view to testing the accuracy of Bede's *History* as a source for this period.

The reign of Aethelberht

The reputedly long reign of Aethelberht, king of Kent from 560 to 616 (*HE* II, 5), has become a well-known feature of early English history, with his marriage to Bertha, Christian daughter of Charibert, king of Paris (561–7), often placed even before 560.[1] Bede says that he was overlord of all the Anglo-Saxon kingdoms south of the Humber (*HE* II, 5) and the length of his reign has made it possible for his supremacy to be thought of as lasting 'for nearly thirty years'.[2] There is evidence, nevertheless, that the conventional chronology of Aethelberht should be drastically revised, and both the duration and geographical extent of his overlordship in southern England significantly curtailed.

Aethelberht, who received the missionaries sent by Pope Gregory under the leadership of Augustine and who, according to Bede, was baptized by them (*HE* I, 26), is the first Anglo-Saxon king to be securely attested by contemporary record. In 601 Pope Gregory wrote to Aethelberht, 'king of the Angles'[3] and to Bertha[4] his wife, advising them on their Christian responsibilities. For much of our information about Aethelberht, however, we are dependent on the later material in the *Historia Ecclesiastica*. It is Bede who first records that the kings of Kent were known as Oiscingas because of their descent from Oisc, reputedly a son or grandson of Hengest, and that Aethelberht was remembered as the son of Eormenric and a descendant of Oisc (*HE* II, 5), though the pedigree of Aethelberht, even as Bede gives it, is confused and unsatisfactory.[5] It may not be without significance, however, that Aethelberht's father 'bore a name famous in Germanic legend'.[6] This looks like a family (see Appendix, Fig.1) which expected to succeed and its claim to have established itself in Britain in the earliest days of the Anglo-Saxon Conquest is an understandable one.

According to Bede, drawing on information supplied by the church of Canterbury, when Aethelberht died in February 616 he had reigned for fifty-six years and was in the twenty-first year from the sending of Augustine in 596 (*HE* II, 5). But Bede also says that Aethelberht's death

31

occurred twenty-one years after his baptism (*HE* II, 5). This could be a simple error or it could indicate that the king was baptized as early as 595, in which case Bede will have been misled into thinking that Aethelberht's conversion was the work of the Gregorian mission.[7] Bede's calculation that Aethelberht died twenty-one years after he accepted the Christian faith, however, on the assumption that Aethelberht was baptized in 597, could indicate that he died in 618, and with this may be compared a statement in the *Anglo-Saxon Chronicle* that Aethelberht reigned fifty-three years from an accession in 565 (*ASC* E, G and *St Neots*, *s.a.* 565). The possibility of alternative traditions behind Bede's uncertainty over the chronology of the reign cannot be discounted. Aethelberht appears to have been thought of as reigning from 560 to 616 or from 565 to 618. When Gregory of Tours says, therefore, that the Frankish princess Bertha married the son of the king of Kent,[8] this has often been understood to mean that she married Aethelberht before 560 (or 565), and if Bede's words that Aethelberht received Bertha from her parents (*HE* I, 35) are taken literally, the marriage would have had to have occurred before 567 when her father, King Charibert, died.

These dates, nevertheless, present problems. It becomes difficult, for example, to see how Bertha could have been the mother of Aethelberht's daughter, Aethelburh, who married Eadwine, king of the northern Angles, and bore him four children in the late 620s and early 630s, for this suggests that Aethelburh was born *c.* 600 or later by which time Bertha would have been in her sixties.[9] Not that Bede does say explicitly that Aethelburh was Bertha's daughter but he implies it, and Aethelburh's dispatch of her son on the death of her husband into the safe-keeping of the Merovingian king, Dagobert, her *amicus* (friend or kinsman) (*HE* II, 20) reinforces the impression that she was. That it is just an impression, however, is worth stressing. Aethelberht's son and successor, Eadbald, is said to have taken as his second wife a Frankish princess,[10] so that King Dagobert's goodwill towards Aethelburh could reflect later relationships. Aethelberht is known to have married again at least once after the death of Bertha. Pope Gregory's letter to Bertha in 601 shows that she was alive *c.* 600/1 but she was evidently dead by 616 (or 618) because Eadbald's first marriage was to his stepmother (*HE* II, 5). Though marriage to a stepmother occasionally occurred in royal circles (for example, Alfred's older brother, Aethelbald, married his stepmother in 858), Eadbald was a pagan at his accession and this highly irregular union in the eyes of the Church was seen as a manifestation of his paganism. The implication is that his stepmother was a pagan also. Aethelburh, on the other hand, was a Christian when she married, and one argument is that she is unlikely to have been the daughter of a pagan mother.[11] But Aethelburh could have become a Christian at any time before her marriage and she did have a Christian father in Aethelberht. It is not inconceivable, therefore, that Aethelburh was the daughter of this unnamed woman.

32

There are other considerations which militate against acceptance of the conventional dating. The reign of fifty-six years ascribed to Aethelberht is a very long one for a king in this period, and though Charibert's father, Chlotar, is credited with a reign of fifty years among the Franks in the sixth century by Gregory of Tours,[12] reservations have been expressed about the historicity of round numbers of years like thirty or fifty when they occur in the records of early Germanic rulers.[13] The reign of the sixth-century Saxon king, Ceawlin, extends over thirty years in the annalistic framework of the *Anglo-Saxon Chronicle*, but the West Saxon Genealogical Regnal List gives him a reign of only seven or seventeen years (see below, p. 50). Some suspicion must attach itself, therefore, to Aethelberht's alleged reign of fifty-six years, and the suggestion has been made that Aethelberht died not in the fifty-sixth year of his reign but in the fifty-sixth year of his life,[14] which would indicate that he was born *c.* 560. According to one late source, Aethelberht was born in 552 (*ASC* F, *s.a.* 552), but it is not known on what evidence or tradition this rests. If he was born *c.* 560, Aethelberht would not have been of marriageable age before *c.* 575–80. Gregory of Tours represents Charibert as king when he married Ingoberg, Bertha's mother, and implies that he separated from her at the time of Bertha's birth,[15] in which case Bertha would have been born *c.* 561–2 and is unlikely therefore to have been given away in marriage much before *c.* 580. If Bertha's marriage to Aethelberht is placed *c.* 580 rather than *c.* 560, it would then certainly have been possible for Aethelburh to have been her daughter.

One difficulty remains. Gregory of Tours records that Ingoberg was about 70 when she died in 589.[16] On this evidence, she was born *c.* 520. On the testimony of Gregory, Charibert had a penchant for young girls and took three of them as his wives after Ingoberg, but if he did not marry Ingoberg until after he become king in 561 she would have been a woman of about 40 at the time. While this is not impossible, it is incongruous. One solution would be to suppose that though Charibert only married her in *c.* 561, he and Ingoberg had been cohabiting for some time, which would mean that the birth of Bertha could have occurred earlier. On the other hand, inconstancy seems to have characterized Charibert's relationship with his wives so that he is unlikely to have remained faithful to Ingoberg for long, and Gregory, who knew Ingoberg and attended on her a few months before her death, places his emphasis very much on Charibert's forsaking of Ingoberg at the time of the birth of Bertha.[17] A further possibility is that the figure of 70 for Ingoberg's age at her death 'may be notional'.[18] The conclusion must be that, though the possibility that Bertha and Aethelberht married some years earlier cannot be entirely excluded, the balance of probability is that they married *c.* 580 and were both aged about 20 at the time. Bede's statement that Aethelberht received Bertha from her parents, therefore, should not be taken literally.

Gregory of Tours is a primary source when he twice refers to Bertha's marriage. In a passage perhaps written in the early 580s, Gregory says only that Bertha married a man from Kent.[19] On a second occasion, writing *c.* 590–1, and recording his meeting with Ingoberg a few months before she died in 589, he says of her that she left one daughter, married to the son of a certain king in Kent.[20] Because it was generally accepted by historians that Bertha's husband was king of Kent across most of the second half of the sixth century, Gregory's failure to mention Aethelberht specifically was ascribed to his ignorance of English affairs, but if Bede's fifty-six years for Aethelberht does represent his age at death and not his regnal length, the date of his accession is unknown. Gregory's second statement presumably reflects how Bertha was spoken of either when Gregory wrote or, perhaps more probably, how Ingoberg referred to her daughter when Gregory saw her in 589, and what it shows is not that Aethelberht was king of Kent at the time, but that his father was. Moreover, Gregory's earlier description of Bertha as married to a man of Kent, without reference even to the fact that her husband was the son of a king, indicates that at the time this was written Eormenric himself was not yet king. Consequently, contrary to the Bedan image of Aethelberht as king from 560 to 616, the indications from Gregory are that Aethelberht's father was not reigning at the time of the marriage *c.* 580 and must have succeeded in the course of the 580s, and that Aethelberht's accession can be placed no earlier than 589.[21] Aethelberht, therefore, had not been king for thirty-seven years when Augustine arrived in Kent in 597, nor married for even longer to Bertha. He had probably been married to Bertha for about seventeen years and king for no longer than eight at the most. The period of time during which he can have been overlord among the southern kingdoms is, of course, correspondingly diminished.

A valuable perspective is obtained on the marriage of Aethelberht and Bertha by the realization that at the time of its arrangement and celebration there may have been no certainty that Aethelberht would become king. Perhaps one of the consequences of the marriage was to bring such Frankish support to Aethelberht and his father in Kent as to guarantee their acquisition of royal power. Merovingian involvement with Saxons returning from Britain to the continent in the early sixth century and the establishment of a Frankish hegemony over the continental Jutes and Saxons seems to have created a context in which Frankish rulers could claim an extension of their political influence across the Channel by the early 550s.[22] When Pope Gregory wrote to the Merovingian kings, Theuderic and Theudebert, concerning the mission of Augustine in 596, he understood that they wished their subjects to be converted to their faith,[23] as if by this date certainly Frankish overlordship of some of the Anglo-Saxons was an acknowledged fact.[24] That Bertha was accompanied to Kent by a Frankish bishop, Liudhard (*HE* I, 25), could be further evidence for this claim to overlordship if Liudhard was intended to represent the Frankish Church in Kent.[25] A Frankish presence or at least a marked cultural Frankish influence has long been detected in the archaeological record of southern England in the sixth century. Gold-rich Kent was clearly engaged in luxury trade with the Franks and able to dominate the commercial life of south-eastern England,[26] and it may well be that a personal link with the Merovingians through marriage was what made possible the political and military ascendancy of Aethelberht. Moreover, the most important common factor among the earliest Anglo-Saxon kings who responded positively to Christianity was their involvement either directly or indirectly in a Christian Frankish sphere of diplomatic and cultural influence which embraced Kent and radiated out into the territories of the eastern and northern Angles. The further removed regions of the hinterland remained in traditional Germanic paganism longer. For Aethelberht, the Frankish connection was probably decisive.

Aethelberht's marriage to Bertha must certainly have played a part in the opening up of Kent to Christian influences, for Bertha and her companion Bishop Liudhard were allowed to practise their faith in the church of St Martin in Canterbury (*HE* I, 25, 26), and Pope Gregory was responding not only emotionally to Anglian slave boys in Rome but also practically to appeals to the Franks by Christians in England when he dispatched Augustine and his companions in 596.[27] Even so, Augustine and his company of nearly forty monks almost returned to Rome at one stage in their journey north, for the Anglo-Saxons possessed a reputation for being a fierce and barbarous people. They were ordered by the pope to continue (*HE* I, 23) and were probably in a state of considerable apprehension when they landed in the spring of 597.[28] This tends to militate against the possibility that Aethelberht had already been baptized before the arrival of Augustine. The letter of Pope Gregory to Bertha in 601 makes it evident that Gregory was critical of the queen for her failure to convert Aethelberht sooner, and a realization that Aethelberht was still a pagan may have been a factor in Augustine's hesitancy in 596–7. The precise date of the conversion and baptism of Aethelberht, who is said to have received the missionaries courteously and to have treated them well, establishing them at Canterbury (*HE* I, 25), has been much debated. Bede implies that the king was baptized quite soon after the arrival of Augustine (*HE* I, 26). When Pope Gregory wrote to Eulogius, patriarch of Alexandria, in June 598, however, though he took pride in the number of converts whom Augustine had baptized, he does not refer to the baptism of the king specifically.[29] Furthermore, the letter of the pope to Bertha implies a greater degree of prevarication on Aethelberht's part than Bede acknowledges; nor is it certain whether Bede knew of the letter.[30] It has been suggested, on the other hand, that the mass baptisms themselves strongly indicate that the king had already been baptized.[31] That he had certainly been converted by the time Pope

Gregory wrote to him in 601 is clear. Aethelberht was addressed as the pope's 'illustrious son' and urged to suppress the worship of idols and to extend the Christian faith among his people (*HE* I, 32).

At whatever moment between 597 and 601 it occurred, the conversion of Aethelberht by the Gregorian mission was an event of immediate significance. It emancipated Aethelberht from the danger of too great a dependence on the representative of the Frankish rulers of Gaul,[32] and was accompanied by a far-reaching programme for the organization of a Church among the Anglo-Saxons. Although Pope Gregory's plan that London and York be created metropolitan sees for the whole of Britain, each with twelve suffragans (*HE* I, 29),[33] could not be implemented (and indeed London never became an archbishopric), Canterbury did emerge as the first archiepiscopal see and the expectation from an early stage may have been that its authority would embrace the whole of Britain (cf., *HE* II, 2 in which Bede styles Augustine 'archbishop of Britain'). The potential for prestige to accrue to Aethelberht must have been immense.[34] He is said to have legislated in Roman fashion (*HE* II, 5) and his lawcode marked the entry of the Kentish kingdom into the league of 'the more advanced Germanic kingdoms of Europe'.[35] Moreover, the Church in Rome at first believed the Britons to be living in accordance with the customs of the Roman Church – only subsequently did it become clear that this was not so – and Pope Gregory intended that Augustine should possess authority as archbishop over 'all the bishops of Britain' (*HE* I, 27). Matters did not proceed, however, as anticipated. The refusal of the British clergy at the conference of Augustine's Oak, somewhere in the valley of the Severn (its precise location uncertain), to accept Canterbury's authority (*HE* II, 2) was a serious blow. Nor did everyone in the Kentish court become or remain a Christian. Though the influence of the Church in the establishment of compensation as an alternative to feud has been perceived in the laws of Aethelberht,[36] the Christian content of these laws, the earliest to survive from an Anglo-Saxon kingdom, is extremely limited. Aethelberht's son and successor, Eadbald, was a pagan at his accession, either because he had never been converted or because he was, as Bede says, an apostate (*HE* II, 5).[37] King Aethelberht's widow, whom Eadbald married, was possibly a pagan or at least a lapsed Christian. Anglo-Saxon paganism retained its royal supporters, who presumably saw no good reason to abandon traditional beliefs, into the mid-seventh century.

Bede's statement that Aethelberht was overlord of the southern kingdoms occurs in his well-known catalogue of rulers who are said to have held an *imperium* over all the Anglo-Saxon kingdoms south of the Humber (*HE* II, 5). Aethelberht is the third to be named after Aelle, king of the South Saxons, and Ceawlin, king of the West Saxons. Though the Humber is no more likely to have defined the extent of his overlordship than Aelle's or Ceawlin's (see above, p. 19), the reality of his *imperium* is well documented.

By 601 when Pope Gregory wrote to him, Aethelberht's authority evidently transcended the boundaries of his own kingdom. The pope urged him to extend the Christian faith not only among his own people but among the kings and peoples subject to him. That Aethelberht was an overlord is thereby established as the central known fact of Anglo-Saxon political life *c.* 600. Moreover, Bede provides information which serves to delineate more precisely the areas which, in varying degrees, recognized Aethelberht's supremacy. Certainly subject to him were the eastern Saxons who were converted to Christianity under their king Saeberht, the son of Sledd (see Appendix, Fig. 2), according to the East Saxon royal genealogy,[38] and Aethelberht's sister, Ricula, Bede specifically describing him as under the authority of Aethelberht (*HE* II, 3); and undoubtedly the acceptance of Christianity by a subject king was an aspect of his political relationship with an overlord.[39] The eastern Saxon kings ruled quite extensive territory north and south of the Thames[40] and should not be thought of as rulers of little consequence at this time, but the marriage of Saeberht's father to Ricula suggests a dependent relationship going back to Eormenric's time. In the early years of the seventh century, London, in the territory of the eastern Saxons, was even established as a bishopric for one of Augustine's helpers, Mellitus (*HE* II, 3). Raedwald, king of the eastern Angles, was converted to Christianity while in Kent, but only partially and without abandoning his pagan gods (*HE* II, 5), which probably means that Aethelberht's influence over the eastern Angles was appreciably less than over the eastern Saxons. By *c.* 602 Aethelberht was in a position to arrange the meeting between Augustine and British bishops at Augustine's Oak on the north-western border of the territory of the western Saxons (*HE* II, 2), which suggests a westerly extension of his authority. However, there is no evidence that Aethelberht was in a position to prevail on the kings of the western or southern Saxons to accept Christianity, even to Raedwald's lukewarm degree, still less upon the Britons to accept his overlordship.

The pagan reaction under Eadbald

Bede describes how, on Aethelberht's death, his son and successor, Eadbald, led a pagan reaction to the recently established Gregorian mission at Canterbury, marrying his stepmother contrary to Church law and refusing baptism. These developments in Kent were evidently paralleled by a similar reaction among the eastern Saxons which resulted in the expulsion of Mellitus, bishop of London, by the three sons and successors of King Saeberht (*HE* II, 5). Mellitus departed for Gaul, accompanied by Justus, bishop of Rochester. Laurentius, Augustine's successor at Canterbury, also contemplated flight and the abandonment of the Gregorian mission but, according to Bede, his miraculous scourging by St Peter so disconcerted

King Eadbald that he abandoned his paganism and was baptized (*HE* II, 6). Justus was restored to Rochester, though not Mellitus to London because of the continuing paganism of the sons of Saeberht, and when Laurentius died, first Mellitus for five years and then Justus succeeded him as archbishop of Canterbury (*HE* II, 7, 8). Some time after, when the pagan Eadwine, described by Bede as a king of the Northumbrians but perhaps more properly regarded as king of the northern Angles, asked for Eadbald's sister, Aethelburh, in marriage, he had to promise to allow her to practise her Christian faith and give an undertaking to consider baptism himself, on the grounds that it was not lawful for a Christian maiden to be given in marriage to a heathen (*HE* II, 9). Bede says that when she travelled north in 625 she was accompanied by Paulinus, already consecrated bishop of York by Archbishop Justus (*HE* II, 9). This account cannot be accepted wholly as it stands.

Eadbald as king of Kent and the heir to Aethelberht's *imperium* was a powerful figure with whom the rulers of the eastern Saxons were probably acting in concert when they expelled Mellitus. A quite substantial shift in attitude across a wide area of south-east England is implied, attendant perhaps upon a rejection by Eadbald of his father's Frankish connections. Unfortunately, Bede's *Ecclesiastical History* does not seek to establish a political dimension to Eadbald's paganism. Nor does Bede's pious legend concerning the scourging of Laurentius by St Peter offer a serious explanation of the recovery of the Gregorian mission in the face of this adversity. The location of the scene of the scourging in the chancel of the church of St Peter and St Paul – that is, St Augustine's, Canterbury – betrays the story as an early piece of hagiography from the monastery of St Augustine. Alcuin, writing much later, declares that Laurentius was 'censured by apostolic authority'.[41] One possibility is that a papal letter ordered Laurentius to remain in Kent, in the same way that Augustine had been ordered to continue on his way there by Pope Gregory. So involved had the papacy been with the mission to the Anglo-Saxons that it is hardly conceivable that the pope was not informed about the crisis facing the Church in Kent as soon as it arose. What cannot be ascertained now is the extent to which the pagan reaction had already been countered by the time that Eadbald was converted. Bede, however, believed that the conversion of Eadbald was a crucial turning-point and so too did the papacy.

The papal correspondence of Boniface V (619–25) sheds further light on these events. His letters to Archbishop Mellitus, Laurentius' successor, and to Justus as bishop of Rochester, to which Bede refers (*HE* II, 7), have not survived but in his *Historia Ecclesiastica* Bede includes copies of Boniface's letter to Justus as archbishop of Canterbury, which mentions a King Aethelwald (*HE* II, 8), and of those to King Eadwine (*HE* II, 10) and his queen, Aethelburh, Eadbald's sister, which mention a King Eadbald (*HE* II, 11). The appearance of quite different names for the king in these letters has raised the possibility that two rulers are being referred to, but the evidence as a whole contradicts this. When the pope wrote to Justus, he congratulated him on missionary successes, saying that he had heard from King 'Aduluald' how he had been brought to a true conversion and a real faith, and sent him a pallium (*HE* II, 8). The use of the second-person plural pronouns *vos* and *vester* in the first part of the letter (dealing with 'Aduluald') but of the singular *tui* and *tuus* in the second (dealing with the pallium) has led to suggestions that a conflation of two letters has occurred, one written to Justus as bishop of Rochester and concerned with the recent conversion of King 'Aduluald', the other written to Justus as archbishop of Canterbury and concerned with the pallium.[42] In other words, the conversion of 'Aduluald' occurred some time before Justus became archbishop. The mixed use of singular and plural pronouns, however, occurs elsewhere in papal letters of this period – one need look no further than Pope Gregory's letter to Aethelberht – and appears to have no obvious significance. This letter to Justus should probably be treated as a single composition.

According to Bede, Justus succeeded Mellitus as archbishop in 624 (*HE* II, 7). This date cannot be independently confirmed, but if Mellitus was archbishop for five years (which figure may derive from an archiepiscopal list) after Laurentius and Aethelberht died in 616, the earliest date at which Justus could have succeeded Mellitus would have been 621/2, if Laurentius lived into 617; and if Aethelberht died in 618, the earliest date for Justus to succeed would have been 623/4, if Laurentius lived into 619. So Bede's date of 624 cannot be wildly inaccurate and the indications are that the pope's letter to Justus was indeed written *c.* 624. What is certain is that it was written at least five years (the length of Mellitus' archiepiscopate) after the death of Laurentius. Who was 'Aduluald'? As Peter Hunter Blair pointed out, 'Aduluald' represents the name Aethelwald. He thought that the letter was written to Justus as bishop of Rochester rather than to Archbishop Mellitus because of the failing health of Mellitus to which Bede refers (*HE* II, 7), and that Aethelwald was an otherwise unknown king with whom Justus had dealings as bishop of Rochester.[43] But the purpose of the letter is to send Archbishop Justus the pallium.[44] Moreover, in the letters to Eadwine and Aethelburh reference is made not to 'Aduluald' but to a king, 'Audubald', who had also recently been converted. Unlike 'Aduluald', 'Audubald' does represent an archaic form of the name Eadbald. Furthermore, both 'Audubald' and 'Aduluald' are described in the papal letters as having peoples subject to them. There can really be little doubt, therefore, that the 'Aduluald' of the letter to Justus is a scribal error for 'Audubald'.[45] The letters to Justus, Eadwine and Aethelburh were evidently all written after the same event, the conversion of King Eadbald. The error with the king's name in the letter to Justus suggests that this letter came from a source or collection other than the one from which those to Eadwine

39

and Aethelburh derived, but there is no reason to suppose that the original letters to Eadwine and his queen were separated in their writing from that to Archbishop Justus by any appreciable interval of time.

In his letter to Eadwine urging him to accept baptism, the pope refers to what was evidently at the time of writing the recent conversion of Eadbald. The pope supposes that Eadwine would be aware of what had been accomplished in the territories of Eadbald because 'your lands are close to one another'. In his letter to Aethelburh, the pope writes that he has been told by those who came to Rome to inform him of the conversion of King Eadbald that her husband still worshipped idols. So Aethelburh was already married when news reached Rome about Eadbald's conversion. In order to avoid impugning the reliability of Bede's narrative at this point, with its emphasis on 625 as the year Aethelburh and Paulinus went to Northumbria, Hunter Blair supposed that, although married earlier, Aethelburh remained in Kent until 625 and that Boniface wrote to her while she was still resident there.[46] But Aethelburh is clearly envisaged by the pope as able to instruct Eadwine personally and continuously in God's commandments. The balance of probability must be that when these letters were written, Aethelburh was residing with her husband among the northern Angles.

The fact is that the survival of copies of papal letters provides the evidence of contemporary documentation, which shows the Bedan narrative to be seriously defective. Bede (or the oral tradition he was using) mistakenly associated the conversion of Eadbald with Archbishop Laurentius' decision to remain in Kent. It was not until after Justus had succeeded Mellitus that Boniface V wrote concerning the conversion of Eadbald. His letter expresses the pope's appreciation of the power of God and the work of Justus which had brought redemption and salvation to those who now received the Gospel. As a consequence of letters from King Eadbald informing him of the way in which Justus had 'guided his soul to a belief in true conversion and real faith', the pope now anticipated the conversion not only of the peoples subject to Eadbald but also of their neighbours, more specifically of King Eadwine, because the pope's letter to Eadwine reveals that he thought of Eadbald and Eadwine as near neighbours (*HE* II, 8).

It is clear that Eadbald was converted not by Laurentius but by Justus. Consequently, though Bede says that Eadbald recalled Mellitus from the continent after a year (*HE* II, 6), this will have been a false inference from the mistaken belief that the king was converted in so short a time. Moreover, the letter to Justus, while written not all that long after Eadbald's conversion, must have been written after the letters to Eadwine and Aethelburh. In these letters the pope had literally just learnt from messengers of the success of the missionaries in Kent. In the letter to Justus he had heard from the king himself. The sequence of events seems to have been the conversion of the king and the sending of messengers to Rome, the writing of letters by the pope to Eadwine and Aethelburh immediately after the arrival of the messengers from Kent, the receipt by the pope of a letter from Eadbald, and the sending of a papal letter with the pallium to Justus in *c.* 624. Eadbald, therefore, was converted not long before *c.* 624. According to Bede, Justus' predecessor, Mellitus, had consecrated a church in Canterbury founded by the king (*HE* II, 6). If this is correct, Eadbald's conversion must have been effected a little before the death of Mellitus, and the founding of a church in Canterbury will have been an immediate public demonstration of his change of heart. The evidence suggests that the conversion of Eadbald, the founding of this church in Canterbury, the death of Mellitus and the election of Justus occurred in rapid succession over a very short span of time. It follows from this, first, that the pagan reaction under Eadbald was more protracted than Bede's single year. It lasted some five or six years (if Eadbald succeeded in 618) or seven or eight (if Eadbald succeeded in 616), which must have been an anxious time for the Gregorian mission. Second, it is difficult to see how Eadbald could have been a Christian when Eadwine asked for the hand of Aethelburh. The pope was writing to Aethelburh on receipt of the news of Eadbald's conversion, by which time she was already married and resident in the north. The date of the marriage cannot now be determined except that it occurred before *c.* 624. Paulinus was certainly not consecrated bishop of York as early as this (see below, p. 107, n. 2). Bede clearly erred when he stated that Aethelburh was accompanied on her journey north by Paulinus as recently consecrated bishop of York (*HE* II, 9), but there is no reason to suppose that Paulinus did not accompany her as her chaplain. If there is anything of substance in Bede's account of the marriage negotiations, therefore, it must have been the Church leaders in Kent, not the king, who dictated terms to Eadwine, and Eadwine's apparent readiness to embrace Christianity may have been one factor which influenced Eadbald's conversion.

The indications are that the Gregorian mission made it increasingly difficult for Eadbald to maintain a pagan posture. Despite the fierceness of the reaction on the death of Aethelberht, the missionaries were not dislodged from their principal remaining seat at Canterbury in the heart of his territory. The refusal of the Church to allow Eadbald's sister to marry a heathen without some guarantee of the latter's readiness to embrace Christianity must have threatened to compromise him in his dealings with Eadwine. Even so, the most decisive force at work in the Kentish court was again probably Frankish. It cannot be without significance that the conversion of Eadbald was evidently accompanied by the setting aside of his first wife and his marriage to a Frankish princess. It may have been Frankish influence which sustained the missionaries at Canterbury during the years of pagan reaction, and in marrying a Frankish princess Eadbald was probably seeking to recreate a relationship established by Eormenric and Aethelberht forty years earlier, only which this time, however, involved his own conversion.

Political developments in the Anglian areas of Britain at the close of Aethelberht's reign were not without their long-term significance but they may not immediately have threatened the heartland of the Kentish *imperium*. The ascendancy of Raedwald and his ability to defeat the northern Anglian ruler, Aethelfrith, in 616 or 617 (*HE* II, 12) (see below, pp. 72-3), was accompanied by a loss of Aethelberht's already limited influence in East Anglia when Raedwald denied him the military leadership of the eastern Angles (*HE* II, 5) (see above, p. 17), but, throughout the years of opposition to the Church, Eadbald appears to have remained a remarkably powerful figure in southern England. Merovingian gold coins were beginning to play a limited monetary role in Kent by the early seventh century and Eadbald was able to arrange the minting of gold coins at London in his own name AVDVARLD (Auduarld).[47] Eadwine's request for Eadbald's sister in marriage may be seen as a measure of Eadbald's continuing prestige among fellow rulers, and the papal letters testify to the Kentish domination of surrounding peoples as late as *c.* 624. But the situation was changing and Eadbald's Frankish marriage may well have been a response to emerging political and military problems. By *c.* 624 the power of the northern Anglian king, Eadwine, may already have been established as a significant force in southern England (see below, pp. 77-8). The fact that the pope wrote to him and to Aethelburh immediately on learning of Eadbald's conversion suggests that Eadwine was by now a ruler of considerable importance. Following his conversion, Eadbald proved quite incapable *c.* 624 of re-establishing the position of the Church among the eastern Saxons. Saeweard and Seaxred, the sons of Saeberht, who appear in the East Saxon royal genealogy as the progenitors of different branches of the East Saxon dynasty (see Appendix, Fig.2), had clearly now broken away from their former dependence on the Kentish king. Bede says that the bishopric of London was not restored because Eadbald had less royal power than Aethelberht (*HE* II, 6). Eadbald's failure to effect a restoration at this time reveals serious limitations to his authority in territories formerly securely under the domination of a Kentish overlord.

The sequel

The political developments of the first half of the seventh century undoubtedly relegated Kent to a position of lesser importance as kings of the northern Angles (Eadwine and Oswald), created new hegemonies. Nevertheless, the kingdom retained its links with the continent and continued to enjoy a rich cultural life in advance of the Anglo-Saxon hinterland. The evidence of the early Kentish laws suggests 'a highly centralized kingdom on which royal lordship had been firmly imposed',[48] and Eadbald's son and successor, Eorcenberht (640–64), was the first ruler among the Germanic peoples in Britain to order the destruction of pagan idols and the observance of Lent (*HE* III, 8). The kings of Kent had a personal involvement in the appointment of successive archbishops of Canterbury. As Bede brings out most clearly in his *History of the Abbots*,[49] Eorcenberht's son and successor, Ecgberht (664–73), or his counsellors, took part in negotiations with the papacy over a new archbishop following the death of Deusdedit in 664 (see below, pp. 104 ff.).

The diplomatic contacts of the royal house were extensive. It may be that Ecgberht was the 'king of the Saxons' with whom the exiled Lombard prince, Pectarit, was seeking refuge in 671 when circumstances unexpectedly permitted him to return to Italy, and whose son, Cunincpert, king of the Lombards (680–700), was married to a woman of Anglo-Saxon race with the Kentish-type name Hermelinda (Eormenhild?).[50] The Kentish court was certainly host to visiting ecclesiastics – for example, Wilfrid and Benedict Biscop (*Vita Wilfridi*, ch. 3)[51] – and it was King Ecgberht who provided an escort under somewhat difficult circumstances for Archbishop Theodore and shortly after for Abbot Hadrian from Gaul to Kent (*HE* IV, 1), where Theodore's party was well received.[52] The prestige of the kings of Kent, therefore, must have remained considerable. They were undoubtedly well connected: to the Merovingian kings of Gaul through the marriages of Aethelberht and Eadbald to Frankish princesses; to the ruling dynasty in East Anglia through Eorcenberht's marriage to Seaxburh, daughter of Anna, king of the eastern Angles (*HE* III, 8); and to the kings of Mercia through the marriage of Eorcenberht's daughter Eormenhild, to Wulfhere, son of Penda, king of the Mercians.[53] In the early 640s Eanflaed, granddaughter of Aethelberht, married Oswiu, king of the northern Angles (*HE* III, 15) and Aebbe (Eafe), the daughter of Eorcenberht's brother, Eormenred, married Merewalh, king of the Magonsaete.[54] The maintenance of a Frankish connection is reflected in the presence of Eorcenberht's daughter, Eorcengota, as a nun at Faremoûtier-en-Brie (*HE* III, 8) and Aebbe's daughter, Mildrith, at Chelles,[55] and as the founders in Kent of the first churches, monasteries and nunneries in England these royal men and women gained great merit in the eyes of the Church.[56] It was probably in the 670s, in response to monetary changes in Gaul, that Kent spearheaded the adoption in Anglo-Saxon territories of a new silver *sceatta* (penny) coinage.[57]

Nor was the political standing of the kings of Kent entirely destroyed by the ascendancy of Anglian *brytenwealdas*, if Bede is correct in specifically excluding Kent from the territories ruled over by Eadwine and Oswald (*HE* II, 5) and this is not simply a gloss to indulge Kentish sensitivity.[58] The indications are that a local Kentish domination of the south-east was maintained by both Eorcenberht and Ecgberht. The sons of Saeberht had broken free from the former dependent relationship of their father on King Aethelberht, but they perished in a campaign against the Gewisse (*HE* II,

5) and thereafter the history of the eastern Saxons is quite obscure until the 650s (*HE* III, 22).[59] Though there is admittedly no evidence for further Christianizing of the eastern Saxons from Kent, it may be that there was some re-establishment for a time at least of Kentish overlordship. Surrey was certainly still in Kentish control when King Ecgberht patronized the monastery of Chertsey (*CS* 34: S 1165).[60] It was not until approximately the last quarter of the seventh century that Kent's influence was further curtailed by more powerful neighbouring rulers, when the consequences of dynastic developments in the early seventh century may have rendered the Kentish kingdom more vulnerable.

It is possible that Eorcenberht shared royal power with his brother, Eormenred,[61] and the claim in the Mildrith legend that Eadbald left the kingdom wholly to Eorcenberht, his younger son,[62] thereby effectively disinheriting Eormenred, may have been part of a later attempt to discredit royal claimants from this branch of the family (see Appendix, Fig.1). There can be no doubt that the murder of Eormenred's sons, Aethelred and Aethelberht, at the instigation of Eorcenberht's son and successor, Ecgberht,[63] was the result of dynastic tension and it certainly seems to have consolidated the kingship in the hands of Eorcenberht's descendants. Ecgberht was succeeded by his brother, Hlothhere (*HE* IV, 5), and Hlothhere by Ecgberht's son, Eadric (*HE* IV, 26), but not one of these princes survived into old age. What is surprising is that they were not challenged, so far as is known, by princes claiming to represent other lines of descent from Eormenric or Oisc, and, certainly, if they were, no rival aetheling (that is, a prince of the royal line) successfully aspired to the kingship. Ecgberht may only have been about 10 years old or so at the time of his accession, for his mother, Seaxburh, is said to have acted as regent on his behalf.[64] Ecgberht's sons, Eadric and Wihtred (*HE* IV, 26), must have been no more than infants when their father died in 673. Indeed, an interregnum of a year appears to have followed Ecgberht's death before the accession of Hlothhere, but probably because of Mercian interference rather than dynastic strife (see below, pp. 113, 115). Hlothhere had served in the retinue of his aunt, Aethelthryth, sister of Seaxburh and the wife of Ecgfrith, king of the northern Angles (*HE* IV, 22), but he was only just over ten years on the throne as king of Kent before his young nephew, Eadric, brought about his death; Eadric survived him only by eighteen months, the kingdom thereafter being exposed to external attack and internal division (*HE* IV, 26) (see below, pp. 118 ff.).

Notes

1 See, for example, K. P. Witney, *The Kingdom of Kent* (London and Chichester, 1982), pp. 85 ff., and J. N. L. Myres, *The English Settlements* (Oxford, 1986), p. 10.

2   F. M. Stenton, *Anglo-Saxon England* (3rd edn, Oxford, 1971), p. 60, though Stenton circumspectly avoided dating precisely Aethelberht's accession or his marriage to Bertha.

3   *Gregorii I papae registrum epistolarum*, ed. P. Ewald and L. M. Hartmann, *MGH Epistolae*, Vols I and II (Berlin, 1887-90), Vol. II, xi, 37 (*HE* I, 32).

4   ibid., Vol. II, xi, 35.

5   P. Sims-Williams, 'The settlement of England in Bede and the "Chronicle"', *Anglo-Saxon England*, vol. 12 (1983), pp. 1–41 (p. 22); cf., N. Brooks, 'The creation and early structure of the kingdom of Kent', in S. Bassett (ed.), *The Origins of Anglo-Saxon Kingdoms* (Leicester, 1989), pp. 55–74 (pp. 58 ff.). B. E. A. Yorke comments in 'Joint kingship in Kent *c.* 560 to 785', *Archaeologia Cantiana*, vol. 99 (1983), pp. 1–19 (pp. 3–4) and also now in *Kings and Kingdoms in Early Anglo-Saxon England* (London, 1990 [forthcoming]), Chap. 2.

6   J. M. Wallace-Hadrill, *Early Germanic Kingship in England and on the Continent* (Oxford, 1971), pp. 25–6.

7   I. N. Wood, *The Merovingian North Sea* (Occasional Papers on Medieval Topics: Alingsås, 1983), p. 15.

8   H. Omont and G. Collon, *Histoire des Francs*, ed. R. Poupardin (Paris, 1913), ix, 26.

9   H. G. Richardson and G. O. Sayles, *Law and Legislation from Aethelberht to Magna Carta* (Edinburgh, 1966), pp. 157–69, draw attention to these chronological difficulties.

10 D. W. Rollason, *The Mildrith Legend: A Study in Early Medieval Hagiography in England* (Leicester, 1982), pp. 33, 92, 114.

11 Richardson and Sayles, *Law and Legislation*, p. 165.

12 *Histoire des Francs*, iv, 14.

13 K. Harrison, *The Framework of Anglo-Saxon History to A.D. 900* (Cambridge, 1976), p. 132.

14 N. Brooks, *The Early History of the Church of Canterbury* (Leicester, 1984), p. 6.

15 *Histoire des Francs*, iv, 19 (26).

16 ibid., iv, 19 (26).

17 This is the clearest chronological point of reference. The matrimonial situation is complicated by the possibility of polygamy in the Merovingian royal family at this time; P. Stafford, *Queens, Concubines, and Dowagers: The King's Wife in the Early Middle Ages* (Athens, Ga, 1983), p. 73. Cf., D. Herlihy, *Medieval Households* (Cambridge, Mass. and London, 1985), p. 49.

18 Wood, *The Merovingian North Sea*, p. 15.

19 *Histoire des Francs*, iv, 19 (26). On the writing of Gregory's *Histories*, see also now W. Goffart, *The Narrators of Barbarian History* (Princeton, NJ, 1988), pp. 119 ff.

20 *Histoire des Francs*, ix, 26.

21 Brooks reaches similar conclusions in 'The creation and early structure of the kingdom of Kent', pp. 65–7.

22 Stenton, *Anglo-Saxon England*, pp. 14, 59; cf., R. Collins, 'Theodebert I', in P. Wormald, D. Bullough and R. Collins (eds), *Ideal and Reality in Frankish and Anglo-Saxon Society* (Oxford, 1983), pp. 7–33 (pp. 10–11). I. N. Wood, 'The end of Roman Britain: continental evidence and parallels', in M. Lapidge and D. Dumville (eds), *Gildas: New Approaches* (Woodbridge, 1984), pp. 1–25, considers that the Franks and the Anglo-Saxons may have enjoyed close legal arrangements from the late fifth century (pp. 23–4). See also E. James, *The Franks* (London, 1988), p. 103.

23 *Gregorii I papae registrum epistolarum*, Vol. II, iv, 49.

24 Stenton, *Anglo-Saxon England*, p. 60. It is true there is 'no evidence that Aethelberht ever became, by a formal act, the man of any Frankish king' (p. 60), but given the paucity of evidence generally this is not surprising. Cf., the observations of Wallace-Hadrill, *Early Germanic Kingship*, pp. 25–6 and Wood, *The Merovingian North Sea*, pp. 11 ff.

25 A. Angenendt, 'The conversion of the Anglo-Saxons', *Angli e sassoni al di qua e al di là del mare*, (Settimane di Studio del centro Italiano di studi sull'alto medioevo, no. 32 (1984); 2 vols, Spoleto, 1986), pp. 747–81 (p.779).

26 C. J. Arnold, *An Archaeology of the Early Anglo-Saxon Kingdoms* (London and New York, 1988), pp. 56 ff., 63 ff. Cf., R. Hodges, *The Anglo-Saxon Achievement: Archaeology and the Beginnings of English Society* (London, 1989), pp. 31–4.

27 *Gregorii I papae registrum epistolarum*, Vol. II, vi, 49. On the Frankish background see J. M. Wallace-Hadrill, *The Frankish Church* (Oxford, 1983), pp. 114 ff.

28 For accounts of the Augustinian mission, see H. Mayr-Harting, *The Coming of Christianity to Anglo-Saxon England* (London, 1972), pp. 51 ff., and Brooks, *The Early History of the Church of Canterbury*, pp. 3 ff.

29 *Gregorii I papae registrum epistolarum*, Vol. II, viii, 29.

30 R. A. Markus, 'The chronology of the Gregorian mission to England: Bede's narrative and Gregory's correspondence', *Journal of Ecclesiastical History*, vol. 14 (1963), pp. 16–30, argues that Bede did not know the letter, but on the possibility that he did, cf., P. Meyvaert, *Bede and Gregory the Great* (Jarrow Lecture, 1964), pp. 245 (n. 40) (reprinted in Meyvaert, *Benedict, Gregory, Bede and Others* (London, 1977)).

31 Brooks, *The Early History of the Church of Canterbury*, p. 8.

32 A point made by B. E. A. Yorke, *Kings and Kingdoms in Early Anglo-Saxon England* Chap. 2.

33 *Gregorii I papae registrum espistolarum*, Vol. II, xi, 39.

34 Cf., on the importance of an archbishop in Germanic society, not least for his ability to convene synods which the bishops of other kingdoms must attend, see A. Angenendt, *Kaiserherrschaft und Königstaufe: Kaiser, Könige und Päpste als geistliche Patrone in der abendländischen Missionsgeschichte* (Berlin and New York, 1984), pp. 187 ff., and 'The conversion of the Anglo-Saxons', p. 772. See also H. Vollrath, *Die Synoden Englands bis 1066* (Paderborn, 1985), pp. 27 ff., 57 ff.

35 Yorke, *Kings and Kingdoms in Early Anglo-Saxon England*, Chap. 2.

36 A. W. B. Simpson, 'The Laws of Aethelberht', in M. S. Arnold *et al.* (eds), *On the Laws and Customs of England*: (New York, 1981), pp. 3–17. For the laws, see *The Laws of the Earliest English Kings*, ed. and trans. F. L. Attenborough (Cambridge, 1922), pp. 4 ff.

37 Angenendt, *Kaiserherrschaft und Königstaufe*, pp. 178 ff., suggests that princes with hopes of succeeding to the kingship remained pagan in case a pagan reaction called for a pagan king; but this does not seem to have been the situation – as Angenendt appreciates (p. 181) – in the family of the northern Anglian king, Eadwine.

38 D. Dumville, 'The West Saxon Genealogical Regnal List: manuscripts and texts', *Anglia*, vol. 104 (1986), pp. 1–32 (pp. 31–2), and B. E. A. Yorke, 'The kingdom of the East Saxons', *Anglo-Saxon England*, vol. 14 (1985), pp. 1–36 (pp. 3–4).

39 Angenendt, *Kaiserherrschaft und Königstaufe*, pp. 176 ff.

40 Yorke, 'The kingdom of the East Saxons', pp. 27 ff. See now also idem, *Kings and Kingdoms in Early Anglo-Saxon England*, Chap. 3.

41 *Epistolae Karol. Aevi*, Vol. II, ed., E. Dümmler, *MGH Epistolae*, Vol. IV (Berlin, 1895), no. 128 (*EHD* Vol. I, no. 203).

42 C. Plummer, *Venerabilis Baedae Opera Historica*, 2 vols (Oxford, 1892, 1896), Vol. II, p. 92. Plummer thought that the first part of the letter could have been that to Mellitus and Justus (*HE* II, 7), this accounting for the use of the plural pronoun, but Bede indicates that Mellitus and Justus each received a letter.

43 P. Hunter Blair, 'The Letters of Boniface V', in P. Clemoes and K. Hughes (eds), *England Before the Conquest* (Cambridge, 1971), pp. 5–13 (reprinted in Blair, *Anglo-Saxon Northumbria*, ed. M. Lapidge and P. H. Blair (London, 1984)).

44 Blair, 'The Letters of Boniface V', stressed that the pope was sending Bishop Justus the pallium with permission to use it only when celebrating mass, 'but not', commented Blair, 'at any other time'(p. 7); but the same reservation is contained in Pope Gregory's letter accompanying the pallium to Augustine (*Gregorii I papae registrum epistolarum*, Vol. II, xi, 39; *HE* I, 29). Cf., Plummer, *Venerabilis Baedae Opera Historica*, Vol. II, pp. 49–50.

45 Cf., J. M. Wallace-Hadrill, *Bede's Ecclesiastical History of the English People* (Oxford, 1988), pp. 64–5, 69, 222.

46 Blair, 'The Letters of Boniface V', p. 12.

47 P. Grierson and M. Blackburn, *Medieval European Coinage*, Vol. I: *The Early Middle Ages* (Cambridge, 1986), pp. 157 ff. Cf., I. Stewart, 'Anglo-Saxon gold coins', in R. A. G. Carson and C. M. Kraay (eds), *Scripta Nummaria Romana* (London, 1978), pp. 143–62.

48 Brooks, 'The creation and early structure of the kingdom of Kent', p. 68.

49 Plummer, *Venerabilis Baedae Opera Historica*, Vol. II, pp. 364 ff.

50 *MGH Script. rer. Langobardicarum*, ed., L. Bethmann and G. Waitz (Hanover, 1878), pp. 155, 157.

51 *The Life of Bishop Wilfrid by Eddius Stephanus*, ed. and trans. B. Colgrave (Cambridge, 1927).

52 Plummer, *Venerabilis Baedae Opera Historica*, Vol. I, p. 367.

53 Rollason, *The Mildrith Legend*, p. 116; M. J. Swanton, 'A fragmentary Life of St Mildred and other Kentish royal saints', *Archaeologia Cantiana*, vol. 91 (1975), pp. 15–27 (pp. 23, 27).

54 Rollason, *The Mildrith Legend*, pp. 93, 115; Swanton, 'A fragmentary Life', pp. 18, 24.

55 Rollason, *The Mildrith Legend*, pp. 98, 120.

56 ibid. (*passim*); cf., Witney, *The Kingdom of Kent*, pp. 128–9 and 'The Kentish royal saints', *Archaeologia Cantiana*, vol. 101 (1984), pp. 1–22.

57 Grierson and Blackburn, *Medieval European Coinage*, Vol. I, pp. 164 ff., 187; Hodges, *The Anglo-Saxon Achievement*, pp. 71 ff.

58 See P. Wormald, 'Bede, the *bretwaldas* and the origins of the *Gens Anglorum*', in Wormald, Bullough and Collins, *Ideal and Reality in Frankish and Anglo-Saxon Society*, pp. 99–129 (p. 127).

59 Yorke, 'The kingdom of the East Saxons', p. 18.

60 For some reservations about this document, see A. Scharer, *Die angelsächsische Königsurkunde im 7. und 8. Jahrhundert* (Vienna, 1982), pp. 135 ff.

61 Rollason, *The Mildrith Legend*, p. 114; Swanton, 'A fragmentary Life', pp. 18, 24; cf., Yorke, 'Joint kingship in Kent', p. 7.

62 Rollason, *The Mildrith Legend*, p. 116.

63 For the legendary accounts of these events, see Rollason, *The Mildrith Legend*, pp. 15 ff., 90 ff., and Swanton, 'A fragmentary Life', pp. 18 ff.

64 Rollason, *The Mildrith Legend*, p. 30. An alternative version describes Seaxburh as regent for Hlothhere (Swanton, 'A fragmentary Life', pp. 24, 27), but this is rejected by Rollason in favour of Ecgberht.

3   The early kings of the western Saxons

When the missionary bishop, Birinus, was sent by Pope Honorius I in the mid-630s to preach the Christian faith in the remotest Anglo-Saxon regions, he may well have journeyed up the Thames *en route* for the Mercians whose slaying of Eadwine, first Christian king of the northern Angles (see below, pp. 83 ff.), had probably precipitated this latest papal initiative. The people among whom he came to rest, however, were the pagan Gewisse, located among those Anglo-Saxons whose presence as a major intrusive element in the archaeological record of the upper Thames valley so impressed E. T. Leeds.[1] It was to the Gewisse that Birinus preached and their king, Cynegils, he baptized, establishing his episcopal see at Dorchester-on-Thames (*HE* III, 7). Another Gewissian leader, Cwichelm – he may have been a king or an aetheling (that is, a prince of the royal line) – was baptized, according to the *Chronicle*, in 636 (*ASC* A, *s.a.* 636). Subsequently, Cenwealh, according to Bede the son and successor of Cynegils, established a second episcopal see at Winchester in Hampshire (*HE* III, 7).

Bede regarded the Gewisse as identical with the West Saxons of his own day.[2] He says that the West Saxons were in earlier days called the Gewisse (*HE* III, 7), and describes the South Saxons as subject in ecclesiastical affairs to the bishop of the Gewisse, 'that is the West Saxons' (*HE* IV, 15). This was certainly the 'official' version of West Saxon history. In later genealogical and annalistic records Cynegils appears as king of the West Saxons. One of his predecessors, Ceawlin, is described as king of the West Saxons by Bede (*HE* II, 5), who also refers to a king, Cwichelm, whom he represents as king of the West Saxons and responsible in the late 620s for an attempt on the life of the northern king, Eadwine (*HE* II, 9). For Bede the terms Gewisse and West Saxon were interchangeable and historians have tended to accept their identification. Bede describes Caedwalla, whom he calls king of the West Saxons (*HE* V, 7), in the late 680s as a vigorous young man from among the Gewisse (*HE* IV, 15), and when he refers to Caedwalla's successor, Ine, as 'of the royal stock' (*HE* V, 7), the royal stock of the Gewisse is undoubtedly meant. By the ninth century both Caedwalla and Ine were seen as descendants of Gewis through Ceawlin and the West Saxon Genealogical Regnal List shows that it was through Ine's brother, Ingild, that Alfred, king of the West Saxons, in the ninth century claimed descent from Gewis (see Appendix, Fig.3).[3] The West Saxon kings, even by the early eighth century and the time of Bede, evidently thought of themselves as the progeny of Gewis, and it is this which explains why the Gewisse and the West Saxons were thought of as identical. But the Gewisse should not necessarily be seen as exclusive of other dynastic lineages.

The history of these western Saxon regions before the arrival of Birinus is really quite obscure and even after the conversion of Cynegils and Cwichelm not well documented. There are no papal letters to illuminate this scene. The influence of Christianity was at first very limited. Cenwealh, king of the western Saxons, and regarded as a son of Cynegils, was still a pagan in the 640s (*HE* III, 7), Centwine, a king of the western Saxons in the late 670s and 80s was not a convert until shortly before his abdication *c.* 685,[4] and Caedwalla who established himself as king in 686, was not baptized until he went as a pilgrim to Rome following his abdication in 688 (*HE* V, 7). Moreover, the extant historical and genealogical material is late and profoundly shaped by the desire of the Alfredian chronicler to trace the history of the kingdom of Wessex back through a single line of kings to the legendary founding-figure of Cerdic, regarded as a descendant of Gewis and the ancestor of all subsequent West Saxon kings. In the late ninth century the West Saxon Genealogical Regnal List and the *Anglo-Saxon Chronicle* together portray the 'political fiction' of a lineal succession to a unified West Saxon kingship from the earliest times.[5]

Bede appears to reveal a much more complex situation when he records, presumably on the basis of evidence supplied by Daniel, bishop of Winchester (*HE* Preface), that on the death of King Cenwealh sub-kings presumed to divide the kingdom of the western Saxons and ruled it for about ten years (*HE* IV, 12). His statement implies a multiplicity of kings in early Wessex, over whom Cenwealh had established a personal hegemony which he was not, however, able to transmit to a successor, and it may be that an overkingship of the western Saxons was a feature of Cenwealh's reign. This particular episode was drawn to Bede's attention because it was the prelude to the subsequent rise of Caedwalla and his successor, Ine, but if there was a multiplicity of kings at this time the situation would almost certainly not have been unique. According to the *Chronicle* D (*s.a.* 626), five kings perished when Eadwine invaded in response to the abortive attempt on his life. One king among the western Saxons whose death is recorded in the *Chronicle* A (*s.a.* 661) in Cenwealh's reign and who must have been either a co-ruler or a subject king of Cenwealh is Cenberht, who appears as the father of Caedwalla. Nor did Ine rule alone in Wessex at the beginning of his reign (see below, p. 122).

The baptism of Cynegils provides the first chronological anchor for the history of the western Saxons. According to Bede, the northern Anglian king, Oswald, was present at the baptism as the king's sponsor and associated himself in the establishment of the see of Dorchester-on-Thames (*HE* III, 7). Since Oswald was still securing himself as king over the northern Angles in the mid-630s, his presence in the Thames valley before the late 630s seems unlikely; the baptism of Cynegils, therefore, should probably be dated to the late 630s, possibly *c.* 640.

For the period before the baptism of Cynegils there is no chronological certainty. The *Anglo-Saxon Chronicle* attempts a framework for West Saxon history which is unacceptable. The annals place the arrival of Cerdic in 495 and again in 514 and he is said to have succeeded to the kingship in 519 (though Aethelweard, translating the *Chronicle* in the late tenth century, offers an alternative date of 500).[6] One way to have attempted to date the beginning of Cerdic's reign, at least theoretically, would have been for Alfredian annalists to subtract the total number of regnal years of the successive kings in the ninth-century West Saxon Genealogical Regnal List from, for example, 871, the year of the accession of Alfred, but in its extant versions the figures in the Regnal List would suggest an arrival for Cerdic *c.* 532 and the assumption of the kingship in 538.[7] If the West Saxon dates were determined in this way, therefore, the Alfredian annalist must have used an altogether different version of the Genealogical Regnal List from those now extant. Alternatively, the chroniclers could have constructed a framework for West Saxon history with reference first to the Dionysian Easter table cycles of nineteen years covering the years 494–512 and 513–31, which suggest 494/5 and 513/14 as starting points for sequences of events.[8] Interestingly, 532 would also have come at the beginning of another Dionysian nineteen-year cycle. The indications are, therefore, that there were a number of alternative schemes for West Saxon chronology by the late ninth century and that none is demonstrably historical. The year 532 for Cerdic's arrival is no more acceptable than 495 or 514 because it depends on the assumption that West Saxon history really was dominated by a single line of kings after Cerdic, ruling in succession, that all their names were known, and that all the regnal figures were correctly preserved. Variants in regnal years in the West Saxon Genealogical Regnal List and evidence for a multiplicity of kings show that this was not the case.

The difficulties do not end with Cerdic. Cynric is associated with Cerdic in the *Chronicle* as his son in all the events in the annals between 495 and 530, and the *Chronicle* knows nothing of Creoda, who appears in the West Saxon Genealogical Regnal List as the son of Cerdic and father of Cynric. Cynric is credited with a long reign of twenty-six or twenty-seven years, though J. N. L. Myres was tempted to dismiss him as 'a ghost figure'[9] so sparse is the annalistic record for him. The backward extension of West Saxon history to 514 or 495 and the omission from the annals of any information about Creoda appears to have resulted in a distended treatment of the material relating to Cynric to fill the resulting gap. A similar process can be seen in the annalistic representation of the career of Ceawlin, the reputed son of Cynric. Ceawlin's regnal length is given in variant readings of the West Saxon Genealogical Regnal List as seven or seventeen years, but in the *Chronicle* his activities as king are distributed across a period of thirty-two years from 560 to 592. Of all these alternatives, the actual regnal length for Ceawlin is thought most likely to have been seven.[10]

There is, therefore, no secure chronology for West Saxon history across the sixth century. Moreover, though the fixed point of *c.* 640 for the baptism of Cynegils is of great value, it cannot dispel the darkness which continues to pervade the chronology of early Wessex across the first half of the seventh century. Cynegils is given a reign of thirty-one years in the West Saxon Genealogical Regnal List and so is Cenwealh, his reputed son and successor. These long reigns of just over thirty years must be regarded with suspicion. The *Chronicle* A places the accession of Cynegils in 611 (*s.a.* 611) and associates a Cwichelm with him in a campaign against the Britons in 614 (*s.a.* 614) and against Penda of Mercia in 628 (*s.a.* 628) (all dates, however, placed too early in the *Chronicle*, as a consequence of the backward extension of West Saxon history in the annals). A prince with the name Cwichelm is said in the *Chronicle* A (*s.a.* 636) to have died in the year he was baptized by Birinus (again, the date is probably too early), and a Cwichelm, son of Cynegils, appears in a genealogy in the annal in the *Chronicle* A for 648. It is generally assumed that the Cwichelm who was baptized by Birinus was the son of Cynegils and had earlier fought beside his father, though this cannot be regarded as absolutely certain. The name was not uncommon. Cynegils' regnal length of thirty-one years, for example, could embrace the reign of an earlier and forgotten King Cwichelm in the 620s. The Cwichelm who fought with Cynegils against the Britons and against Penda could have been this King Cwichelm, or another prince of the same name, or Cynegils' son. A range of possibilities exists. Chronology remains as uncertain as personal identities. If the regnal length of thirty-one years for Cenwealh is rejected as unreliable,[11] the year when he began to reign is unknown. He was certainly established as king by *c.* 651/2, at the latest, however, because after being expelled by Penda, king of the Mercians, he spent three years in exile at the court of Anna, king of the eastern Angles (*HE* III, 7), and Anna was slain in battle in 654 or 655 by Penda who himself perished in the battle of the *Winwaed* in 655 or 656 (*HE* III, 18) (see below, pp. 92–5). Nor is it only regnal chronology which is uncertain. That of the West Saxon bishops also seems to have been incorrectly represented. Though the *Chronicle* places the death of Haeddi, bishop of Winchester, in 703, Bede indicates that he died in 705 (*HE* V, 18).[12] Confirmation of an inaccuracy occurs when the *Chronicle* records that Wine became bishop (of Winchester) for three years in 660 (A *s.a.* 660), which cannot be correct for Wine was still bishop when he assisted at the consecration of Chad *c.* 665 (*HE* III, 28).

According to Bede, the sub-kings who divided and ruled the territory of the western Saxons on Cenwealh's death were conquered at the end of a ten-year period and Caedwalla took the kingship himself but abdicated to go as a pilgrim to Rome in 688 after a reign of two years (*HE* V, 7). This

51

is a most important dating reference though one not without difficulties. A three-year reign for Caedwalla in the West Saxon Genealogical Regnal List becomes immediately suspect as an artificial extension of an earlier, shorter regnal length; so when the *Chronicle* A (*s.a.* 685) says that Caedwalla began to contend for the kingship in 685 the possibility that the correct year was 686 is very strong. Bede's ten-year period gives rise to some chronological difficulty. All the texts of the *Chronicle* place Cenwealh's death in 672 – but if Caedwalla established himself as king in 686 at the end of a ten-year period which began with the death of Cenwealh, the implication could be that Cenwealh died *c.* 676. Bede associates the death of Cenwealh with a return of the Northumbrian, Benedict Biscop, from one of his several journeys to the continent, specifically with Benedict's return to England in 672;[13] but Benedict returned from the continent again in 675 after another visit[14] and Cenwealh's death could have occurred on the occasion of Benedict's return in that year.[15]

Barbara Yorke, however, has challenged the assumption that Bede necessarily means that it was Caedwalla who suppressed the sub-kings. A ten-year period from the end of the reign of Cenwealh, if he died in 672, would end in 682 in the reign of Caedwalla's predecessor, Centwine. She suggests that it was Centwine who terminated the independence of the sub-kings.[16] If correct, this would place Centwine in a wholly new light. Centwine was certainly a not insignificant warrior. The *Chronicle* A (*s.a.* 682) records that he put the Britons to flight as far as the sea, and Aldhelm, writing at the end of the seventh century, attributes three victories to him over his enemies.[17]

The *Chronicle* represents Cenwealh as succeeded in 672 by his widow, Seaxburh, for one year, after whom Aescwine, son of Cenfus, reigned from 674–6, followed by Centwine, son of Cynegils, from 676–85 (the year in which Caedwalla is said to have begun to contend for the kingship); but the information of the Genealogical Regnal List is that after Cenwealh, Seaxburh reigned for a year, Aescwine for two and Centwine for seven or nine, while the *Chronicon ex Chronicis*, citing what it calls the *dicta* of King Alfred, records Seaxburh for one year, Cenfus for two, Aescwine for nearly three and Centwine for seven.[18] The impression is that regnal lengths were modified with relative impunity. Firmer ground is provided by the *Chronicle* A which records (*s.a.* 675) that in 675 Aescwine fought Wulfhere, king of the Mercians, at *Biedanheafde*, a battle which must have occurred in 675 at the latest because Wulfhere died in that year, an important event because it represented the only known challenge to Wulfhere in southern England (see below, p. 116). This would seem to push Cenwealh's death back to at least some time before the mid-670s. Aescwine's battle with Wulfhere in 675 suggests that, if he were one of the sub-kings who had asserted his independence, he was even so a formidable figure. It is difficult to see why he should have been relegated to the role of an upstart sub-king rather than honoured as a leader of the western Saxons who endeavoured to check the military advance of the Mercians.

One explanation, however, may be proposed. Bede's disparagement of Cenwealh's successors is very reminiscent of his statement that usurpers seized royal power in Kent in the late 680s until the rightful king, Wihtred, established himself (*HE* IV, 26), despite the fact that one of these 'usurpers' was of the Kentish royal family though not of Wihtred's own branch (see below, p. 123). In other words, Bede's comment about the Kentish succession – almost certainly derived from Canterbury – was extremely partisan. Similarly, therefore, it may well be the case that the Bedan view – derived undoubtedly from Daniel, bishop of Winchester – of Cenwealh's successors as sub-kings who presumed to elevate themselves unduly and who had to be forcibly removed, represents the partisan point of view of the supporters of Caedwalla and Ine. There must exist a strong possibility that they regarded Cenwealh's immediate successors as inferiors (whether including Centwine or not it is impossible to say in view of Bede's failure to mention him), primarily because they were not of the same branch of the royal family or even perhaps of the same royal family as Cenwealh, Caedwalla and Ine. Bede's account is not so much a record of the fracturing of the unity of the kingdom as a reflection of deep divisions of loyalty among the western Saxons, torn between rival dynastic factions.

The relationship between these early kings, of course, is not at all certain. Cenwealh is described by Bede as the son of the Cynegils whom Birinus baptized (*HE* III, 7). More than one Cynegils, however, appears in the West Saxon genealogical record. The annal for 611 in the *Chronicle* A describes the Cynegils whom Birinus baptized as a son of Ceola, son of Cutha, son of Cynric (see Appendix, Fig. 4.1) The genealogy of King Centwine in the A annal for 676 describes Centwine as the son of a Cynegils, son of Ceolwulf (see Appendix, Fig. 4.2), but the West Saxon Genealogical Regnal List refers to King Ceol as the brother and predecessor of King Ceolwulf and describes Birinus' King Cynegils as the son of the brother of King Ceolwulf.[19] If Centwine's father, Cynegils, was the son not of Ceolwulf, therefore, but of a brother of Ceolwulf (Ceol/Ceola) (see Appendix, Fig. 4.3), there would be a possibility that Centwine was regarded as a descendant of the Cynegils whom Birinus baptized. When Aldhelm wrote a poem between 689 and 709 in honour of a church founded by Bugga, daughter of King Centwine, however, he praised her father who had built churches and abdicated to become a monk,[20] but did not refer to her grandfather, Cynegils, as he surely would have done if he knew him to have been the first Christian king in the region. This suggests either that Centwine's father was not the Cynegils whom Birinus baptized but only later came to be identified as such in some circles, or indeed that Centwine was only subsequently represented as a son of Cynegils by a West Saxon genealogist who had no knowledge of his true paternity.

In the annal for 688 a Cynegils is referred to as the brother of King Ine's grandfather, Ceolwald, son of Cuthwine, son of Ceawlin, son of Cynric (see Appendix, Fig. 4.4). There is a variant of this genealogy in the annal for 855 in the *Chronicle* A when Ceolwald is described as the son of Cutha, son of Cuthwine, son of Ceawlin (see Appendix, Fig. 4.5), and another in the West Saxon Genealogical Regnal List which represents Ceolwald as the son of Cuthwulf, son of Cuthwine, son of Ceawlin (see Appendix, Fig. 4.6). Though it is not explicitly stated that Cynegils, son or grandson of Cuthwine, was regarded as the Cynegils of Bede's narrative, the specific reference to a Cynegils as the brother of Ine's grandfather suggests that a special significance attached to him. There is a possibility, therefore, that the ninth century West Saxon kings, who regarded themselves as the descendants of Ine's brother, Ingild, thought of the first Christian king of the West Saxons as the brother of their forebear, Ceolwald, and the son or grandson of Cuthwine, son of Ceawlin. This is likely to have become the received tradition of the West Saxon dynasty. It cannot be regarded as any more certain that the first Christian king among the western Saxons was a son of Cuthwine and the brother of Ceolwald than that he was a son of Ceol/Ceola. None of these alleged relationships can be relied upon.[21]

The impression is that West Saxon tradition knew of several princes of the name of Cynegils but was uncertain which was the first Christian king of the West Saxons in a situation in which every family claiming a prince of that name among its ancestors or among the close relatives of its ancestors regarded that prince as the patron of Birinus. The evidence seems to suggest that the Cynegils of Bede's *Ecclesiastical History* was a ruler from whom any aspiring dynasty would wish to claim descent or associate itself with in kinship. The same is almost certainly true of Ceawlin, who came to be seen in one genealogical tradition at least as the grandfather or great-grandfather of Cynegils. The annals in the *Chronicle* do not specifically say that Ceawlin was a son of Cynric – they simply associate the two together on one occasion in a battle against the Britons – but the genealogical material shows that by the late ninth century Ceawlin was regarded as Cynric's son. The received genealogical tradition, however, is almost certainly the consequence of a desire to accommodate Ceawlin at an appropriate point within the royal pedigree of the kings of Wessex and no more certainty attaches to Ceawlin's place in this pedigree as the grandson of Cerdic than it does to that of Cynegils as Ceawlin's grandson or great-grandson. Bede, who probably had no information on the relationship between Ceawlin and Cynegils, does refer to Cenwealh as the son of Cynegils, but it could be that even here one generation has been omitted. Cenwealh, that is, might be chronologically more intelligible as a grandson of Cynegils. Cuthred, son of Cwichelm, son of Cynegils, to whom Cenwealh is said (*ASC* A *s.a.* 648) to have given 3,000 hides of land near Ashdown, provides evidence that one prince certainly who was Cenwealh's contemporary was thought of as a grandson of Cynegils.

A feature of early West Saxon history is the varied geographical setting of its dynastic traditions. The material concerning Cerdic and Cynric in the *Chronicle* places them in Wiltshire, at the head of an advance from Southampton Water to Old Sarum (*ASC* A, *s.a.* 552). The mission of Birinus to the Gewisse was centred on Dorchester-on-Thames. Cenwealh established an episcopal see at Winchester in Hampshire. It seems likely that these Anglo-Saxon settlements – in Wiltshire, Hampshire and the upper Thames valley – were at first politically quite independent of one another (indeed, southern Hampshire would seem to have been originally a province of the Jutish kingdom of Wight).[22] They constituted some of the groups out of which the kingdom of the West Saxons eventually coalesced, and it is difficult to envisage the West Saxons of a later period as exclusively identical with any of them, even the Gewisse.

From quite an early period these different territories were among those periodically brought under subjection to an overlord. Bede places two Saxon rulers at the head of his list of *brytenwealdas*, Aelle, whom he calls king of the South Saxons, and Ceawlin, whom he calls king of the West Saxons. Bede's description of Aelle as king of the South Saxons suggests that his area of domination was based on a position of coastal strength and the *Anglo-Saxon Chronicle* A (*s.a.* 491) associates him with the siege and capture of the Saxon shore fort of *Anderida* (Pevensey). Though the geographical extent of his *imperium* is unknown,[23] it is unlikely to have been confined solely to coastal areas and may well have extended northwards across Hampshire to the upper Thames valley. Ceawlin's domination of much of the Saxon south obscures his origin-centre. An original base in the upper Thames valley might make the best sense of the military activities attributed to him in the *Chronicle* – the capture of Gloucester, Cirencester and Bath (*ASC* A, *s.a.* 577) and the campaign to *Fethanleag* (Stoke Lyne) in north-east Oxfordshire (*ASC* A, *s.a.* 584), with which must be associated the capture by a certain Cuthwulf of Limbury, Aylesbury, Bensington and Eynsham in the Thames valley itself (*ASC* A, *s.a.* 571) – though the historicity of each of these events has been questioned,[24] nor is it known for certain how Cuthwulf and Ceawlin were related (if at all), and a battle between Ceawlin and the Britons took place at Barbury Castle in Wiltshire (*ASC* A, *s.a.* 556). Ceawlin was eventually expelled, however, after a battle at Woden's Barrow (Adam's Grave) (*ASC* A, *s.a.* 592) overlooking the Vale of Pewsey, so that what could well be interpreted as a day of reckoning for him took place in Wiltshire, not in the upper Thames valley. Ceawlin, that is, may have been a Thames valley leader who came to dominate Wiltshire and much of southern England.

The chronology of all these events is extremely imprecise. The archaeological evidence suggests Saxon settlement in Sussex from the mid-fifth century onwards,[25] and if Aelle was associated with this primary settlement he must belong to the fifth century. Fundamentally, however, Aelle inhabits a chronological vacuum, for the basis for the South Saxon dates in the *Chronicle* A is unknown.[26] All the other overlords in Bede's list followed one another in relatively rapid chronological sequence, which could indicate that Aelle was an older contemporary of Ceawlin were it not for his traditional association with the attack on *Anderida* and the possibility that Bede's list of overlords is incomplete. Ceawlin was an older contemporary of Aethelberht of Kent. He fought against Aethelberht and defeated him, most likely *c.* 590 before Aethelberht had securely established himself as a powerful ruler in his own right. Despite all the reservations about dates in the *Chronicle*, therefore, those for Ceawlin's last years may not be all that inaccurate. The *Chronicle* A places Ceawlin's overthrow in 592 (*s.a.* 592) and his death in 593 (*s.a.* 593). At most these events must have occurred less than a decade later for Aethelberht's overlordship was established by the time Pope Gregory wrote to him in 601. Ceawlin's ascendancy across seven or at most seventeen years must certainly have disturbed existing political structures, and the eclipse of Ceawlin is likely to have been one of the factors which enabled Aethelberht to create a Kentish *imperium*. The later sixth century, therefore, seems to have witnessed fundamental changes in the distribution of power and authority in southern Saxon England.

Where Ceawlin met his death the year after his expulsion is unknown (*ASC* A, *s.a.* 593), but his opponent at Woden's Barrow is likely to have been the Ceol who is credited with a reign of five or six years in the West Saxon Genealogical Regnal List. The beginning of the reign of Ceol (or Ceola), described as a son of Cutha, son of Cynric (*ASC* A, *s.a.* 611), is placed in the *Chronicle* A the year before the battle at Woden's Barrow (*s.a.* 591). According to the West Saxon Genealogical Regnal List his brother, Ceolwulf, reigned after him for seventeen years – though the *Annals of St Neot* accord him fourteen years and the *Chronicle*, which places his accession in 597 and his death in 611, also adopts a fourteen-year period for his reign. These are the princes who seem to have displaced Ceawlin. Though the evidence is too imperfect to admit of anything other than the most speculative of hypotheses, the possible association of Ceol with the defeat of Ceawlin at Woden's Barrow and the representation of him as a grandson of Cynric, whose associations seem to have been with Wiltshire, could connect both Ceol and Ceolwulf with the Wiltshire Saxons rather than with those of the upper Thames valley.[27] In southern England the overthrow of Ceawlin is likely to have resulted in political fragmentation and the heir to Ceawlin's position as *brytenwealda* was Aethelberht of Kent; but it may be that Ceolwulf began to construct among the groups which comprised the western Saxons a regional overkingship which foreshadowed Cenwealh's. The statement in the *Anglo-Saxon Chronicle* that Ceolwulf fought Angles, Britons, Picts and Scots (A *s.a.* 597) reads like a misplaced reference to Bede's account of the Northumbrian overlords (*HE* II, 5), but it could conceivably serve to identify Ceolwulf as a significant warrior-king among the western Saxons in the early seventh century.

Despite the fall of Ceawlin, therefore, the western Saxon groups remained militarily and politically significant. Under King Ceolwulf they were at war with the South Saxons, the *Chronicle* placing the campaign in 607, perhaps ten years or so too early. The Gewisse of the upper Thames valley were certainly a force to be reckoned with. In the early years of the seventh century, *c.* 620, they defeated and slew the three sons of Saeberht, the kings of the eastern Saxons (*HE* II, 5). By the third quarter of the century their king, Cenwealh, was secure enough in much of Hampshire to establish a second episcopal see at Winchester (*HE* III, 7), not far to the north of the boundary with the mainland Hampshire territory of the kingdom of Wight.[28] In the west, the *Chronicle* A records in an annal for 658 that Cenwealh fought the Britons at *Peonnum*, probably in the vicinity of Penselwood, and drove them in flight as far as the River Parrett. Allowing again for the slight chronological inaccuracy of the *Chronicle* across these years, this event may be dated *c.* 660. The annal implies that by this date Cenwealh dominated the Saxons of Wiltshire and beyond. He had evidently emerged as the ruler of quite extensive territory, in a position to grant 3,000 hides of land in Berkshire to his kinsman, Cuthred. Thus, he must have re-assembled some of the territories which had once been under the domination of Ceawlin.

His authority, however, was circumscribed by developments elsewhere, in particular the extension of Anglian influence. Some at least of those who made up the southern Mercians must have experienced the impact of Ceawlin's commanding position in southern England, but in the first half of the seventh century it was the western Saxons who were under attack from their more northerly neighbours. King Cwichelm, possibly a predecessor of Cynegils and whom Bede accuses of attempting to deprive the northern Anglian king, Eadwine, of life and kingdom, was presumably responding to unwelcome interference in the valley of the upper Thames by Eadwine when he plotted his assassination (*HE* II, 9). Eadwine retaliated with a military campaign in which, Bede says, he either slew all who had plotted his death or forced them to surrender. But the most serious danger to the kings of the western Saxons came from the Mercians, among whom Penda established himself as king in 633 or 634, in which year he slew Eadwine in battle (*HE* II, 20) (see below, pp. 83-4). In an annal which is dated to 628, undoubtedly again a number of years too early, the *Chronicle* A records that Penda fought Cynegils and Cwichelm at Cirencester and that they afterwards came to terms. If the *Chronicle* is to be believed, Ceawlin had campaigned in the vicinity of Cirencester and captured the town together with Gloucester and Bath, but this agreement appears to have given Penda control of the lower Severn.[29] It marked a substantial loss of influence on the part of the western Saxon kings which was never made good.

For so long as the northern king, Oswald, could lay claim to the *imperium* which had been Eadwine's, the Gewisse were probably able to maintain their position in the Thames valley as his allies in the face of pressure from Penda of Mercia. Oswald stood sponsor to Cynegils at his baptism *c.* 640 and was associated in the establishment of Dorchester-on-Thames as an episcopal see for Birinus. He married Cynegils' daughter, Cyneburh (*HE* III, 17). The relationship between Oswald and Cynegils, therefore, may have been relatively cordial and an example of an arrangement between an overlord and a dependant which was mutually beneficial.[30] With the overthrow of Oswald, however, again by Penda, and the confinement of his successor, Oswiu, to a more restricted northern sphere of influence (see below, pp. 91–2 ff.), the Gewisse found themselves dangerously exposed to Mercian aggression. The still-pagan Cenwealh was already within the Mercian orbit to the extent of having married Penda's sister, but, emboldened perhaps by an increase of territory under his control, he repudiated her and married another. Penda's response was to expel Cenwealh, vividly demonstrating thereby the strength of his position along the valley of the upper Thames, and Cenwealh spent three years in exile among the eastern Angles, who were also subject to Mercian pressure, and among whom he was converted to Christianity at the court of King Anna (*HE* III, 7). The princes who ruled among the Gewisse during Cenwealh's years in exile are unknown but it seems reasonable to conclude that they would have been subject to Penda and perhaps among the thirty *duces* who accompanied him to the battle of the *Winwaed* (*HE* III, 24) (see below, p. 93). Anna was slain in battle by Penda (*HE* III, 18) the year before the battle of the *Winwaed* according to the chronological scheme of the *Chronicle*, and it seems reasonable to suppose that Cenwealh was unable to return to his own kingdom until Penda perished at the *Winwaed* in 655 or 656. It is likely that Cenwealh was reasonably secure from external danger in the immediate aftermath of the battle and, interestingly, he evidently then enjoyed quite extensive contacts with Northumbrian court circles – with King Oswiu's son, Ealhfrith, and with Wilfrid (*Vita Wilfridi*, ch. 7),[31] as well as with Benedict Biscop.[32] It is possible that he had taken refuge among the northern Angles on the eve of *Winwaed*.

Whatever temporary respite the overthrow of Penda brought to the Gewisse, however, was relatively short-lived. Mercian influence in the upper Thames valley was re-established by Penda's son and eventual successor, Wulfhere (see below, p. 115). What Bede describes as a division of Cenwealh's kingdom into two dioceses with the founding of Winchester (*HE* III, 7) was in reality part of the slow abandonment of Dorchester-on-Thames. Agilbert, a Frank whom Cenwealh had made bishop of Dorchester on his restoration, was the last bishop of Dorchester. He subsequently quarrelled with the king over the establishment of a second see at Winchester, on which he had not been consulted, and departed for

Gaul. The approximate date of this can be inferred. Wine held the bishopric for three years and was still bishop in Wessex in 665 when he consecrated Chad bishop of York (*HE* III, 28), so he could have been consecrated as early as 662 or as late as 665. Indeed, he could have been established in his see while Agilbert was attending the synod of Whitby in 664 (*HE* III, 25). It is often thought that Agilbert went to Northumbria after he had abandoned Cenwealh, but it seems just as likely that from Dorchester he returned directly to the continent where he became bishop of Paris.

In the mid-660s, therefore, the see of Dorchester was abandoned and a fundamental dislocation in the history of the Gewisse is thereby revealed. They were falling under Mercian control and their ruling dynasty had been effectively displaced.[33] The *Chronicle* A (*s.a.* 661) records that Wulfhere harried Ashdown in 661. The date is again probably inaccurate by a matter of three or four years, but the annal testifies to a Mercian military presence in the Thames valley by the mid-660s. There is some evidence that by the early 670s Wulfhere possessed a royal residence at Thame to the north-east of Dorchester (*CS* 34: S 1165). In the late 670s Dorchester functioned for a time as a Mercian see under Bishop Aetla (*HE* IV, 23)[34] and somewhat belatedly the relics of Birinus were translated to Winchester (*HE* III, 7). The pervasive character of Mercian influence in the region at this time is demonstrated by the way in which Wine, when he too quarrelled with Cenwealh and was expelled from his bishopric, *c.* 665–8, sought refuge with Wulfhere, king of the Mercians, and acquired from him the see of London (*HE* III, 7). It is the eclipse of Gewissian power in its traditional heartland that provides the context for the political tensions among the western Saxons which followed the death of Cenwealh.

Notes

1 E. T. Leeds, 'The West Saxon invasion and the Icknield Way', *History*, vol. 10 (1925–6), pp. 97–109, and cf., idem, *The Archaeology of the Anglo-Saxon Settlements* (Oxford, 1913; reprinted 1970).
2 Cf., H. E. Walker (who also argued that the Gewisse and the West Saxons were wholly identical), 'Bede and the Gewissae: the political evolution of the heptarchy and its nomenclature', *Cambridge Historical Review*, vol. 12 (1956), pp. 174–86.
3 The West Saxon Genealogical Regnal List is edited by D. Dumville, 'The West Saxon Genealogical Regnal List: manuscripts and texts', *Anglia*, vol. 104 (1986), pp. 1–39 and discussed by him in 'The West Saxon Genealogical Regnal List and the chronology of early Wessex', *Peritia*, vol. 4 (1985), pp. 21–67.
4 *Aldhelmi Opera Omnia*, ed. R. Ehwald *MGH Auctores Antiq.*, Vol. XV (Berlin, 1919), pp. 14–15; trans. M. Lapidge and J. L. Rosier, *Aldhelm, The Poetic Works* (Woodbridge, 1985), pp. 47–8.
5 Dumville, 'The West Saxon Genealogical Regnal List and the chronology of early Wessex', p. 57.
6 A. Campbell (ed.), *The Chronicle of Aethelweard* (Edinburgh and London, 1962), p. 11.
7 Dumville, 'The West Saxon Genealogical Regnal List and the chronology of early Wessex', pp. 38–9, 44–6, 49 ff.
8 P. Sims-Williams, 'The settlement of England in Bede and the "Chronicle"', *Anglo-*

Saxon England, vol. 12 (1983), pp. 1–41 (pp. 34 ff).

9 J. N. L. Myres, *The English Settlements* (Oxford, 1986), p. 153.

10 Dumville, 'The West Saxon Genealogical Regnal List and the chronology of early Wessex', pp. 27, 39–40, 46, 50–1.

11 Cf., ibid., p. 8.

12 The argument of M. Lapidge and M. Herren, *Aldhelm: The Prose Works* (Ipswich, 1979), p. 10, that Haeddi died in 706 rests on the view that Aldfrith, king of Northumbria, died in 705, not 704, but see below, p. 145. Cf., also H. Edwards, *The Charters of the Early West Saxon Kingdom* (BAR British series 198, 1988), pp. 109–10.

13 C. Plummer (ed.), *Venerabilis Baedae Opera Historica*, 2 vols (Oxford, 1892, 1896), Vol. I, p. 367.

14 ibid., Vol. II, p. 68–9.

15 As suggested by D. P. Kirby, 'Problems of early West Saxon history', *English Historical Review* vol. 80 (1965), pp. 10–29 (p. 18).

16 B. E. A. Yorke, *Kings and Kingdoms in Early Anglo-Saxon England* (London, 1990 [forthcoming]), Chap. 7.

17 *Aldhelmi Opera Omnia*, p. 15; trans. Lapidge and Rosier, *Aldhelm, The Poetic Works*, p. 48.

18 Dumville, 'The West Saxon Genealogical Regnal List: manuscripts and texts', p. 25; *Florentii Wigorniensis monachi Chronicon ex Chronicis*, ed. B. Thorpe, 2 vols (London, 1848), Vol. I, p. 272.

19 Dumville, 'The West Saxon Genealogical Regnal List: manuscripts and texts', p. 22.

20 *Aldhelmi Opera Omnia*, pp. 14–15; trans. Lapidge and Rosier, *Aldhelm, The Poetic Works*, pp. 47–8.

21 For a different interpretation of the genealogical evidence concerning the early kings of the western Saxons, see Yorke, *Kings and Kingdoms in Early Anglo-Saxon England*, Chap. 7.

22 B. E. A. Yorke, 'The Jutes of Wight and Hampshire and the origins of Wessex', in S. Bassett (ed.), *The Origins of Anglo-Saxon Kingdoms* (Leicester, 1989), pp. 84–96. See also now, idem, *Kings and Kingdoms in Early Anglo-Saxon England*, Chap. 7.

23 Cf., on Aelle, M. G. Welch, 'The kingdom of the South Saxons: the origins', in S. Bassett (ed.), *The Origins of Anglo-Saxon Kingdoms*, pp. 75–83; 'any attempt to map the territory he may have dominated is doomed to failure' (p. 83).

24 Sims-Williams, 'The settlement of England in Bede and the "Chronicle"', pp. 29–34.

25 M. C. Welch, *Early Anglo-Saxon Sussex*, vol. i (BAR British Series 112(i), 1983), p. 259; idem, 'The kingdom of the South Saxons: the origins', p. 81.

26 Cf., the suggestion that Aelle's chronological position in the *Anglo-Saxon Chronicle* may have been dictated by the inclusion of annals relating to West Saxon-British warfare from Cerdic to Ceawlin, P. Sims-Williams, 'Gildas and the Anglo-Saxons', *Cambridge Medieval Celtic Studies*, vol. 6 (1983), pp. 1–30 (p.26), and 'The settlement of England in Bede and the "Chronicle"', p. 26.

27 For an earlier consideration of this material, see D. P. Kirby, 'Problems of early West Saxon history', *English Historical Review*, vol. 80 (1965), pp. 10–29, but note the observations of Sims-Williams, 'The settlement of England in Bede and the "Chronicle"', p. 28, n. 118, who doubts the possibility of establishing from the confused and inadequate source-material 'the true state of affairs'.

28 Yorke, 'The Jutes of Hampshire and Wight and the origins of Wessex', p. 93.

29 F. M. Stenton, *Anglo-Saxon England* (3rd edn, Oxford, 1971), p. 45.

30 Cf., the comments of A. Angenendt on sponsoring: *Kaiserherrschaft und Königstaufe: Kaiser, Könige und Päpste als geistliche Patrone in der abendländischen Missionsgeschichte* (Berlin and New York, 1984), pp. 176–7, 183–6 and 'The conversion of the Anglo-Saxons', *Angli e sassoni al di qua e al di là del mare* (Settimane di Studio del centro Italiano di studi sull'alto medioevo, no. 32 (1984); 2 vols, Spoleto, 1986), Vol. I, pp. 747–81 (p. 766).

31 *The Life of Bishop Wilfrid by Eddius Stephanus*, ed. and trans. B. Colgrave (Cambridge, 1927).

32 Plummer, *Venerabilis Baedae Opera Historica*, Vol. I, p. 367.

33 Cf., H. P. R. Finberg, *The Early Charters of Wessex* (Leicester, 1964), p. 215.

34 Plummer, *Venerabilis Baedae Opera Historica*, Vol. II, pp. 245–6.

4   The Anglian territories in the late sixth and early seventh centuries

Though to the Irish and the Welsh all the Germanic peoples in Britain whether in the north or the south were Saxons, for Bede the settlers in eastern midland and northern England were Angles, and the widespread scatter of cremation cemeteries,[1] in association with various categories of archaeological material (pottery and brooches),[2] has tended to be regarded as evidence for a distinct Anglian cultural province at least by the sixth century 'north of an approximate line from the mouth of the Stour on the east coast of England . . . to the valley of the Avon'.[3] It does not seem inappropriate, therefore, to retain the term Angle for the Germanic peoples in this region.

The Angles and Saxons did not lose their association with their continental homelands following their settlement in Britain. Maritime communications remained of great importance. In the mid-sixth century Procopius heard of a king of the Angles in Britain who was said to have equipped his sister with a fleet and an army to go in pursuit of her betrothed, a prince of the continental Varni who was about to abandon her.[4] The bride of a king of the northern Angles in the mid-seventh century was brought from Kent by sea (*HE* III, 15). Moreover, Anglian communities in northern or midland England may have participated along with the eastern Angles in their probably long-established contacts with north-European commerce which are revealed by the range of goods from the famous East Anglian boat-burial of the early seventh century in the Sutton Hoo barrow cemetery.[5] Even so, in the late sixth century the Anglian communities in Britain were perhaps more isolated than the men of Kent and the south-east. Arguments from silence can be misleading. Were it not for two references in Adomnán's *Life of Columba* to 'Saxons' on Iona in the lifetime of Columba, who died in 597,[6] nothing would be known of an Anglo-Saxon presence there before the end of the sixth century. So far as is known, however, no sixth-century king of the Angles in Britain married a Frankish princess. No Anglian king is known to have made laws at this time. In his letter to the northern King Eadwine, the earliest contemporary evidence for a king of the Angles in Britain apart from that of Procopius, Pope Boniface V (619–25) contemplated with some excitement the extension of Christianity into 'nations at the extremities of the earth'

(*HE* II, 20). Taken together, these would seem to be indicators of relative remoteness.

The situation began to change by as early as *c.* 600 as Frankish influence was disseminated through Kent into the immediate Anglian hinterland. Raedwald, king of the eastern Angles, 'was almost certainly in contact with the Merovingians'.[7] One of his sons, Sigeberht, possessed a name not uncommon in Merovingian royal circles and fled into exile in Gaul during the reign of his half-brother, Eorpwald (*HE* II, 15). Frankish coins were included among the treasure in the Sutton Hoo ship-burial. A royal marriage to a Frankish princess in Raedwald's time, therefore, does become a possibility. But caution is necessary. The northern Anglian prince, Eadwine, took for his first wife a daughter of Cearl, a neighbouring Anglian king of the Mercians (*HE* II, 14). Subsequently as king and in search of a second wife, his request not for a kinswoman of Raedwald's but for the sister of the king of Kent – Aethelburh, sister of Eadbald (*HE* II, 9) – was probably inspired by the continuing prestige of Eadbald and a desire to secure the best access to the more sophisticated economic and political world of the south-east and beyond.

Moreover, if the clearest manifestation among the Anglo-Saxons of meaningful diplomatic and cultural contact with advanced society on the continent in this period was a readiness to become part of the Christian Catholic world of Frankish west Europe, this was not immediately apparent in Anglian territories. Raedwald, in his maintenance of two altars, one a Christian, the other a pagan, was at best only a partial convert and both his sons, Eorpwald and Sigeberht, were still pagans when he died, Sigeberht's conversion only taking place during his subsequent exile in Gaul (*HE* II, 1 5). Among the northern Angles, even Eadwine appears to have prevaricated until the late 620s. This evidence, therefore, tends to confirm the impression of the Anglian areas of Britain as further removed from west European cultural values than the more advanced kingdom of Kent. Still more would this have been true of the Anglian hinterland – the territory of the Mercians – and the Saxon areas along and south of the Thames. These were among the real backwoods of early seventh-century England. The missionary bishop, Birinus, is said by Bede to have been specially directed by the papacy to preach in the remotest regions where no teacher had yet been (*HE* III, 7) and, though he settled among the Saxons of the upper Thames valley, his original intention may have been to go to Mercia. In the late sixth and early seventh centuries the Mercian kingdom remained a peripheral force in the struggle towards political cohesion in the Anglian territories north of the Thames, and much of the Mercian aggression of the mid-seventh century and later may be attributable not only to the need to secure control of a coastline, resources and emerging ports of trade[8] but also to the need to achieve a greater political cohesion within Mercia and to create satellite dependencies in the surrounding territories.

The struggle for political and military leadership

The survival of contemporary documentary evidence means that events in Kent and the south-east in the later years of the sixth century and the early years of the seventh can be relatively well established, but this must not obscure the fact that important developments were occurring elsewhere in England at this time. No contemporary documents illustrate the upheaval in the Anglian world which brought Eadwine of Deira to the throne among the northern Angles, but Bede has preserved a considerable body of tradition about this event in the form current just over a hundred years later.

Eadwine's predecessor, Aethelfrith of Bernicia, was the father of three of the kings who reigned among the northern Angles after Eadwine – Eanfrith, Oswald and Oswiu, the grandfather of two – Ecgfrith and Aldfrith, sons of Oswiu, and the great-grandfather of two – Osred, son of Aldfrith, and Osric (see Appendix, Fig. 6.2). These men dominated the kingship of the northern Angles down to 716. Aethelfrith was remembered as a brave ruler who subjected more land to the Angles than any king (presumably northern) before him, defeating the Scots of Dál Riata at *Degsastan* (*HE* I, 34), and the men of Powys at Chester (*HE* II, 2). He was also remembered as someone who had persecuted Eadwine and driven him into exile, seeking to destroy him. When Eadwine found refuge at the court of Raedwald, king of the eastern Angles, Aethelfrith offered Raedwald large sums of money to put Eadwine to death, threatening to make war on him if he did not. Bede regarded Raedwald as the grandson of Wuffa, the reputed founder of the East Anglian dynasty of the Wuffingas (*HE* II, 15) (see Appendix, Fig. 5). According to the tradition Bede received, he was on the point of complying with Aethelfrith's demands when his queen dissuaded him by arguing that to do so would be dishonourable; instead, therefore, Raedwald marched against Aethelfrith and slew him in battle on the east bank of the River Idle (*HE* II, 12). Writing some twenty years or so before Bede, the author of a Northumbrian *Life* of Pope Gregory[9] describes King Aethelfrith as a tyrant and implies that Eadwine's exile at the court of Raedwald was even then a well-known fact of Northumbrian history (ch. 16). This *Life*, which was intended to reflect the interests of the monastic community at Whitby under the direction of Abbess Aelfflaed, Eadwine's granddaughter, leaves no doubt that in circles where the cult of a saintly Eadwine flourished Aethelfrith continued to be regarded with hostility. The Whitby *Life* and Bede's narrative can give an impression of the conflict on the Idle as a clash purely and simply between Aethelfrith and Raedwald over the person of Eadwine. It was, however, more than this. It reflected not only serious rivalries among the northern Angles but on a wider stage it was part of a protracted struggle to determine the military and political leadership of the Anglian peoples in the first half of the seventh century.[10]

For Bede, Aethelfrith and Raedwald were kings respectively of the Northumbrians (*HE* I, 34) and East Angles (*HE* II, 5). It is doubtful if these terms were used in the late sixth and early seventh centuries. On one occasion Bede refers to Raedwald simply as king of the Angles (*HE* II, 12), possibly inadvertently for Raedwald had been king of the East Angles to the writer of the Whitby *Life* of Pope Gregory, where, however, 'king of the Angles' also occurs in the account of Eadwine's exile at Raedwald's court in which archaic features could have been preserved (ch. 16). Certainly, it is likely that Raedwald was known to his contemporaries simply as *rex Anglorum*, 'king of the Angles', the description Pope Gregory applied to Aethelberht of Kent. The political cohesion of the Northumbrian and East Anglian kingdoms at the end of the sixth century and the beginning of the seventh should not be exaggerated. It is inconceivable that the settlement and political development of such large areas was a fully co-ordinated process and the former existence of now unknown and originally independent principalities within their spheres of influence is a strong possibility. It will also have taken considerable time for the boundaries of the territory of the eastern Angles with other neighbouring groups to be defined adequately enough for their communities to be characterized specifically as 'East' Anglian, and even thereafter in the ninth century Aethelstan and Eadmund, kings of the East Angles, were still *Rex An[glorum]* on their coins.[11]

The northern king, Ecgfrith, is styled in the record of the proceedings of the council of Hatfield in 679 or 680 not king of the Northumbrians but *rex Humbronensium*, 'king of the Humbrians' (*HE* IV, 17), and the term Humbrians survived into the early eighth century when it was used by the author of the Whitby *Life* of Pope Gregory (ch. 12). Asser's description of York as on the north bank of the Humber, and the naming of a tributary of the Don as Humber Head Dyke, indicates that the Humber was conceived of as extending more widely than at present.[12] The region of *Heathfeld land* or Hatfield Chase, stretching southwards from the Rivers Idle, Don and Trent and through which passed Ryknield Street linking York and Doncaster to Lincoln, was certainly of particular strategic significance for the early warring Anglian principalities. Bede says that the east bank of the Idle was the Mercian border (*HE* II, 12) and it cannot be without significance that Aethelfrith made a stand here – perhaps near Austerfield, not far from the junction of road and river – against Raedwald and that subsequently Eadwine was also brought to bay by the Mercians in Hatfield Chase.[13] Certainly, the later Northumbrian frontier was as far south as Dore, near Sheffield, where the Northumbrians are said to have submitted to the West Saxons in 829 (*ASC* A, *s.a.* 827) and the poem on the West Saxon King Edmund's redemption of the Five Boroughs in the 940s describes Mercia as bounded by Dore and Whitwell (*ASC* A, *s.a.* 942). By the late seventh century, therefore, the Humbrians would seem to have been the peoples on both sides of the Humber and the authority of the king of the Humbrians extended over the territories along the Humber and its tributaries. The Humberside territory of the Lindesfara, the men of Lindsey, was under the domination of the king of the northern Angles from at least the early seventh century before it passed into a Mercian orbit and was finally lost to the Mercians in 679 or 680 (*HE* IV, 21). The Mercians themselves were arguably seen as Humbrians, 'for their territory included the Middle Trent valley, which was as much an extension of the Humber as the rivers of Yorkshire',[14] and the statement in the early ninth-century *Historia Brittonum* that Penda, king of the Mercians in the first half of the seventh century, was the first to separate the kingdom of the Mercians – the Southumbrians as the Northumbrians called them[15] – from that of the northerners (*HB* ch. 65), presupposes an earlier interdependent relationship. Not, however, that such interdependence necessarily goes back to the earliest period of settlement. The authority of the king of the northern Angles over the Humbrians was only established by degrees as political groupings coalesced and principalities were defined. Eadwine married Cwoenburh, daughter of Cearl, king of the Mercians, while he was an exile and in flight from Aethelfrith (*HE* II, 14). As Nicholas Brooks observed, 'the Mercian king Cearl can scarcely have been subject to Aethelfrith when he allowed his daughter to marry the exiled Deiran prince.'[16] This would suggest that a Humbrian confederacy under the domination of a king of the northern Angles had not fully emerged at that time.

Part of the explanation for this may be that in the early seventh century the influence of the eastern Angles was a significant force at least as far inland as the Trent, for the archaeological indications are that some of the settlers along the Trent had penetrated the eastern midlands from the fenlands around the Wash.[17] If there is any connection between the Icel who was regarded as the founding-figure of Penda's Mercian dynasty – the Iclingas (*Vita Guthlaci*, ch. 2) – and the place-names of eastern England which contain the name-element *Icel*, it may be that Penda's family derived from eastern Anglian lands rather than from the region of the Humber,[18] but this is extremely tenuous. What can be said is that the east midlands, the area which came to be known as the territory of the Middle Angles and which embraced Leicestershire and Northamptonshire, had cultural affinities with the eastern Anglian territories; archaeologically the same 'Anglo-Saxon amalgam' is said to have prevailed 'throughout East and Middle Anglia'.[19] The embryonic Mercian kingdom was probably a meeting-ground, therefore, of contrary political influences from the north and from the east.

Raedwald was more than just a king of the eastern Angles. According to Bede, he was the fourth overlord of the Anglo-Saxon kingdoms south of the Humber. His emergence as an overlord did not entirely shatter the Kentish hegemony which – even if somewhat contracted – evidently continued to exist side by side with Raedwald's (see above, p. 42), but it was nevertheless a development of very great significance. How Raedwald established his authority over the various groups within the eastern Anglian region – some of them going back to the earliest phase of Germanic settlement in eastern Britain[20] – to create so powerful an overkingship is not known, though the possibility of Frankish support must be recognized, nor is it certain where the centre of his power lay. It has become almost conventional to associate him with Sutton Hoo. Located by the River Deben and near the East Anglian royal residence at Rendlesham (*HE* III, 12), the Sutton Hoo treasure affords a 'mighty impression of barbarian magnificence'.[21] Its large quantity of imported Mediterranean silver, its military accoutrements, its rich Germanic ornamentation and apparent regalian character has suggested to many that the Sutton Hoo ship-burial was the cenotaph or (as some think now) the grave[22] of Raedwald. The Merovingian coins found among the grave-goods appeared to date no later than *c.* 625, and Raedwald's death has also tended to be placed *c.* 625.[23] There are, however, difficulties. Raedwald may have been dead before *c.* 625, before *c.* 624 even (see below, p. 77), and some of the coins are now thought to belong to the years *c.* 626–9.[24] Earlier uncertainties about the interpretation of the regalia[25] have been compounded by recognition of the possibility that it may be only a local 'status-seeking' chieftain whose worldly goods have been gathered together in this burial.[26] It could be that trade and coastal-based power were what gave Raedwald his paramountcy and Sutton Hoo was in an area distinguished by trading settlement at Ipswich and by commercial activity;[27] alternatively, he could have been primarily a ruler of Angles astride the Icknield Way who imposed his overlordship on the Angles of Suffolk as well as on those of Middle Anglia.[28] He almost certainly controlled the Middle Angles by the time he fought Aethelfrith on the Idle,[29] and perhaps it was the protection of Raedwald which enabled Cearl to give his daughter in marriage to Eadwine. Again, as with Aelle and Ceawlin, the political geography of Raedwald's world has been obscured by later developments. Certainly, however, Raedwald's ascendancy signalled the first recorded appearance of an overlord whose power-base was in the Anglian territories north of the Thames rather than in the Saxon or Jutish lands south of it. The replacement of this eastern by a northern Anglian hegemony, which occurred when Eadwine established his own pre-eminence as the first of a succession of northern overlords, represented a secondary though important recrystallization of power north of the Thames among the Anglian communities. A further restructuring occurred from the second half of the seventh century onwards when the contours of Anglian political life were again redrawn to create the supremacy of the Mercian kings of the central midlands.

Deirans and Bernicians

Eadwine was a prince of the ruling family of the Deirans (see Appendix, Fig. 6.1) between the Humber and the Tees and Aethelfrith the ruler of the Bernicians north of the Tees (see Appendix, Fig. 6.2). The Deirans, like the men of Lindsey and the eastern Angles, included communities whose ancestors were established in Britain in the earliest days of Germanic settlement but after Soemil they only re-emerge into recorded history under what could have been a new dynasty with King Aelle, father of Eadwine.[30] According to the *Anglo-Saxon Chronicle* A, Aelle became king in 560, reigned for thirty years (*s.a.* 560) and died in 588 (*s.a.* 588). Clearly, this record cannot be entirely correct and it is complicated further by the fact that Bede thought that Aelle was alive when Augustine arrived in 597.[31] Again according to the *Chronicle* A (*s.a.* 588), Aelle was succeeded by an Aethelric who reigned for five years, from 588 to 593, in which year the *Chronicle* places the accession of Aethelfrith as king of 'Northumbria'. The year 593 seems to have been inferred from Bede who says that Aethelfrith was in his eleventh year in 603 (*HE* I, 34), so that ten years could have been deducted from 603 to give the date of his accession.[32] The belief that Aethelfrith succeeded Aethelric, who succeeded Aelle, compelled the chronicler to deduct five from 593 to obtain 588 for Aelle's death. The chronicler's Deiran chronology was here controlled by that for the Bernician Aethelfrith.

The Northumbrian king-list from the early eighth century accords Eadwine a reign of seventeen years[33] but does not provide details of Deiran regnal succession before Eadwine. The *Anglo-Saxon Chronicle* D (*s.a* 617) places the accession of Eadwine in 617, but a chronology based on the Northumbrian king-list would indicate 616 for Eadwine's accession and 633 for his death. This was clearly the chronological scheme adopted by Bede who also places Eadwine's death in October 633 after a reign of seventeen years (*HE* II, 20). There is a possibility, however, that Eadwine was still alive in 634 and that his death occurred in the October of that year. Eadwine was converted in the late 620s by Paulinus, bishop of York, and Pope Honorius I (625–38) wrote to him (*HE* II, 17) and simultaneously to Honorius, archbishop of Canterbury (*HE* II, 18), concerning the sending of two pallia at the request of King Eadwine and King Eadbald, one for Paulinus and one for Honorius. The letter to Honorius is precisely dated to June 634. If Eadwine was killed in October 633, it is surprising that the pope had not been informed of this by June 634. It is important not to exaggerate the time it would take a messenger (or a relay of messengers) travelling post-haste to cover the distance from Kent to Rome. Pope Gregory I had heard by 28 July 598, at the latest, of the baptism of converts in Kent by Augustine at Christmas 597.[34] The balance of probability must be, therefore, that the pope would have heard of the death of Eadwine by June 634 if the king had perished eight months before. Consequently, the likelihood exists – to put it no stronger – that Eadwine was killed in October 634. In this case his accession will have occurred in 617 (see Appendix, Fig. 7.3).

The Bernicians, representing an intrusive force probably from Anglian communities further south, were establishing themselves in the north from the mid-sixth century under their leader, Ida, traditionally regarded as the ancestor of the later Bernician kings (*HE* V, 24). The regnal figures in the Northumbrian king-list indicate 547 for the beginning of the twelve-year reign of Ida (cf., *HE* V, 24), which would need to be emended to 548, however, if it were to be kept in line with 617 as opposed to 616 for the accession of Eadwine (see Appendix, Fig. 7.2). Oesa, who is represented in the Anglian genealogies as the grandfather of Ida,[35] is said to have been the first of his line to come to Britain,[36] but nothing further is known of him and Bernician history begins with Ida. According to the *Chronicle* A (*s.a.* 547) (cf., *HB* ch. 61) Ida built Bamburgh (which was later named after Bebba, wife of Aethelfrith (*HE* III, 6, 17: *HB* ch. 63)). He is said to have had twelve sons, a claim to distinction shared with Pybba, father of the Mercian king, Penda (*HB* chs 57, 60), which indicates not so much the historicity of so numerous a progeny as that many princely lines later traced their ancestry back to him (and to Pybba), including the descendants of Aethelfrith who regarded Aethelfrith as the son of Aethelric, son of Ida (see Appendix, Fig. 9).[37]

The immediate successors of Ida were Glappa, with a reign of one year, and Adda with one of eight, after whom the Northumbrian king-list includes an Aethelric with a reign of four years (subsequently misread as seven).[38] This regnal chronology indicates 568–72 for Aethelric's reign, possibly to be emended to 569–73 (see Appendix, Fig. 7.2). The Bernician Aethelric, father of Aethelfrith, and the Deiran Aethelric, the successor of Aelle, were regarded on occasion as one and the same person. The *Chronicon ex Chronicis* accorded Aethelric a reign of two years in Bernicia and five in Deira and held him responsible for the expulsion of Eadwine, son of Aelle, from Deira.[39] The two Aethelrics, however, were quite separate. Aelle had one brother called Aelfric (*HE* III, 1) and Aethelric, Aelle's successor, may have been another. Aethelfrith's father, Aethelric, on the other hand, was one of a succession of Bernician chiefs who made war on the northern Britons from advance bases at Bamburgh and on the island of Lindisfarne. His immediate successors were Theodric with a reign of seven years, Frithuwald with one of six (subsequently misread as seven), and Hussa with one of seven. Hussa's successor, Aethelfrith, who is credited with a regnal length of twenty-four years (subsequently misread as twenty-seven or twenty-eight),[40] reigned from 592 to 616, on the basis of this same regnal chronology, possibly to be emended to 593 to 617. According to the *Historia Brittonum* (ch. 63) Aethelfrith reigned for twelve years among the Bernicians before he established himself also in Deira. If this statement can be accepted, and depending on whether Aethelfrith began to rule in Bernicia in 592 or 593, he would have extended his authority into Deira only in 604 or 605 (see Appendix, Fig. 7.2). It is from 604 or 605, therefore, on the basis of this evidence that the chronology of the reigns of the Deiran Aelle and Aethelric should be inferred, indicating a reign for Aethelric from 599 to 604 or from 600 to 605 and for Aelle, assuming a regnal length of twenty-eight or thirty years (neither of which span has anything very much to commend it), a range of alternative dates for an accession between 569–72 (see Appendix, Fig. 7.1).

Quite apart from the suspicion which attaches to round regnal numbers such as Aelle's thirty, the example of the changes which occur in the figures for the regnal years of the Bernician Aethelric and Aethelfrith demonstrate how inexact such figures can sometimes be, so that dates deduced from king-lists do not inspire absolute confidence. Nevertheless, Aelle's son, Eadwine, was 47 years old when he was killed (*HE* II, 20), so that he was born *c.* 586/7, which would seem to confirm the likelihood that Aelle belongs to the late rather than the mid-sixth century. Similarly, Eadwine's sister, Acha, married Aethelfrith (*HE* III, 6), no later than *c.* 604/5 for her son, Oswald, was 37 at his death in the early 640s (*HE* II, 9), suggesting that she also was born in the mid-580s. It is not at all inconceivable, therefore, that Aelle was reigning when Augustine landed in 597 (see Appendix, Fig. 7.1).

The wars with the northern Britons

Bamburgh and Lindisfarne were in the territory of the Votadini, which extended originally from the Tees to the Firth of Forth. This area had been in the forefront of wars with the Picts in the early fifth century and may have been accustomed to population displacement. British kings of the first dynasty to reign in Gwynedd in north Wales are said to have claimed descent from Cunedda, allegedly a fifth-century migrant chieftain from Manau Gododdin, the plain of the Votadini between the Avon and the Carron rivers at the head of the Firth of Forth.[41] If the region was highly unstable this might provide a context for the suggestion that the Votadini invited the first Angles to be established in their territory to settle there or at least acquiesced in such settlements,[42] but it is difficult to associate Ida and his successors with such an initial phase, which is more likely to have characterized the fifth rather than the mid-sixth century. North-east of Votadini territory was the kingdom of the Dumnonii, later Strathclyde, with its centre at Dumbarton but the frontiers of which eventually extended as far north as the head of Glen Falloch by Loch Lomond and eastwards to the neighbourhood of the Votadini stronghold of Stirling.[43] To the south of Strathclyde was the kingdom of Rheged, its precise geographical extent unknown but the heartland of which seems to have been the Eden valley and the land bordering on the Solway.[44] Well to the south of Rheged was the British territory of Elmet, the name of which still survives in place-names of the former West Riding of Yorkshire.[45] Many of these British principalities were now threatened by the newly arrived Bernician warlords.

According to the *Historia Brittonum* (ch. 63),[46] four British kings, Rhydderch, Urbgen, Gwallawg and Morcant fought, though not necessarily all at the same time, against the successors of Ida. Rhydderch was king of the Strathclyde Britons.[47] The bardic poems traditionally ascribed to Taliesin[48] associate Urbgen, otherwise Urien, with Rheged as 'Rheged's protector'[49] and Gwallawg is portrayed as a 'judge over Elmet'.[50] Morcant may have been a prince of the Votadini. Aethelric's successor in Bernicia, Theodric (572–9 or 573–80) (see Appendix, Fig. 6.2), is said in the *Historia Brittorium* to have responded vigorously, and Urien was assassinated by Morcant during a three-day siege of Lindisfarne, allegedly because Morcant was jealous of his military reputation. Bardic images are of fierce fighting – and on the part of the Angles of 'frequent loss and great suffering'[51] – but it is unlikely that the Bernicians should be thought of as entirely isolated or contained in the vicinity of Lindisfarne and Bamburgh. Bamburgh was certainly a frontier fortress, but the Bernicians must have controlled from an early date the land routes south to Hadrian's Wall and the Tyne, linking up overland as well as by sea with Anglian settlements in Deira. An adversary of Urien, who appears in two of the poems of Taliesin as 'Flamebearer',[52] could have been one of the Bernician leaders at Bamburgh or a commander at any point along a fairly extended line of command.

It is certainly likely that the Deirans should be thought of as supporting and giving military aid to this northward thrust of fellow Angles beyond the Wall. The image preserved in the poem (or collection of poems), the *Gododdin*, attributed to the bard Aneirin, at least in its longer version, is of Bernicians and Deirans together in the battle of *Catraeth* (generally thought to be Catterick) against a Votadini-led army of British warriors from the northern stronghold of *Din Eidyn* (Edinburgh).[53] The absence of any reference to the battle of *Catraeth* outside the *Gododdin*, the location of Catterick (if this is the site of *Catraeth*) so deep in Anglian territory, and the uncertain historicity of the poem[54] make it difficult to place the undated event it purports to describe in a historical context. However, the Votadini must certainly have been in the front line of any war with Deira and Bernicia, and it would make greater sense of Bernician successes in the north if the Bernicians received Deiran assistance.

If an historical event does lie behind the poem, it seems more likely than not that it occurred no later than the early years of Aethelfrith in Bernicia. Bede thought of Aethelfrith as a Northumbrian King Saul because of the extent of his conquests of British territory (*HE* I, 34),[55] and some of these wars belong to the period when Aethelfrith was king only of Bernicia. So substantial were his conquests that they provoked a response from Áedán, son of Gabrán, king of the Scots of Dál Riata, which led to the major conflict at *Degsastan*, possibly Dawston in Liddesdale,[56] in 603, according to Bede (*HE* I, 34). The date 603 will need to be emended to 604 if Northumbrian regnal chronology is to be adjusted consistently. This battle occurred the year before Aethelfrith established himself in Deira. For some years the Scots had been campaigning in southern Pictland far outside the frontiers of their western kingdom, and *c.* 598 Domangart, son of Áedán, was slain fighting the Angles.[57] Hostilities are likely to have become acute as both Dalriadic Scots and Bernicians began to converge on territories bordering on the Forth. One discontented Bernician aetheling, Hering, son of Hussa, appears to have been prepared to take advantage of the situation to challenge Aethelfrith; Hussa is almost certainly the Hussa who reigned in Bernicia, on the evidence of the Northumbrian king-list, immediately before Aethelfrith[58] from 585 to 592 or 586 to 593 (see Appendix, Fig. 7.2), but concerning whose reputed ancestry nothing is known. Hering is said to have led Áedán's army to *Degsastan* (*ASC* D, *s.a.* 603). Bede records that the Scots advanced with an immense army, but, though Aethelfrith lost a brother in the battle (*ASC* D, *s.a.* 603), the Irish annals[59] confirm that Áedán was decisively defeated (*AU s.a.* 599: *AT* p. 163: *CA* p. 142). It is not impossible that Aethelfrith gained victory solely with Bernician forces; traditional accounts of the battle could have exaggerated the size of Áedán's army. Nevertheless, Deiran support would certainly help to explain what seems to have been a shattering defeat of the Scots. Bede declares that after *Degsastan* no Scottish king dared to attack the Northumbrians.

Against a background of possible Deiran–Bernician co-operation, the extension of Aethelfrith's kingship over both territories appears as a formalization of a previous relationship. The circumstances under which Aethelfrith established himself in 604 or 605 as king also of the Deirans to create a new northern Anglian overkingship are quite unknown, but two aspects of the situation deserve comment. First, the support of Hering, son of Hussa, for the Dalriadic Scots suggests serious dynastic tensions among the Bernicians. This may have destabilized the existing relationship between the Deirans and the Bernicians. Second, Aethelfrith's marriage to Aelle's daughter, Acha, was either the prelude to the forging of a closer relationship or the consolidation of a position recently achieved. The expulsion of Eadwine did not necessarily follow immediately and Aethelfrith's hostility to his wife's kinsmen probably manifested itself only by degrees. Even so, a development important for subsequent Northumbrian history had occurred: Bernician domination of the Deirans had been established in the first years of the seventh century and was to prove a fundamental feature of political life among the northern Angles. The military and political eclipse of the more settled and prosperous Deira by the Bernician war-zone created long-enduring tensions within the Anglian polity north of the Humber which it took much of the century to resolve and then not necessarily completely.

The extent to which Aethelfrith crushed the surrounding Britons may not have been quite as total as Bede implies. During Aethelfrith's last years Eadwine's nephew, Hereric, was in exile with his wife, Breguswith, and infant daughter, Hild, in the British kingdom of Elmet (*HE* IV, 23). Gwallawg's successors continued to rule there until Eadwine as king took Elmet and drove out King Ceretic (*HB* ch. 63), whose death the Welsh annals[60] place (albeit too early) in 616 (*AC s.a.* 616). Hereric is said to have been poisoned while at the court of Ceretic (*HE* IV, 23) and Eadwine's attack on Elmet perhaps carried with it undercurrents of vengeance. The murder of Hereric may have occurred in response to bribes and threats from Aethelfrith of the kind deployed ultimately to no avail against Raedwald, but it is important to stress the continued independent existence of Elmet across these years. Nevertheles, Aethelfrith, king of the Bernicians and now of the Deirans, was a very powerful warlord. In *c.* 616 he advanced with his army to Chester where he defeated the army of the king of Powys, Selyf 'Serpent of battles' ap Cynan, slaying both Selyf and an otherwise unknown king, Cetula, and putting to the sword a company of monks from the neighbouring monastery of Bangor-is-coed who had come to pray for the British army (*HE* II, 2; *AU s.a.* 613: *CA* p. 143).[61] What lay behind Aethelfrith's attack is unknown, but this conflict with the men of Powys represented a deep thrust into disputed territory, perhaps to protect Anglian settlers in Lancashire[62] or to bring an emerging independent Anglian principality beyond the Pennines under Aethelfrith's authority. It shows Aethelfrith, perhaps with the support of Anglo-Saxon settlers, close to the border with the men of Powys, operating to the north of the Wocensaete or Wreocensaete, who came to dominate north Shropshire, and possibly in the territory of the Westerna.[63] His victory at Chester confirms the impression of him as the dominant figure in the early seventh century among the northern Angles over a very wide territory indeed.

What Aethelfrith had achieved was a position of authority in the north analogous to Raedwald's over the eastern Angles and their immediate neighbours. His advance to the River Idle against Raedwald in 616 or 617 could indicate that he was now beginning to establish a transhumbrian overkingship in some of the lands south of the Humber. It may be that Eadwine's flight into the territory of Raedwald occurred when Aethelfrith's power began to impinge on Cearl or his successors among the Mercians. The conflict between Raedwald and Aethelfrith, therefore, was about more than Raedwald's protection of Eadwine. It was a confrontation between two powerful rulers and it was resolved in what was probably a sensitive border area. Bede says that Raedwald assembled a large army but did not give Aethelfrith time to gather his whole army together, and in this clash of Titans on the banks of the Idle it was Aethelfrith who was defeated and slain (*HE* II, 12). The victory must have marked an important stage in the establishment of Raedwald's *imperium*. It is likely that it enabled him to impose his authority over some if not all of the Mercians and at least as far north as the Humber, with Eadwine established in what may have been at first a dependent capacity as king of the northern Angles. The key to Eadwine's ability not only to acquire the kingship of the Deirans but to expel Aethelfrith's sons from Bernicia (*HE* III, 1), (there were seven according to genealogical tradition [*ASC* E, *s.a.* 617]), and thereby recreate Aethelfrith's overkingship may have lain in the continuing support of Raedwald. Without it, Eadwine could probably not have established himself so securely. The history of the northern Angles in the seventh century as a whole shows clearly that the Bernicians were the dominant force for most of that time. Eadwine's accession was contrary to the prevailing tendency and temporarily frustrated Bernician aspirations.

Notes

1 J. N. L. Myres, *The English Settlements* (Oxford, 1986), pp. 110 ff.
2 J. Hines, *The Scandinavian Character of Anglian England in the pre-Viking Period* (BAR British Series 124, 1984), pp. 5 ff. Cf., E. T. Leeds, 'The distribution of the Angles and Saxons archaeologically considered', *Archaeologia*, vol. 91 (1945), pp. 1–106.
3 Hines, *The Scandinavian Character of Anglian England*, p. 13. Cf., C. Hills, 'The archaeology of Anglo-Saxon England in the pagan period', *Anglo-Saxon England*, vol. 8 (1979), pp. 297–329 (p. 316).
4 *History of the Wars*, ed. H. B. Dewing (5 vols, London, 1914–40), vol. 5, pp. 254–5; but for a note of scepticism see A. Russchen, *New Light on Dark Age Frisia* (Drachten, 1967), p. 34, and E. A. Thompson, 'Procopius on Brittia and Britannia', *Classical Quarterly*, vol. 30 (1980), pp. 498–507 (p. 504).
5 Hines, *The Scandinavian Character of Anglian England*, p. 289. On Sutton Hoo, see now the major volumes, *The Sutton Hoo Ship-Burial*, ed. R. L. S. Bruce-Mitford, 3 vols (British Museum, 1975–83), but note also the important paper by M. O. H. Carver, 'Sutton Hoo in context', *Angli e sassoni al di qua e al di là del mare* (Settimane di Studio del centro Italiano di studi sull'alto medioevo, no. 32 (1984); 2 vols, Spoleto, 1986), vol. I, pp. 77–123. Cf., also A. C. Evans, *The Sutton Hoo Ship-Burial* (British Museum, 1986).
6 *Adomnan's Life of Columba*, ed. and trans. A. O. and M. O. Anderson (Edinburgh and London, 1961), III, 10, 22.
7 I. N. Wood, *The Merovingian North Sea* (Occasional Papers on Medieval Topics I: Alingsås, 1983), p. 14.
8 C. J. Arnold, *An Archaeology of the Anglo-Saxon Kingdoms* (London and New York, 1988), pp. 171, 188; R. Hodges, *The Anglo-Saxon Achievement: Archaeology and the Beginnings of English Society* (London, 1989), pp. 57–8.
9 *The Earliest Life of Gregory the Great by an Anonymous Monk of Whitby*, ed. and trans. B. Colgrave (Lawrence, 1968).
10 Cf., P. Hunter Blair, 'The Northumbrians and their southern frontier', *Archaeologia Aeliana*, vol. 26 (1948), pp. 98–126 (p. 118) (reprinted in Blair, *Anglo-Saxon Northumbria*, ed. M. Lapidge and P. H. Blair (London, 1984)).
11 H. E. Pagan, 'The coinage of the East Anglian Kingdom from 825 to 870', *British Numismatic Journal*, vol. 52 (1982), pp. 41–83.

12 J. N. L. Myres, 'The Teutonic settlement of northern England', *History*, vol. 20 (1935–6), pp. 250–62 (p. 251); cf., Blair, 'The Northumbrians and their southern frontier', p. 116.

13 S. Revill, 'King Edwin and the battle of Hatfield', *Transactions of the Thoroton Society*, vol. 79 (1975), pp. 40–9 (p. 48); cf., B. Eagles, 'Lindsey', in S. Bassett (ed.), *The Origins of Anglo-Saxon Kingdoms* (Leicester, 1989), pp. 202–12 (p. 212).

14 P. H. Sawyer, *From Roman Britain to Norman England* (London, 1978), p. 38.

15 Blair, 'The Northumbrians and their southern frontier', pp. 105 ff., and cf., N. Brooks, 'The formation of the Mercian kingdom', in Bassett, *The Origins of Anglo-Saxon Kingdoms*, pp. 159–70 (p. 160).

16 Brooks, 'The formation of the Mercian kingdom', p. 166.

17 ibid., p. 162; and Myres, *The English Settlements* p. 183.

18 ibid., p. 185; and Brooks, 'The formation of the Mercian kingdom', p. 164.

19 Myres, *The English Settlements*, p. 100.

20 M. Carver, 'Kingship and material culture in early Anglo-Saxon East Anglia', in Bassett, *The Origins of Anglo-Saxon Kingdoms*, pp. 141–58 (p. 147).

21 J. Campbell, 'The first Christian kings', *The Anglo-Saxons* (Oxford, 1982), pp. 45–69 (p. 66).

22 V. I. Evison, 'The body in the ship at Sutton Hoo', *Anglo-Saxon Studies in Archaeology and History*, no. 1, ed. S. C. Hawkes, D. Brown and J. Campbell (BAR British Series 72, 1979), pp. 121–38.

23 Raedwald's death, however, even on this reconstruction, was 'uncomfortably near' the date of the minting of the later coins; A. C. Evans, *The Sutton Hoo Ship-Burial*, p. 110.

24 D. Brown, 'The dating of the Sutton Hoo coins', *Anglo-Saxon Studies in Archaeology and History*, no. 2, ed. D. Brown, J. Campbell and S. C. Hawkes (BAR British Series 92, 1981), pp. 71–86.

25 J. M. Wallace-Hadrill, *Early Medieval History* (Oxford, 1975), pp. 47–56. Cf., B. Arrhenius in *Medieval Archaeology*, vol. 22 (1978), p. 194.

26 Carver, 'Sutton Hoo in context', p. 88.

27 R. Hodges, 'North Sea trade before the Vikings', in K. Biddick (ed.), *Archaeological Approaches to Medieval Europe* (Kalamazoo, 1984), pp. 193–202 (p. 194). See also idem, *The Anglo-Saxon Achievement*, pp. 55–6.

28 Cf., for a possibility that Sutton Hoo was on the periphery of the kingdom of the eastern Angles, Carver, 'Sutton Hoo in context', pp. 88 ff., and discussion pp. 119 ff.

29 Cf., D. Dumville, 'Essex, Middle Anglia and the expansion of Mercia', in Bassett, *The Origins of Anglo-Saxon Kingdoms*, pp. 123–40 (p. 132).

30 D. N. Dumville, 'The Anglian collection of royal genealogies and regnal lists', *Anglo-Saxon England*, vol. 5 (1976), pp. 23–50 (p.35).

31 *Chronica Majora*, ed. T. Mommsen, *Chronica Minora*, Vol. III, *MGH Auctores Antiq.*, vol. XIII (Berlin, 1898), p. 309; M. Miller, 'The dates of Deira', *Anglo-Saxon England*, vol. 8 (1979), pp. 35–61 (pp.46–7)

32 P. Hunter Blair, 'The *Moore Memoranda* on Northumbrian history', in C. Fox and B. Dickens (eds), *The Early Cultures of North-West Europe* (Cambridge, 1950), pp. 245–57 (p. 247) (reprinted in Blair, *Anglo-Saxon Northumbria*).

33 Blair, 'The *Moore Memoranda*', p. 246; Dumville, 'The Anglian collection of royal genealogies', pp. 32, 36.

34 Gregorii I papae registrum epistolarum, ed. P. Ewald and L. M. Hartmann, *MGH Epistolae*, Vols I and II (Berlin, 1887–90), Vol. II, viii, 29.

35 Dumville, 'The Anglian collection of royal genealogies', pp. 32, 36.

36 D. N. Dumville, 'A new chronicle-fragment of early British history', *English Historical Review*, vol. 88 (1973), pp. 312–14 (p. 314); see also idem, 'The origins of Northumbria', in Bassett, *The Origins of Anglo-Saxon Kingdoms*, pp. 213–22 (p. 218).

37 Dumville, 'The Anglian collection of royal genealogies', pp. 30, 32, 35. The *Historia Brittonum* (ch. 63) represents Aethelfrith as the grandson of Ida's son, Adda, but Adda here is probably an error for Ida; cf., Miller, 'The dates of Deira', p. 48.

38 Blair, 'The *Moore Memoranda*', p. 246; Dumville, 'The Anglian collection of royal genealogies', pp. 32, 36.

39 *Florentii Wigorniensis monachi Chronicon ex Chronicis*, ed. B. Thorpe, 2 vols (London, 1848), Vol. I, pp. 6, 8.

40 Blair, 'The *Moore Memoranda*', p. 246; Dumville, 'The Anglian collection of royal genealogies', pp. 32, 36.

41 I. A. Richmond, *Roman and Native in North Britain* (London, 1958), pp. 64, 139, 153; A. H. A. Hogg, 'The Votadini', in W. F. Grimes (ed.), *Aspects of Archaeology in Britain and Beyond* (London, 1951), pp. 200–20. M. Miller, 'The foundation legend of Gwynedd in the Latin texts', *Bulletin of the Board of Celtic Studies*, vol. 27 (1976–8), pp. 515–32; D. P. Kirby, 'The political development of Ceredigion, *c.* 400–1081', in J. L. Davies and D. P. Kirby (eds), *Cardiganshire: A County History*, Vol. I (forthcoming).

42 L. Alcock, 'Gwŷr y Gogledd: an archaeological appraisal', *Archaeologia Cambrensis*, vol. 132 (1983), pp. 1–18 (reprinted L. Alcock, *Economy, Society and Warfare among the Britons and Saxons* (Cardiff, 1987), pp. 234–54). On the archaeological evidence for Anglo-Saxons in Bernicia, see now R. Miket, 'A re-statement of evidence for Bernician Anglo-Saxon burials', in P. Rahtz, T. Dickinson and L. Watts (eds), *Anglo-Saxon Cemeteries* (BAR British Series 82, 1980), pp. 289–306.

43 W. J. Watson, *The Celtic Place-Names of Scotland* (Edinburgh, 1926), p. 206; K. H. Jackson, 'The sources for the life of St. Kentigern', in N. K. Chadwick (ed.), *Studies in the Early British Church* (Cambridge, 1958), pp. 273–327 (pp. 305, 307–9).

44 K. H. Jackson, 'The Britons in southern Scotland', *Antiquity*, vol. 29 (1955), pp. 77–88 (p. 82).

45 Cf., E. Kolb, 'Elmet: a dialect region in northern England', *Anglia*, vol. 91 (1973), pp. 285–313 and G. R. J. Jones, 'Early territorial organization in Gwynedd and Elmet', *Northern History*, vol. 10 (1975), pp. 3–27.

46 Though D. N. Dumville, 'The historical value of the *Historia Brittonum*', *Arthurian Literature*, vol. 6 (1986), pp. 1–26, is sceptical of the accuracy of the *Historia*'s chronological synchronizations at this point (p. 23).

47 Cf., R. Bromwich, *Trioedd Ynys Prydein: The Welsh Triads* (Cardiff, 1978), pp. 504–5.

48 *Canu Taliesin*, ed. Ifor Williams (Cardiff, 1960), with English version by J. E. Caerwyn Williams, *The Poems of Taliesin* (Dublin, 1968). For other bardic material relating to Urien, see J. Rowland, *Early Welsh Saga Poetry: A Study and Edition of the Englynion* (Woodbridge, 1990), pp. 75–119, 419–28, 477–82.

49 *Canu Taliesin*, poem III, l.11.

50 ibid., poem XII, l.21.

51 ibid., poem III, ll.10–13.

52 ibid., poem VI, l.3 and poem X, l.11.

53 *Canu Aneirin*, ed. Ifor Williams (Cardiff, 1938): trans. K. H. Jackson, *The Gododdin: The Oldest Scottish Poem* (Edinburgh, 1969) and more recently A. O. H. Jarman, *Aneirin: Y Gododdin* (Llandysul, 1986).

54 T. M. Charles-Edwards, 'The authenticity of the *Gododdin*: an historian's view', in R. Bromwich and R. Brinley Jones (eds), *Astudiaethau ar yr Hengerdd: Studies in Old Welsh Poetry* (Cardiff, 1978), pp. 44–71, argues that the poem is the authentic work of Aneirin, but see now D. N. Dumville, 'Early Welsh poetry: problems of historicity', in B. F. Roberts (ed.), *Early Welsh Poetry: Studies in the Book of Aneirin* (Aberystwyth, 1988), pp. 1–16. Cf., also, the comments of L. Alcock, 'Gwŷr y Gogledd: an archaeological appraisal', pp. 16–17 (*Economy, Society and Warfare*, pp. 252–3).

55 Cf., on the Saul image, J. M. Wallace-Hadrill, *Early Germanic Kingship in England and on the Continent* (Oxford, 1971), pp. 76–8, and A. Johnson, 'Bede and Aethelfrith of Northumbria', *Trivium*, vol. 22 (1987), pp. 5–17.

56 But see I. M. Smith, 'Brito-Roman and Anglo-Saxon: the unification of the borders', in P. Clack and J. Ivy (eds), *The Borders* (CBA Group 3: Durham, 1983), pp. 9–48, who suggests Addinston in Berwickshire (p. 9).

57 J. Bannerman, *Studies in the History of Dalriada* (Edinburgh and London, 1974), pp. 80 ff.

58 Blair, 'The *Moore Memoranda*', p. 246; Dumville, 'The Anglian collection of royal genealogies', pp. 32, 36.

59 For relevant Irish annals, see the *Annals of Ulster* (hereafter abbreviated as *AU*), ed. S. Mac Airt and G. Mac Niocaill (Dublin, 1983) and the *Annals of Tigernach* (hereafter abbreviated as *AT*), ed. W. Stokes, *Revue Celtique*, vol. xvii (1896); and K. Grabowski and D. Dumville, *Chronicles and Annals of Medieval Ireland and Wales* (hereafter abbreviated as *CA*) (Woodbridge, 1984). References in the text to the *Annals of Ulster* are by annal, according to the *Annals of Ulster's* uncorrected dates, but to the *Annals of Tigernach* and *Chronicles and Annals* by page.

60 For the text of the *Annales Cambriae*, the Welsh annals (hereafter abbreviated as *AC*), see E. Phillimore (ed.), 'The *Annales Cambriae* and the Old Welsh genealogies from *Harleian MS 3859*', *Y Cymmrodor*, vol. 9 (1888), pp. 141–83, and *Annales Cambriae*, ed. J. W. ab Ithel (Rolls series: London, 1860). The Harleian annals are translated J. Morris, *Nennius* (London and Chichester, 1980). The texts of the *Brut y Tywysogyon* (hereafter abbreviated as *ByT*) are ed. and trans. by T. Jones, *Brut y Tywysogyon or The Chronicles of the Princes* (Board of Celtic Studies, University of Wales History and Law Series), nos VI (Peniarth MS 20) (1941), XI (Peniarth MS 20 (trans.)) (1952), XVI (Red Book of Hergest) (1955), and XXV (Brenhinedd y Saesson) (1971). References in the text are by annal, according to their own dates.

61 On the battle, see J. E. Lloyd, *A History of Wales from the Earliest Times to the Edwardian Conquest*, 2 vols (3rd edn, London, 1939), Vol. I, pp. 179 ff., and N. K. Chadwick, 'The battle of Chester', in N. K. Chadwick (ed.), *Celt and Saxon: Studies in the Early British Border* (Cambridge, 1963), pp. 167–85.

62 J. M. Dodgson, 'The English arrival in Cheshire', *Transactions of the Historical Society of Lancashire and Cheshire*, vol. 119 (1967), pp. 1–37 (pp. 32–4 and n. 122).

63 M. Gelling, 'The early history of western Mercia', in Bassett, *The Origins of Anglo-Saxon Kingdoms*, pp. 184–201 (p. 192).

5 The northern Anglian hegemony in the seventh century

The dominance in the seventh century of Anglian political and military power in southern as well as northern England was accompanied by an extension of Anglian influence into British territories and over the Picts and Scots beyond the Forth.

The Humbrian overlordship of Eadwine

Deira, as Bede appreciated, remained Eadwine's essential power-base (*HE* III, 1). The leader of Eadwine's pagan priests was in charge of the sanctuary at *Godmunddingaham*, possibly Goodmanham, near York, and when Eadwine was converted he was baptized at York (*HE* II, 13). He conquered the still-surviving British kingdom of Elmet (*HB* ch. 63) and extended over the men of Lindsey (among whom the missionary Paulinus baptized at Lincoln and Littleborough (*HE* II, 16)), a lordship which must soon have come to embrace the Mercians north of the Trent and, no doubt by slower degrees, those south of it. Even more so than Aethelfrith, Eadwine established himself as a Humbrian king. Nor did his ambition rest here. For Bede he became the fifth overlord of all the Anglo-Saxons south of the Humber (*HE* II, 5).

The period immediately following the death of Raedwald among the eastern Angles was one of internal strife between Raedwald's son and successor, Eorpwald, and his half-brother, Sigeberht (see Appendix, Fig. 5), who was driven into exile in Gaul, and probably also one of tension between pagan and Christian factions as the kingdom lapsed further into paganism under Eorpwald (*HE* II, 15), so that Eorpwald was not able to maintain the influence that had been Raedwald's. It is not known when Raedwald died but it must be significant that when Eadwine sought a new bride (before *c.* 624 (see above, p. 41)), he did not do so at the court of the king of the eastern Angles but at that of the still-powerful Eadbald, king of Kent, whom he seems to have continued to treat with considerable respect. Bede specifically excludes Kent from the kingdoms south of the Humber which he regarded as subject to Eadwine (*HE* II, 5) (see above, p. 43). Nevertheless, Eadwine's overtures to Eadbald for the hand of his sister Aethelburh (*HE* II, 9) suggest a northern ruler already prestigious in his own right. The impression is very strong that Raedwald was dead by now and Eadwine well on his way to establishing a dominant position amongst the Angles. He was a significant enough figure by *c.* 624 for Pope Boniface V to write to him and his queen (*HE* II, 10, 11). Even so, good diplomatic relations were consolidated with the eastern Angles, also in part through marriage. Hereswith, the daughter of Eadwine's nephew, Hereric, married Aethelric, Raedwald's nephew (see Appendix, Fig. 5), to become the mother of Ealdwulf, later king of the eastern Angles (*HE* IV, 23). The probability indeed is that the eastern Angles either had been or were in the process of being brought into a dependent relationship with Eadwine by the time of his marriage to Aethelburh or at least not long after. The way in which Eadwine was able eventually to induce Eorpwald, king of the eastern Angles, to accept Christianity (*HE* II, 15) would suggest that the eastern Anglian court was more amenable to Eadwine's influence than the Mercian upon which Eadwine could not prevail in the same way. The possibility arises of a special relationship between Eadwine and his former benefactors, the eastern Angles, so that an alliance between Eadwine and Eorpwald, though one in which the northern Anglian rather than the eastern Anglian king was now the dominant party, may have come to characterize Eadwine's ascendancy as an overlord.

It was probably with his authority already established over the Angles of the east and the midlands that Eadwine also aspired to subject to his rule the Saxons of the upper Thames valley. This process was under way by *c.* 625–6 when Cwichelm, styled by Bede king of the West Saxons but perhaps more correctly thought of as a king in the upper Thames valley (see above, pp. 48 ff.), sought to have Eadwine assassinated; Eadwine's retaliating attack, when he is said to have slain or subdued all those who had plotted against him (*HE* II, 9), confirms that he was reaching the height of his power by the mid-620s.

The *Ecclesiastical History* places the baptism of Eadwine in York at Easter in the twelfth year of his reign, which Bede, who dated Eadwine's accession to 616, considered to be 627 (*HE* II, 14), but if Eadwine's accession were not in 616 but in 617 this date would need to be corrected to 628. Less is known about the circumstances of his conversion than the relatively copious material suggests. Bede's account of Eadwine's successive 'conditional promises' (as they have been called) to accept Christianity – if he should find it acceptable after marrying Aethelburh (*HE* II, 9), if he should be victorious in the campaign against Cwichelm (*HE* II, 9), and if his counsellors should advise it after consultation (*HE* II, 10) – carries with it an air of literary artificiality.[1] The *Historia Brittonum* (ch. 63) states that Eadwine was baptized with thousands of his people by a Briton, Rhun, son of Urbgen (possibly to be identified with Urien, lord of Rheged), but this may rest on a confusion of Bede's account of mass-baptisms by Paulinus in the River Glen near Yeavering (*HE* II, 14) with the occasion of the baptism of Eadwine which took place in York (*HE* II, 14). While it is possible that the missionary who baptized in the River Glen was the Briton, Rhun, and that Bede was mistaken when he located Paulinus at Yeavering, the statement about Rhun in the *Historia Brittonum*, inserted as it is in a somewhat garbled account seemingly extrapolated from the *Ecclesiastical History*, cannot be regarded as undoubtedly signifying this and it is uncertain what weight can be attached to it. There clearly was quite an extended period between Eadwine's marriage to Aethelburh – some time before *c*. 624 - and his baptism by Paulinus in 627 or 628.

Despite the fact that Aethelburh was accompanied north when she married by Paulinus as her chaplain, and that Paulinus was subsequently consecrated bishop of York by Archbishop Justus in 625 or 626 (*HE* II, 9),[2] Eadwine did not hasten to embrace the new faith and it needs to be emphasized that his eventual baptism was untypical among the Anglo-Saxons at this time. Eorpwald, king of the eastern Angles, was a pagan. The Mercians were pagan. There was no Christian king anywhere in England outside Kent. That the most northerly of the Anglian kings should have been the first non-Kentish ruler to adopt Christianity in the 620s is, at the very least, surprising. It was part of Eadwine's success, however, that he was in tune with the more advanced trends of contemporary political life. The standard which was borne before him as he progressed through his kingdom was reminiscent of Rome (*HE* II, 16). His marriage to Aethelburh gave him a connection with cross-Channel diplomacy and his children by Aethelburh were kinsfolk of a Merovingian king in Gaul. His wife's Christian beliefs put him in touch with Rome itself, and even before 625 made him and his wife recipients of papal letters and gifts from the head of the Christian Church in the West. It will have been in the aftermath of this contact with the papacy that Eadwine, though still a pagan, allowed an episcopal see to be established at York for Paulinus, and in itself this shows the direction in which Eadwine was moving. His prestige, like Aethelberht's before him, could now find further expression in the diffusion of the new religion among the territories subject to him and through his personal participation in ecclesiastical affairs at the highest level.

Paulinus preached and baptized in the dependent territory of Lindsey and his activities there – and in Bernicia, if Bede is correct in placing him at Yeavering – serve to delineate where Eadwine had most effective control outside Deira. The success experienced among the eastern Angles with the conversion of Eorpwald may have been due in part at least to the influence of older patterns established by missionaries in the time of Raedwald, but nevertheless it testifies to Eadwine's real influence in the East Anglian area at this time. There was also continuing close contact between Eadwine's court and that of Eadbald, king of Kent. It has been suggested that one reason for Eadwine's preferential treatment of the Kentish kingdom was the location there of the southern archbishopric at Canterbury,[3] and there certainly emerged at this time a clear intention to implement Pope Gregory the

Great's original plan for two archiepiscopal sees among the Anglo-Saxons. Paulinus consecrated Honorius, archbishop of Canterbury, at Lincoln, after which Eadwine joined with Eadbald in requesting a pallium for Honorius and another for Paulinus (*HE* II, 17, 18). This would have had the effect of endowing York with metropolitan status as Pope Gregory the Great had originally intended and it is likely that Eadwine, on Bede's testimony a thoughtful and sagacious individual (*HE* II, 9), appreciated the significance of this development. The pope despatched two pallia in June 634 (*HE* II, 18), but the death of Eadwine in battle in Hatfield Chase against combined Welsh and Mercian forces, either in October 633 or more likely October 634, and the subsequent collapse of the ecclesiastical community at York with the flight of Paulinus to Kent (*HE* II, 20) (see below, p. 83 ff.), terminated this phase in the history of the church of York and arrested its development as an archiepiscopal see for a hundred years. It is important not to allow this to obscure the fact that, at the height of his power, Eadwine had embarked on an ecclesiastical programme to establish a separate northern province of the Anglo-Saxon Church.

The overthrow of Eadwine was the consequence of further shifts in the political equilibrium of the Anglian world. Eorpwald, king of the eastern Angles, was slain by a pagan, Ricberht, soon after his conversion and a period of three years elapsed before Eorpwald's half-brother, Sigeberht, who had been baptized during his exile in Gaul, became king and Felix, a Burgundian, was appointed bishop of the eastern Angles by Honorius, archbishop of Canterbury. The date of these events can be inferred only by the episcopal chronology of the bishops of the eastern Angles. Felix was bishop for seventeen years and his successor, Thomas, for five, and then Berhtgils (or Boniface) was consecrated by Archbishop Honorius, who died on 30 September 653 (*HE* III, 20). On these figures, Felix must have become bishop by 631 at the latest, so that three years before this gives 628 for the slaying of Eorpwald, whose conversion would have followed very rapidly indeed on Eadwine's and his assassination very swiftly on his conversion. But the figures should not be deployed too rigidly. It is not even certain that Honorius was archbishop in 631. The pope did not send him a pallium until June 634 and, given the long-standing papal concern with the well-being of the church of Canterbury, a three-year interval between Honorius' appointment and the sending of a pallium would seem to be rather a long time. A date *c.* 632–3 for Honorius' appointment is perhaps more likely. There are other considerations. The three–year period, for example, between the death of Eorpwald and the accession of Sigeberht, could signify that Sigeberht succeeded in the third year after Eorpwald's assassination. Felix may have died in his seventeenth year or Thomas in his fifth. There is a possible error here of some three years in the calculations. The assassination of Eorpwald could easily have taken place as late as 630/1. Even so, the sequence of events remains rapid and Eorpwald's death must have constituted a serious threat to Eadwine's position south of the Humber. The paganism of the eastern Angles over the next two or three years suggests that Eadwine's influence in the region was no longer what it had been in Eorpwald's lifetime. Indeed, a factor of some importance in the slaying of Eorpwald may have been hostility to the way in which the kingdom of the eastern Angles had sunk under his rule to satellite status. Nor can it be assumed that Eadwine found new allies among the eastern Angles in *c.* 632/3 when Eorpwald's half-brother, Sigeberht, returned from Gaul to partition the kingdom with his kinsman, Ecgric. Bede has much to say about Sigeberht's Christian patronage within his kingdom (*HE* III, 18) but nothing of Ecgric's, and the probability is that Ecgric was and remained a pagan. Sigeberht's position was possibly insecure because he was only Eorpwald's maternal brother[4] – that is, he was Raedwald's step-son – and before long he abdicated to enter a monastery, and Ecgric ruled alone (*HE* III, 18).

Deprived of the support of the ruler of the eastern Angles, Eadwine was vulnerable also to undercurrents of restlessness in other parts of the Anglian world. The coalescence of the Mercians across the first half of the seventh century into a powerful midland kingdom radically reshaped the patterns of power among the Angles and provided a serious long-term challenge not only to the authority of the northern Anglian kings but also to any hopes of a revival of eastern Anglian power. This process was beginning in Eadwine's last years. Penda – 'a most vigorous young man of the royal race of the Mercians', as Bede calls him (*HE* II, 20) – was aspiring to royal power. When the British king of Gwynedd in north Wales, Cadwallon ap Cadfan, invaded Eadwine's territory in 633 or 634, Penda joined him and participated in the overthrow of Eadwine in battle at Hatfield Chase (*HE* II, 20).

Descent from Icel was claimed for Penda, certainly in the course of time, through his father Pybba, also reputedly the father of Eowa and Coenwealh.[5] The kings of the Mercians until at least the time of Ceolwulf (821–3) claimed descent from either Penda or one of his brothers (see Appendix, Fig. 8). The chronology of Penda's reign has been confused by a variety of different regnal lengths.[6] According to Bede, who records the death of Penda in the battle of the *Winwaed*, which he places in 655 (*HE* III, 24), Penda ruled the Mercian nation for twenty-two years from his victory at Hatfield to his defeat at the *Winwaed* (*HE* II, 20), that is from 633 to 655. If Eadwine was slain not in 633 but in 634, the battle of the *Winwaed* will have occurred not in 655 but in 656, so that Bede's 633–55 may need to be emended accordingly to 634–56. The attribution of a thirty-year reign to Penda in the *Anglo-Saxon Chronicle* A (*s.a.* 626), however, would indicate an accession in 625 (reckoning back from 655) or (if Penda was thought of as having died in his thirtieth regnal year) 626. By contrast, the *Historia Brittonum* claims only a ten-year reign for Penda, dating it evidently from the battle of *Cogwy* (ch. 65) – Bede's *Maserfelth*, which Bede dates to 642 but which again may need to be emended (in accordance with any adjustment of Bede's other Northumbrian dates) to 643 (*HE* III, 9: V, 24). Nevertheless, neither the *Chronicle* nor the *Historia Brittonum* provides an acceptable alternative to the Bedan chronology. The *Chronicle* A represents Penda as 50 years old when he began his thirty-year reign, and grave suspicion attaches to both round numbers.[7] The image of Penda as an octogenarian at the *Winwaed* but still with two young sons (Wulfhere and Aethelred) has not proved a credible one to historians.[8] The Welsh annals misdate the battle of *Cogwy* (that is, *Maserfelth*) by two years, to 644 (*AC s.a.* 644) as opposed to Bede's 642, and place the death of Penda in 657 (*AC s.a* 657), but the interval here between the alleged date of Penda's accession and his death is more than ten years. Moreover, when the *Historia Brittonum* (ch. 65) accords Ecgfrith, son of Oswiu, a reign of nine years, this is an error for fourteen (viiii for xiiii);[9] x years for Penda could conceivably be a partial transcription of xxii. There can be no doubt that twenty-two years is a sounder regnal length for Penda than either ten or thirty and that neither of the two latter present a significant challenge to Bede's figure. It seems most likely, therefore, that Penda was king of the Mercians from 633 to 655 or from 634 to 656. Who had reigned over the Mercians in the period before 633/4 is unknown. Cearl had probably died some years earlier. The complete absence of information makes it very difficult to uncover the processes of change which may have been at work among the peoples north and south of the Trent during the reign of Eadwine, but it is inconceivable that Eadwine was able to extend his hegemony southwards without first achieving domination of the Mercians.

If the battle in which Penda fought Cwichelm and Cynegils at Cirencester, dated to 628 in the *Chronicle* A (*s.a.* 628) (which is almost certainly a few years too early), can be safely placed before 633/4, Penda was already a formidable force before Hatfield, but even if it were to date to a little after 633/4 it still reveals the wide-ranging character of Penda's early activities. Whether the progression was from Cirencester to Hatfield or from Hatfield to Cirencester, here was a Mercian leader whose military exploits far transcended those of his obscure predecessors. Terms were agreed at Cirencester by which, it would seem, the western Saxons lost control of Cirencester and the lands along the Severn which became part of the territory of the Hwicce, so that the kingdom of the Hwicce has come to be regarded as a Mercian creation of the time of Penda.[10] It is true that the Hwicce appear to have been within the sphere of influence of the Mercian king from the reign of Wulfhere at the latest and Penda's presence at Cirencester *c.* 630 certainly reveals Mercian involvement with the region at a still earlier date. Nevertheless, though Penda may have embarked on a programme of domination of the south-west midlands, there is no evidence that he was responsible for the formation of the Hwiccian kingdom.[11] In the course of time the Mercian kingdom also came to embrace much of the territory, for example, of the Wocensaete or Wreocensaete, who took their name from the Wrekin and dominated the north Shropshire plain, and it would probably be the case, if charter-material had survived for this area of north-west Mercia analogous to that which has survived for the Hwicce, that kings of the Wreocensaete emerged in varying degrees of dependence on or subjection to the Mercian ruler. Unless it is to be assumed that all these territories represent kingdoms established by the Mercians, what the evidence indicates is that the Mercian leaders were extending their influence into originally independent kingdoms on their borders. Penda's presence in the environs of Cirencester against the kings of the Gewisse, at about the time he became king of the Mercians, provides a glimpse of how advanced this process was even by the early seventh century. As David Dumville comments, 'the creation of a Midland hegemony was achieved by a remarkable series of expansionist campaigns in a number of directions almost simultaneously'.[12]

Eadwine's British wars

In 633 or 634 (see above, pp. 67–8 and Appendix, Fig. 7.3) on 12 October Eadwine, king of the northern Angles, was defeated and slain in battle in Hatfield Chase by Cadwallon ap Cadfan, king of the Britons of Gwynedd, acting in concert with a Mercian force under Penda. This was an event which was to have profound repercussions. Bede says that the affairs of Northumbria were thrown into confusion by the disaster (*HE* II, 20). He describes how one of Eadwine's sons, Osfrith, perished with his father and another, Eadfrith, surrendered to Penda, while the queen, accompanied by Paulinus, took flight for Kent with her daughter, Eanflaed, and her young son, Uscfrea, and Osfrith's young son, Yffi. Bede also records that Osric, son of Eadwine's uncle, Aelfric, took the kingship of the Deirans, and Eanfrith, son of Aethelfrith, that of the Bernicians (see Appendix, Fig. 6.1 & 6.2), thereby fracturing Eadwine's overkingship. Osric certainly continued the war with Cadwallon, and besieged him in a fortified stronghold. It was not until the following summer that Cadwallon surprised Osric's forces and slew the Deiran leader, thereafter ravaging widely across Anglian territory and slaying Eanfrith when he came to sue for peace (*HE* III, 1). Eanfrith and Osric are said by Bede to have reverted to paganism on their accession, but it may be that Paulinus and the queen did not take flight immediately upon the death of Eadwine but only on the death of Osric.[13] This was the moment when the Deiran royal court was destroyed. Nor, indeed, did the young Deiran princes survive to claim their inheritance. Uscfrea and Yffi died in infancy in Gaul among the Franks, where they had been sent for greater safety (*HE* II, 20). Into the power-vacuum created by the slaying of Osric and Eanfrith stepped Eanfrith's brother, Oswald, who slew Cadwallon in the battle of 'Heavenfield' near Hexham in the autumn of either 634 (if Eadwine was killed in 633) or 635 (if Eadwine did not perish until 634) (see Appendix, Fig. 7.3), and assumed the kingship of both the Deirans and the Bernicians (*HE* III, 1, 2).

The outline of these events is well known. Bede's account of them – the unexpected defeat of Eadwine, the emergence of apostate kings, the ravages of Cadwallon, and the recovery of the northern Angles under Oswald, a Christian who prayed to God on the eve of the battle of 'Heavenfield' – constitutes one of the most dramatic and best-known parts of the *Ecclesiastical History*. There are, however, some enigmas. What brought a king of Gwynedd on such a far-flung military campaign along the banks of the Humber and north to the vicinity of Hadrian's Wall? How was it that one of the exiled sons of Aethelfrith was so close at hand (and another not far behind) and in a position to assume the kingship of the Bernicians when Eadwine fell?

According to Bede, Eadwine not only established himself as overlord of all the kingdoms south of the Humber with the exception of Kent, but he also ruled over all the inhabitants of Britain, Angles and Britons alike (*HE* II, 5). It is difficult to evaluate this very general statement. There is no evidence, for example, that Eadwine's influence was felt among the Britons of Dumnonia, on the one hand, or of Strathclyde, on the other. Oswald's achievement was certainly magnified. Bede represents Oswald as bringing under his sway all the peoples of Britain, divided by language into Angles, Britons, Picts and Irish (*HE* III, 6), but elsewhere writes that it was his brother and successor, Oswiu, who made tributary the Picts and the Scots who inhabited the northern parts of Britain (*HE* II, 5). He seems to have allowed his awareness of the different native languages of Britain to lead him into defining Oswald's Anglo-British *imperium* in excessive terms. Even his description of Oswiu's overlordship in Britain may convey an inflated impression of military activity under Oswiu. When Bede came to write further of him, he referred only to his subjection of the Picts (*HE* III, 24). It was certainly a Northumbrian claim, however, that the Scots as well as the Picts had been subject to Northumbrian domination. Bede says that after the defeat and death of Oswiu's son and successor, Ecgfrith, in the battle of *Nechtanesmere* in 685, the Picts recovered their land which the Angles had held and the Scots who lived in Britain and certain of the Britons (perhaps of Strathclyde) their independence (*HE* IV, 26). The implication of the evidence as a whole could be that it was only in the reign of Ecgfrith that Northumbrian overlordship embraced the Strathclyde Britons and the Scots. There was undoubtedly a tendency to push back in time the establishment of a far-flung military hegemony. Alcuin, possibly basing his statement on the words of Bede (*HE* II, 5), later claimed that Eadwine subjected Saxons, Britons, Picts and Scots.[14] Bede's material was certainly leading in this direction.

The ecclesiastical jurisdiction of the church of York was thought of as having been advanced by the military conquests of successive northern kings. Bede says of the episcopal authority of Bishop Wilfrid in the reign of Oswiu that it embraced Northumbrians and Picts as far as the power of Oswiu extended (*HE* III, 3), and the *Life of Wilfrid* that in the reign of Ecgfrith it widened still further so that Wilfrid was bishop of the Saxons (that is, the Northumbrians) in the south and the Britons, Scots and Picts in the north (*Vita Wilfridi*, ch. 21).[15] A close connection was evidently established between the territories dominated by the northern Anglian king and the claims of the church of York to wide-ranging ecclesiastical authority in north Britain, these claims perhaps encouraging a tendency to exaggerate the extent of the Northumbrian hegemony. In addition there is no indication in the *Ecclesiastical History* that Bede thought of Eadwine's successors as failing to maintain Eadwine's overlordship of all the Britons. He allows his readers to infer that the position he attributes to Eadwine was little changed before the battle of *Nechtanesmere*; Oswald ruled the same territory as Eadwine and Oswiu 'almost' the same (*HE* II, 5). The impression is conveyed of an 'imperial' view of Northumbrian history in which the age of Northumbrian supremacy formed an essentially unbroken continuum from the reign of Eadwine to that of Ecgfrith. Such a view necessarily underscored the battle of *Nechtanesmere* in 685 as an overwhelming catastrophe.

There can be no doubt, however, about the far-reaching character of Eadwine's impact in some British territories. The king's residence at Yeavering in the Cheviots reveals the solidity of his royal presence in the British hinterland of Bernicia.[16] It is uncertain what weight can be placed on the evidence of a medieval Welsh triad which refers to Eadwine as nurtured in Môn (Anglesey), implying that he had spent some time – perhaps while in exile – on the island,[17] but set into the earliest surviving Welsh tradition is the memory of armed conflict between Eadwine and Cadwallon. The Welsh annals (*s.a.* 629) refer to the besieging of Cadwallon on the island of Ynys Lannog (Priestholm) and Bede says that Eadwine brought under Anglian rule the Mevanian Islands, by which Môn (Anglesey) and Man are meant (*HE* II, 5), making it clear that the northern Anglian king must have established an impressive naval and military presence in the Irish Sea. Welsh bardic tradition was that he carried his offensive into the heartland of Gwynedd.

Two early poems appear to shed some light on what happened. *Marwnad Cadwallon* ('Lament for Cadwallon')[18] is a battle-poem which catalogues Cadwallon's exploits against Britons and Saxons. Cadwallon is described as 'a fierce affliction to his foe, a lion of hosts over the Saxons'. His 'camp on the uplands of Mount Digoll' – that is the Long Mountain, near Welshpool, in Powys in the centre of a district called Meigen – is recalled in the references in the Welsh triads to the 'action of Digoll' between

Cadwallon and Eadwine.[19] It would seem that the region of Powys in north-east Wales remained as much in the front-line of warfare with the northern Angles in the time of Eadwine as it had been when Aethelfrith defeated the men of Powys at Chester. Indeed, Eadwine may have used Chester as a base for his attack. A second and earlier poem *Moliant Cadwallon* ('In Praise of Cadwallon'),[20] possibly by Cadwallon's bard, Afan Ferddig, celebrates Cadwallon's victorious progress against Eadwine 'the deceitful' after his return from Ireland, where he may have been in exile, though an alternative possibility is that he had been gathering reinforcements there. Cadwallon is 'lwydawc Prydain' – 'battle-hosted one of Britain' or 'ruler of the armies of Britain', Eadwine '(m)vneir Prydein' – 'lord of Britain'. Cadwallon's people are the Cymru and their land is 'Cadwallon's land'. Cadwallon has gathered a victorious host and appears to have been encamped on Môn (Anglesey) with a fleet nearby. He refuses to treat with the men of Bernicia, for Eadwine is a too deceitful leader. In the face of Cadwallon's army, Eadwine is depicted as retreating, if not fleeing, many of his army being slain as the Britons pursued them across the salt sea, and Cadwallon advances to *Caer Caradog*, even setting York ablaze. The poem makes no reference to the slaying of Eadwine. If it is to be regarded as a genuine composition from the court of Cadwallon, it would seem to belong to the very eve of Hatfield. A fragment of yet another poem alludes to the bringing of Eadwine's severed head to Aberffraw (principal residence of the kings of Gwynedd on Môn (Anglesey)) and clearly refers to a moment after the battle of Hatfield Chase.[21]

What lay behind Eadwine's assault on the kingdom of Gwynedd is never made clear, but Aethelfrith had campaigned as far afield as Chester against the men of Powys and the Anglian attack on the north Britons was a continuing process. In *Moliant Cadwallon* Gwallawg, Taliesin's 'judge over Elmet', and 'the sadness of *Catraeth* of great honour' are recalled. By the early ninth century at the latest, the kings of the first dynasty of Gwynedd were regarded as descendants of Cunedda from Manau Gododdin (the plain of the Votadini between the Rivers Avon and Carron) in the territory of the Votadini (*HB* ch. 62).[22] If Cadwallon believed himself to be descended from a Votadini chieftain, he may well have wished to support the Votadini in their continuing war with the northern Angles. It would certainly add a significant dimension to Eadwine's attack on Gwynedd and the retaliation of Cadwallon if Eadwine saw in Cadwallon a powerful king likely to offer substantial military aid to the north Britons who were resisting the Anglian advance.

Cadwallon evidently sought to strengthen himself in his war with Eadwine by a series of alliances. That he invaded Eadwine's territory with the support of Penda, a Mercian aetheling, is well known (*HE* II, 20). It may be that other disaffected Anglian elements also gave assistance and it would be surprising if no help had been forthcoming from the men of Powys, who cannot have been unaffected by Aethelfrith's victory at Chester and the recent warfare between the northern Angles and the king of Gwynedd. Moreover, it must be of considerable significance that when Eadwine was slain in Hatfield the sons of Aethelfrith were nearby to take advantage of the situation. They had taken flight on Eadwine's accession into exile among the Picts and Scots (*HE* III, 1), Oswald and Oswiu finding refuge in Scottish Dál Riata (*HE* III, 3, 25) and Eanfrith evidently in Pictland where his son, Talorcan, subsequently reigned as king of the Picts in the mid-650s.[23] The reappearance, first and most immediately, of Eanfrith and subsequently of Oswald in Bernician territory at so crucial a moment in the history of the northern Angles could imply military assistance for them from the Picts or the Scots or both and even perhaps a certain ability to act in concert with the British king, Cadwallon. One common denominator is Ireland. There is some evidence that Oswald, while an exile, may have fought in Ireland – according to one story in the retinue of the Uí Néill king of Tara[24] – and *Moliant Cadwallon* refers obliquely to Cadwallon's sojourn in Ireland during the time of Eadwine's attack on Gwynedd. The probability is, therefore, that a wide-ranging set of alliances was entered into in the period immediately preceding the final conflict between Cadwallon and Eadwine, involving not only Cadwallon and his allies, including Penda, but the Bernician royal exiles with likely Pictish and Scottish support, possibly even contingents of Irish troops.[25]

The alliances did not survive the overthrow of Eadwine for any length of time. How long Penda remained in the territory of the northern Angles is unknown but he probably returned swiftly to Mercia to secure himself as king. He took with him Eadwine's son, Eadfrith (*HE* II, 20), thereby retaining an interest in the royal succession among the Deirans, but his immediate military involvement was over. When Cadwallon finally slew Osric in the summer of 634 or 635, the exact year depending on whether Eadwine fell in 633 or 634 (see Appendix, Fig. 7.1), this should have been his signal to withdraw. Instead, he began to ravage more widely. The slaying of Eanfrith, which followed soon after, may have been an important turning-point. Until that moment the sons of Aethelfrith had possibly been in alliance with the British leader. What now became clear was that Cadwallon was prepared to tolerate neither the family of Eadwine nor that of Aethelfrith as rulers of the northern Angles. The site of the battle of 'Heavenfield', in the vicinity of Hexham, shows that Cadwallon advanced north against Oswald, presumably intending to deal with the Bernician aethelings before they could consolidate their position further. This may be what lies behind Bede's statement that Cadwallon intended to destroy the whole nation (*HE* II, 20). Despite his immense forces (though Bede or his sources may have exaggerated Cadwallon's numerical superiority for dramatic effect), it was Cadwallon who proved the more vulnerable, far from home and by now an isolated member of the alliance which had conspired to defeat Eadwine. Oswald commended himself and his men to God and his victory over Cadwallon established a new Christian king over the northern Angles.

The reign of Oswald

Oswald, whom Bede regarded as the fifth overlord of the peoples south of the Humber and described as ruling within the same bounds as Eadwine (*HE* II, 5), clearly became on this testimony as powerful a ruler as Eadwine had been, but on his accession he faced an immediate challenge in midland and eastern England from Penda. It may be that eastern Anglian influence among the middle Angles was still appreciable and resented by Penda. Penda's invasion of the territory of the eastern Angles in 635/6 or 636/7, when he slew in battle both King Ecgric and the ex-king, Sigeberht, who had been brought out of his monastery to lead the army with Ecgric (*HE* III, 18),[26] terminated, as far as can be seen, the exercise of royal power among the eastern Angles by the direct descendants of Raedwald (see Appendix, Fig. 5), and made the repression of Penda's ambition imperative if Oswald were to reconstruct the paramount position which had been Eadwine's.

The first stage must have been the re-establishment of Eadwine's Humbrian confederacy to embrace Lindsey, for example, over which Oswald certainly established himself as a conqueror (*HE* III, 11), and to bring the Mercians back into a dependent relationship; and the second to restore Eadwine's position of dominance in southern England. It seems likely that Oswald achieved the same accord as Eadwine with Eadbald, king of Kent. In a bid to protect them from possible attack by Oswald and Eadbald, acting in collusion, Aethelburh sent the Deiran princes for greater protection to the Frankish king, Dagobert I, for fear specifically of Oswald and Eadbald (*HE* II, 20). Of Oswald's dealings with the eastern Angles nothing is known, but it was probably the case that Anna, son of Eni, Raedwald's nephew (*HE* II, 15: III, 18),[27] was established as king of the eastern Angles with northern Anglian assistance. The presence of members of Anna's family in Gaul at the nunnery of Farmoûtier-en-Brie (*HE* III, 8) emphasizes the continuing Frankish orientation of his kingdom and throughout his reign Anna appears to have been involved in opposition to the Mercians. It could be that the Christianizing of the Middle Angles began under the auspices of the eastern Angles in Anna's reign.[28] He gave shelter to Cenwealh when he was driven out of the territory of the upper Thames valley Saxons by Penda (*HE* III, 7) and he was eventually slain in battle by Penda (*HE* III, 18). Certainly, Oswald was a significant force at least as far south as the upper Thames valley where *c.* 640 he stood sponsor to King Cynegils at his baptism and joined with Cynegils in giving Dorchester-on-Thames to the missionary bishop, Birinus (*HE* III, 7) (see above, p. 48). Oswald's marriage to Cyneburh,[29] daughter of Cynegils, reveals clearly that relatively cordial relations could prevail between an overlord and a dependant if both stood to gain from the relationship. The Thames valley Saxons must have been as anxious as Oswald and Anna to contain Penda.

Even so, in three important respects Oswald's reign represented a break with Eadwine's. First, there is no evidence that Oswald was ever the presence in north Wales which Eadwine appears to have been. When Penda fled before Oswald in Oswald's final campaign and took refuge among the Welsh,[30] the northern Anglian king advanced no further than the vicinity (possibly) of Old Oswestry (see below, p. 90). Second, according to Adomnán's *Life of Columba*, Oswald is said, reputedly on his own testimony, to have had a vision of St Columba on the eve of the battle of 'Heavenfield',[31] and as soon as he was established as king he sent a request to Columba's monastic foundation on Iona among the Dalriadic Scots for a bishop, receiving in due course Aidan (*HE* III, 3). Oswald had been brought up as a Christian prince in Celtic lands from the age of 12, so it was perhaps natural for him to look to an Irish religious foundation for ecclesiastical and spiritual direction, and it may be that these overtures to Iona also reflect a dependence on Dalriadic military support at the time of his accession. The Church in Bernicia and Deira was now brought within the *familia* of Iona and subject to the authority of the abbot of Iona.[32] The assimilation of the northern Anglian area within the diocesan structure of the *ecclesia Anglorum*[33] was consequently halted. Aidan's episcopal see was on the island of Lindisfarne near the Bernician royal stronghold of Bamburgh (*HE* III, 5, 6). There was no attempt to revive the church of Paulinus at York and no further pursuit at this time of a pallium for a northern archbishop.[34] This was a development which also disseminated throughout northern England the idiosyncratic customs of the clergy of the Celtic regions of the British Isles which the Church of Rome, as it comprehended them over time, came increasingly to view as schismatic – not simply a different, more archaic method of calculating the date of Easter (which Iona retained long after other Irish communities had abandoned it), but a whole range of differences in ritual practice and, in the absence of an established ecclesiastical hierarchy of bishops and archbishops, a barely recognizable ecclesiastical order.[35] Third, within the territory of the northern Angles a Bernician leadership had reasserted itself and the political centre of gravity shifted northwards away from the plain of York. Oswald and (probably) his brother, Oswiu, were the sons of Aethelfrith by Acha, sister of Eadwine (*HE* III, 6), and this may have facilitated acceptance of Oswald as king among the Deirans and the restoration of an overkingship, but the deaths of many of the Deiran royal family will have left a political vacuum at the heart of the Deiran kingdom which cannot have been immediately filled by Aethelfrith's sons.

It may have been in the early 630s, when Oswiu was in his late teens, that he married Riemmelth, granddaughter of Rhun (*HB* ch. 57), for he had a son, Ealhfrith, and a daughter, Ealhflaed, old enough to be married *c.* 650 (*HE* III, 21). Rhun is thought to have been a son of Urien of Rheged (see above, p. 78), and Oswiu's marriage to Riemmelth may have cemented an alliance with the north British principality of Rheged as another important strand in the web of alliances which conspired to overthrow Eadwine.[36] If the rulers of Rheged were able to preserve a role as Oswiu's allies, this may have directed the main thrust of the Bernician attack on British territory at this time towards the Forth. The Bernicians may have reached the Firth of Forth under Oswald, for in 638 the Irish annals record the siege of *Eten* (*AU s.a.* 637: *AT* p. 184: *CA* p. 144), which is to be identified with Edinburgh in the territory of the Votadini, and the siege has been interpreted as probably marking the capture of this important British stronghold by the northern Angles.[37] Before the mid-650s the Anglian frontier had also been extended to include *Iudeu* or *Giudi*, identified as probably Stirling;[38] Oswiu retreated here on the eve of the battle of the *Winwaed* (*HB* chs 64, 65). Possession of Stirling, the natural fortress at the head of the navigable waters of the Forth and commanding the crossing of the Forth by the Roman road leading north into Pictland, implies the annexation of *Manau Gododdin*. If *Manau Gododdin* was annexed by Oswald and Oswiu at this time, the Anglian frontier in the north would now march with those of the Britons of Strathclyde to the west and the Picts to the north. It may have been the Anglian advance towards Stirling which tempted Domnall Brecc, grandson of Áedán, son of Gabrán, and king of Scottish Dál Riata, to attack the Strathclyde Britons in 642 (*AU s.a.* 641: *AT* p. 186: *CA* p. 144).[39] Domnall's death in Strathcarron underlines the strategic importance of this 'the central cross-roads of Scotland',[40] where Britons, Scots and Angles intermingled. Indeed, the possible conjunction of the northern Anglian princes and Domnall Brecc in the same area could imply that an alliance between Angles and Scots or at least concerted action between them was the key to Anglian success in north Britain in the reign of Oswald.

Oswald was vulnerable, however, south of the Humber. In 642 or 643 (depending on whether he became king in 634 or 635) (see Appendix, Fig. 7.3) he was slain fighting Penda at the battle of *Maserfelth* (*HE* III, 9) or *Maes Cogwy* (*HB* ch. 65; *AC s.a.* 644),[41] traditionally though not certainly Old Oswestry,[42] and his body dismembered. Oswald's adversaries here may have included Cynddylan ap Cyndrwyn, a prince of Powys. It is unfortunate that the verse saga ascribed to Llywarch Hen, which celebrates Cynddylan's defence of the River Tern in Shropshire on the Powys border and laments the destruction of his residence at *Pengwern*, situated perhaps on the Wrekin or at nearby Wrockwardine,[43] is essentially unhistorical, but the statement, 'I saw armies on the ground of the field of Cogwy [*Maes Cogwy*] and the battle full of affliction: Cynddylan was an ally',[44] may possess value as an independent fragment.[45] Bardic tradition certainly associated members of the Cyndrwynyn kindred with (probably) the battle of Chester and a battle in *Meigen* in the time of Eadwine.[46] Moreover, *Marwnad Cynddylan* ('Lament for Cynddylan'), perhaps by the bard, Meigant, may be of seventh-century date or at least no later than the ninth. It recalls what was evidently a memorable expedition – 'magnificent combat, great the booty' – to Caer Lwytgoed (Lichfield), when there was no escape for 'book-holding monks'.[47] But Cynddylan does appear as an ally of the family of Pyd (Pybba), father of Eowa and Penda, in *Marwnad Cynddylan* which declares, 'when the son of Pyd desired, how ready he was', almost certainly meaning that Cynddylan was prepared, when the opportunity arose, to join forces with the Mercians.[48] So Cynddylan's presence at *Maes Cogwy* is a possibility.

When the twelfth-century bard, Cynddelw, recalled 'the clash of Powys . . . with Oswald',[49] he was looking back on an episode which had considerable significance not only for the Welsh but also for the Mercians. For it was not only Oswald who perished in the battle but also Eowa, king of the Mercians and Penda's brother (*AC s.a.* 644). It has been suggested that Penda's political power was in eclipse at the time and that Eowa was the dominant ruler among the Mercians as a subject king of the northern Angles from the mid-630s until his death, possibly in Oswald's army, in the battle at *Maserfelth*,[50] but there is no reason why Penda and Eowa should not have been ruling jointly, with Eowa as king possibly of the northern Mercians and Penda as king of the southern. It was over the southern Mercians that Oswiu, king of the northern Angles, later established Penda's son, Peada, in the aftermath of Penda's death at the battle of the *Winwaed* (*HE* III, 24) (see below, pp. 96–7). The Mercians may always have been ruled by more than one king, possibly several, before the mid-seventh century, and Bede certainly thought of Penda as king at the time of his attack on the eastern Angles in the late 630s (*HE* III, 18).[51] Following Oswald's ascendancy it is difficult to imagine that Penda and Eowa were other than both subject to his overlordship. Whether Eowa was in alliance with Oswald in 642 or 643, it is impossible to say.

The first consequence of the battle of *Maserfelth* was that Penda was left as sole king of the Mercians, without question the most powerful Mercian ruler so far to have emerged in the midlands. A second consequence was that the northern Humbrian confederacy fragmented when, as the *Historia Brittonum* records, Penda separated the Southumbrians from the Northumbrians (*HB* ch. 65), and Oswald's brother, Oswiu, was able to assume royal power only among the Bernicians. This constituted a further major dislocation of the northern Anglian hegemony and seriously destabilized the dynastic situation within Deira and Bernicia. Though Bede considered Oswald's brother and successor, Oswiu, to have been the sixth of the overlords of the Anglo-Saxons (*HE* II, 5), it is clear that it was many years before Oswiu could securely establish himself as king even over all the northern Angles let alone as overlord of his southern neighbours and that this latter position was very shortlived.

Penda had taken Eadfrith, son of Eadwine, into Mercia with him after the battle of Hatfield, possibly with the intention of restoring him one day in Deira as a dependent ruler, but perhaps ill-advisedly put him to death during the reign of Oswald (*HE* II, 20) – though conceivably prevailed upon to do so by Oswald.[52] Nevertheless, despite the decimation of Eadwine's family, a Deiran prince, Oswine, son of Eadwine's cousin, Osric, emerged as king among the Deirans (*HE* III, 14) (see Appendix, Figs 6.1 and 7.1), though he was evidently unable or disinclined to revive the Canterbury mission at York. If Bede is to be believed, Oswine proved an attractive ruler who gained the admiration of Aidan, which suggests that Oswiu faced a dangerous rival in this Deiran king whom he eventually out-manoeuvred and slew by treachery the ninth year of the latter's reign (*HE* III, 14). To Bede, for whom Oswald became king in 634 and died in 642, Oswine's ninth year was 651 (*HE* V, 24), but again, if Eadwine was killed in 634, not 633, and Oswald perished in 643, not 642, Oswine's ninth year would be 651/2 and the year of his death, therefore, might need to be emended to 652 (see Appendix, Fig. 7.1). It was no doubt in part at least to consolidate himself dynastically in the face of the threat posed by Oswine that Oswiu married Eanflaed, daughter of Eadwine and Aethelburh, and therefore of part-Deiran, part-Kentish extraction, *c.* 644 (her son, Ecgfrith was in his fortieth year in 685) (*HE* III, 15). This must also have secured for Oswiu an important diplomatic contact with the Kentish court of King Eorcenberht (640–64), son of Eadbald, and re-established the former relationship which had prevailed in the time of Eadwine and Eadbald. Eanflaed's kinship with Oswine subsequently obliged Oswiu to found a monastery at the place of Oswine's death at Gilling in Yorkshire in expiation of his murder (*HE* III, 24). On (or soon after) Oswine's death Oswiu's nephew Oethelwald, son of Oswald, secured the kingship in Deira (*HE* III, 23) (see Appendix, Figs 6.2 and 7.1), though whether appointed to this position by Oswiu or acquiring it in opposition to his uncle is unknown. His elevation to the kingship may have been a manifestation of the support he could command in his own right among the northern Angles as the son of the victor of 'Heavenfield'.

The battle of the Winwaed

In the context of this dramatic eclipse of northern Anglian military might, Penda experienced a steady increase in power. By November of the year 655 or 656 – Bede gives 655 (*HE* III, 24) but again this date may need to be emended in the same way as Bede's other Northumbrian dates (see Appendix, Fig. 7.3) – Penda was able to challenge Oswiu at the battle of the

Winwaed with a mighty coalition, for he had spent the intervening thirteen years consolidating his position. The Middle Anglian communities passed under Mercian rule and out of any possible eastern Anglian orbit and Penda appointed his son, Peada, their ruler (*HE* III, 21). The eleventh-century claim that Merewalh, king of the Magonsaete, was also a son of Penda[53] cannot be authenticated, even though in the 740s Aethelbald, king of the Mercians, appears to describe Mildrith (later regarded as the daughter of Merewalh and Aebbe (Eafe), a Kentish princess) as his kinswoman (*CS* 177: S 91); and the likelihood is not that the Magonsaete were a Mercian creation but that Mercian control was being imposed upon their territory across the mid-seventh century.[54] It is not inconceivable that Merewalh was the son of a sister of Penda. Penda gave one sister in marriage to Cenwealh, king of the upper Thames valley Saxons, and when Cenwealh repudiated her he drove him out of his kingdom by *c.* 650/1 and into exile among the eastern Angles (*HE* III, 7), an important stage in the establishment of the upper Thames valley as a Mercian sphere of influence. Whether Penda was able to dominate Sigeberht the Little, king of the eastern Saxons (*HE* III, 22) (see Appendix, Fig. 2), is unknown. He attacked the eastern Angles between 649/50 and 652[55] and expelled King Anna whose unexpected return temporarily checked the Mercian advance,[56] though only until 654 or 655[57] when Penda invaded East Anglian territory again and this time slew him (*HE* III, 18). It is possible that he now established Anna's brother, Aethelhere (see Appendix, Fig. 5) in his place, to judge from Aethelhere's presence in Penda's army at the *Winwaed*, if not as a dependent ruler at least as an ally (*HE* III, 24).[58] An alliance with the Welsh leaders was also concluded. Though it has been suggested that Cynddylan may have been among Penda's British allies at the *Winwaed*,[59] there is no direct evidence for this, but when Penda attacked Oswiu in the mid-650s he is said to have been supported by British kings (*HB* ch. 64), principal among whom was Cadafael ap Cynfedw, king of Gwynedd (*HB* ch. 65).[60] According to Bede, Penda led thirty *duces* into battle at the *Winwaed*, including Oethelwald, king of Deira, allied with those who had slain his father rather than with his uncle against them (*HE* III, 24). It was, therefore, a most impressive and formidable army which the Mercian king marshalled against the Bernicians.

Relations between Penda and Oswiu in the years between the death of Oswald and the battle of the *Winwaed* had been variable. At an unknown date, but before the death of Aidan, Penda campaigned deep into Bernicia, storming Bamburgh and endeavouring to fire it (*HE* III, 16). There may well have been other such incidents. In the early 650s, however, Oswiu's son, Ealhfrith, married Penda's daughter, Cyneburh, after which Penda's son, Peada, now ruler of the Middle Angles, requested in marriage Oswiu's daughter, Ealhflaed, and received missionaries in her company, being urged to accept Christianity not least by his recently acquired brother-in-law, Ealhfrith (*HE* III, 21). It may be that it was the removal of Oswine which enabled Oswiu and Penda to treat on these equal terms. A precise chronology is impossible, but Bede says it was in 653 – by which 654 may need to be understood, for Bede also says it occurred two years before the death of Penda (in 655 or 656) – that Peada was converted (*HE* V, 24).

What is striking is that Peada was baptized by Fínán, Aidan's successor as bishop of Lindisfarne, at *Ad Murum* in the vicinity of Hadrian's Wall, and that he took back with him four priests, Cedd, Adda, Betti and Diuma, to work among the Middle Angles, the Irishman Diuma receiving consecration from Fínán, according to Bede, as bishop of the Middle Angles and the Mercians (*HE* III, 13). The Mercian prince had clearly not turned southwards to Canterbury for religious advice and ecclesiastical direction. His political and cultural orientation was still northwards, his world essentially that of the Humbrians. Moreover, for Diuma to have been consecrated bishop of the Middle Angles *and* Mercians (assuming that Bede has not made an error here), while Penda remained a heathen, must have been tantamount to treating Penda's territory as a northern Anglian sphere of influence. Simultaneously with the conversion of Peada, Oswiu was also prevailing upon Sigeberht the Good, king of the eastern Saxons (see Appendix, Fig. 2), the successor of Sigeberht the Little, to accept Christianity. Sigeberht paid regular visits to King Oswiu's court and was also eventually baptized at *Ad Murum* by Bishop Fínán, Oswiu then sending priests to the eastern Saxons, most notably Cedd, who was now detached from the Middle Anglian mission and subsequently consecrated bishop of the eastern Saxons by Fínán (*HE* III, 22). A new wave of evangelization was carrying the influence of the church of Lindisfarne deep into southern England, symbolizing a new political initiative on the part of Oswiu. Furthermore, the consolidation of Bernician domination of the northern Britons had probably been proceeding unhindered. For Oswiu, driven north when Penda's attack materialized in the autumn of 655 or 656, *Iudeu* (probably Stirling) (see above p. 90) proved a safe refuge (*HB* ch. 65). Nor was Oswiu necessarily without allies in the north of Britain. Though there is no specific reference to Dalriadic support for Oswiu in these years, the suspicion that a Dalriadic alliance was a constant factor in the Bernician situation under Oswald and Oswiu must be a strong one. In addition, in 653, Oswiu's nephew, Talorcan, son of his brother, Eanfrith, became king of the Picts.[61] It must be regarded as extremely probable that Oswiu was able to seek help in the confrontation with Penda not only from the Scots but also from the Picts, possibly even from the Irish (see also below, p. 99).

Oswiu certainly needed all the support he could attract. What precipitated the final crisis with Penda and the attack on Oswiu which culminated at the *Winwaed* on 15 November in 655 or 656 is obscure but Penda was almost certainly the primary moving force, the centre of a coalition which included Cadafael, king of Gwynedd (*HB* ch. 65), Aethelhere, king of the eastern Angles, and Oethelwald, king of the Deirans (*HE* III, 24).

A passage in Bede's account attributing responsibility as the author of the war to Aethelhere, is now generally regarded as corrupt,[62] but Oethelwald's support for Penda certainly implies a complexity of factors. It may also be that the aims and intentions of Penda and his allies were mixed. For Cadafael, king of Gwynedd, Oswiu's domination of the north Britons, perhaps particularly the Votadini, may have been of principal concern. Among the Mercians there must be a reasonable probability that Penda regarded Oswiu's activities in general as contrary to Mercian interests – in particular his involvement, for example, with the eastern Saxons, and possibly his likely reception of Cenwealh from the upper Thames valley whom Penda had expelled (see above, p. 58). It may also be that whereas the British kings intended to replace Oswiu with a more acceptable candidate, Penda sought only to reduce Oswiu to the status of a dependant and at the same time effectively to establish territories such as Lindsey as falling within a southumbrian Mercian orbit.

Penda was no stranger to Bernician terrain across which he had campaigned before (*HE* III, 16), and his army successfully traversed the whole length of Oswiu's kingdom to besiege him at *Iudeu*. He obliged Oswiu not only to give his son, Ecgfrith, aged 10, as a hostage – Penda sending the boy into the keeping of his queen, Cynewise, in Mercia (*HE* III, 24) – but also to part with great treasure to Penda and his allies (*HB* ch. 65). Bede says that Oswiu was forced to pay this tribute as the price of peace on condition that Penda would cease to devastate his kingdom and withdraw (*HE* III, 24). Penda and his allies had left Oswiu's territory by the time Oswiu, with his son, Ealhfrith, and a much smaller force, according to Bede, caught up with them. Oswiu seems to have taken them by surprise and brought them to bay on the banks of the River *Winwaed*, now swollen by autumnal rains, and probably to be identified with the River Went, a tributary of the Don.[63] The invading army was evidently homeward bound and perhaps disinclined for a renewed engagement, which may explain why Cadafael (*HB* ch. 65) and Oethelwald (*HE* III, 24) withdrew before battle was joined. There may even have been some dissatisfaction among Penda's allies with what had been achieved at *Iudeu*. But not all Penda's allies deserted. Aethelhere, king of the eastern Angles, and the majority of Penda's *duces* perished in the ensuing battle in which, according to Bede, more died in the flood-waters of the river than were slain by the sword (*HE* III, 24).[64] There must at least be a possibility that Penda's decapitation by Oswiu was an avenging of Penda's earlier dismemberment of Oswald's Gody.[65]

The last phase of northern domination in southern England

The repercussions of Oswiu's victory at the *Winwaed* were profound. Oethelwald is not heard of again after the battle and Oswiu re-established an overkingship of the northern Angles with his son, Ealhfrith, as co-ruler or sub-king over the Deirans (*Vita Wilfridi*, chs 7, 10). In the mid-660s, Ealhfrith was replaced by Oswiu's younger son, Ecgfrith (see below, p. 103), but the territory remained firmly in Bernician control. When Ecgfrith succeeded his father, he appears to have established his younger brother, Aelfwine, in his place (*HE* IV, 22; *Vita Wilfridi*, chs 17, 24). Following Aelfwine's death in the battle of the Trent against the Mercians in 679 or 680 (*HE* IV, 21; *Vita Wilfridi*, ch. 24) (see below, p. 117), Deira was ruled from then on directly by the Bernicians (see Appendix, Fig. 7.1). The Mercian kingdom was divided, Oswiu entrusting the southern Mercians to Penda's son, Peada, his son-in-law, but retaining north Mercian territory in his own hands. The following spring Peada was murdered at Easter, allegedly, according to Bede, through the treachery of his wife, Oswiu's daughter, Ealhflaed (*HE* III, 24). The whole of Mercia (and Middle Anglia) now passed under Oswiu's control. At the same time the Welsh annals record that 'Oswiu came and took booty' (*AC* *s.a.* 658), presumably in the Welsh marches, and possibly from Cadafael, king of Gwynedd, and the contemporary rulers of Powys.

Clearly Oswiu experienced a tremendous increase in personal power and prestige following his victory at the *Winwaed*. First, it must have enabled him to consolidate his hold on Anglian territories north of the Humber, establishing himself securely now not only in Deira but also presumably over the more outlying regions of his kingdom. When Ecgfrith and his brother, Aelfwine, gave estates to the church of Ripon in the early 670s on the occasion of its consecration by Wilfrid (on whom see below, pp. 101 ff.), they granted transpennine estates in the presence of sub-kings (*Vita Wilfridi*, ch. 17). One such sub-king was the Beornhaeth who campaigned with Ecgfrith against the Picts in the early 670s (*Vita Wilfridi*, ch. 19) (see below, p. 100), and whose territory may have adjoined the southern Pictish frontier. It seems highly probable that the northern kingdom achieved a greater cohesion and a more rigorously defined hierarchy of power in the decade or so after *Winwaed*. Second, Bede says that Oswiu established his rule over the southern Anglo-Saxon kingdoms for three years after Penda's death (*HE* III, 24) – on Bede's chronology 655–8 but perhaps to be emended to 656–9. Unfortunately, very little evidence bears on Oswiu's standing in southern England during these years. If it was in the aftermath of Penda's death that Cenwealh re-established himself as king of the Thames valley Saxons, it is likely that he did so with Oswiu's approval and even support. The eastern Saxons are almost certain to have remained at this time within the orbit of Oswiu and it may also be the case that Aethelwald, the brother of Aethelhere (*HE* III, 22) (see Appendix, Fig. 5), received Oswiu's support as the new king of the eastern Angles; it is certainly not at all impossible that he ruled at first in a dependent relationship. There is no evidence which bears on the position of Eorcenberht, king of Kent, though Bede, who exempted Kent from the area of Eadwine's hegemony, implies that Kent's special position was maintained during the reigns of Oswald and Oswiu (*HE* II, 5). But Bede himself appears to limit Oswiu's southern *imperium* chronologically to the three years following Penda's overthrow. At the end of that period Penda's young son, Wulfhere, came to power in a coup in Mercia which expelled Oswiu's governors and threw off Oswiu's overlordship (*HE* III, 24). Oswiu had attempted a re-assimilation of the Mercians into the Humbrian federation from which Penda had earlier broken free, dispensing with a Mercian king and governing through his own agents in a dramatic extension of the powers of an overlord in one of the major kingdoms of the Anglo-Saxon heptarchy. It is not surprising that he failed.

The successful seizure of royal power by Wulfhere reflected a substantial change in the situation. New political patterns began to emerge in southern England. This was probably the time when Cenwealh established his own overkingship of the western Saxons. Sigeberht the Good, king of the eastern Saxons, over whom Oswiu's influence had been considerable, was murdered at an unknown date (but well before 664 for Sigeberht's successor was dead by 664) and replaced by Swithhelm, son of Seaxbald (*HE* III, 22) (see Appendix, Fig. 2). Aethelwald, king of the eastern Angles, seems to have made the most of his opportunity to extend his authority into Swithhelm's territory, for when Cedd baptized Swithhelm he did so among the eastern Angles in the royal manor of Rendlesham, near Sutton Hoo, in the presence of King Aethelwald, who was his sponsor (*HE* III, 22).[66] The foundation of a monastery at Barking in Essex for Aethelburh by her brother, Eorcenwald, later bishop of London (*HE* IV, 6), could indicate an extension also of Kentish influence into the territory of the eastern Saxons.[67] Both Aethelburh and Eorcenwald, if not of Kentish royal extraction,[68] had Kentish connections, for Eorcenwald was founding-abbot with the support of Ecgberht, king of Kent, of the monastery of Chertsey in the Kentish-controlled territory of Surrey (*HE* IV, 6) (*CS* 34: S 1165). The date of the founding of Barking is uncertain but it would seem to have been *c.* 660 if the king, Swithfrith, who appears to have given a foundation gift to the monastery (*CS* 87: S 1246), was a co-ruler with King Swithhelm who died *c.* 664 (*HE* III, 30).[69] Until Wulfhere was able to establish a dominant position for himself among the southern kings (see below, pp. 114 ff.), the evidence suggests a multiplicity of regional overlordships. Oswiu's involvement must have been minimal in all of them.[70]

Oswiu died on 15 February 670, according to Bede (*HE* IV, 5), reckoning a reign of twenty-eight years (*HE* III, 14) from an accession in 642, but if Oswiu became king in 643 he would have died in 671 (see Appendix, Fig. 7.3). There is some evidence that this may have been the case. Ecgfrith, his successor, is given a reign of fifteen years in the Northumbrian regnal list,[71] but Bede says that he was killed on 20 May 685 in his fifteenth year

(*HE* IV, 24), and that Ecgfrith was indeed in his fifteenth year in 685 is confirmed by the inscription at Jarrow which records the dedication of the church on 23 April (which fell on a Sunday in 685), a month before his death, in his fifteenth year.[72] What was meant by the year of a king? The first year of a king ran from the day of his accession in one calendar year to the eve of the anniversary of that accession in the following, his second from the first anniversary of his accession to the eve of his second, and so on. The eighth-century Northumbrian annals in the *Historia Regum*[73] and the *Anglo-Saxon Chronicle* D (*s.a.* 761) show that Aethelwald Moll began to reign as king of Northumbria on 5 August 759, and the battle of Eildon, which lasted from 6–9 August 761, is described as taking place 'at the beginning' of his third year.[74] Aethelwald's third year clearly extended from 5 August 761 to 4 August 762. In Ecgfrith's case, by the same principle, if he was killed in the fifteenth year of his reign and had only been king fourteen years, he may have become king in 671 and certainly could not have done so before 21 May 670. If Oswiu died on 15 February 670, an interval will have occurred before Ecgfrith succeeded[75] and, though an *ex silentio* argument is not conclusive, evidence for such an interval or interregnum is lacking. Moreover, a date for the death of Eadwine in 634 as opposed to 633 would have the cumulative effect of pushing the year of Oswiu's death from 670 into 671. In this case, Ecgfrith would have succeeded his father almost immediately in early 671 and only just begun his fifteenth year as king when he was slain. It has been suggested that Bede, in order to synchronize diverse chronological tradition, 'considered the whole year of the Incarnation, in which a king died, as his last year and reckoned the next year of the Incarnation as the first of his successor',[76] so that if, for example, Oswiu died in 670, the whole of 671 was Ecgfrith's first year for Bede and the whole of 685 his fifteenth.[77] The ultimate clue to Ecgfrith's regnal chronology, however, is the documentary report of the council of Hatfield which Bede includes in the *Ecclesiastical History* (IV, 17) and which demonstrates, by reference to Ecgfrith in his tenth year on 17 September in a year which can only be 680 (see below, p. 113), that Ecgfrith certainly succeeded no earlier than 17 September 670 – which introduces an even longer interregnum if Oswiu had died in the February of that year and makes his death in February 671 more likely still. Given this degree of ambiguity in the chronological indicators, it certainly cannot be regarded as out of the question that Oswiu died and Ecgfrith became king in the early months of 671.

Military recovery in north Britain under Oswiu and Ecgfrith

It is to the period immediately following the battle of the *Winwaed* that Oswiu's wars with the Picts should probably be assigned. Bede places

Oswiu's subjection of the Picts in the same context as his domination of the southern kingdoms, in the years immediately after the battle of the *Winwaed* (*HE* III, 24). The death of Oswiu's nephew, Talorcan, king of the Picts, in 657 (*AU s.a.* 656: *AT* p. 195) could well have been the signal for an attack. If Donuel (Domnall), father of Talorcan's successors in the kingship of the Picts, first Gartnait and then Drest, could be securely identified as Domnall Brecc, formerly king of Dál Riata, Gartnait and Drest could perhaps be viewed as the beneficiaries of an alliance between the Scots and the northern Angles against the Picts; but Donuel's identification with Domnall Brecc is not certain,[78] and what seems to have been a break in the succession of kings of the Picts occurred from 663 to 665/6 between the death of Gartnait and the accession of Drest.[79] It may be this which signals the high-water mark of Oswiu's intervention in Pictland, analogous to his activities in Mercia in the three years after Penda's death, and it does not imply an obvious community of interest between Oswiu and the sons of Donuel. It seems reasonable to assume that Oswiu certainly brought into subjection to himself the Pictish kingdom of Fortriu (between the Forth and the Tay), for Bridei, the son of Bili, king of Strathclyde,[80] and Ecgfrith's cousin (*HB* ch. 57),[81] who became king of the Picts on the explusion of Drest and later fought against Ecgfrith, is described specifically in the Irish annals as 'king of Fortriu' at his death in 692 (*AU s.a.* 692: *AT* p. 212). The kingdom of Fib (Fife) with Forthreve (Kinrossshire), possibly a dependent territory of Fortriu[82] and one which the Northumbrian Cuthbert visited as prior of Melrose in the course of his pastoral responsibilities,[83] was probably also subjugated. It must also be borne in mind that in 685 Ecgfrith was able to invade through Strathmore as far as *Nechtanesmere* (Dunnichen), near Forfar, which will have been in the more northerly kingdom of Circinn (between the Isla and the Dee).[84] The impact of the northern Angles on the Picts, therefore, should not be underestimated.

Though Bede says at one point that Oswiu also made tributary the Scots (of Dál Riata) (*HE* II, 5), there is no direct evidence for this. Even Adomnán's reference to 'strangers' holding sway among the Dalriadic Scots[85] cannot be construed as a reference to the agents of King Oswiu (or Ecgfrith)[86] because these strangers are represented as oppressing Dál Riata from *c.* 639 to 'this day', that is, Adomnán's time of writing, *c.* 700,[87] which is some time after the power of the northern Angles beyond the Forth had been shattered at *Nechtanesmere* in 685, and the reference is rather to the failure of the kings of Scottish Dál Riata to regain control of Irish Dál Riata in Antrim. This territory was lost when Domnall Brecc was defeated at the battle of Moira c.639 by the Uí Néill ruler, Domnall, son of Áed, king of Tara.[88] Oswiu's campaigns beyond the Forth were almost certainly confined to the Picts. It may even be that he received Dalriadic assistance. This would have been in keeping with the likely pattern of Bernician–Dalriadic relations. The Pictish king, Talorcan, son of Eanfrith, had defeated the Scots in 654 (*AU s.a.* 653: *AT* p. 193: *CA* p. 145), and a divided Dalriadic kingdom across the period *c.* 650–60[89] may have left Conall Crandomna, Domnall Brecc's brother, joint king of Dál Riata, anxious to preserve good relations with Oswiu, who was, after all, his brother's protégé. Such a state of affairs may also have prevailed throughout the reign of Domangart, son of Domnall Brecc, from 660 to 673.

Oswiu's son and successor, Ecgfrith, rather than Oswiu himself, is far more likely to have asserted his lordship over the Scots in the wake of his suppression of a Pictish revolt *c.* 672. The Picts are said to have fiercely resented their subjection to the Saxons and attacked Ecgfrith who defeated them with the help of his sub-king (*subregulus*), Beornhaeth (*Vita Wilfridi*, ch. 19), probably between the Avon and the Carron (in Manau of the Gododdin).[90] This episode occurred early in Ecgfrith's reign and is probably to be associated with the expulsion of Drest, king of the Picts, in 672 (*AU s.a.* 671: *AT* p. 202).[91] Ecgfrith was a king who was prepared to send his army in 684 under a military commander, the *dux* Berht (*HE* IV, 26), probably to be identified with Berhtred, *dux regius* (*HE* V, 24), son of Beornhaeth (*AU s.a.* 697: *AT* p. 26), to ravage in Ireland (including the Uí Néill territory of Meath) (*HE* IV, 26: *AT s.a.* 684: *AT* p. 202). He must have been well placed to advance from the re-establishment of his supremacy over the Picts in 672 to the imposition of it also on the Scots, and an opportunity may have been provided when Domangart was slain in 673 and his nephew, Máeldúin, son of Conall Crandomna, became king.[92] Maelduin reigned until his death in 689 (*AU s.a.* 688). He was king at the time, therefore, of the battle of *Nechtanesmere*, after which Bede says the Scots recovered their independence. If there were any Scots with the Pictish army in 685 Máeldúin would have sent them. Indeed, for all that is known to the contrary, Ecgfrith may have been facing a Pictish–Scottish alliance in 685. Such a transformation of allegiances would help to explain the reversal of northern Anglian military fortunes beyond the Forth at this time and could well have been provoked by the changed relationship between the Angles and the Dalriadic Scots. The probable father-and-son relationship between Beornhaeth, who was associated with Ecgfrith in his defeat of the Picts in the early 670s, and Berht, who led the Northumbrian forces into Uí Néill territory in Ireland in 684, even suggests Irish support for the Picts in their wars with the northern Angles. Furthermore, an additional factor is likely to have been British support for Bridei, king of the Picts, as the son of Bili, former king of Strathclyde. Territory was lost, possibly to the Britons, by the Northumbrians along the south bank of the Forth, whence Bishop Trumwine was expelled from his bishopric at Abercorn in the aftermath of *Nechtanesmere* (*HE* IV, 26).

Ecclesiastical politics

The military involvement of the northern Angles against the Picts may have been a factor in the success of Wulfhere's coup in Mercia in 658 or 659 and in the disintegration thereafter of Oswiu's southern *imperium*. Nor was the eclipse of Oswiu's influence in southern England without repercussions among the northern Angles themselves. It cannot be entirely coincidental that the following years witnessed the heightening of tensions which threatened to divide Oswiu's kingdom from within. The council of Whitby, which Bede places in 664, symbolizes this. According to Bede this meeting to adjudicate between the Roman Easter and the by now largely obsolescent Easter observances of Iona was held in Oswiu's twenty-second regnal year, thirty years after the arrival of Scottish monks (*HE* III, 26). Bede's reckoning from 642 for the accession of Oswiu would suggest to him the year 664, but if Oswiu did not succeed until 643 the reference to his twenty-second year would point to 665 as the year of the council. The indications are, however, that in this instance 664 is the correct year. The year of the council was the year of an eclipse (*HE* III, 27), which took place on 1 May 664, and an outbreak of plague (*HE* III, 27). Either, therefore, Oswiu did become king in 642, as Bede says, or Bede was able to date the council of Whitby to 664 by reference to the eclipse and plague of that year and he calculated Oswiu's regnal year at this point for himself on his own assumption of a succession for Oswiu in 642. Cedd, who acted as interpreter at the council, died in this plague (*HE* III, 23), probably on 26 October 664,[93] and so did Tuda, appointed bishop of Lindisfarne in succession to Colmán who returned to Iona after Oswiu had given his decision at Whitby in favour of the Catholic Easter (*HE* III, 27).

Oswiu's queen, Eanflaed, observed Easter according to Catholic custom within the paschal limits of the nineteen-year tables of Dionysius Exiguus, with her chaplain, Romanus, and James the Deacon, a survivor from the mission of Paulinus. Oswiu and his son, Ealhfrith, adhered to Iona's older fourth-century eighty-four-year cycle (*HE* III, 25).[94] Ealhfrith must have been about 20 years old at the time of the battle of the *Winwaed*, after which he became king of Deira, taking over the former territory of his cousin, Oethelwald. It was very soon after this that he began to show signs of dissatisfaction with the ecclesiastical situation in the north. He was on good terms with Cenwealh, king of the Thames valley Saxons (*Vita Wilfridi*, ch. 7), whose first bishop was Agilbert, a Frank and later bishop of Paris, a Catholic bishop, therefore, observing the customs and practices of the Roman Church. It was Cenwealh who recommended to Ealhfrith *c*. 658 Wilfrid, a young Northumbrian recently returned from the continent where he had visited Rome and received the Petrine tonsure in Gaul (*Vita Wilfridi*, chs 3, 7).[95] Wilfrid was already well versed in Roman orthodoxy, and well aware of differences of observance among Irish and

101

Britons, whom his biographer calls 'schismatics' (*Vita Wilfridi*, ch. 5). At some point before 664 Ealhfrith ejected Eata, abbot of Melrose and a pupil of Aidan (*HE* III, 16), and his companion, Cuthbert, who would not accept the Catholic Easter and other canonical rites of the Roman Church, from his new foundation at Ripon and committed it instead to Wilfrid (*HE* III, 25: V, 19).[96] It was with Ealhfrith that Bishop Agilbert and his priest, Agatho, stayed when they visited the northern Angles prior to arguing in favour of the Dionysian Easter at the council of Whitby (*HE* III, 25). Hence, Ealhfrith began to favour Roman tradition while his father, Bede says, considered that nothing was to be preferred to the teachings of the Scottish clergy (*HE* III, 25).

Oswiu's decision at Whitby in favour of the Roman Easter indicates an appreciation of the need to bring the Church among the northern Angles into some degree of greater conformity with the Church of Rome, though he evidently envisaged a relatively slow process of accommodation to Catholic requirements under the Irish Tuda as the new bishop of Lindisfarne. Tuda wore a Petrine tonsure and observed the Roman Easter. The issue between the Roman and the Celtic clergy, however, turned at this time as much if not more on the question of the validity of orders as on the date of Easter or the shape of the tonsure. Tuda's episcopal consecration in southern Ireland would not for long have been acceptable. When the highly orthodox Wilfrid was sent, evidently with Oswiu's consent, to be consecrated as Ealhfrith's bishop, he went to Gaul in the absence (after the death of Deusdedit, archbishop of Canterbury, on 14 July 664) of bishops in England of recognized orthodox and canonical soundness (*HE* III, 28: V, 19: *Vita Wilfridi* chs 11, 12). Though there is an element of ambiguity about the whereabouts of Wilfrid's see, it is most likely that Ealhfrith intended him to be bishop of York, the significance of which is unlikely to have been lost on Wilfrid and his royal patron if Pope Gregory's original plan to establish York as an archbishopric was known to them. It was not until *c.* 666 that Wilfrid returned to Deira by which time Tuda had died and King Oswiu had appointed Chad, the brother of Cedd, as bishop of York. Chad had received consecration from Wine, bishop of the western Saxons, and two British bishops (*HE* III, 28). The abandonment of Lindisfarne by Oswiu in favour of a bishop at York implies an awareness on the part also of Oswiu of the importance of York in the Gregorian scheme for two metropolitan provinces in England. Chad was a northern Angle and undoubtedly orthodox in matters of the tonsure and the date of Easter, but his readiness to accept consecration from the British bishops reveals a continuing failure in Oswiu's entourage to appreciate the importance of canonical rectitude. Archbishop Theodore made this quite clear when he subsequently re-ordained him through every ecclesiastical grade (*Vita Wilfridi*, ch. 15), which was in effect to treat Chad as a layman despite his previous consecration.

Wilfrid withdrew to Ripon and, although he acted on occasion as bishop for Wulfhere among the Mercians and even ordained priests and deacons in Kent, he did not at this time exercise episcopal functions north of the Humber (*HE* III, 28; *Vita Wilfridi*, ch. 14). Moreover, nothing further is heard of Ealhfrith. At some point in the mid-660s he was forbidden by his father to go to Rome with Benedict Biscop, who was later to found the monastery of Wearmouth and Jarrow.[97] The conclusion might have been that Ealhfrith abdicated in a voluntary acceptance of the religious life were it not for Bede's silence on the matter and his statement that Oswiu was attacked in the course of his reign by the Mercians, his nephew, Oethelwald, and by his own son, Ealhfrith (*HE* III, 14). There is a possibility, therefore, that Ealhfrith lost his life in a rebellion against his father while Wilfrid was receiving consecration in Gaul.[98] Such a disturbance could help to explain Wilfrid's delayed return. Ealhfrith's personal religious predilections need not necessarily have borne undertones of political dissatisfaction but the differences on ecclesiastical matters between father and son, coming as they did at a time of profound change in Oswiu's former position of influence in southern England, probably reflected a crisis of potentially serious dimensions. Oswiu's appointment of Chad to York suggests that he was moving towards a re-affirmation of his authority in the whole northern Church, not least in Deira. Ealhfrith may also have been apprehensive about his father's plans for his younger half-brother, Ecgfrith, who appears to have married Aethelthryth, widowed daughter of Anna, king of the eastern Angles, *c.* 660.[99] A young man in his late teens by the time of the council of Whitby and the son of the reigning king in Bernicia by Eanflaed, daughter of Eadwine, Ecgfrith was almost certainly in a position to attract support not only among the Bernicians but also among the Deirans in the territory of Ealhfrith,[100] and in the last years of his reign Oswiu did make him sub-king of Deira.[101] Another larger issue could well have been the major redirection of Bernician military might and political power needed to secure an advance north of the Forth. Despite the earlier campaigns to the Forth against the Britons, this further offensive and the resources which it required and continued to require while Mercian strength increased in southern England represented a serious dislocation of northern Anglian royal aspirations, especially at a time when Oswiu remained committed to the maintenance of his influence south of the Humber, at least in ecclesiastical affairs.

Bede's statement that Chad was sent by Oswiu to the archbishop of Canterbury to be consecrated, only to find that Deusdedit had died (*HE* III, 28), is unlikely to be correct because Wilfrid had known that Deusdedit was dead when he was earlier seeking consecration as Ealhfrith's bishop and the probability must be that Oswiu's court would have known this too.[102] Indeed, it could well have been the death of Archbishop Deusdedit in July 664 which rendered it essential for Oswiu, faced by the resurgence of Mercian power under Wulfhere, to establish his Catholic orthodoxy at

Whitby if he was to play a part in finding a replacement for Deusdedit.[103] Nevertheless, there is no reason to doubt that Chad was sent to Canterbury. Oswiu's appointment of Chad to Paulinus' former bishopric at York instead of Lindisfarne represents a most important change of direction on the king's part, and his immediate dispatch of Chad to Kent suggests a desire to renew an older relationship with the archiepiscopal community there.

Moreover, Oswiu appears to have entered into immediate relations with the papacy. In his *History of the Abbots* Bede says that Ecgberht, king of Kent, sent a certain Wigheard to Rome where he wished him to be consecrated archbishop,[104] and only subsequently in the *Ecclesiastical History* does Bede report that Oswiu and Ecgberht consulted together on what action to take about a successor to Deusdedit and that they agreed on the choice of one of Deusdedit's clergy, Wigheard, whom they sent to Rome to be consecrated (*HE* III, 29). Wigheard and all his companions, however, including a messenger of Oswiu's, died shortly after their arrival in Rome, presumably in a local epidemic.[105] The involvement of the northern king is confirmed by Pope Vitalian's letter to King Oswiu (*HE* III, 29).[106] The pope acknowledges Oswiu's conversion to orthodoxy and the Roman Easter, thanks him for the gifts he has sent but grieves that the bearer of these gifts had died in Rome, and regrets that he has not been able at the time of writing to find someone suitable to send as Wigheard's replacement. The pope envisaged that whomsoever he sent would eradicate all that required uprooting throughout 'your island' – that is, Britain – and such wide jurisdiction at this time belonged only to Canterbury. This seems to have been a major attempt on the part of Oswiu, by associating himself with Ecgberht's archbishop-elect and by a recognition of the authority of Canterbury, to establish a new beginning for the Anglo-Saxon Church. For Oswiu it was perhaps preparatory to a request for a pallium for the bishop of York.

Following Wigheard's death, Abbot Hadrian of *Hiridanum* recommended Theodore of Tarsus to the pope for the vacant see of Canterbury and Theodore, accompanied by Hadrian, left Rome on 27 May 668. He arrived in Canterbury on 27 May 669, having been escorted from Gaul, where he had been staying with Agilbert, by a representative of King Ecgberht, not of Oswiu (*HE* IV, 1). Theodore was determined to assert his authority throughout the whole Anglo-Saxon Church[107] and it must have become immediately apparent that Oswiu's influence over the new archbishop was minimal. Chad, Oswiu's bishop at York, was deposed and Wilfrid installed. Though a reconsecrated Chad was shortly afterwards appointed bishop of Lichfield with Oswiu's consent, this must have seemed to the northern king a high-handed way for the new archbishop to act. The consequence of Oswiu's decision at Whitby, therefore, was the destruction of the authority of Iona in Anglo-Saxon territory and the restoration of the authority of the archbishop of Canterbury over the northern Angles. There is no evidence at this time of any further move towards the provision of a pallium for the bishop of York.

The reign of Ecgfrith witnessed a working out of the tensions which had emerged under Oswiu. The authority of the archbishop of Canterbury continued to bear on the Northumbrian Church. Theodore behaved not unreasonably. He treated Lindsey as subject to a Mercian bishop when Wulfhere controlled it and as part of Ecgfrith's kingdom *c.* 678–9 when Ecgfrith held it (*HE* IV, 12). Though committed to increasing the number of bishops in England since the council of Hertford in 672 (*HE* IV, 5), he did not attempt (so far as is known) to partition Wilfrid's vast diocese of York until Ecgfrith quarrelled with Wilfrid and expelled him in 678 and even then king and archbishop appear to have been in agreement about the subdivision (*HE* IV, 12: V, 19, 24; *Vita Wilfridi,* ch. 24).

Wilfrid, however, reacted passionately, if not to the partition of his diocese then to his expulsion and to the bishops who were appointed from communities other than his own[108] – Eata, who had been obliged to leave a new monastic foundation at Ripon to make way for Wilfrid in Ealhfrith's time, now consecrated bishop in Bernicia with his see at Wilfrid's monastic foundation at Hexham; Eadhaed, a former companion of Chad (*HE* III, 28), bishop of Lindsey; and Bosa, trained at Whitby where the community under Abbess Hild had opposed acceptance of the Roman Easter at the council of Whitby, bishop of Deira at York (*HE* IV, 12). Though these men were perfectly acceptable to Theodore, Wilfrid is said to have declared himself unable to serve God in unity with them because he regarded them as strangers to the Catholic Church (*Vita Wilfridi,* ch. 30).[109] They were in the ecclesiastical tradition which would have prevailed in the north if Wilfrid had not been forcibly installed at York by Theodore in place of Chad. It was impossible for Theodore to maintain the integrity of Wilfrid's position while at the same time attempting to conserve the tradition which Eata, Eadhaed and Bosa represented, and in the years which followed it was the latter which was consolidated. Though in 681 Tunberht, formerly one of Wilfrid's monks at Ripon and subsequently abbot of Gilling (and the brother of Bede's abbot, Ceolfrith), was made bishop of Hexham (*HE* IV, 12), he was deposed in 685 (*HE* IV, 28). When Ecgfrith lost control of Lindsey, Eadhaed became bishop of Ripon and when Tunberht was appointed to Hexham, Eata moved to Lindisfarne, while Trumwine, whose antecedents are unknown (though he was remembered in Cuthbert's circle and his subsequent retirement to Whitby suggests a background similar to Bosa's), became bishop of Ecgfrith's Pictish subjects at Abercorn on the Forth (*HE* IV, 12, 26). On Tunberht's deposition in 685, Eata's companion, Cuthbert, was appointed bishop of Hexham but allowed to remain at Lindisfarne while Eata returned to Hexham (*HE* IV, 27, 28). Undoubtedly, this reorganization of the Northumbrian Church pleased Theodore, who secured the establishment of additional bishoprics north of the Humber, and Ecgfrith, who was not only rid of a bishop whom he did not want but able also to secure the appointment of men whom he personally favoured, men generally prepared to deal sensitively with the legacy of the Scottish mission in a post-Whitby era. Indeed, these appointments both enhanced and stabilized the Church in Deira and Bernicia and defined its character into the eighth century. The crisis of 678, however, was very much a consequence of Theodore's intervention in 669. Moreover, the approval of Theodore remained crucial at every stage. It was Theodore who consecrated Bosa, Eata and Eadhaed, Theodore who appointed Tunberht and Trumwine, and Theodore who consecrated Cuthbert.

From 669 to 678, as bishop of York with its former metropolitan associations (cf., *Vita Wilfridi*, ch. 10), Wilfrid, lord also of his own great monastic foundations at Ripon and Hexham, had dominated the northern Church. He was, according to his biographer, second to none in largesse (*Vita Wilfridi*, ch. 21), and his retinue of armed followers was considered by Ecgfrith's second queen, Iurminburh, to be the equal of a king's (*Vita Wilfridi*, ch. 24). His fall from power in 678 was not unique among the bishops of this period. In the final analysis, the king's power was greater than the bishop's. Ecgfrith was able to imprison Wilfrid (*Vita Wilfridi*, ch. 34), even allegedly plan his death (*Vita Wilfridi*, ch. 27). Nevertheless, the expulsion of a bishop was a relatively rare phenomenon. Nor is it at all clear why Ecgfrith and Wilfrid quarrelled. It may well be that Wilfrid was no more acceptable to Ecgfrith than he had originally been to Oswiu.[110] In addition, it is likely that all bishops were deeply involved in the politics of the day. Shortly before he became bishop of Lindisfarne, Cuthbert is said to have been asked by Aelfflaed, abbess of Whitby and daughter of Oswiu and Eanflaed, who would succeed her brother (who had no son).[111] It is salutory to note the political involvement of even this reputedly other-worldly figure. Cuthbert was evidently able to remind Aelfflaed (if she really needed reminding) of the existence of Aldfrith, illegitimate son of King Oswiu, at that time resident among the islands of Britain. There were many branches of the Northumbrian dynasty, however, and many noble families who claimed descent from Ida and thereby expressed aspirations to the kingship. Aelfflaed's question to Cuthbert reveals the ambition of this family, which had possessed royal power continuously for fifty years since 634 or 635, to hold on to it. Rather than asking Cuthbert ingenuously who would succeed Ecgfrith, Aelfflaed was probably testing his loyalties.

It may be that an element in the antipathy of Ecgfrith and his queen, Iurminburh, to Wilfrid was that Wilfrid was not committed enough to Ecgfrith's family. To whom might he have been more attached? One possibility is Oswald's family. The patronage of royal saintly cults implied dynastic predispositions and one cult highly favoured in Wilfridian circles and at Hexham in particular was Oswald's.[112] Wilfrid could well have transferred his allegiance to an otherwise unknown prince of Oswald's line when he lost his patron in Ealhfrith. Or Ealhfrith could have left sons. Osric, king of Northumbria (718–29), could have been a descendant of Ealhfrith (see below, p. 147). Another possibility is that Wilfrid's sympathies lay with descendants of the Deiran royal family of Eadwine. Aethelwald Moll, who became king of Northumbria in 759, may have been of Deiran royal descent; his power-base certainly seems to have been in Deira (see below, p. 150). One of his forebears could have won the support of Wilfrid. When Wilfrid was a prisoner in the late 670s in the custody of Aebbe, abbess of Coldingham, uterine sister of Oswald and Oswiu,[113] the daughter of Eadwine's sister, Acha (*HE* III, 6),[114] it was Aebbe who was instrumental in procuring his release (*Vita Wilfridi*, ch. 39). In other words, it was a kinswoman of the Bernician royal family, but one with strong Deiran connections, who interceded on this occasion for Wilfrid. It may even be that the Eadwulf who challenged the accession of Osred, son of Aldfrith, in 704 and whose son was with Wilfrid at Ripon at the time (*Vita Wilfridi*, ch. 59) (see below, p. 146), was of royal Deiran extraction.

It is not possible to demonstrate adequately a specific hypothesis but one fact is certain: Wilfrid so earned the enmity of Ecgfrith that despite an appeal to Rome which endorsed the justice of his case, he remained in exile and was still an outcast from his church when Ecgfrith fell in battle against the Picts on 20 May 685.

Notes

1 N. K. Chadwick, 'The conversion of Northumbria', in N. K. Chadwick (ed.), *Celt and Saxon: Studies in the Early British Border* (Cambridge, 1963), pp. 138–66.

2 Bede gives 625 as the year of Paulinus' consecration but this may need to be emended to 626 in keeping with a chronological rearrangement by one year of all Eadwine's regnal dates. According to Bede, Paulinus was consecrated bishop on 21 July 625 and died on 10 October 644 after an episcopate of 19 years, 2 months and 21 days (*HE* II, 9: III, 14), but these figures indicate 20 July for his consecration, which was a Saturday in 625. However, 20 July 626 was a Sunday. The indications are that Paulinus was consecrated bishop on 20 July 626, and died on 10 October 645; cf., D. P. Kirby, 'Bede and Northumbrian chronology', *English Historical Review*, vol. 78 (1963), pp. 514–27 (p. 518).

3 A. Angenendt, 'The conversion of the Anglo-Saxons', *Angli e sassoni al di qua e al di là del mare* (Settinare di Studio del centro Italiano di studi sull'alto medioevo, no.32, (1984), 2 vols, Spoleto, 1986), vol. I, pp. 747–81 (pp. 772–3).

4 *Florentii Wigorniensis monachi Chronicon ex Chronicis*, ed. B. Thorpe, 2 vols (London, 1848), Vol. I, p. 260.

5 D. N. Dumville, 'The Anglian collection of royal genealogies and regnal lists', *Anglo-Saxon England*, vol. 5 (1976), pp. 23–50 (pp. 30–1, 33, 36–7).

6 N. Brooks, 'The formation of the Mercian kingdom', in S. Bassett (ed.), *The Origins of Anglo-Saxon Kingdoms* (Leicester, 1989), pp. 159–70 (pp. 165–6) reviews the relevant material.

7 K. Harrison, *The Framework of Anglo-Saxon History to A.D. 900* (Cambridge, 1976), p. 132, n. 10.

8   Brooks, 'The formation of the Mercian kingdom', pp. 165–6, thinks that the figure 50 has relevance as the age of Penda not at his accession but at his death.

9   Cf., Kirby, 'Bede and Northumbrian chronology', p. 517.

10 F. M. Stenton, *Anglo-Saxon England* (3rd edn, Oxford, 1971), p. 45. Cf., H. P. R. Finberg, *The Early Charters of the West Midlands* (Leicester, 1961), pp. 167 ff.

11 S. Bassett, 'In search of the origins of Anglo-Saxon kingdoms', in idem, *The Origins of Anglo-Saxon Kingdoms*, pp. 3–27 (p. 6).

12 D. N. Dumville, 'Essex, Middle Anglia and the expansion of Mercia', in Bassett, *The Origins of Anglo-Saxon Kingdoms*, pp. 123–40 (pp. 128–9).

13 Cf., S. Woods, 'Bede's Northumbrian dates again', *English Historical Review*, vol. 98 (1983), pp. 280–96 (p. 291).

14 *Alcuin, The Bishops, Kings and Saints of York*, ed. P. Godman (Oxford, 1982), pp. 14–15.

15 *The Life of Bishop Wilfrid by Eddius Stephanus*, ed. and trans. B. Colgrave (Cambridge, 1927).

16 B. Hope Taylor, *Yeavering: An Anglo-British Centre of Early Northumbria* (London, 1977). For some recent comments see L. Alcock, *Bede, Eddius and the Forts of the North Britons* (Jarrow Lecture, 1988), pp. 7–9, and R. Hodges, *The Anglo-Saxon Achievement: Archaeology and the Beginnings of English Society* (London, 1989), pp. 58–9.

17 *Trioedd Ynys Prydein: The Welsh Triads*, ed. R. Bromwich (2nd edn, Cardiff, 1978), pp. 47, 48. Cf., the reservations of M. Miller, 'The dates of Deira', *Anglo-Saxon England*, vol. 8 (1979), pp. 35–62 (pp. 49–50).

18 J. Gwenogvryn Evans (ed.), *The Poetry in the Red Book of Hergest*, Vol. I (Series of Old Welsh Texts, vol. xi, 1911), cols 1043–4, and now by R. G. Gruffydd, 'Canu Cadwallon ap Cadfan', in R. Bromwich and R. Brinley Jones (eds), *Astudiaethau Ar Yr Hengerdd: Studies in Old Welsh Poetry* (Cardiff, 1978), pp. 25–43 (p. 34 ff.). There is a translation in R. Barber, *The Figure of Arthur* (London, 1972), pp. 98–9. See also for text and translation, however, J. Rowland, *Early Welsh Saga Poetry: A Study and Edition of the Englynion* (Woodbridge, 1990), pp. 169–73, 446–7, 495–6, 613–16.

19 Bromwich, *Trioedd Ynys Prydein*, pp. 182–3; Rowland, *Early Welsh Saga Poetry*, pp. 127–8.

20 Ed. I. Williams, 'Hengerdd', *Bulletin of the Board of Celtic Studies*, vol. 7 (1933), pp. 23–32, then by G. C. J. Thomas, 'Dryll o hen lyfr Ysgrifen', *Bulletin of the Board of Celtic Studies*, vol. 23 (1970), pp. 309–16 and most recently by R. G. Gruffydd, 'Canu Cadwallon ap Cadfan', *Astudiaethau Ar Yr Hengerdd*, p. 27 ff. For some comments in English on the poem, see Bromwich, *Trioedd Ynys Prydein*, p. 294, I. Ll. Foster, 'The emergence of Wales', in I. Ll. Foster and G. Daniel (eds), *Prehistoric and Early Wales* (London, 1965), pp. 213–25 (pp. 230–1), and *Astudiaethau Ar Yr Hengerdd*, pp. 3–4. On this material as 'the oldest Gwynedd verse and likely to be authentic', see J. T. Koch, 'When was Welsh literature first written down?', *Studia Celtica*, vol. 20/1 (1985/6), pp. 43–66 (pp. 63–4).

21 Gruffydd, 'Canu Cadwallon ap Cadfan', pp. 41–3 (cf. p. 3). Bede says that Eadwine's head was subsequently (not necessarily immediately) taken to York and placed in the church of St Peter (*HE* II, 20), which suggests ignorance of or indifference to the Welsh poetic tradition. For a further poetic fragment, see G. C. J. Thomas, 'A verse attributed to Cadwallon fab Cadfan', *Bulletin of the Board of Celtic Studies*, vol. 34 (1987), pp. 67–9.

22 See above, p.75, n. 41.

23 M. O. Anderson, *Kings and Kingship in Early Scotland* (Edinburgh, 1973), pp. 170, 248, 262, 266, 273, 281, 287.

24 H. Moisl, 'The Bernician royal dynasty and the Irish in the seventh century', *Peritia*, vol. 2 (1983), pp. 103–26 (pp. 110–12).

25 ibid., p. 116.

26 That this event occurred in 635/6 or 636/7 is clear from the *Liber Eliensis*, ed. E. O. Blake (London, 1962), p. 18, in which Anna is said to have been in the nineteenth year of his reign when he fell in battle. This was in a year the *Chronicle* A gives as 654 (*s.a.* 654), the year before the battle of the *Winwaed*. The battle of the *Winwaed*, however, may have taken place in 656. If Anna was slain in 655 in his nineteenth year,

he succeeded in 636 or 637. There is no certainty, on the other hand, that Anna's death was dated by reference to the *Winwaed* and if Anna fell in 654, he succeeded in 635/6. The Irish annals place 'the battle of Anna' in 655 (*AU s.a.* 656).

27 Cf., Dumville, 'The Anglian collection of royal genealogies and regnal lists', pp. 31, 33, 37.

28 B. E. A. Yorke, *Kings and Kingdoms in Early Anglo-Saxon England* (London, 1990 [forthcoming]), Chap. 4.

29 Bede mentions the marriage (*HE* III, 7) but the twelfth-century *Vita Oswaldi* first names Oswald's queen; *Symeonis Monachi Opera Omnia*, ed. T. Arnold, 2 vols (Rolls series: London, 1882, 1885), Vol. I, p. 349.

30 This reconstruction by the author of the *Vita Oswaldi* seems a reasonable one; *Symeonis Monachi Opera Omnia*, Vol. I, p. 350.

31 *Adomnan's Life of Columbus*, ed. and trans. A. O. and M. O. Anderson (Edinburgh and London, 1961), I, 1.

32 On the organization of the church of Iona, see J. Duke, *The Columban Church* (Oxford, 1932), pp. 119–21, R. Sharpe, 'Some problems concerning the organization of the church in early Ireland', *Peritia*, vol. 3 (1984), pp. 230–70 (pp. 244–6), and M. Herbert, *Iona, Kells and Derry: The History and Hagiography of the Monastic Familia of Columba* (Oxford, 1988).

33 Cf., H. Vollrath, *Die Synoden Englands bis 1066* (Paderborn, 1985), p. 48.

34 Cf., A. Angenendt, *Kaiserherrschaft und Königstaufe: Kaiser, Könige und Päpste als geistliche Patrone in der abendländischen Missionsgeschichte* (Berlin and New York, 1984), pp. 190 ff.

35 There is a vast literature on the difference of observance and practice among the clergy in Celtic lands; see, for example, L. Gougaud, *Christianity in Celtic Lands* (London, 1932) and H. Mayr-Harting, *The Coming of Christianity to Anglo-Saxon England* (London, 1972); cf., D. P. Kirby, 'The Church in Ceredigion: Introduction', in J. L. Davies and D. P. Kirby (eds), *Cardiganshire: A County History*, Vol. I (forthcoming) for some general comments.

36 A. P. Smyth, *Warlords and Holy Men: Scotland A.D. 80–1000* (London, 1984), p. 23.

37 K. H. Jackson, 'Edinburgh and the Anglian Occupation of Lothian', in P. Clemoes (ed.), *The Anglo-Saxons* (Cambridge, 1959), pp. 35–42.

38 K. H. Jackson, 'Bede's *Urbs Giudi*: Stirling or Cramond?', *Cambridge Medieval Celtic Studies*, vol. 2 (1981), pp. 1–7.

39 Cf., on Domnall, Anderson, *Kings and Kingship in Early Scotland*, pp. 152–3.

40 *Royal Commission on the Ancient and Historical Monuments and Constructions of Stirlingshire* (Edinburgh, 1963), Vol. I, p. 6.

41 Cf., I. Williams, 'A reference to the Nennian Bellum Cocboy', *Bulletin of the Board of Celtic Studies*, vol. 3 (1926–7), pp. 59–62, and Bromwich, *Trioedd Ynys Prydein*, pp. 321–2.

42 See, however, M. Gelling, *Signposts to the Past* (London, 1978), pp. 186–7, and idem, 'The early history of western Mercia', in Bassett, *The Origins of Anglo-Saxon Kingdoms*, pp. 184–210 (pp. 188–9).

43 For Wrockwardine, see G. R. J. Jones, 'Continuity despite calamity: the heritage of Celtic territorial organization in England', *Journal of Celtic Studies*, vol. 3 (1981), pp. 1–30 (pp. 22 ff.).

44 I. Williams, *Canu Llywarch Hen* (Cardiff, 1935), pp. 48, 242. There is a translation of the relevant stanza by K. H. Jackson, 'On the Northern British section in Nennius', in N. K. Chadwick (ed.), *Celt and Saxon: Studies in the Early British Border* (Cambridge, 1963), pp. 20–62 (p. 39) and cf. I. Williams, *The Beginnings of Welsh Poetry*, ed. R. Bromwich, (2nd edn, Cardiff, 1980), p. 149. See also, however, Rowland, *Early Welsh Saga Poetry*, pp. 445, 494.

45 Rowland, *Early Welsh Saga Poetry*, p. 125.

46 The history of the Cyndrwynyn has been reconstructed by Rowland, *Early Welsh Saga Poetry*, pp. 120 ff.

47 This important poem was first edited by I. Williams, 'Marwnad Cynddylan', *Bulletin of the Board of Celtic Studies*, vol. 6 (1934), pp. 134–41, and subsequently included in

Canu Llywarch Hen, no. XIII; and then by R. G. Gruffydd, 'Marwnad Cynddylan', *Bardos*, ed. R. G. Gruffydd (Cardiff, 1982), pp. 10–28. The most recent edition and translation of *Marwnad Cynddylan* is by J. Rowland, *Early Welsh Saga Poetry*, pp. 175–9. The significance of the expedition to Lichfield is difficult to determine: Rowland, op. cit., pp. 133–5.

48 On Pyd (Pybba), Rowland, *Early Welsh Saga Poetry*, p. 184.

49 ibid., p. 124.

50 Brooks, 'The formation of the Mercian kingdom', pp. 166–7.

51 On the date, see above, n. 26.

52 Cf., T. M. Charles-Edwards, 'Bede, the Irish and the Britons', *Celtica*, vol. 15 (1983), pp. 42–52 (p. 51), who suspects that Oswald was here pursuing the vendetta.

53 D. W. Rollason, *The Mildrith Legend: a Study in Early Medieval Hagiography in England* (Leicester, 1982), pp. 93, 115.

54 Cf., the varying interpretations of Stenton, *Anglo-Saxon England*, p. 47, and 'Pre-Conquest Herefordshire', *Preparatory to Anglo-Saxon England*, ed. D. M. Stenton (Oxford, 1970), pp. 193–202 (pp. 194–5), and Finberg, 'The princes of the Magonsaete', *The Early Charters of the West Midlands*, pp. 217 ff.

55 For the date, D. Whitelock, 'The pre-Viking church in East Anglia', *Anglo-Saxon England*, vol. 1 (1972), pp. 1–22 (p. 6).

56 *MGH Script. rer. Merovingicarum*, Vol. IV, ed. B. Krusch (Hanover and Leipzig, 1902), p. 449 (cf., L. Bieler, *Ireland: Harbinger of the Middle Ages* (London, 1963), p. 99).

57 See above, n. 26.

58 M. Carver, 'Kingship and material culture in early Anglo-Saxon East Anglia', in Bassett, *The Origins of Anglo-Saxon Kingdoms*, pp. 141–58, suggests that Penda's East Anglian expeditions 'should be seen in the light of interfactional struggles within East Anglia' (p. 155).

59 Rowland, *Early Welsh Saga Poetry*, pp. 131–2.

60 Cf., Bromwich, *Trioedd Ynys Prydein*, pp. 289–90.

61 Talorcan died in 657 according to the Irish annals (*AU s.a* 656: *AT* p. 195), and the Pictish king-lists accord him a reign of four years.

62 J. O. Prestwich, 'King Aethelhere and the battle of the *Winwaed*', *English Historical Review*, vol. 83 (1968), pp. 89–95, suggested an emendation to Bede's text which would confirm Penda's responsibility; cf., however, the reservations of J. M. Wallace-Hadrill, *Bede's Ecclesiastical History of the English People* (Oxford, 1988), p. 121.

63 A. H. Smith, *The Place-Names of the West Riding of Yorkshire*, part VII (English Place-Name Society, vol. 36; Cambridge, 1962), p. 35, n. 1. Cf., J. W. Walker, 'The battle of Winwaed AD 655', *Yorkshire Archaeological Journal*, vol. 36 (1944–7), pp. 394–408. K. H. Jackson, 'On the northern British section in Nennius', pp. 35–6, unravels some of the confusion in the *Historia Brittonum* account.

64 For some interesting comments on certain of Bede's details concerning the battle of the *Winwaed*, not least the figure thirty for the number of *duces* who are said to have accompanied Penda, see J. McClure, 'Bede's Old Testament kings', in P. Wormald (ed.), *Ideal and Reality in Frankish and Anglo-Saxon Society* (Oxford, 1983), pp. 76–98 (pp. 89–90).

65 Cf., Wallace-Hadrill, *Bede's Ecclesiastical History of the English People*, pp. 122–3.

66 Cf., Angenendt, *Kaiserherrschaft und Königstaufe*, p. 185.

67 Cf., C. R. Hart, 'The Early Charters of Barking Abbey', *The Early Charters of Eastern England* (Leicester, 1966), pp. 117 ff.

68 ibid., pp. 117–18, and D. Whitelock, *Some Anglo-Saxon Bishops of London* (London, 1975), p. 5, but Yorke, *Kings and Kingdoms in Early Anglo-Saxon England*, Chap. 3, suggests rather that they were members of the East Saxon royal family.

69 On Swithfrith, see B. E. A. Yorke, 'The kingdom of the East Saxons', *Anglo-Saxon England*, vol. 14 (1965), pp. 1–36 (p. 19).

70 Cf., N. Brooks, *The Early History of the Church of Canterbury* (Leicester, 1984), p.70.

71 P. Hunter Blair, 'The *Moore Memoranda* on Northumbrian history', in C. Fox and B. Dickens (eds), *The Early Cultures of North-West Europe* (Cambridge, 1950), pp. 245–57 (p. 246); Dumville, 'The Anglian collection of royal genealogies', pp. 32, 36.

72 K. Harrison, *The Framework of Anglo-Saxon History* (London, 1976), pp. 84–5.

73 T. Arnold (ed.), *Symeonis Monachi Opera Omnia*, 2 vols (Rolls series: London, 1882, 1885), Vol. II, pp. 30 ff. (trans. J. Stevenson, *Church Historians of England*, Vol. III, Part II (London, 1855)).

74 *Symeonis Monachi Opera Omnia*, Vol. II, p. 41.

75 Harrison favours the idea of an interregnum: *Framework of Anglo-Saxon History*, p. 84 (cf., idem, 'The reign of Ecgfrith', *Yorkshire Archaeological Journal*, vol. 43 (1971), pp. 79–84).

76 W. Levison, *England and the Continent in the Eighth Century* (Oxford, 1946), p. 271.

77 Cf., Woods, 'Bede's Northumbrian dates again', pp. 281 ff. See also below, p. 159, n. 24.

78 Cf., Anderson, *Kings and Kingship in Early Scotland*, p. 172.

79 D. P. Kirby, 'per universas Pictorum provincias', in G. Bonner (ed.), *Famulus Christi: Essays in Commemoration of the Thirteenth Centenary of the Birth of the Venerable Bede* (London, 1976), pp. 286–324 (p. 290).

80 *Chronicles of the Picts and Scots*, ed. W. F. Skene (Edinburgh, 1867), p. 409.

81 On this relationship, cf., Anderson, *Kings and Kingship in Early Scotland*, pp. 170 ff., and Kirby, 'per universas Pictorum provincias', pp. 289, 303 ff. The relationship is generally thought to have been through Eanfrith, father of Talorcan, but Smyth, *Warlords and Holy Men*, p. 63, suggests a possible kinship through the princes of Strathclyde.

82 Anderson, *Kings and Kingship in Early Scotland*, pp. 141–2.

83 D. P. Kirby, 'Bede and the Pictish Church', *Innes Review*, vol. 24 (1973), pp. 6–25 (pp. 10–11).

84 Cf., Anderson, *Kings and Kingship in Early Scotland*, p. 143.

85 *Adomnan's Life of Columba*, ed. and trans. A. O. and M. O. Anderson, III, 5.

86 As suggested by Anderson, *Kings and Kingship in Early Scotland*, pp. 156–7.

87 J. M. Picard, 'The purpose of Adomnán's *Vita Columbae*', *Peritia*, vol. I (1982), pp. 160–77 (pp. 167–9).

88 J. Bannerman, *Studies in the History of Dalriada* (Edinburgh and London, 1974), pp. 99–103.

89 Anderson, *Kings and Kingship in Early Scotland*, pp. 155–7.

90 *Adomnan's Life of Columba*, Anderson and Anderson, p. 52.

91 Cf., Kirby, 'per universas Pictorum provincias', p. 290.

92 For Máeldúin, Anderson, *Kings and Kingship in Early Scotland*, p. 15.

93 *Florentii Wigorniensis monachi Chronicon ex Chronicis*, Vol. I, p. 27.

94 Harrison, *The Framework of Anglo-Saxon History*, pp. 30 ff., 52 ff. Cf., also D. Ó Cróinín, 'The Irish provenance of Bede's Computus', *Peritia*, vol. 2 (1983), pp. 229–47, Wallace-Hadrill, *Bede's Ecclesiastical History of the English People*, pp. 125, 228, 235, and also P. Hunter Blair, 'Whitby as a centre of learning in the seventh century', in M. Lapidge and H. Gneuss (eds), *Learning and Literature in Anglo-Saxon England* (Cambridge, 1985), pp. 3–32 (pp. 17–22).

95 D. H. Farmer, 'Saint Wilfrid', in D. P. Kirby (ed.), *Saint Wilfrid at Hexham* (Newcastle-upon-Tyne, 1974), pp. 35–60.

96 On the date of this expulsion, R. Abels, 'The council of Whitby: a study in early Anglo-Saxon politics', *Journal of British Studies*, vol. 23 (1983), pp. 1–25 (p. 9 and n. 43).

97 C. Plummer, *Venerabilis Baedae Opera Historica*, 2 vols (Oxford, 1982, 1986), Vol. I, p. 365.

98 Contrary to earlier opinion, there are no grounds for regarding the inscription on the Bewcastle cross as commemorating Ealhfrith; R. I. Page, 'The Bewcastle Cross', *Nottingham Medieval Studies*, vol. 4 (1960), pp. 36–57.

99 *Florentii Wigorniensis monachi Chronicon ex Chronicis*, Vol. I, p. 24. Her translation, probably on Sunday, 17 October 695 (C. Plummer, *Venerabilis Baedae Opera Historica*, Vol. II, p. 239) was sixteen years after her death; she had been abbess for seven years, being appointed a year after she took the veil, and she had lived with Ecgfrith for twelve years before that (*HE* IV, 19).

100 Cf., Abels, 'The council of Whitby', p. 7.

101 *Liber Eliensis*, p. 21.
102 Abels, 'The council of Whitby', p. 23.
103 ibid., pp. 11 ff.
104 Plummer, *Venerabilis Baedae Opera Historica*, Vol. I, p. 366.
105 ibid.
106 J. Campbell, 'Bede', in T. H. Dorey (ed.), *Latin Historians* (London, 1966), pp. 159–90 (p. 187) (reprinted in Campbell, *Essays in Anglo-Saxon History* (London and Ronceverte, 1988), pp. 1–27). This matter is also discussed by Vollrath, *Die Synoden Englands*, pp. 60 ff.
107 Cf., ibid., pp. 29, 66.
108 M. Gibbs, 'The decrees of Agatho and the Gregorian plan for York', *Speculum*, vol. 48 (1973), pp. 213–46 (pp. 227, 233).
109 Vollrath reviews the career of Wilfrid, *Die Synoden Englands*, pp. 68 ff., 415–18, and considers that Wilfrid regarded himself as heir to Paulinus and rightfully archbishop of York in accordance with Pope Gregory's original plan. W. Goffart, *The Narrators of Barbarian History* (Princeton, NJ, 1988), p. 287, associates an interest in the metropolitan status of York with those who commissioned the *Life* of Wilfrid rather than with Wilfrid himself.
110 Gibbs, 'The decrees of Agatho and the Gregorian plan for York', argues that Wilfrid's intention was to revive the metropolitan status of York in accordance with Pope Gregory the Great's plan for the Anglo-Saxon Church, but that Ecgfrith preferred Theodore as sole archbishop of Britain under his protection as *bretwalda* (pp. 224 ff.). It must be regarded as doubtful whether the political situation even in 678 would have justified any such aspiration on Ecgfrith's part and quite unlikely that it did on Aldfrith's in 690.
111 *Two Lives of St Cuthbert*, ed. and trans. B. Colgrave (Cambridge, 1940), pp. 102–5, 234–7.
112 See further on this, Kirby, 'Northumbria in the time of Wilfrid', idem, *Saint Wilfrid at Hexham*, pp. 1–34 (pp. 26–8), and Goffart, *The Narrators of Barbarian History*, p. 261.
113 *Two Lives of St Cuthbert*, Colgrave, pp. 188–9.
114 *Florentii Wigorniensis monachi Chronicon ex Chronicis*, Vol. I, p. 268.

6 The southumbrian kingdoms from the mid-seventh to the mid-eighth century

By their action in rebelling against King Oswiu and setting up Penda's young son, Wulfhere, as their king (see Appendix, Fig. 8), the Mercians again broke free from the northern Anglian Humbrian federation and re-entered the arena of southern politics.

The reign of Wulfhere

Wulfhere was probably in his mid-teens when he became king three years after the battle of the *Winwaed*. If *Winwaed* was fought in 656 not 655 (see above, p. 92), the revolution which led to the expulsion of Oswiu's agents from Mercia occurred in 659 not 658. According to Bede, Wulfhere reigned seventeen years (*HE* III, 24), which led him to 675 for Wulfhere's death, reckoning forward from 658, but if Wulfhere did not bcome king until 659 a seventeen-year reign would suggest 676 for his death. Some light on the date of the accession of Wulfhere's brother and successor, Aethelred, is shed by the proceedings of the council of Hatfield, dated by reference to 17 September of the Eighth Indiction and by the tenth year of Ecgfrith, king of the Humbrians, the seventh of Hlothhere, king of Kent, and the sixth of Aethelred, king of the Mercians (*HE* IV, 17). The year of the Indiction could be 679, if the Greek Indiction was being used, or 680, if the Caesarean. Bede's methods led him to give 680 for a year he would otherwise have thought of as 679.[1] A charter of Hlothhere, however, refers to 1 April 675 as 'in the first year of our reign' (*CS* 36: S 7), which means that he became king in 674 at the earliest and 17 September in his seventh year can have fallen no earlier than 680. If, therefore, 17 September 680 fell in Aethelred's sixth year, Aethelred began to reign at some point after 17 September 674 and before the anniversary of that date in 675. Bede presents Aethelred as abdicating to become a monk in 704 after a reign of thirty years (*HE* V, 24), but the *Anglo-Saxon Chronicle* A (*s.a.* 704) states that he held the kingdom for twenty-nine years, that is, he died in his thirtieth year. Taken together this evidence indicates 675–704 for the reign of Aethelred and makes reasonable the conclusion that Wulfhere

113

did not reign seventeen years but died in his seventeenth year, so that his reign will have been 659–75.[2]

It is perhaps not without significance that Wulfhere's queen was Eormenhild, daughter of Eorcenberht, king of Kent (640–64),[3] a marriage probably intended to bring the Mercians more closely into association with the Anglo-Frankish world of the Kentish court at a time when their kingdom was being Christianized under Wulfhere. No details are known of the conversion of Wulfhere but he reigned as a Christian king with a succession of bishops - Trumhere, Jaruman, Chad and Wynfrith – with their seat, at least from the time of Chad, at Lichfield (*HE* III, 24: IV, 3). For a time Wilfrid, exiled bishop of York, acted as Wulfhere's bishop (*Vita Wilfridi*, ch. 14)[4] before Archbishop Theodore provided the king with Chad *c.* 669 (*HE* IV, 3). Perhaps some of Wilfrid's monasteries in Mercia (*Vita Wilfridi*, ch. 64) date back to this period in his life for Wulfhere was a patron of monasticism. He gave land to Chad at Barrow in Lindsey for the building of a monastery (*HE* IV, 3), and when Chad died Wynfrith, who succeeded him as bishop, was evidently abbot of Barrow (*HE* IV, 6).

Wulfhere's reign is primarily distinguished in the surviving record, however, by his re-establishment of the Mercians as a significant political and military force in southern England and it is difficult to envisage Oswiu, king of the northern Angles, maintaining after *c.* 664 more than a shadow of the influence in southern England which had been Eadwine's or Oswald's. Attempts were made by Wulfhere to detach the kingdom of Lindsey from its dependency on the north Anglian king, for Chad probably and Wynfrith (672–c. 674)[5] certainly, successive bishops of Lichfield, exercised episcopal authority over the Lindesfara (*HE* IV, 3) and the political foundations for this may have been laid in the 660s. Nothing is known of Wulfhere's power among the eastern Angles, where the accession *c.* 664 of Ealdwulf (in his seventeenth regnal year at the time of the council of Hatfield (*HE* IV, 17)), son of Anna's brother, Aethelric, brought to royal power a new branch of the royal family (see Appendix, Fig. 5), but Ealdwulf's Northumbrian connection – he was the son of a Deiran princess (see above, p. 78) and in continuing contact with Northumbria (*HE* II, 15) – did not necessarily enable him to exist independently of Wulfhere's sphere of influence. Despite a reign of about fifty years – he died in 713[6] and was succeeded by his son, Aelfwald – almost nothing is known about him. The kingdom of the eastern Saxons, however, certainly passed into a Mercian orbit. When Swithhelm, king of the eastern Saxons, died *c.* 664 to be succeeded by his kinsmen, Sigehere and Saebbi (see Appendix, Fig.2), and Sigehere and his people lapsed into paganism in the plague of 664, it was Wulfhere who organized their reconversion (*HE* III, 30). With domination of the eastern Saxons went control also of London. Wulfhere was in a position by *c.* 665–8 to sell the bishopric of London to Wine, recently expelled from his bishopric at Winchester (*HE* III, 7). Archbishop Theodore was to appoint his own choice, Eorcenwald, abbot of Chertsey, as bishop of London in succession to Wine, probably in 675 (*HE* IV, 6), but there can be no doubt about the reality of Mercian power in Wulfhere's last years not only north but also south of the Thames, facilitated in all probability by the death of Ecgberht, king of Kent, in 673 (see above, p. 44) and the disintegration of the overkingship of Cenwealh among the western Saxons across the years 672–5 (see above, pp. 52 ff.).

The province of Surrey, most recently under the control of King Ecgberht appears to have passed under the domination of Wulfhere at this time. Between 673 and 675 Wulfhere is found at his royal residence at Thame in Oxfordshire confirming a grant by which Frithuwald, sub-king of Wulfhere in the province of Surrey, gave land to Chertsey in the company of three other sub-kings, most probably of the regions bordering on Surrey – Osric, Wigheard and Aethelwald, all representing territories soon to be wholly subsumed within larger political creations (*CS* 34: S 1165). The occasion of Wulfhere's intervention in Surrey is likely to have been the death of King Ecgberht, which appears to have been followed by an interregnum or at least a contested succession. Ecgberht's two sons, Eadric and Wihtred, must have been very young in 673 – infants of perhaps 2 or 3 years of age – and Ecgberht's brother, Hlothhere, did not become king of Kent until 674. Such an interruption of the Kentish regnal succession may reflect disturbed conditions attendant on Wulfhere's annexation of Surrey for Wulfhere, the uncle of Eadric and Wihtred, could well have been hostile to Hlothhere's succession in Kent. It may even be that in Kent for about a year after Ecgberht's death, 'Wulfhere could have been the effective ruler'.[7] Among the witnesses of Frithuwald's grant to Chertsey was his son, Frithuric. The appearance of a Frithuric among the Middle Angles in the reign of Wulfhere's successor, Aethelred, giving *Bredun*, probably Breedon on the Hill in Leicestershire, to the monastery of Peterborough in the time of Seaxwulf, Wynfrith's successor as bishop of Lichfield, and Breedon's connection with the monasteries of Bermondsey and Woking in Surrey,[8] raises the intriguing possibility that Frithuwald was a Middle Anglian intruded into Surrey by Wulfhere or at the very least that Frithuwald represented a ruling family in Surrey which had strong Middle Anglian connections.[9] Frithuwald was certainly a man of some importance. There is evidence to suggest that the territory for which he was responsible under Wulfhere extended across the Thames into north Buckinghamshire and the environs of Thame.[10]

It is clear that Wulfhere's presence in the Thames valley placed the Gewisse of the upper Thames under very serious pressure (see above, pp. 58 ff.). According to the *Anglo-Saxon Chronicle* A (*s.a.* 661), Wulfhere harried Ashdown in 661, in which year he is also said to have attacked the Isle of Wight and given it to Aethelwealh, king of the southern Saxons. Bede, however, says that Wulfhere's attack on Wight and the gift of the island to Aethelwealh occurred 'not long before' the mission of Wilfrid to the southern Saxons in the mid-680s (*HE* IV, 13), which suggests that Wulfhere's actions should be placed later in the reign than 661.[11] One of the regions adjacent to Surrey which is referred to in Frithuwald's charter is Sonning, the province of the Suningas in east Berkshire,[12] and it is possible that one of the three sub-kings who witnessed with Frithuwald ruled here, in which case Wulfhere's presence in Berkshire was already established at the time of Frithuwald's grant. Indeed, given a campaign by Wulfhere as far as the coast, it is difficult to see how the whole extent of the northern territory of the western Saxons from Berkshire to Somerset could have escaped Mercian pressure in these years, creating perhaps precedents for further Mercian involvement in these districts at a later time.

Wulfhere's subsequent advance to the Isle of Wight suggests a near-total collapse of political and military order south of the Thames. According to Bede, Wulfhere was able to give the Isle of Wight and the territory of the Meonware in the Meon valley of Hampshire opposite the Isle of Wight to Aethelwealh, king of the southern Saxons on the occasion of his baptism in Mercia in the presence of the Mercian king, possibly on the occasion of Aethelwealh's marriage to Eafe, a Hwiccian Christian princess (*HE* IV, 13). The later hostility of Caedwalla and the western Saxons to Arwald, king of the people of Wight, and indeed to his family (*HE* IV, 16), suggests that the ruling dynasty of the Isle of Wight responded favourably to these arrangements and welcomed the conjunction of Mercian and southern Saxon interests. It seems likely, therefore, that the men of Wight and the Meonware were allies of Wulfhere who helped to make his advance possible. Clearly, important diplomatic contacts were being established which were designed to benefit both the Mercians and the southern Saxons through the creation of a new hierarchy of power in southern England. At this point the historic West Saxon kingdom of the eighth century could have been stillborn or at least confined to political insignificance beyond Selwood, but there was not enough time for Wulfhere to consolidate his position south of the Thames before a major crisis confronted him. The new king of the northern Angles, Ecgfrith, son of Oswiu, represented a challenge to the Mercian hold on Lindsey. Despite the presence in his army of southern leaders – the *Life of Wilfrid* says that he stirred up 'all' the southern kingdoms - Wulfhere was defeated by Ecgfrith *c.* 674 (*Vita Wilfridi*, ch. 20) and Lindsey passed temporarily out of Mercian control (*HE* IV, 12). Wulfhere's position in the south was immediately weakened. In 675 the *Chronicle* A (*s.a.* 675) records that Aescwine, son of Cenfus, one of the kings of the western Saxons, fought him at *Biedanheafde*. Though the outcome of the battle is not recorded, Wulfhere's premature death (in his mid-thirties) that same year and the inability of Aethelred, his brother and successor (*HE* V, 24), to maintain Wulfhere's southern hegemony enabled the kings of the western Saxons to survive without further serious dismemberment of their territory. Nor is there any evidence that Saebbi, king of the eastern Saxons, continued to acknowledge the overlordship of the Mercian ruler.[13]

Aethelred's initial acts on becoming king should perhaps be seen as primarily a securing of Mercian border territories. His devastation of Kent in 676, in the course of which Rochester was ransacked (*HE* IV, 12), may have been partly designed at least to deter the Kentish king from attempting to repossess Surrey.[14] Moreover, though married to Osthryth, sister of King Ecgfrith (*HE* IV, 21), in 679 or 680 Aethelred fought against the northern Anglian king and by a victory on the Trent, in which battle Ecgfrith's brother, Aelfwine, was slain, secured Lindsey – permanently as it turned out - for the Mercians (*HE* IV, 12). This defeat of Ecgfrith represented a decisive stage in the delineation of the frontier between Mercians and northern Angles - so that henceforth the power of the king of the northern Angles was more narrowly defined as north-Humbrian – and went some way towards redressing the débâcle of Wulfhere's last year or so. There was probably some extension of Mercian influence into northern Wiltshire and the territory of the western Saxons at this time also, for Aethelred (and possibly his kinsman, Cenfrith (*CS* 58: S 73)) may have given land *c.* 681 to Malmesbury (*CS* 59: S 71),[15] and a certain Berhtwald, possibly the nephew of Aethelred, who befriended Wilfrid for a time *c.* 680 (*Vita Wilfridi,* ch. 40), appears in a charter of doubtful authenticity[16] in the same area as a sub-king of Aethelred (*CS* 65: S 1169).

The late 670s and early 680s were remarkably free of political and military disturbance in contrast with what had gone before and what came after. These years were more a time of disturbance within the Church as Archbishop Theodore sought to reorganize its diocesan structure. The canons of the synod of Hertford (672) established a model for good episcopal order (*HE* IV, 5) and subdivision of the great kingdom-dioceses proceeded as opportunity presented itself. The diocese of the eastern Angles was divided in the mid-670s on the illness of Bishop Bisi (*HE* IV, 5), the Mercian diocese likewise, probably on the deposition of Bishop Wynfrith and the appointment of Seaxwulf, abbot of Peterborough, as bishop, *c.* 674–5 (*HE* IV, 6),[17] and the territory of the northern Angles was partitioned in 678 following King Ecgfrith's expulsion of Wilfrid, bishop of York (*Vita Wilfridi,* ch. 24: *HE* IV, 12). Theodore thereby gave a wholly new dimension to the authority of the archbishop of Canterbury within the Anglo-Saxon Church. He also moderated political conduct, mediating peace between Ecgfrith and Aethelred in 679 following the battle of the Trent at a time when Ecgfrith was otherwise honour-bound to pursue hostilities to avenge Aelfwine (*HE* IV, 21). The relative peace of these years, therefore, may have owed much to Theodore's influence.

The ascendancy of Caedwalla and its aftermath

This quiescent phase in the political life of the Anglo-Saxon kingdoms came to an end in the mid-680s. The western Saxons, one of whose kings, Centwine, was still a pagan in the mid-680s until shortly before his abdication *c.* 685–6 when the pagan Caedwalla came to power, and the southern Saxons under a Christian king, Aethelwealh, but still otherwise largely a pagan people, appear to have been beyond the range of Theodore's metropolitan power. It was from these territories that further political disruption derived, affecting directly the kingdom of Kent but drawing Mercians and eastern Saxons into a new power-struggle.

The kingdom of Kent had enjoyed political stability for some time. According to Bede, Eorcenberht (640–64) ruled the kingdom 'most nobly' (*HE* III, 8) and his son and successor, Ecgberht (664–73), afforded a secure base from which Theodore could embark as archbishop of Canterbury on his work of ecclesiastical reorganization. The court of Ecgberht was in touch not only with Rome (*HE* III, 29) but also with Frankish Gaul (*HE* IV, 1), and possibly Lombard Italy, its continuing economic vitality reflected in the adoption of the silver *sceatta* (see above, p. 43). Dynastic tension within the kingdom, however, was a source of weakness. With the example before him of the exclusion from the succession of the line of Eorcenberht's brother, Eormenred, and the murder of Eormenred's sons, Aethelred and Aethelberht, Eadric, son of Ecgberht, may have feared exclusion by his uncle, Hlothhere (see Appendix, Fig. 1). There is no certain evidence that Hlothhere shared royal power as king of Kent with his nephew. The laws of Hlothhere and Eadric appear in their extant version as a single code issued jointly by Hlothhere and Eadric as kings of Kent,[18] but they may represent a conflation of two originally separate sets of laws or even a confirmation by Eadric of the dooms of his uncle. They reveal the Kentish kings still with commercial interests in London under the supervision of a royal reeve, and suggest that Hlothhere was a ruler of some standing. In the mid-680s, Eadric, probably by now a youth of about 15, attacked him. He did so with the support of the southern Saxons and, after a reign of eleven years and seven months (*HE* IV, 5), Hlothhere died from wounds received in battle either on 6 February 685 (*HE* IV, 26) (if, as Bede believed, he became king in July 673) or 686 (if he did not become king until 674). Eadric now assumed royal power. He was the nephew of Wulfhere and it is reminiscent of the political alignments of Wulfhere's day that the southern Saxons should have supported him against Hlothhere. Moreover, what this episode testifies to is a resurgence of the power of the southern Saxons as they sought to further their own ascendancy in the south-east, the foundation of which had been laid by Wulfhere, and it seems likely that Eadric was established as king in Kent as a southern Saxon satellite. The impact of these events on the church of

Canterbury is unknown but Theodore's increasing ill-health (*Vita Wilfridi*, ch. 43) may have meant a serious diminution in Canterbury's influence at this time.

The single most dynamic individual in southern England in the mid-680s, however, was neither Eadric nor Aethelwealh but Caedwalla who both frustrated southern Saxon expansion and furthered the creation of a new overkingship of the western Saxons which was the foundation of the West Saxon kingdom of King Ine. Caedwalla first appears in the records as a noble exile in the forests of Chiltern and Andred (*Vita Wilfridi*, ch. 42). Remembered as a son of the King Cenberht who had been a co-ruler of the western Saxons with Cenwealh before his death in the 660s (see above, p. 49), he may have been as much a victim of the impact of earlier Mercian expansion under Wulfhere as of internal strife. He was in his mid-twenties in 685, still a pagan and the leader of what was evidently a powerful fighting force.

It was while in exile in Andredsweald that Caedwalla encountered Wilfrid, exiled bishop of York, who had come *c.* 680–1 into the territory of the southern Saxons where he enjoyed the patronage of King Aethelwealh and where he was engaged in converting the people to Christianity (*Vita Wilfridi*, chs 41, 42: *HE* IV, 13). The author of the *Life of Wilfrid*, who represents Wilfrid as persuading the king and queen to accept the word of God and as preaching to a people who had never before heard the Gospel, undoubtedly exaggerates the paganism of the southern Saxons, for Bede reveals from non-Wilfridian sources, first, that Aethelwealh had married a Christian princess and had been baptized himself and, second, that a number of ealdormen and thegns had likewise received baptism, with the priests, Eappa, Padda, Burghelm and Aeddi ministering to the common people either at the time of Aethelwealh's conversion or subsequently (*HE* IV, 13). The account of Wilfrid's activities among the South Saxons in his *Life*, therefore, must be used with caution.[19] Nevertheless, that Wilfrid enjoyed good relations with Aethelwealh is confirmed by Bede who records the king's gift to him of 87 hides of land for a monastery at Selsey (*HE* IV, 13), the site of the bishopric subsequently established among the south Saxons in the time of Daniel, bishop of Winchester (*HE* V, 18). Wilfrid's dealings with Aethelwealh were at about the time of Aethelwealh's involvement in Kent in support of Eadric when a new southern Saxon hegemony extending from Wight into Kent could conceivably have challenged the existing political map of south-east England.

While a beneficiary of Aethelwealh's patronage, however, Wilfrid is said to have been sought as a spiritual father by Caedwalla (*Vita Wilfridi*, ch. 42). Though Caedwalla remained unbaptized until after his abdication as king in 688, it is not inconceivable that he approached Wilfrid in such a capacity, and certainly by the time of his abdication Caedwalla had resolved to seek baptism in Rome itself. He was presumably influenced in this direction by the churchmen around him, among whom Wilfrid is conspicuous for his known familiarity with the see of St Peter. It was against this background that Caedwalla attacked the southern Saxons. He was at first driven out by the *duces*, Berhthun and Andhun, but it was not long before he attacked again and slew King Aethelwealh (*HE* IV, 15). Berhthun and Andhun then governed the kingdom, possibly as kings. Aethelwealh's possession of Wight and the Meon valley since before 675 and the consequent shift in political and military relationships were almost certainly the reason for Caedwalla's hostility, together with a desire to prevent a further extension of southern Saxon influence in the south-east. That he was able to summon the military force necessary for this invasion of southern Saxon territory, however, is surprising and a vivid demonstration of power by an exiled aetheling. One possibility is that he had already begun to campaign in western Saxon territory and that additional troops joined him from his supporters there. It is not necessary to suppose that Wilfrid behaved treacherously to Aethelwealh in associating with Caedwalla; the warfare between the two was probably outside his control. The impression conveyed by Wilfrid's career in these years is of a Church still very dependent in the pursuit of its own interests, certainly in territories outside Canterbury's sphere of influence, on the unpredictable inclination of the princes with whom it had to deal. There is no indication that Wilfrid exercised any influence on Caedwalla's secular and military activities. Nevertheless, it is likely that he was quick to accommodate himself to the victor and to profit from a new source of patronage.[20]

The *Chronicle* A (*s.a.* 685) says that Caedwalla began to contend for the kingship in 685, but it was not until 686 that he established himself as king over the western Saxons. The West Saxon Genealogical Regnal List allocates him a reign of three years, with one variant reading of two,[21] but Bede also says that Caedwalla reigned for two years before his abdication in 688 (*HE* IV, 12: V, 7) (see also above, p. 51). His predecessor, Centwine, abdicated on his conversion to enter a monastery,[22] but of the details of the process by which Caedwalla established himself over the western Saxons nothing is known. It certainly should not be thought that he overthrew all other kings. If the evidence, admittedly not here of the best, of land-grants can be accepted, Bealdred, a king in the region of Somerset and west Wiltshire *c.* 681 (*CS* 61: S 236), was still reigning in 688 (*CS* 71: S 1170),[23] and Cenred, the father of Ine, also appears to have been ruling as a king somewhere in Wessex in Ine's early years (*CS* 78: S 45).[24]

In 686 Caedwalla ravaged Kent with his brother, Mul (*ASC* A, *s.a.* 686). A second invasion of southern Saxon territory, in which Berhthun was slain (*HE* IV, 15), may also belong to that year. The Isle of Wight was also attacked (*ASC* A, *s.a.* 686) and Bede gives details (*HE* IV, 16). Caedwalla attempted, according to Bede, to exterminate the natives and replace them with inhabitants of his own kingdom, vowing, though still a pagan, that he would give a fourth part of the island and the booty seized to the Church if he were successful. This vow he fulfilled by granting extensive estates to Bishop Wilfrid. Among the casualties of Caedwalla's attack on Wight were Arwald, king of the island, and his two young brothers who escaped to the opposite mainland where they were captured and put to death after Caedwalla had first allowed them to receive baptism. It is conceivable that it was Arwald's accession as a young king which was the signal for Caedwalla's attack. In Kent, after a reign of a year and a half (*HE* IV, 26), Eadric died either in 686 (if he succeeded Hlothhere in 685) or 687 (if he succeeded Hlothhere in 686) on 31 August.[25] Mul was evidently established as king in Kent[26] but he was burnt to death there and Caedwalla responded with a second invasion in 687 (*ASC* A, *s.a.* 687) and may then have ruled Kent directly for a time. Bede says that he reduced the southern Saxons to a more grievous servitude on the death of Berhthun (*HE* IV, 15), and the situation in Kent may have been similar, the kingdom reduced to economic and political disarray.[27]

Caedwalla's presence in the south-east was sustained. He is represented as granting land at Hoo in Kent to an Abbot Ecgbald (*CS* 89: S 233),[28] and a grant of land at Farnham, perhaps dating to 686, for the founding of a monastery reveals him with authority in Surrey (*CS* 72: S 235).[29] It was in 686, in the second year of King Aldfrith (*Vita Wilfridi*, ch. 44: *HE* IV, 19), that Wilfrid returned to Northumbria. Theodore's reconciliation with Wilfrid took place in the context of Caedwalla's dramatic ascendancy in southern England and if it is true that he expressed the wish that Wilfrid succeed him at Canterbury (*Vita Wilfridi*, ch. 43)[30] this may have been in recognition of Caedwalla's new regime with which Wilfrid was associated. Eorcenwald, bishop of London, is said to have been privy to discussions between Theodore and Wilfrid (*Vita Wilfridi*, ch. 43). It is becoming clear how important was Eorcenwald's role in the evolution of the diplomatic form of early Anglo-Saxon charters in the 680s and thereafter; indeed he may have been responsible for drafting Caedwalla's charter to Farnham.[31] The presence of such individuals in Caedwalla's entourage confirms the Gewissian prince as a significant political figure. Not only had he transformed the political situation among the western Saxons but he had also established himself as the most powerful ruler in southern England. If his achievement had been consolidated, a new and formidable political and military order might have been established which could have proved resilient to subsequent Mercian attack. The grant of Oethelred, a kinsman of Saebbi, king of the eastern Saxons, to Abbess Aethelburh of Barking, Eorcenwald's sister, which was possibly drawn up by Eorcenwald, has West Saxon witnesses (including Bishop Haeddi) and would seem to belong to 686–8 (*CS* 81: S 1171) (see above, p. 20). Together with Caedwalla's grant of land in Battersea in Surrey, also to the monastery of Barking (*CS* 87: S 1246), it constitutes the first sign of an extension of western Saxon influence north of the Thames and an indication of potential development. Not surprisingly, Aldhelm was to describe Caedwalla some years after as 'renowned in war and arms . . . a powerful occupant of the throne'.[32] Whatever brought about Caedwalla's abdication in 688, therefore, probably changed the political direction of the southern kingdoms in the late seventh century. The most likely explanation is that the illness which took his life within ten days of his baptism in Rome on 10 April 689 was of long standing and that Caedwalla abdicated in the knowledge that his health was failing. What is striking about it is that he is the first Anglo-Saxon king known to have abdicated to go to Rome and that he went to Rome not as a baptized Christian but to seek baptism. He was remarkable not only in his military achievement but in the circumstances of his renunciation of power.

The abdication of Caedwalla created a power-vacuum in southern England. Among the western Saxons Ine may not have acquired royal power until the following year; he abdicated in 726 and the West Saxon Genealogical Regnal List gives him a reign of thirty-seven years[33] which implies an accession in 689, not 688. He was the son of and seems to have been co-ruler with his father, King Cenred (see Appendix, Fig. 3), whose advice he acknowledges in his laws which date to the period before 693/4 (when Eorcenwald, bishop of London, whose help he also acknowledges, died). Unsettled conditions among the western Saxons, therefore, may have prevailed in the aftermath of Caedwalla's abdication.

A disturbed situation also reveals itself in the south-east. In Kent a prince of the native line emerged in Oswine, a descendant, so it would seem, of Eormenred, brother of King Eorcenberht. In a record of a grant of land in Thanet in January 690[34] to Aebbe (Eafe), daughter of Eormenred and now abbess of Minster-in-Thanet, Oswine refers to her as his kinswoman (*CS* 35: S 13), and in another charter granting land to Aebbe which had once belonged to Eormenred he expresses gratitude at his restoration to the kingdom of his fathers (*CS* 40: S 14). Oswine, therefore, was probably Aebbe's nephew.[35] In January 690 he was in the second year of his reign, so his accession took place in 688, no doubt in the immediate aftermath of Caedwalla's abdication. In this venture, Oswine appears to have had the support of the king of the Mercians. Land he gave to St Augustine's, Canterbury, in 689, which had come to him from his parents, had been confirmed in his possession by King Athelred (*CS* 73: S 12). Denied an opportunity to intervene since 676, Aethelred was clearly seeking to re-establish a Mercian presence in Kent. Simultaneously, however, into Kent came princes of the eastern Saxons. Sigehere, king of the eastern Saxons (*HE* III, 30), appears there with Swaefheard, son of his co-ruler Saebbi (so identified in *CS* 42: S 10), confirming the grant of land Caedwalla had made at Hoo (*CS* 89: S 233) (see Appendix, Fig. 2). Swaefheard first emerges in the circle of Oswine, witnessing Oswine's grant to St Augustine's in 689 and that to Abbess Aebbe in January 690, but if he was in the second year of his reign by March 690 (*CS* 42: S 10) he must have succeeded before March 689. Oswine's power was clearly already weakening by January 690 for he refers in the grant to Abbess Aebbe at that time to those Kentish nobles who were able to be with him. Swaefheard, on the other hand, had the support of his father, King Saebbi (*CS* 42: S 10). It is not clear how far these princes of the eastern Saxons were operating in Kent on their own initiative or to what extent they were under Aethelred's control. With the rulers of the eastern Saxons possibly free of subjection to Aethelred for the last ten years or more, their presence in Kent suggests a revival of eastern Saxon power and implies at the very least that Aethelred needed their assistance. Even though, therefore, in 691 Aethelred confirmed a grant of land by Swaefheard to Abbess Aebbe in 690 (*CS* 42: S 10), and confirmed also the successive donations to Hoo (*CS* 89: S 233), it may be that he was not entirely master of the situation.

The disarray in Kent at this time is reflected in the failure on the death of Archbishop Theodore on 19 September 690 to elect a successor until 1 July 692 (*HE* V, 8). The fundamental weakness in Oswine's position was not necessarily so much the challenge from Swaefheard as the lack of support within the kingdom for a prince of Eormenred's line. Bede, drawing on Canterbury sources, says that when Eadric died, various usurpers or foreign kings plundered the kingdom until the rightful king, Wihtred, son of Ecgberht, established himself on the throne (*HE* IV, 26). The usurpers or foreign kings will have included Caedwalla and Swaefheard and his family. They will also have included Oswine. Wihtred, a descendant of Eorcenberht rather than Eormenred (see Appendix, Fig. 1), was evidently viewed as the legitimate heir in a way in which Oswine never was. The weight of the church of Canterbury was behind Wihtred and it may have been this which ensured his success. Wihtred was in his sixth regnal year in April 697 (*CS* 96: S 18), so he secured the kingship either early in 692 or after April 691, when he will have been a young man of about 20. At first he reigned with Swaefheard. Bede records that when Beorhtwald, abbot of Reculver, was elected archbishop of Canterbury on 1 July 692, Wihtred and Swaefheard were ruling in Kent (*HE* V, 8). There is no trace of Swaefheard in Kent, however, after this date. Saebbi, king of the eastern Saxons, died in 694 and was succeeded by his sons, Sigeheard and Swaefred[36] (*HE* IV, 11) (see Appendix, Fig. 2), and Wihtred was left in Kent as sole ruler.[37]

It is clear that the Mercians under Aethelred had been unable to assert Mercian authority in Kent in the confused circumstances of these years and the limits to Mercian power in this area had been strikingly reaffirmed. Nevertheless, Mercian overlordship of the eastern Saxons was consolidated. Aethelred granted land to Eorcenwald's successor, Wealdhere, bishop of London, in the period 693–704 (S 1783) and in 704 consented to a grant by King Swaefred in Middlesex, subsequently confirmed by Aethelred's successors, Coenred (704–9) and Ceolred (709–16) (*CS* 111: S 65). Coenred also confirmed with Sigeheard, king of the East Saxons, a grant by Tyrhtil, bishop of Hereford, to Wealdhere (S 1785). Offa, king of the East Saxons (*c.* 705–9), whose father, Sigehere, may have married into the ruling family of the Hwicce,[38] gave land as sub-king in the territory of the Hwicce to the church of Worcester in the reign of Coenred (*CS* 123: S 64).

Reconstruction

With the re-establishment of stable kingship in Kent and among the West Saxons under Wihtred and Ine respectively and the confinement of Mercian power, a period of relatively peaceful consolidation followed which lasted for a quarter of a century during which time kings in southern England embarked on that redefinition of their realms which is embodied in the extant laws of Wihtred and Ine.

In 694 the people of Kent came to terms with Ine by which a payment of 30,000 pence, signifying approximately 7,200 shillings and the value of an aetheling's life, was made to the western Saxons in compensation for the burning of Mul (*ASC* A, *s.a.* 694). This agreement may have involved the ceding of border territory and Ine seems to have retained Surrey, referring to Eorcenwald, bishop of London, whose diocese included Surrey, as 'my bishop' in the preface to his laws.[39]

Wihtred's long reign, though devoid of known incident, is distinguished as a period of close co-operation between the royal court and the Church in Kent under Archbishop Beorhtwald. Bede's statement that Wihtred was the rightful king of Kent who brought the rule of the usurpers to an end (*HE* IV, 26) reflects the viewpoint of a Church thoroughly committed to him. In return, Wihtred's laws, issued at Bearsted on 6 September 695, freed the Church in Kent from taxation and concerned themselves extensively with religious matters, pronouncing against irregular marriage unions, non-observance of Sunday as a day of rest, and continuing pagan worship.[40] Wihtred, it has been said, 'legislated with the Church in the forefront of his mind'.[41] Four years later he granted immunity from all royal burdens to the churches of Kent (*CS* 99: S 20).[42] At the same time 'a sharply punitive element' and 'a new authoritarianism'[43] has been detected in the secular clauses of his laws in which royal judgement could transcend normal procedures and supplant the payment of compensation.

The contemporary laws of Ine, king of the western Saxons, while not unconcerned with religious matters – baptism, observance of Sunday, rights of sanctuary, Church taxes – deal more than do the Kentish with a range of civil as well as criminal matters, including aspects of agrarian economy.[44] Wihtred was heir to a legislative tradition in Kent which went back to Aethelberht but no king among the western Saxons is known to have legislated before Ine. His achievement in bringing together such an elaborate code has been highly regarded, Stenton describing it as 'the work of a responsible statesman'.[45] Richardson and Sayles thought Ine's legislation 'more mature, less experimental in some ways, than the surviving body of Kentish law'.[46] The laws of Ine and Wihtred contain one clause in common concerning the need for a stranger to shout or blow his horn if straying off the trackway if he did not wish to be mistaken for a thief. This clause and the adoption in Wihtred's laws of the West Saxon term *gesith* for noble in place of the *eorlcund* of the laws of Aethelberht, Hlothhere and Eadric perhaps strengthen a possibility that some degree of collaboration attended the drawing up of these codes. Certainly, it seems very possible that both were produced in a period of reconstruction immediately following the termination of hostilities and the payment of compensation for Mul. If it is true that kings only legislated when faced with an urgent need to enhance their standing with their subjects by prestigious acts of law-making,[47] the appearance of royal codes of law in Kent and Wessex at this time may reflect something of the very considerable crisis through which these regions had recently passed. It seems reasonable to suspect that a certain political and military stability had first to be achieved and that the capacity to make law required consensus and mature counsel among the wiser men of the realm who advised the king which transcended his purely personal ambition. Both Wihtred and Ine were evidently alive to the importance of ecclesiastical support and the need to secure the goodwill of their great men in preserving, as the laws of Ine put it, 'the security of our kingdom'.

It is not possible to reconstruct a detailed history of Ine's reign but the indications are that he ruled with firmness. Bede says that he subjected the kingdom of the southern Saxons to severe oppression and their bishopric was soon absorbed within the diocese of Winchester (*HE* IV, 15). The southern Saxons appear to have been divided among more than one king at this time – King Nothhelm (otherwise Nunna) is found in association with a King Watt in the 690s (*CS* 78: S 45) and a King Aethelstan *c.* 714 (*CS* 132: S 42). The description of Nothhelm as Ine's kinsman in an annal recording Nothhelm's assistance to Ine in his war with Geraint, king of Dumnonia, in 710 (*ASC* CDE, *s.a.* 710), indicates that the two ruling families were now connected by marriage. Their campaign was part of a military advance into British territory by Ine which brought the West Saxon frontier in the west to the Tamar.[48] On his eastern border, Ine brought pressure to bear on the eastern Saxons who were sheltering exiles from his kingdom. A letter of Wealdhere, bishop of London, to Archbishop Beorhtwald in 704–5 reveals a state of estrangement between Ine and the eastern Saxon rulers, Sigeheard and Swaefred; in return for the expulsion of the exiles, Ine undertook not to inflict vengeance on the eastern Saxons and a forthcoming council at Brentford, to be attended by the kings and their leading men both ecclesiastical and lay, was expected to resolve the crisis.[49] Indirectly this must have represented a challenge to the influence of Aethelred of Mercia in the East Saxon region. Ine was the patron of several churches in his kingdom – Malmesbury, Muchelney and Glastonbury appear to have been beneficiaries – and a genuine act of general exemption from secular burdens may lie behind the suspect extant privilege to West Saxon churches and monasteries of 704 (*CS* 108: S 245).[50] He seems to have worked well with leading churchmen – such as Eorcenwald and Haeddi whom he acknowledges in the prologue to his laws – and Wynfrith, a monk at Exeter, later known in the course of his mission to the continental Germans as Boniface. According to his *Life*,[51] Boniface entered the public arena *c.* 710–15 as King Ine's envoy to the archbishop of Canterbury (*Vita Bonifatii*, ch. 4). There can be no doubt that it was Ine who set the seal on the creation of the historic kingdom of Wessex and defined its horizons as a Christian realm in which monasticism and men of letters flourished amid active involvement in an overseas mission. Ine did not allow the displeasure of Canterbury at his failure to agree to a partition of the diocese of Winchester to drive him into action on the matter, despite threats of excommunication.[52] It was not until the death of Bishop Haeddi in 705 that the territory of the western Saxons was partitioned between Aldhelm (at Sherborne) and Daniel (at Winchester) (*HE* V, 18). Ine appears as a hard-headed, resilient leader in rigorous pursuit of his own interests. His kingdom had come some considerable way from the remote and backward region it had been at the beginning of the seventh century. By *c.* 700 the area of circulation of the *sceatta* or penny, introduced probably in Kent in the 670s, was widening to embrace the Thames valley[53] and *Hamwic*, near Southampton, was emerging as an important trading settlement to become within a few decades 'possibly the largest and most densely populated town in eighth-century England'.[54]

One of the unexpected features of this period is the relative quiescence of the Mercians. This is all the more surprising in view of the fact that the northern king, Aldfrith, was now confined largely north of the Humber, the Northumbrians preoccupied with their own problems of reconstruction following the Pictish victory at *Nechtanesmere* in 685 and seemingly unable even to take possession of Lindsey again. Despite this absence of distractions to the north, however, Aethelred, king of the Mercians, exhibited no further expansionist leanings in the south. It could be that he too was preoccupied nearer home, for example, in wars with the Welsh and the *Life of Guthlac* may provide evidence of this.[55] It was also at this time that the Hwicce (and possibly other border peoples such as the Magonsaete and Wreocensaete) were brought more completely under Mercian control. Among the Hwicce, Osric ruled as king (*HE* IV, 23) from the mid-670s when he granted land to the abbess of Bath (*CS* 43: S 51),[56] and Oshere granted land as king of the Hwicce to Cuthswith, abbess of Bath, in 693 (*CS* 85: S 53). But Aethelred's consent was being sought from the mid-670s (*CS* 43: S 51) and there can be no doubt that he regarded Oshere as his sub-king (*CS* 156: S 1429; *CS* 217: S 1255). A letter to Boniface, written *c.* 680 by a suppliant, Ecgburh, expresses her grief at the loss some time before of her brother, Oshere, whom a bitter and cruel death had taken from her,[57] and it may be that her brother was Oshere, king of the Hwicce. It is likely, therefore, that Aethelred was involving himself quite extensively in the affairs of the Hwicce across these years, being personally associated, for example, if the relevant document has an authentic base, with the founding of the monastery of St Peter, Gloucester, in 681 (*CS* 60: S 70).[58] In the 690s Aethelred granted land in Hwiccian territory to Oftfor, bishop of Worcester, seemingly without reference to any local prince (*CS* 76: S 76; *CS* 75: S 77); Aethelbald was certainly doing so at the beginning of his reign in 716-7 (*CS* 137: S 102).[59] Withdrawal from southern England, therefore, may have been accompanied by a period of consolidation in the more immediately adjoining territories around the Mercian heartland,[60] analogous to processes at work in northern and southern England.

Aethelred is best known in his later years for his support for Wilfrid, exiled bishop of York. His marriage to Osthryth, the sister of King Ecgfrith, inhibited him from bestowing royal favour on Wilfrid until Archbishop Theodore engineered a reconciliation of offended parties in 686. Following his subsequent quarrel with King Aldfrith *c.* 692, Wilfrid took refuge with Aethelred who made him bishop of the Middle Angles (*Vita Wilfridi*, ch. 45; *HE* IV, 23) and stood by him when Wilfrid refused to submit to Aldfrith and Archbishop Beorhtwald at the council of Austerfield *c.* 702 (*Vita Wilfridi*, chs 46–8). Aethelred's reasons for so doing are not made clear, but Wilfrid was head of a chain of monasteries which extended into Mercia (*Vita Wilfridi*, ch. 64).[61] To support Wilfrid was also to engage in a protracted dispute which must have been a long-term embarrassment both to the Northumbrian king and the archbishop of Canterbury. It is conceivable that Aethelred would have preferred Wilfrid as archbishop of Canterbury to Beorhtwald and associated Beorhtwald with that eclipse of Mercian influence in Kent which is a feature of the early 690s. When Wilfrid returned from his final visit to Rome Aethelred had abdicated but he summoned his nephew and appointed successor, Coenred, to meet Wilfrid and is said to have urged him to uphold Wilfrid's cause (*Vita Wilfridi*, ch. 57).

Wilfrid was resident in Mercia at the time that Queen Osthryth was murdered by Mercian nobles in 697 (*HE* V, 24). This could have been a vengeance slaying for the killing of Peada forty years before, allegedly by the treachery of his wife, Ealhflaed, the sister of Osthryth (*HE* III, 21, 24), but no further details are known. It was seven years later, in 704, that Aethelred abdicated to become a monk and abbot at Bardney in Lincolnshire (*HE* V, 19, 24: *ASC* A, *s.a.* 716), to which monastery Queen Osthryth had earlier translated some of the relics of Oswald, former king of the northern

Angles and her uncle (*HE* III, 11) and where she herself was buried.[62] Again, Aethelred was clearly much involved with a territory bordering on Mercia which he was in the process of bringing into closer dependence.

Coenred, son of Wulfhere,[63] was a man of at least 30 years of age, possibly older, who abdicated five years later in 709 to live as a monk at Rome (*HE* V, 19, 24) and who was succeeded by Aethelred's son, Ceolred. Ceolred is said not to have been a son of Osthryth,[64] so that if he were the son of Aethelred by a subsequent marriage after Osthryth's death, he would have been aged only about 10 or 11 at his accession. He did not acquire a good reputation. A visionary at Much Wenlock, on the testimony of Boniface, proclaimed in Ceolred's lifetime that the angels surrounding him had withdrawn their protective shield and abandoned him to demons because of the multitude of crimes he had committed.[65] Thirty years after his death in 716, Boniface criticized him for his disregard of the laws of the Church and for his personal immorality and depicted him as struck with madness while feasting with his nobles, so that he died 'gibbering with demons and cursing the priests of God'.[66] Boniface expresses a body of tradition violently hostile to the king. The visionary at Much Wenlock was a member of a community founded, according to its own tradition, by Mildburh, daughter of Merewalh and a princess of the Magonsaete.[67] The animosity of the community to the king is evident and reflects perhaps the resentment of a dependent people. Perhaps Boniface was also prejudiced by one particular episode. Ceolred evidently felt secure enough to attack deep into the territory of King Ine in 716, fighting against him in battle at Woden's Barrow (Adam's Grave) overlooking the Vale of Pewsey (*ASC* A, *s.a.* 716). The outcome is quite unknown but Ceolred was unquestionably the invader and it should not be assumed that Ine won.

Ceolred was remembered in some quarters at least as a profligate, but Wilfridian circles seem to have believed that Wilfrid could have worked well with him (*Vita Wilfridi*, ch. 64). Ceolred's father, Aethelred, had become a monk and abbot and his cousin, Coenred, had renounced his kingdom to go to Rome. This is a paradox characteristic of Mercian history at this time. When Coenred went to Rome he went in the company of Offa, son of Sigehere and king of the eastern Saxons, who abdicated at the same time (*HE* V, 19), and the harmony which appears to have prevailed between Coenred and Offa is another salutary warning not to describe relations between overlords and their royal dependants in this period as one of constant hostility. On the other hand, Ceolred's attack on Ine demonstrated the harsher reality of that desire for military prestige and territorial aggrandizement which is the more constant feature of Anglo-Saxon political history in this period. It ended the era of peaceful co-existence among the southumbrian kingdoms and inaugurated what has become known as the age of Mercian supremacy.

The reign of Aethelbald

Ceolred was not without at least one rival as king of the Mercians, namely Aethelbald, son of Alwih, who is depicted in the genealogies of the kings of Mercia as a descendant of Penda's brother, Eowa (see Appendix, Fig. 8).[68] The *Life of Guthlac*, written after *c.* 721 at the earliest and dedicated to Aelfwald, king of East Anglia, who died in 749,[69] describes Aethelbald as of a famous progeny, whom Ceolred drove into exile and pursued (*Vita Guthlaci*, chs 40, 49). Aethelbald, probably a young man in his teens, took refuge in the fens of the east midlands with his companions in the vicinity of Crowland and the cell of Guthlac. Guthlac himself was of distinguished Mercian stock and a descendant of the Iclingas, the Mercian royal dynasty (*Vita Guthlaci*, chs 1, 2), and formerly an exile in the time of Ceolred's father, Aethelred, among the Britons (*Vita Guthlaci*, ch. 34). The *Life of Guthlac* claims that Guthlac – reputedly appearing after his death in a vision to Aethelbald – prophesied that he would receive the kingdom from the hand of God, who had foreshortened Ceolred's life for its wickedness, and triumph over his foes (*Vita Guthlaci*, ch. 49). If this prophecy conveys anything of the sentiments of the Crowland community at the time, it must have been from congenial company hostile to Penda's descendants that Aethelbald emerged to establish himself as king in Mercia, if not when Ceolred died (*ASC* A, *s.a.*, 716) then certainly when an otherwise unknown Ceolwald, who may have succeeded Ceolred, died or was driven out.[70] Aethelbald's accession broke the monopoly of royal power in Mercia by Penda and his descendants which had lasted over seventy years. It is a striking coincidence that in the same year that Aethelbald came to power among the Mercians, the assassination of Osred, son of Aldfrith, in Northumbria and the accession there of Coenred also broke the entrenched power of the family of Aethelfrith which had dominated the kingship of the northern Angles for more than seventy years (see below, pp. 47 ff.). Changes of some significance were evidently affecting the established dynasties of the northern and Mercian Angles as new princes emerged to dominate the Anglo-Saxon kingdoms in the early eighth century.

Sir Frank Stenton was of the opinion that with Aethelbald's accession 'the history of southern England enters upon a new phase'.[71] For Stenton, the half century before 716 when no Anglo-Saxon king had been able to establish more than a local ascendancy, had 'little significance in English political history'[72] because it had given no promise of the great advance, as he saw it, towards the unity of England which was to be made by the Mercian kings before the end of the eighth century. A preoccupation with the unification of England, however, in which the desire to unify was perceived as a guiding factor in a succession of early but powerful kings has channelled much of the study of pre-Viking history into too narrow an appreciation of political activity in the several kingdoms of the Anglo-Saxon heptarchy. The half century before 716, in fact, is full of political interest. The southumbrian kingdoms could have developed in any number of directions, three of which in particular seem to stand out: a southern England could have emerged, the domination of which was shared between the Mercians and the South Saxons (this was the prospect in the reign of Wulfhere if the trends of that time had been maintained); or even a south-eastern England dominated by the South Saxons (this was perhaps a prospect in late 670s); or a southern England dominated from the reign of Caedwalla by the West Saxons (the prospect in the mid-680s). In the event, not one of these possibilities for the immediate future materialized and a period of balance emerged in which the three principal southumbrian kingdoms – Kent, Wessex and Mercia – existed in a state of political equilibrium and the stability of Kent and Wessex was in striking contrast to the volatility of the recent past. It could be argued, therefore, that the rise of Mercia in the eighth century represented a serious destabilization of the southumbrian situation before the return to a new balance between the Mercians and the West Saxons in the first half of the ninth.

Absence of record material obscures Aethelbald's earliest years as king. Until the mid-730s he is described only as king of the Mercians but in an important charter of 736 concerning the granting of land in the territory of the Hwicce, the oldest Mercian original text to survive, Aethelbald is variously 'king not only of the Mercians but also of all the provinces which are known by the general name South Angles', 'king of the South Angles' and 'king of Britain' (*CS* 154: S 89).[73] The other charters in which Aethelbald is styled 'king of the South Angles' (*CS* 157: S 94; *CS* 163: S 101) are either not necessarily earlier than 736 or not certainly genuine (*CS* 164: S 103).[74] This spate of exalted titles for Aethelbald, which finds no echo elsewhere in texts from centres other than Worcester, could well be a purely local phenomenon in the mid-730s, peculiar to Worcester, with little direct bearing on the chronology of the process by which Aethelbald made himself master of the southern kingdoms. There is no reason to suppose, therefore, that a moment of particular significance in the reign of Aethelbald was reached in 736 or that the mid-730s constituted a watershed in the political history of the time. Bede shows that, even by 731 as he drew the *Ecclesiastical History* to a close, all the kingdoms south of the Humber were subject to Aethelbald, king of the Mercians (*HE* V, 23). That nothing of the process by which Aethelbald mastered southern England is directly revealed by the *Ecclesiastical History* or by annals or even by charters is a vivid demonstration of how incomplete the evidence can be for this early period of Anglo-Saxon history.

What may be said is that among the West Saxons the reign of Ine did not move peacefully towards its close. It was marked by rebellion and by internal dynastic division as rival aethelings came forward to challenge his authority. It was because of a rebellion that the young Boniface had been sent as Ine's envoy to the archbishop of Canterbury *c.* 710–15. In 721 Ine slew the aetheling, Cynewulf, whose relationship to Ine is unknown (*ASC* A, D, *s.a.* 721). In 722 the *Chronicle* A (*s.a.* 722) records that Ine's queen, Aethelburh, demolished Taunton which the king had built. This could suggest a domestic crisis, for the *Chronicle* records immediately after that the aetheling, Ealdberht, whom Ine had exiled, went into Surrey and Sussex and it is not inconceivable that Ealdberht was either Ine's son or the son of his brother, Ingild, who died in 718, seeking recognition perhaps as Ine's heir.[75] This rebellion was serious enough to involve disaffected groups in Surrey and Sussex and in 725 Ine fought against the South Saxons and slew Ealdberht (*ASC* A, *s.a.* 725). That this aetheling could find refuge in Surrey and among the South Saxons suggests a change in the situation in the south-east since Ine's earlier years as king. These territories appear to have been breaking free from West Saxon domination and it may be that Ine's weakening hold on Surrey at this time reflects either renewed Kentish influence in the area or a stage in the growth of the power of Aethelbald. The following year Ine abdicated to go to Rome (*ASC* A, *s.a.* 728), an event strangely not referred to by Bede. He left behind him a disputed succession between his kinsman, Aethelheard (*ASC* A, *s.a* 726) and a rival aetheling, Oswald, allegedly a descendant of Ceawlin (*ASC* A, *s.a.* 728), who survived until 730 (*ASC* A, *s.a* 730: cf., D, *s.a.* 730). Such a civil war would create exactly the conditions for the Mercian ruler to consolidate any advantage gained in the south-east at Ine's expense.

The situation in Kent was also changing. The death of Wihtred in 725, the year before Ine's abdication, leaving three sons as his heirs – Aethelberht, Eadberht and Ealric (*HE* V, 23) (see Appendix, Fig. 1) – resulted in a partition of the kingdom. The Eadberht, king of Kent, who was in his thirty-sixth regnal year in 761 (*CS* 190: S 28; cf., *CS* 189: S 29), was presumably the son of Wihtred. He ruled at first in a subordinate position to his brother, Aethelberht (*CS* 159: S 27), but whether or not the Aethelberht, king of Kent, who died in 762 (*ASC* A, *s.a.* 760), is to be identified with Aethelberht, son of Wihtred, has been disputed.[76] Another Eadberht, styled king of Kent, died in 748 (*ASC* A, *s.a.* 748) and an Eardwulf, son of Eadberht (*CS* 176, 199: S 31), reigned from *c.* 747 (*CS* 175: S 30) to some unknown date after the death of Boniface in 754.[77] So here also circumstances may have been more susceptible to external pressure. The years immediately following 725/6 must have been a crucial period in the establishment of Aethelbald of Mercia's domination of southern England.[78]

It is evident from the *Life of Guthlac* that a harmonious relationship prevailed for some time after Aethelbald became king between the Mercian king and Aelfwald, son of Ealdwulf, king of the East Angles, otherwise it would be difficult to explain the dedication of the *Life* of a Mercian saint to King Aelfwald. Perhaps an alliance with the East Angles was the cornerstone of Aethelbald's ascendancy. It is unfortunate that the *Life* of Guthlac cannot be more closely dated. Though the *Life* says that Aethelbald's happiness as king had grown in succeeding years (since his accession) (*Vita Guthlaci*, ch. 52), it is not certain that this means that Aethelbald was 'apparently at the height of his power',[79] and it is not impossible that the *Life* dates to a period before Aethelbald had asserted his authority outside his own kingdom – perhaps *c.* 725. If the *Life* is later than that and if it belongs to the 730s or even 740s, however, it would again demonstrate that the relationship between a dependant or sub-king and his overlord was not inevitably confrontational but on occasion at least perfectly acceptable to both sides for as long, presumably, as it remained of mutual benefit.

The charters of the kings of Kent reveal no trace of Aethelbald's over-lordship, though an Eadberht, king of Kent, consented to Aethelbald's remission of tolls on half a ship (probably in London) for the abbess of Minster-in-Thanet in 748 (*CS* 177: S 91). That Aethelberht, king of Kent, exercised authority over his brother, Eadberht, is clear from the way in which it was necessary for Ealdwulf, bishop of Rochester, to secure confirmation of a grant of land from Eadberht in 738 from Aethelberht and Nothhelm, archbishop of Canterbury, acknowledging that he had erred in not doing so sooner (*CS* 159: S 27), but nothing is said of any necessity to secure Aethelbald's confirmation. It may be simply that no document has survived in which Aethelberht was required to acknowledge Aethelbald as his overlord, but so far as can be seen there was no restriction on the power of the Kentish king to grant land to whomsoever he wished.[80] Nor, on the evidence of a rather poor run of West Saxon charters was there any such restriction on the power of the West Saxon king to do so. There are very few South Saxon charters from this period and again none which reveals any necessity to secure the consent of Aethelbald.

If it did not manifest itself in this particular way, however, Aethelbald's power was none the less real. The election of Tatwine, a priest in the monastery of Breedon on the Hill in the territory of the Middle Angles, to be archbishop of Canterbury on the death of Beorhtwald in early 731 (*HE* V, 23), should perhaps be seen as an expression of Aethelbald's influence, and likewise that of Nothhelm, a priest of London, to Canterbury in 734–5, and of Cuthbert, probably the former bishop of Hereford, to Canterbury in 740.[81] There is no evidence that the East Saxons under Swaefberht, who seems to have succeeded Offa (see above p. 124) and who died in 738,[82] and then under Selered (see Appendix, Fig. 2), who died in 746 (*ASC* A, *s.a.* 746),[83] were anything other than subject to the Mercians at this time and Aethelbald appears to have been master of the land of the Middle Saxons (*CS* 182: S 100). He granted a number of remissions of tolls on ships in the port of London – to the bishop of London (S 1788), for example, to the bishop of Rochester (*CS* 152: S 88), to the abbess of Minster-in-Thanet (*CS* 149: S86; *CS* 150: S 87; CS 177: S 91) and to the bishop of Worcester (*CS* 171: S 98). Among the West Saxons it may be that it was Aethelbald's support which enabled Aethelheard to defeat the aetheling, Oswald, and that this established both Aethelheard and his brother,[84] Cuthred, who subsequently succeeded Aethelheard in 739,[85] as Aethelbald's dependants or at least obliged them to make territorial concessions. In 733, Aethelbald occupied Somerton (*ASC* A, *s.a.* 733), probably a seizure of West Saxon territory by the Mercian king.[86] Subsequently both Aethelbald and Cuthred witnessed the sale of land to Glastonbury with Aethelbald's consent (*CS* 168: S 1410) and in 746 Aethelbald gave unidentified estates to the abbot of Glastonbury (S 1679).[87] He gave the monastery of Cookham in Berkshire to Christ Church, Canterbury (*CS* 291: S 1258), indicative of control also of this area.[88] The impression these records give is that Aethelbald brought certain West Saxon territories directly under his own authority. The Mercians would seem to have had influence in Berkshire at an earlier date in the reign of Wulfhere and the same may well have been true of Somerset, in which case what Aethelbald was doing was appropriating border territories traditionally in dispute between the Mercians and the western Saxons. In 756–7 he granted land, probably at Tockenham in Wiltshire, another area in which Mercian influence had been a feature of the recent past, to Eanberht, possibly abbot of Malmesbury (*CS* 81: S 96).[89] It must be regarded as probable, therefore, that under Aethelbald the Mercian position in areas bordering on other kingdoms was consolidated at the expense of surrounding neighbours. Presumably a similar border dispute lay behind Aethelbald's attack on Northumbrian territory in 740.[90]

At the same time, however, domination of the West Saxon kings by Aethelbald was certainly a feature of Aethelbald's overlordship. In agreeing to the sale of land to Glastonbury with Cuthred, Aethelbald's consent was what was crucial and his precedence over Cuthred is clear (*CS* 168: S 1410). The charter recording Aethelbald's grant of land to the monastery of Abingdon in Berkshire between 726 and 737, in which he is styled 'king of the Angles of Britain' (*CS* 155: S 93), is a forgery and unacceptable as an authentic record, but its attestation by Aethelheard, king of the West Saxons, while on expedition beyond the Severn against the Britons, could derive from a genuine fragment.[91] The *Chronicle* A (*s.a.* 743) records that in 743 Aethelbald and Cuthred, king of the West Saxons, fought the Britons. It may be that these West Saxon kings were obliged to join the Mercian ruler on occasion at least in his military campaigns, as indeed earlier kings had assisted Penda and Wulfhere. Though in the mid-850s Burgred, king of Mercia, and the West Saxon king, Aethelwulf, joined together in a campaign against the Welsh without any indication of the subordination of one to the other (see below, p. 195), the evidence as a whole suggests a West Saxon subjection to the Mercians in the mid-eighth century. Cuthred is said to have fought bravely against Aethelbald (*ASC* A, *s.a.* 741) and in his twelfth year, which the *Chronicle* gives as 752 (*ASC* A, *s.a* 752) but which may need to be corrected to 751,[92] to have defeated and put the Mercian king to flight at the battle of *Beorhford*. This action, elsewhere characterized as an insurrection,[93] probably established Cuthred as an independent ruler. It is not impossible that on Cuthred's death in 755[94] Aethelbald supported Cynewulf against Sigeberht in the ensuing struggle for the West Saxon kingship.[95] In 756[96] Cynewulf was able to seize the kingdom from Sigeberht, confining him to the region of Hampshire where he perished soon after (*ASC* A, *s.a.* 755); but he was obliged in 756–7 to witness Aethelbald's grant of land in Wiltshire to Abbot Eanberht (*CS* 181: S 96). That Aethelbald's position in southern England at the end of his reign was still a dominant one is suggested by the description of him in the record of this grant as 'king not only of the Mercians but also of the surrounding peoples', but it may be that a diminution of power in the early 750s played a part in exposing him to assassination in Mercia a few years later.[97]

What happened in East Anglia on Aelfwald's death in 749 is not clear. The kingdom is said to have been divided among three kings, Hun, Beonna and Aethelberht,[98] of whom Aethelberht was still reigning in 794 (*ASC* A, *s.a.* 792) (which would give him a reign of forty-five years). The later *Lives* of Aethelberht place his accession in 779[99] so that the suspicion must arise that this note is perhaps based on a misreading of a king-list which concluded by simply listing these names and misled the annalist into thinking that the kingdom had been partitioned among them. Beonna may have come to power *c.* 758.[100] The minting of his own coins by Beonna could suggest that he too broke free for a time from Aethelbald's domination. These coins can be dated no more closely than the late 750s or early 760s,[101] but they are possibly to be associated with the disintegration of Aethelbald's *imperium* in southern England following his death.

Aethelbald is alleged in a ninth-century list of benefactions from Gloucester abbey to have slain the kinsman of a Mercian abbess (*CS* 535: S 1782) and his eventual assassination at Seckington, near Tamworth, by his own bodyguard in 757 (*ASC* A, *s.a.* 755)[102] has tended to reflect unfavourably upon him. He was buried in state at Repton[103] but a contemporary visionary pictured him in hell.[104] This impression of a somewhat unpleasant individual is strengthened by the letter which Boniface and seven other missionary bishops among the continental Germans wrote to the king in 746/7, which is intensely critical of him.[105] Aethelbald was rebuked by Boniface for his failure to take a lawful wife and more especially for his violation of nuns and virgins. The letter implies that some of these nuns were themselves leading immoral lives but this in no way exonerated Aethelbald in Boniface's eyes. Gloomy prognostications of Aethelbald's life being in danger of passing away like a shadow and his soul into eternal perdition – although conventionally expressed – imply an unhappy conclusion to his life as a real possibility.

Boniface wrote to Ecgberht, archbishop of York, authorizing him to amend the letter in any way he thought desirable,[106] and to Herefrith, a priest, who was to make known Boniface's views to Aethelbald by reading the letter to him and explaining it – Herefrith being one to whom Aethelbald was prepared to listen.[107]

The letter raises the suspicion that there was a threat to Aethelbald's life in 746–7 and that Boniface was responding to a potentially dangerous situation in Mercia at that time when any personal idiosyncrasy of behaviour on the part of the king, which was unacceptable to Christian morality, would be magnified. This attack on the king is part of a general condemnation by Boniface of the adulterous life of many Anglo-Saxons, but Aethelbald is also censured for his violation of the privileges of churches and monasteries, including the seizure of revenues, and violence done to monks and priests. Boniface was looking back to an age in which the privileges of the churches of the Anglo-Saxons had been untouched and inviolate, or so it was thought, and he saw this age as ending – as he tells Aethelbald – in the time of Ceolred, king of the Mercians, and Osred, king of the Northumbrians (both of whose reigns ended in 716), whom Boniface accuses of behaving as Aethelbald was now doing and as a consequence of which they both perished miserably. Boniface's perspective was shared by Bede a decade or so earlier. Bede regarded the period after the death of King Aldfrith – that is, beginning with the reign of Osred – as one in which the monastic life was abused by laymen.[108] It is difficult to ignore this combined perspective on Anglo-Saxon society in the early eighth century and its implication that it had entered 'a highly unstable phase'.[109] But Osred provides a useful example of a king who could be sharply criticized for character defects in some Northumbrian circles though remembered as a generous patron of an ecclesiastical community in others (see below, p. 147). Aethelbald similarly was well regarded at Crowland and by no means wholly unacceptable to Boniface; he performed good works, gave very many alms, prohibited theft, perjury and rapine, defended the widows and the poor and maintained a firm peace in his kingdom. For all these things, Boniface commended him.

Moreover, the king was indeed associated with Church reform. Boniface's concern about the state of the Church in England generally is revealed by his letter to Cuthbert, archbishop of Canterbury, which, it has been said, 'amounts to a far-reaching critique of the English Church'.[110] Boniface informed the archbishop about the holding of Frankish synods and sent him a copy of their decrees, particularly those of the council of 747,[111] urging him to reform the behaviour of bishops and condemning their adornment of dress and propensity for drunkenness. He pronounced against secular control of monasteries and the forced labour of monks on royal buildings and other works, 'a thing unheard of anywhere' except among the Angles.[112] The whole tone of the letter appears designed to urge

135

Cuthbert to hold a synod – as Boniface had done among the Franks – the implication being that he had not recently done so. Perhaps to some extent in response to this letter and certainly with the decrees of the Frankish synod of 747 in mind, Archbishop Cuthbert did hold a synod at *Clofesho* in 747, attended by all the bishops of the southern province of the Anglo-Saxon Church, in the presence of King Aethelbald. Among other matters it dealt with lay control of monasteries, excesses of dress among churchmen, and the immorality and drunkenness of Anglo-Saxon clergy, and ordered the holding of diocesan synods to implement the decrees of the council.[113] At the council of Gumley in Leicestershire two years later, possibly as a response to some of Boniface's criticisms, Aethelbald issued a grant of privileges to the churches in Mercia, conceding immunity from royal food-rents and from all works and burdens except the building of bridges and the defence of fortresses against enemies (*CS* 140, 178: S 92).[114] Aethelbald's association with these councils does not give the impression of a king so totally outside contemporary conventions as Boniface's letter to him seems to imply.

There is no evidence that *sceattas* circulated widely in the Mercian hinterland and some reason to suggest in the light of a multiplicity of distinctive *sceatta* coinages in eastern and southern England that Aethelbald, who may have minted in Canterbury, failed to impose his authority over the issue of coins by others, 'a critical commentary', perhaps 'on what Bede asserts, and on Aethelbald's own claims'.[115] It may be that from *c.* 714 on, however, Anglo-Frankish trade was prejudiced by a greater degree of political instability in Gaul.[116] At a time when only the Northumbrians, and then only for a time in the reign of Eadberht (737–58), minted coins of pure silver, southern England experienced a decline in the quality of its *sceattas*. From *c.* 730 progressive debasement of *sceattas* reduced their silver content quite dramatically and, if there was a decline in the silver available from *c.* 730 onwards, this could have been a factor in the aggressive policies of Aethelbald in southern England at this time.[117]

Notes

1 K. Harrison, *The Framework of Anglo-Saxon History to AD 900* (Cambridge, 1976), pp. 41, 83.
2 Cf., D. P. Kirby, 'Bede and Northumbrian chronology', *English Historical Review*, vol. 78 (1963), pp. 514–27 (p. 520).
3 *Florentii Wigorniensis monachi Chronicon ex Chronicis*, ed. B. Thorpe, 2 vols (London, 1848), Vol. I, pp. 32, 259.
4 *The Life of Bishop Wilfrid by Eddius Stephanus*, ed. and trans. B. Colgrave (Cambridge, 1927).
5 On the date 674, cf., C. Plummer, *Venerabilis Baedae Opera Historica*, 2 vols (Oxford, 1892, 1896), Vol. II, p. 215.
6 ibid., p. 107; D. N. Dumville, 'The Anglian collection of royal genealogies and regnal lists', *Anglo-Saxon England*, vol. 5 (1976), pp. 23–50 (pp. 31, 33, 37).
7 Harrison, *The Framework of Anglo-Saxon History*, p. 145; cf., K. P. Witney, *The Kingdom of Kent* (Chichester, 1982), pp. 146–7.

8 F. M. Stenton, 'Medeshamstede and its colonies', in D. M. Stenton (ed.), *Preparatory to Anglo-Saxon England* (Oxford, 1970), pp. 179–92 (pp. 181 ff.).

9 Cf., P. Wormald, 'Bede, the bretwaldas and the *Gens Anglorum*', in P. Wormald, D. Bullough and R. Collins (eds), *Ideal and Reality in Frankish and Anglo-Saxon Society* (Oxford, 1983), pp. 99–129 (p. 112) and H. Vollrath-Reichelt, *Königsgedanke und Königtum bei den Angelsachsen* (Cologne, 1971), p. 124.

10 J. Blair, 'Frithuwald's kingdom and the origins of Surrey', in S. Bassett (ed.), *The Origins of Anglo-Saxon Kingdoms* (Leicester, 1989), pp. 99–107.

11 Cf., S. C. Hawkes, H. R. E. Davidson and C. F. C. Hawkes, 'The Finglesham man', *Antiquity*, vol. 39 (1965), pp. 17–32 (p. 32, n. 62) and M. G. Welch, *Early Anglo-Saxon Sussex*, vol. i (BAR British series 112(i), 1983), p.260.

12 F. M. Stenton, *Anglo-Saxon England* (3rd edn, Oxford, 1971), pp. 294, 301 (cf., Stenton, *Preparatory to Anglo-Saxon England*, pp. 230, 232).

13 Cf., B. E. A. Yorke, 'The kingdom of the East Saxons', *Anglo-Saxon England*, vol. 14 (1985), pp. 1–36 (p.32).

14 D. W. Rollason, *The Mildrith Legend: A Study in Early Medieval Hagiography in England* (Leicester, 1982), p. 39, accepts Aethelred as uncle of the murdered sons of Eormenred (because their sister, Eafe, married Merewalh, supposedly the brother of Wulfhere and Aethelred – though this relationship is not certain and Merewalh, if anything, may have been their brother-in-law) and attributes to him in this campaign a desire for vengeance.

15 P. Wormald, *Bede and the Conversion of England: The Charter Evidence* (Jarrow Lecture, 1984), p. 25, regards this charter as among the 'broadly trustworthy' texts. R. R. Darlington associated *CS* 58: S 73 with it, and for his observations on these documents and on Cenfrith, see 'Anglo-Saxon Wiltshire', *A History of Wiltshire*, Vol. II, ed. R. B. Pugh and E. Crittall (The Victoria County History of England: London, 1955), pp. 3–4. Cf., also, however, A. Scharer, *Die angelsächsische Königsurkunde im 7. und 8. Jahrhundert* (Vienna, 1982) pp. 148 ff., and, more recently still, H. Edwards, *The Charters of the Early West Saxon Kingdom* (BAR British series 198, 1988), pp. 90–2.

16 Scharer, *Die angelsächsische Königsurkunde*, p. 93 n. 47, but see also Edwards, *The Charters of the Early West Saxon Kingdom*, pp. 93–4.

17 *Florentii Wigorniensis monachi Chronicon ex Chronicis*, Vol. I, p. 239, gives 679 for the creation of additional Mercian sees but in favour of 674–5 cf., P. Sims-Williams, 'St Wilfrid and two charters dated AD 676 and 680', *Journal of Ecclesiastical History*, vol. 39 (1988), pp. 163–83 (p. 168).

18 *Laws of the Earliest English Kings*, ed. and trans. F. L. Attenborough (Cambridge, 1922), pp. 18 ff.

19 D. P. Kirby, 'The Church in Saxon Sussex', in P. F. Brandon (ed.), *The South Saxons* (Chichester, 1978), pp. 160–73 (pp. 167 ff.). For some comments with a different emphasis, see H. Mayr-Harting, 'St Wilfrid in Sussex', *Studies in Sussex Church History* (1981), pp. 1–17 (p. 15).

20 On Caedwalla's grant of estates in Sussex to Wilfrid (*CS* 50: S 230), generally regarded as spurious, see now G. T. Dempsey, 'Legal terminology in Anglo-Saxon England: the *Trimoda Necessitas* charter', *Speculum*, vol. 57 (1982), pp. 843–9.

21 D. N. Dumville, 'The West Saxon Genealogical Regnal List: manuscripts and texts', *Anglia*, vol. 104 (1986), pp. 1–32 (p. 23): idem, 'The West Saxon Genealogical Regnal List and the chronology of early Wessex', *Peritia*, vol. 4 (1985), pp. 21–66 (p. 48).

22 *Aldhelmi Opera Omnia*, ed. R. Ehwald, *MGH Auctores Antiq.*, Vol. 15 (Berlin, 1919), p. 15; trans. M. Lapidge and M. Herren, *Aldhelm, the Poetic Works* (Woodbridge, 1985), p. 48.

23 Edwards, *The Charters of the Early West Saxon Kingdom*, pp. 11–15, 94–7.

24 ibid., pp. 292–9 (cf., p. 233).

25 Certain annals give 687 as the year of Eadric's death (*MGH Scriptores*, Vol. 4, ed. G. Pertz (Berlin, 1841), p. 2), noted by C. Plummer, *Venerabilis Baedae Opera Historica*, Vol. II, p. 264, but the same annals give 685 for the death of Hlothhere and 685 and 687 cannot both be correct.

26 B. E. A. Yorke, 'Joint kingship in Kent', *Archaeologia Cantiana*, vol. 99 (1983), pp. 1–19 (p. 7), and idem, *Kings and Kingdoms in Early Anglo-Saxon England* (London,

1990 [forthcoming]), Chap. 2.

27 R. Hodges, *The Anglo-Saxon Achievement: Archaeology and the Beginnings of English Society* (London, 1989), p. 76.

28 Stenton, 'Medeshamstede and its colonies', p. 189, but cf., Scharer, *Die angelsächsische Königsurkunde*, pp. 84 ff. See also Edwards, *The Charters of the Early West Saxon Kingdom*, pp. 300–5.

29 On this document, see Scharer, *Die angelsächsische Königsurkunde*, pp. 138 ff., and Edwards, *The Charters of the Early West Saxon Kingdom*, pp. 132–7.

30 Cf., the comments of M. Gibbs. 'The decrees of Agatho and the Gregorian plan for York', *Speculum*, vol. 48 (1973), pp. 213–46 (pp. 238–9), and N. Brooks, *The Early History of the Church of Canterbury* (Leicester, 1984), p. 77. See also H. Vollrath, *Die Synoden Englands bis 1066* (Paderborn, 1985), pp. 90, 108.

31 Wormald, *Bede and the Conversion of England*, pp. 9 ff.

32 *Aldhelmi Opera Omnia*, p. 15; Lapidge and Herren, *Aldhelm, the Poetic Works*, p. 48.

33 Dumville, 'The West Saxon Genealogical Regnal List: manuscripts and texts', p. 23.

34 On the date of this and other related Kentish charters of these years, see D. Whitelock, cited in Harrison, *The Framework of Anglo-Saxon History*, p. 142.

35 On Oswine, see G. Ward, 'King Oswine – a forgotten ruler of Kent', *Archaeologia Cantiana*, vol. 50 (1938), pp. 60–5, and more recently Witney, *The Kingdom of Kent*, pp. 155 ff.

36 Cf., on Swaefred, K. Bascombe, 'Two charters of King Suebred of Essex', in K. Neale (ed.), *An Essex Tribute: Essays Presented to F. G. Emmison* (London, 1987), pp. 85–96.

37 Yorke, 'The kingdom of the East Saxons', p. 21, n. 11.

38 H. P. R. Finberg, 'Offa of Essex', in H. P. R. Finberg (ed.), *Early Charters of the West Midlands* (Leicester, 1961), pp. 182–3.

39 Stenton, *Anglo-Saxon England*, p. 73; Witney, *The Kingdom of Kent*, p. 164.

40 Attenborough, *The Laws of the Earliest English Kings*, pp. 24 ff.

41 J. M. Wallace-Hadrill, *Early Germanic Kingship in England and on the Continent* (Oxford, 1971), p. 67.

42 See further on this, Brooks, *The Early History of the Church of Canterbury*, p. 78 (cf., Scharer, *Die angelsächsische Königsurkunde*, pp. 97 ff.). Wihtred's grant of privilege to the churches and monasteries of Kent at the council of Bapchild (*CS* 91, 92: S 22), however, is a spurious document, probably from the first half of the ninth century: Brooks, op. cit., pp. 191 ff.

43 Witney, *The Kingdom of Kent*, pp. 165–6.

44 Attenborough, *The Laws of the Earliest English Kings*, pp. 36 ff.

45 Stenton, *Anglo-Saxon England*, p. 72.

46 H. G. Richardson and G. O. Sayles, *Law and Legislation from Aethelberht to Magna Carta* (Edinburgh, 1966), p. 14.

47 P. Wormald, '*Lex Scripta* and *Verbum Regis*: legislation and Germanic kingship from Euric to Cnut', in P. H. Sawyer and I. N. Wood (eds), *Early Medieval Kingship*, (Leeds, 1977), pp. 105–38.

48 H. P. R. Finberg, 'Sherborne, Glastonbury and the Expansion of Wessex', in H. P. R. Finberg (ed.), *Lucerna* (London, 1964), pp. 95–115 (pp. 100–2).

49 *Councils and Ecclesiastical Documents Relating to Great Britain and Ireland*, ed. A. W. Haddan and W. Stubbs, 3 vols (Oxford, 1869–71), Vol. III, pp. 274–6 (*EHD*, Vol. I, no. 164); see P. Chaplais, 'The letter of Bishop Wealdhere of London to Archbishop Brihtwold of Canterbury: the earliest original "Letter Close" extant in the West', in M. B. Parkes and A. G. Watson (eds), *Medieval Scribes, Manuscripts and Librarians* (London, 1978), pp. 3–23 (reprinted Chaplais, *Essays in Medieval Diplomacy and Administration* (London, 1981)).

50 H. Edwards, 'Two documents from Aldhelm's Malmesbury', *Bulletin of the Institute of Historical Research* 59 (1986), pp. 1–19, and idem, *The Charters of the Early West Saxon Kingdom*, pp. 107–14.

51 W. Levison (ed.), *M.G.H. Scriptores rer. Germanicarum in usum scholarum* (Hanover, 1905) (trans. C. H. Talbot, *The Anglo-Saxon Missionaries in Germany* (London and New York, 1954)).

52 *Councils and Ecclesiastical Documents*, Vol. III, p. 275. Cf., Vollrath, *Die Synoden Englands*, p. 102.

53 D. M. Metcalf, 'Monetary expansion and recession: interpreting the distribution-patterns of seventh- and eighth-century coins', in J. Casey and R. Reece (eds), *Coins and the Archaeologist* (BAR 4, 1974), pp. 206–23 (pp. 208–10), (reprinted and revised, 2nd edn (London, 1988), pp. 230–53 (pp. 234–6)). See also P. Grierson and M. Blackburn, *Medieval European Coinage*, Vol. I: *The Early Middle Ages* (Cambridge, 1986), pp. 164 ff., and Hodges, *The Anglo-Saxon Achievement*, pp. 77–8.

54 J. Haslam, *Anglo-Saxon Towns in Southern England* (Southampton, 1984), p. 335. Cf., Hodges, *The Anglo-Saxon Achievement*, pp. 80 ff.

55 See the comments of B. Colgrave, *Felix's Life of St Guthlac*, ed. and trans. B. Colgrave (Cambridge, 1956), pp. 3, 178.

56 H. P. R. Finberg, 'Princes of the Hwicce', in his *The Early Charters of the West Midlands*. pp. 167–80 (pp. 172–4); see now also, P. Sims-Williams, 'Continental influence at Bath monastery in the seventh century', *Anglo-Saxon England*, vol. 4 (1975), pp. 1–10, and idem, 'St Wilfrid and two charters dated AD 676 and 680', pp. 165 ff.

57 *MGH Epistolae Selectae* I, ed. M. Tangl (Berlin, 1955), no. 13. (Selections of the letters of Boniface are translated in E. Emerton, *The Letters of Saint Boniface* (Columbia, 1940) and Talbot, *The Anglo-Saxon Missionaries in Germany*.)

58 Finberg, 'The early history of Gloucester Abbey', in his *Early Charters of the West Midlands*, pp. 153–66.

59 On these documents, see, however, Scharer, *Die angelsächsische Königsurkunde*, pp. 152 ff., 162, 170 ff.

60 B. E. A. Yorke, *Kings and Kingdoms in Early Anglo-Saxon England*, Chap. 6, examines Mercian management of neighbouring satellite provinces.

61 E. John, 'The social and economic problems of the early English Church', *Agricultural History Review*, vol. 18 (1970): Supplement; in J. Thirsk (ed.), *Land, Church and People*, pp. 39–63.

62 D. W. Rollason, 'Lists of saints' resting-places in Anglo-Saxon England', *Anglo-Saxon England*, vol. 7 (1978), pp. 61–93 (p. 89). N. K. Chadwick comments on Aethelred and Osthryth's association with Bardney in 'The conversion of Northumbria', in N. K. Chadwick (ed.), *Celt and Saxon: Studies in the Early British Border* (Cambridge, 1963), pp. 138–66 (pp. 143–5, 152–5).

63 *Florentii Wigorniensis monachi Chronicon ex Chronicis*, Vol. I, p. 265.

64 *Chronicon Abbatiae de Evesham*, ed. W. D. Macray (Rolls series: London, 1863), p. 73.

65 *Epistolae Selectae*, Vol. I, ed. M. Tangl, no. 10.

66 ibid., no. 73 (the phrasing of the translation is by Talbot, *The Anglo-Saxon Missionaries in Germany*, p. 125).

67 H. P. R. Finberg, 'St Mildburg's Testament', in his *Early Charters of the West Midlands*, pp. 197–216.

68 Dumville, 'The Anglian collection of royal genealogies', pp. 31, 33.

69 *Felix's Life of St Guthlac*, Colgrave, pp. 15–19.

70 *Hemingi Chartularium Ecclesiae Wigorniensis*, ed. T. Hearne, 2 vols (Oxford, 1723), Vol. II, p. 369; see Yorke, *Kings and Kingdoms in Early Anglo-Saxon England*, Chap. 6, who draws attention to the inclusion of a Ceolwald in this regnal list.

71 F. M. Stenton, 'The supremacy of the Mercian kings', in Stenton, *Preparatory to Anglo-Saxon England*, pp. 48–66 (p. 53).

72 Stenton, *Anglo-Saxon England*, p. 202.

73 Cf., now Scharer, *Die angelsächsische Königsurkunde*, pp. 169 ff.

74 Cf., ibid., pp. 174 ff.

75 According to Henry of Huntingdon, Ealdberht had been besieged in Taunton by Queen Aethelburh, escaping from there to Surrey: *Henrici Archidiaconi Huntendunensis Historia Anglorum*, ed. T. Arnold (Rolls series: London, 1879), p. 112.

76 Yorke, 'Joint kingship in Kent *c.* 560 to 785', p. 10.

77 *Epistolae Selectae*, Vol. I, ed. M. Tangl, no. 122.

78 Cf., Scharer, *Die angelsächsische Königsurkunde*, pp. 168 ff.

79 *Felix's Life of St Guthlac*, Colgrave, p. 19.

80 Cf., Vollrath-Reichelt, *Königsgedanke und Königtum*, p. 133.
81 Cf., Brooks, *The Early History of the Church of Canterbury*, p. 80.
82 *Symeonis Monachi Opera Omnia*, ed. T. Arnold, 2 vols (Rolls series: London, 1882, 1885), Vol. II, p. 32.
83 Yorke, 'The kingdom of the East Saxons', p. 23.
84 *Symeonis Monachi Opera Omnia*, Vol. II, p. 32.
85 This is the date given by the *Historia Regum* (*Symeonis Monachi Opera Omnia*, Vol. II, p. 32) as opposed to the 740 of the *Anglo-Saxon Chronicle* (or the 741 of A). Aethelheard is given a reign of fourteen years in the West Saxon Genealogical Regnal List and he may have reigned 726–40 but the *Historia Regum* could be embodying contemporary northern annals (cf., Dumville, 'The West Saxon Genealogical Regnal List and the chronology of early Wessex', pp. 42–3). Moreover, the West Saxon Genealogical Regnal List gives Aethelheard's successor, Cuthred, a reign of sixteen years, his successor, Sigeberht, a reign of one year, and Sigeberht's successor, Cynewulf, a reign of thirty-one years, but the *Chronicle*, with 740–56 for Cuthred, 756–7 for Sigeberht and 757 (*s.a.* 755) to 786 (*s.a.* 784) for Cynewulf, only allows Cynewulf a reign of twenty-nine years (cf., Dumville, art. cit., pp. 43, 48). If Aethelheard died in 739, however, he would have died in his fourteenth year. The *Historia Regum* also places Cuthred's death in 755 not 756 (*Symeonis Monachi Opera Omnia*, Vol. II, p. 40), when he would have reigned sixteen years if he succeeded in 739, and this would mean that Sigeberht reigned 755–6 not 756–7 and Cynewulf 756–86, so that he could have died in his thirty-first year. This may be as close to chronological precision as we can get.
86 Stenton, *Anglo-Saxon England*, p. 204.
87 Edwards, *The Charters of the Early West Saxon Kingdom*, pp. 41–5.
88 ibid., pp. 272–3.
89 ibid., pp. 124–6. See also the comments of Vollrath-Reichelt, *Königsgedanke und Königtum*, pp. 140 ff.
90 *Bede's Ecclesiastical History of the English People*, ed. and trans. B. Colgrave and R. A. B. Mynors (Oxford, 1969), pp. 572–5.
91 Cf., Edwards, *The Charters of the Early West Saxon Kingdom*, pp. 178–9.
92 See above, n. 85.
93 *Bede's Ecclesiastical History of the English People*, Colgrave and Mynors, pp. 574–5.
94 See above, n. 85.
95 Edwards, *The Charters of the Early West Saxon Kingdom*, p.126.
96 See above, n. 85.
97 H. Vollrath-Reichelt, *Königsgedanke und Königtum*, taking a minimal view of the significance of *CS* 181: S 96, regards Cynewulf and Aethelbald as equals (p. 141), and considers it by no means certain that Aethelbald sustained his southern hegemony until the end of his reign (p. 151). Cf., Edwards, *The Charters of the Early West Saxon Kingdom*, p. 126.
98 *Symeonis Monachi Opera Omnia*, Vol. II, p. 39.
99 M. R. James, 'Two Lives of St Ethelbert, king and martyr', *English Historical Review*, vol. 32 (1917), pp. 214–44 (p. 241). Yorke, *Kings and Kingdoms in Early Anglo-Saxon England*, Chap. 4, has used this evidence to date the beginning of Aethelberht's reign.
100 *Florentii Wigorniensis monachi Chronicon ex Chronicis*, Vol. I, p. 57, records under the year 758 that Swithred, king of the East Saxons, Osmund, king of the South Saxons, and Beorn (*recte* Beonna), king of the East Angles, reigned at that time, but this piece of dating evidence should not be too narrowly treated; Osmund was still alive *c.* 770 (see below, p. 167), and *c.* 758 could signal Beonna's accession.
101 Grierson and Blackburn, *Medieval European Coinage*, Vol. I, pp. 277–8.
102 *Bede's Ecclesiastical History of the English People*, Colgrave and Mynors, pp. 574–5.
103 On Aethelbald's tomb, see M. Biddle, 'Archaeology, architecture and the cult of saints in Anglo-Saxon England', in L. A. S. Butler and R. K. Morris (eds), *The Anglo-Saxon Church* (CBA Research Report, no. 60, 1986), pp. 1–31 (p. 22).
104 *Epistolae Selectae*, Vol. I, ed. M. Tangl, no. 115.
105 ibid., no. 73 (*EHD*, Vol. I, no. 177).

106 ibid., no. 74 (*EHD*, Vol. I, no. 178).
107 ibid., no. 75 (*EHD*, Vol. I, no. 179).
108 Plummer, *Venerabilis Baedae Opera Historica*, Vol. I, p. 416.
109 Hodges, *The Anglo-Saxon Achievement*, p. 110.
110 Brooks, *The Early History of the Church of Canterbury*, p. 84. Vollrath, *Die Synoden Englands*, pp. 151 ff., however, stresses rather Boniface's high regard for the Anglo-Saxon Church and minimizes his concern to reform it.
111 W. Levison, *England and the Continent in the Eighth Century* (Oxford, 1946), p. 86.
112 *Epistolae Selectae*, Vol. I, ed. M. Tangl, no. 78.
113 *Councils and Ecclesiastical Documents*, Vol. III, pp. 363–71.
114 N. Brooks, 'The development of military obligations in eighth- and ninth-century England', in P. Clemoes and K. Hughes (eds), *England Before the Conquest* (Cambridge, 1971), pp. 69–84.
115 D. M. Metcalf, 'Monetary circulation in southern England in the first half of the eighth century', in D. Hill and D. M. Metcalf (eds), *Sceattas in England and on the Continent* (BAR British series 128, 1984), pp. 27–69 (p. 46).
116 Hodges, *The Anglo-Saxon Achievement*, p. 90.
117 D. M. Metcalf, 'Monetary affairs in Mercia in the time of Aethelbald', in A. Dornier (ed.), *Mercian Studies* (Leicester, 1977), pp. 87–106, and D. M. Metcalf, 'Monetary expansion and recession: interpreting the distribution-patterns of seventh- and eighth-century coins', in T. Casey and R. Reece (eds), *Coins and the Archaeologist* (2nd edn), p. 239. Cf., Grierson and Blackburn, *Medieval European Coinage*, Vol. I, pp. 184 ff. See also Hodges, *The Anglo-Saxon Achievement*, p. 91.

7 Northumbria in the eighth century

King Ecgfrith was advised by Cuthbert, bishop of Lindisfarne, and presumably informed circles among the northern Angles not to invade Pictland in 685 (*HE* IV, 26), and Cuthbert's personal familiarity with the *Niduari* Picts in Fib (Fife) affords a glimpse of the probably extensive contacts between northern Anglian circles and Pictish communities immediately north of the Forth.[1] Ecgfrith remained undeterred, however, and his army had traversed Strathmore when it turned aside to experience total defeat on 20 May at *Nechtanesmere*, otherwise known as Dún Nechtain (*AU s.a.* 684: *AT* p. 209) and as the Lake of the Heron (*HB* ch. 57), now Dunnichen in Forfarshire.

F. T. Wainwright commented that 'it is easy to over-estimate the political significance of *Nechtanesmere*'.[2] It is certainly true that one strand at least in a Northumbrian view of the past seems to have thought of *Nechtanesmere* as destroying the position of military dominance originally achieved by Eadwine in the first half of the seventh century (*HE* II, 5), whereas Eadwine's ascendancy over the Britons in Wales had disappeared by the mid-630s and an overlordship of the southern English kingdoms, restored only temporarily in the late 650s, was lost long before 685 (see above, p. 85). Nevertheless, the defeat of Ecgfrith was obviously a serious military setback for the northern Angles. Bishop Trumwine fled from his bishopric at Abercorn, which was never restored (*HE* IV, 26). The Dalriadic Scots and the Britons, probably of Strathclyde, whom Ecgfrith had almost certainly driven into alliance with the Picts in 685 through his claims to supremacy over them (see above, p. 100), regained their independence, and the Picts threw off the overlordship of the northern Anglian king and recaptured territory formerly held by the Angles (*HE* IV, 26). The Northumbrians never retrieved their pre-685 military position in North Britain (cf., *HB* ch. 57). In 698 the *dux regius* Berhtred, son of Ecgfrith's sub-king, Beornhaeth, a Northumbrian ealdorman and probably the Berht who had led Ecgfrith's raiding party to Ireland (*HE* IV, 26), was killed by the Picts (*HE* V, 24; *AU s.a.* 697: *AT* p. 26). Ecgfrith's brother and successor, Aldfrith (see Appendix, Fig. 6.2), appears to have accepted that he could restore his kingdom only within narrower bounds (*HE* IV, 26). Given all this, however, the successors of Ecgfrith preserved and maintained a secure realm within what were still wide-ranging frontiers. Northumbria remained rich, politically stable and intellectually gifted enough under

Aldfrith and his immediate successors to enable that creative synthesis of Celtic, Anglo-Saxon and Mediterranean art – which is so striking a feature of post-conversion Northumbrian civilization – to achieve its maximum expression in the renaissance of the late seventh and first half of the eighth centuries.[3] Moreover, so far as can be seen a Northumbrian hegemony continued to prevail between the Humber and the Forth and across to the west, above and below the Solway from the Mersey to the borders of Strathclyde,[4] at least until the mid-eighth century. The somewhat stormy dynastic history of Northumbria should not be allowed to obscure this important aspect of the history of the northern Angles.

Aldfrith, known to the Irish as Fland (*AU s.a.* 703: *AT* p. 219: *CA* p. 148), was an illegitimate son of King Oswiu[5] by Fín, daughter, according to genealogical tradition, of the northern Uí Néill king in Ireland, Colmán Rímid, who died *c.* 604.[6] If this were correct, Aldfrith would probably have been born *c.* 630, when Oswiu would have been about 18 years of age, and Fín already at least 26, or not long after. In this case, Aldfrith would have been in his early fifties when he became king, yet his marriage to Cuthburh, sister of Ine, king of the West Saxons (*ASC* A, *s.a* 718) (unlikely to have occurred earlier), and his subsequent fathering of Osred, born *c.* 696, and of other sons, Osric (possibly) and Offa (see Appendix, Fig. 6.2), may suggest a somewhat younger man. If Fín were the granddaughter rather than the daughter of Colmán Rímid, however, these dates and ages would lose their element of incompatibility. She might then have been younger than Oswiu and her liaison with him could have occurred *c.* 650. Aldfrith would then have been a man in his early thirties at his accession in 685, which seems more credible.[7] If this reconstruction is sound, Oswiu's encounter with Fín occurred at about the time that he may have been seeking Irish support against the forces of Penda.

Aldfrith appears to have been very much on the periphery of Northumbrian dynastic life before his accession. On the eve of Ecgfrith's campaigns against the Picts in 685 he was living on Iona.[8] Bede says that he was in exile for the purposes of study[9] and he subsequently described him as a most learned man (*HE* V, 12). For the author of the *Life of Wilfrid*[10] (chs 44, 45) and for the Irish annalist (*AU s.a.* 703: *CA* p. 148) he was *sapiens*, 'wise'.[11] According to Alcuin he was devoted to the pursuit of learning from his earliest years, a wise man who was both king and teacher.[12] In Bede's opinion, Aldfrith was most learned in the Scriptures (*HE* IV, 26). After he became king, Aldhelm wrote a treatise on metre for him in the form of a letter to Arcircius (Aldfrith)[13] and Adomnán, abbot of Iona, gave him a copy of his work on *The Holy Places* (*HE* V, 15). Abbess Aelfflaed's question to Cuthbert, bishop of Lindisfarne, as to who would succeed the childless Ecgfrith[14] need not imply that she had otherwise forgotten about Aldfrith's existence, but rather that she was testing Cuthbert to ascertain that his loyalties lay in the right place. Cuthbert's oblique reference to Aldfrith in his reply seems to have satisfied her. Here was a family determined if at all possible to keep royal power in its own hands. Its prolonged domination is really quite amazing, and the way it held on to power at this time is an impressive lesson in dynastic skill. On Oswiu's death, so far as we know, the succession passed peacefully to his son, Ecgfrith, but concern for what would happen on the death of Ecgfrith is likely to have been acute. Though the prestige of Aldfrith's descent from the Uí Néill will not have been negligible, he was born out of wedlock and there must have been many legitimate sons of other Northumbrian lords who claimed descent from Ida.[15] The prestige of Oswiu's family, or else its capacity for intimidation, must have been very considerable for Aldfrith to return and rule in what seems to have been domestic peace. Bringing Aldfrith back was a master-stroke for those who wished to perpetuate the monopoly of royal power in the hands of Oswiu's family. It seems likely that they received support from parties within the Uí Néill territory in Ireland, even from among the Dalriadic Scots and perhaps the Picts, anxious to have the bellicose Ecgfrith replaced by a more pacific figure.[16]

Aldfrith certainly possessed some of the qualities of a diplomat. Ecgfrith had sent a raiding party to Meath in 684 despite the exhortation not to of the Northumbrian priest, Ecgberht, who was residing among the Irish (*HE* IV, 26). In 687 and again in 688 Adomnán, abbot of Iona, visited Aldfrith and secured the release of those whom the Northumbrians had seized during this expedition and kept in captivity (*AU s.a.* 686: *AT* pp. 210, 211: *CA* p. 134).[17]

At Theodore's urging in 686, Aldfrith also made an attempt to resolve the outstanding quarrel with Wilfrid and Theodore certainly seems to have prevailed on the king to restore Wilfrid first of all to Hexham (during a vacancy there, Eata having died, though in 687 John of Beverley, a monk of Whitby, was appointed bishop); then to York (from which see Bosa, who was still alive in 704 (*Vita Wilfridi*, ch. 54), was removed) and Ripon (from where Eadhaed was also removed) (*Vita Wilfridi*, ch. 44). When Cuthbert died (also in 687) Wilfrid administered Lindisfarne as well for a year until the appointment of Bishop Eadberht in 688 (*HE* IV, 29). The final position, therefore, was that Wilfrid had been restored to York and had regained control of Ripon. This represented a quite remarkable compromise which required the co-operation of Aethelred, king of the Mercians, who restored Wilfrid's Mercian possessions, and Aelfflaed, abbess of Whitby, whose influence with King Aldfrith is likely to have been considerable (*Vita Wilfridi*, ch. 43), but it may have been a manifestation of the insecurity of Aldfrith in the years immediately following his accession. By 692 the king felt politically strong enough to countenance the seizure of some of the estates of the church of Ripon and project its restoration as a bishopric.[18] Refusing to accept dismemberment of his remaining territory, Wilfrid took himself into Mercia where he acted for King Aethelred as bishop of the

Middle Angles (*HE*, IV, 23; *Vita Wilfridi*, ch. 45). A bishopric was not re-created at Ripon (perhaps because a papal privilege was now recognized as protecting the monastery there),[19] but Wilfrid was never restored to York during Aldfrith's reign. Rather, Bosa again presided in his place. A further attempt at a settlement was made at the council of Austerfield in Northumbria *c.* 702–3, Archbishop Beorhtwald presiding, but the terms are said to have been that Wilfrid relinquish his episcopal office and retire to his monastery at Ripon and they were unacceptable (*Vita Wilfridi*, chs 46–7). Wilfrid withdrew into Mercia and from there resumed his appeal in person at Rome where he appears now to have expressed a readiness to relinquish his bishopric provided he could retain Ripon and Hexham (*Vita Wilfridi*, ch. 51).[20]

The quarrel between Aldfrith and Wilfrid cannot have been without its political dimension. It is not known who was the mother of Osred, Aldfrith's son and successor, nor when Aldfrith's queen, Cuthburh, parted from him to found a nunnery at Wimborne (*ASC* A, *s.a.* 718). Aldfrith may not have had an obvious heir across the late 680s and early 690s, for Osred was only about 8 years old on his father's death and not born, therefore, until *c.* 696. It must always have been a real hope on Wilfrid's part that a king of Northumbria from another branch of the royal family or from a noble line claiming royal descent would be more favourably disposed towards him than the descendants of Oswiu. When Aldfrith died, a certain Eadwulf, unfortunately of unknown descent, became king. Wilfrid was at Ripon with Eadwulf's son, probably the Earnwine, son of Eadwulf, who was killed in 740.[21] Osred with his supporters, led by a nobleman, Berhtfrith (possibly a son of the Berhtred who perished fighting the Picts in 698), was at Bamburgh. It is made quite clear in the *Life of Wilfrid* that Wilfrid was intending to give his support to Eadwulf (*Vita Wilfridi*, ch. 59).

The Northumbrian regnal list gives Aldfrith a reign of twenty years[22] and Bede correspondingly assigned him a reign from 685 to 705 (*HE* IV, 26; V, 18), but Bede also knew, perhaps from knowledge of a more precise regnal figure, that Aldfrith really reigned nineteen years (*HE* V, 1) and died before the end of his twentieth regnal year (*HE* V, 18). Aldfrith, therefore, almost certainly died in 704. His death occurred on 14 December (*ASC* D, *s.a* 705). He succeeded Ecgfrith some time after 20 May 685. If he died on 14 December 705 he would have reigned a full twenty years and probably several months as well. Only if he succeeded after 14 December 685 would he not have completed twenty years by 14 December 705. Consequently, it has been suggested that Aldfrith did not succeed until after 14 December 685.[23] He was certainly living on Iona on the eve of Ecgfrith's final campaign, and there may well have been a delay of a month or so before he became king, but to suppose a delay of seven months or more seems unwarranted. At such a critical time Aldfrith would surely have returned to Northumbria with all speed. The Irish annals also place Aldfrith's death in 704 (*AU s.a.* 703: *AT* p. 219: *CA* p. 148).[24] However, since Osred's reign began in 705, no further dislocation of Northumbrian chronology occurs at this point.

Aldfrith appears to have governed well. The coins which bear his name are the first Northumbrian silver coins.[25] His failing health, however, by late 704 presented a serious crisis for his immediate family, for his son Osred was very young and this time there was certainly a rival for the throne in the person of Eadwulf. According to the testimony of Abbess Aelfflaed, it was Aldfrith's dying wish that his successor should come to terms with Wilfrid (*Vita Wilfridi*, ch. 59). It may be that Wilfrid's personal support could still be of assistance to an aspiring aetheling, but it is interesting that Eadwulf spurned Wilfrid's overtures. Wilfrid's failure to secure a sympathetic hearing suggests that it was not only Oswiu's family which found him unpalatable. The nobleman Berhtfrith subsequently attributed Osred's victory over his enemies at Bamburgh to the decision of Osred's party to do justice by Wilfrid (*Vita Wilfridi*, ch. 60) and the indications are that Wilfrid came to an understanding with Osred's party following his rejection by Eadwulf. Osred even became Wilfrid's adopted son (*Vita Wilfridi*, ch. 59). Once secure in power, however, the new regime, with which Abbess Aelfflaed was closely associated, did not prove particularly generous. In Osred's first year a council was held on the banks of the River Nidd, again presided over by Archbishop Beorhtwald, at which both Aelfflaed and Berhtfrith spoke in Wilfrid's favour; Wilfrid was not restored to York, of which John of Beverley, bishop of Hexham, became bishop, but he was allowed to retain his former possessions of Ripon and Hexham as bishop of Hexham (*HE* V, 19: *Vita Wilfridi*, ch. 60).[26] He lived quietly during his remaining years, dying on a visit to his Mercian possessions, probably in 710.[27]

The *Life of Wilfrid* offers two versions of Aldfrith's dying injunction concerning Wilfrid which may reflect two stages in its production. In the first, which the author derived from Abbess Aelfflaed, herself an eye-witness, who died in 713 (*HE* III, 24; *AU s.a.* 712: *AT* p. 222), Aldfrith is said to have urged his successor, whoever he might be, to come to terms with Wilfrid (*Vita Wilfridi*, ch. 59), and in the second, seemingly later version, to have urged his son and heir, Osred, to do so (*Vita Wilfridi*, ch. 60). Aelfflaed's testimony suggests that Aldfrith had not certainly engineered his son's succession and that Osred's triumph over Eadwulf was the work of a powerful faction at court devoted to the preservation of royal power in the hands of the descendants of Oswiu. Its influence must have been very considerable for the boy to have been so successfully supported for the kingship against an adult rival. As a consequence of its success, the Northumbrian establishment which had been responsible for the débâcle of *Nechtanesmere* and the limited recovery under Aldfrith

146

perpetuated itself in power a little longer and sporadic warfare with the Picts was resumed. Berhtfrith *praefectus*, almost certainly the Berhtfrith who fought on Osred's side at Bamburgh and who later spoke in favour of a settlement with Wilfrid at the council on the Nidd (*Vita Wilfridi*, ch. 60), perhaps also a kinsman of Berhtred, son of Beornhaeth, was involved in a conflict in 711 in what had been *Manau Gododdin* between the Rivers Avon and Carron when the Picts were defeated (*HE* V, 24; *ASC* D, *s.a.* 710; *AU s.a.* 710: *AT* p. 222). Continuing Pictish–Northumbrian military confrontation was a part of the background, therefore, of Osred's reign. Osred was slain in 716 'to the south of the border' (*ASC* D, *s.a.* 716), which may refer to a boundary with the Picts.

The contrasting images which survive of Osred are probably a reflection of the increasing divisions within the Northumbrian kingdom at this time. Bede welcomed him as a new Josiah, the king of Judah in whose reign a religious reform movement purified the Temple worship,[28] but came to lament the decline, as he saw it, of ecclesiastical standards after the death of Aldfrith,[29] sentiments echoed later by Boniface. At Beverley, where John of Beverley was bishop of York throughout the reign, Osred was remembered for his benefactions;[30] but the picture given in Aethelwulf's *De Abbatibus*, written in the early ninth century, is of an uncontrollable youth who slew many of his nobles and drove others to seek refuge in monastic life.[31] The explanation for such divergent viewpoints may lie not in Osred's reign as a particularly inauspicious period so much as in the dynastic rivalries of this time, accompanied by a failure to sustain Aldfrith's silver coinage under Osred or his immediate successors. The slaying of Osred in 716 at the age of 19 or 20 was certainly an event of some significance for it broke the monopoly of royal power which the descendants of Aethelfrith had maintained since the accession of Oswald. The accession of Coenred (716–18) (*HE* V, 22), son of Cuthwine, son of Leodwald, a representative of a hitherto obscure line of Bernician aristocrats who appears in the Anglian genealogies as a descendant of Ida,[32] set a new pattern. Osric, king of Northumbria (718–29) (*HE* V, 23), no details of whose reign are known, could have been a son of Ealhfrith or of Aldfrith,[33] and either way his accession will have represented a restoration of Oswiu's family to royal power (even if, in the former case, of a branch which had been in political eclipse for half a century), but his successor Ceolwulf (729–37) was a brother of Coenred (*HE* V, 23) and Ceolwulf's successor, Eadberht (737–58), son of Eata, son of Leodwald, was Ceolwulf's first cousin.[34] A substantial shift of power had occurred within Northumbrian royal circles and families formerly excluded from power now held the kingship (see Appendix, Fig. 9).

Though Ceolwulf abdicated in 737, he lived until 764,[35] and so was probably only in his early twenties at the most when he succeeded Osric.[36] It is unfortunate that knowledge of this important phase in Northumbrian dynastic history is so slight but Bede says that Osric nominated Ceolwulf as his successor (*HE* V, 23), and Bede appears to have welcomed his accession, sending him a draft version of the *Ecclesiastical History* for his comments and criticism and dedicating the finished work to him (*HE* Preface). Bede perceived in Ceolwulf a love of religion and recommended him to Ecgberht, bishop of York, in 734 as a willing helper in the work of ecclesiastical reform and organization.[37] Certainly, there were significant developments at this time. It was in Ceolwulf's reign that the church of York finally acquired archiepiscopal status in 735.[38] That this was a matter of interest and concern in Northumbria in the early 730s is clear from Bede's letter to Ecgberht in 734 in which Bede expounded at length on the necessity for more bishops and a proper organization of the Northumbrian Church under an archbishop at York.[39] The creation of a northern province ended Canterbury's sole direction of the Anglo-Saxon Church, which had characterized the archiepiscopates of Theodore and Beorhtwald, and an important stage in the development of the Church in England was reached with the establishment of the Northumbrian kingdom as an independent ecclesiastical community within the Catholic order of western Europe.

Relations with the Picts across these years changed dramatically. No later than early 716 Nechtan, son of Derilei, king of the Picts, approached Ceolfrith, abbot of the monastery of Wearmouth and Jarrow, for guidance on Dionysian Easter tables and the Roman dating of Easter (*HE* V, 21) – probably at the time that the Northumbrian priest, Ecgberht, was persuading the church on Iona to adopt the same (*HE* III, 4; V, 22, 24) – and in 717 expelled the Columban communities from Pictland into Dál Riata (*AU* s.a. 715, 716: *AT* p. 225).[40] These developments almost certainly signalled the inauguration of a more peaceful period in Pictish–Northumbrian relations with the accession of Coenred. The seal on this *rapprochement* was set with a treaty of peace with the Picts to which Bede refers in the penultimate chapter of the *Ecclesiastical History* as a significant aspect of the situation in 731 (*HE* V, 23). This treaty was probably made either before 724 or after 729, for during the intervening years Pictland was torn by the dynastic in-fighting among rival princes which preceded the ascendancy of the powerful Pictish king, Óengus, son of Forgus. Bede's reference to it in the context of the situation in 731 could suggest, on balance, that it was concluded when Ceolwulf became king or very soon after.

There would seem to have been, therefore, some important and substantial developments within Northumbria during Ceolwulf's reign. At the close of the *Ecclesiastical History* Bede wrote that such serious commotions had characterized the beginning and course of the reign that it was impossible to know what to say about them or anticipate their eventual outcome (*HE* V, 23). These words were probably written after the capture

and tonsuring of the king in 731 by unnamed opponents who kept him
for a while in a monastic centre, somewhere presumably in Northumbria.
The same year, Wilfrid's former companion, Acca, bishop of Hexham, was
expelled.[41] It is not known whether Acca's expulsion was connected with
the temporary deposition of Ceolwulf or with his subsequent restoration
in the same year, or whether it was a totally unrelated crisis. It was
undoubtedly serious. Though Acca lived until 740, he was never restored
to Hexham and in 734 Ecgberht, bishop of York, consecrated Frithuberht
to the still vacant see.[42] Acca's continuing exile from his see would suggest
that he did not enjoy the favour of Ecgberht and that Ceolwulf was either
too ineffective to arrange his return or hostile to him. The probability must
be that Ceolwulf and Ecgberht were in accord over the future of the diocese
of Hexham and that both approved of Acca's continued exclusion. What
we do not know is who came to power in Northumbria during Ceolwulf's
temporary deposition nor whether there was any connection between the
controversies surrounding Wilfrid and those now involving Acca.

In 737 Ceolwulf abdicated and was tonsured, apparently this time at his
own request, to become a monk on Lindisfarne.[43] His successor was his
cousin, Eadberht, the brother of Archbishop Ecgberht, but it is not possible
to say whether his powerful relatives brought pressure to bear on him to
resign. Ceolwulf may genuinely have wished to renounce the world. He
granted several estates to the monastery of Lindisfarne when he entered it
and was subsequently venerated as a saint, his relics being removed in the
ninth century to Norham with those of St Cuthbert[44] – and eventually to
Durham.

Eadberht was Ceolwulf's cousin, according to the Anglian genealogies
which give his alleged descent from Ida (see Appendix, Fig. 9).[45] The
indications are that he only began to reign in 738, for an eclipse of the sun,
followed by a lunar eclipse, which occurred in January 753, is described
in the eighth-century Northumbrian annals as happening in his fifteenth
year,[46] whereas Eadberht's fifteenth year if he succeeded in 737 would have
been 751–2. Moreover, an attack by Eàdberht, in alliance with Óengus, son
of Forgus, king of the Picts, on Dumbarton is placed in 756 in Eadberht's
eighteenth year,[47] whereas his eighteenth year, again if he succeeded in 737,
would have been 754–5. What is most probable is that Ceolwulf resigned
the kingship at the very end of 737 and that Eadberht's accession occurred
in early 738. Eadberht's son and successor, Oswulf, perished on 24 July
758 but his successor, Aethelwald Moll, did not begin to reign until 5
August.[48] Despite the survival of eighth-century Northumbrian annals,
without Bede's informative *Ecclesiastical History* and in the absence also
of Northumbrian charters, only the most skeletal account of post-Bedan
Northumbrian history can be reconstructed. Even so, it is clear that
Eadberht, in contrast to Ceolwulf, was a warrior-king who reversed the
quiescent policies of his immediate predecessors and extended the bounds

of his kingdom,[49] annexing the plain of Kyle in Ayrshire in 750 together with other territories.[50] His military expeditions were sometimes ill-fated. While he was attacking the Picts in 740, Aethelbald, king of the Mercians, devastated part of Northumbria.[51] In 756, after successfully campaigning against the Britons of Strathclyde and besieging Dumbarton at the time of the alliance with Óengus, son of Forgus, king of the Picts, almost the whole of Eadberht's army perished at Newburgh on the Tyne, perhaps at the hands of the Britons.[52] Some recently acquired territory may have been lost at this time or soon after. Despite these reverses, however, a revival of seventh-century northern imperial ambition had evidently occurred among the Northumbrians at the court of Eadberht, and though the dominance of Óengus, son of Forgus, in Pictland probably impeded its fulfilment, the indications are that Eadberht was bringing new prosperity to his kingdom. This can be seen in the revival (at an unknown date)[53] of a substantial regal silver coinage in Northumbria together with an archiepiscopal coinage combining Eadberht's name with that of his brother, Archbishop Ecgberht, which has been described as 'ahead of its age' in its fineness.[54]

Dynastic tension, however, had not abated. The killing of Earnwine, son of Eadwulf, in 740 may have been a prolongation of older rivalries which sparked off a new cycle of vendetta. In 750 Eadberht imprisoned Cynewulf, bishop of Lindisfarne, at Bamburgh, and besieged Offa, son of Aldfrith, in the church of Lindisfarne until, almost dead with hunger, he was dragged from sanctuary.[55] This episode reveals a deep and continuing rift between the descendants of Oswiu and the kings of Leodwald's line. There can be no doubt that such hostilities were having important consequences; they created opportunities for new dynastic families to emerge.

Eadberht abdicated of his own accord in 758, handing the kingdom over to his son, Oswulf, and becoming a cleric at York (where he died in 768),[56] but Oswulf was killed within the year by his own household in 759 near the unidentified settlement of *Methel Wongtun*[57] and replaced by Aethelwald Moll, who is likely to have been associated with those who were responsible for Oswulf's murder; nor did Eadberht's descendants recover royal power for twenty years. Oswulf's overthrow seems to have been the consequence of challenge to the monopoly of royal power by the descendants of Leodwald as dynamic new forces entered the arena of Northumbrian dynastic politics. Aethelwald's ancestry is unrecorded. His power-centre appears to have been located in Deira. He is probably to be identified with the 'patrician' (the term signifies an individual of very high standing indeed) called Moll to whom King Eadberht and Archbishop Ecgberht gave the monasteries of Stonegrave and Coxwold in Yorkshire, seized by them from Moll's brother, Abbot Forthred, for which action Pope Paul I reproved them.[58] In 762 he married a certain Aethelthryth at Catterick.[59] It may be that Aethelwald's genealogy does not survive because his family did not claim descent from Ida and it is possible that he was descended from

Oswine of Deira. If he was of Deiran royal descent, he ended more than a century of Bernician domination. Alternatively, he may have represented a powerful aristocratic family descended from neither the Deiran nor the Bernician royal family and which was aspiring to royal power for the first time, though the likelihood is that some such affinity was at least claimed. The high standard of Eadberht's coinage declined before his reign ended,[60] but these years immediately following Eadberht's abdication were not so disruptive of Northumbrian political life that Aethelwald was unable to mint.[61] Nevertheless, he faced rebellion, possibly a challenge from a rival aspirant to the throne, in 761 when, after a three-day conflict, he defeated and slew a certain Oswine, who is otherwise unknown, at Eildon on 9 August;[62] and in 765 the annals record that he lost the kingdom of the Northumbrians at *Pincanheale* on 30 October.[63] *Pincanheale* was the site of two Northumbrian church councils in 787 and 796,[64] and it may be that Aethelwald was overthrown at a gathering there of his magnates and leading churchmen. According to the Irish annals he was tonsured (*AT* p. 262: *CA* p. 137).

It was not, however, a descendant of Leodwald who replaced him. Instead royal power passed now to Alhred, a representative, according to the Anglian genealogies, of a quite separate line of descent from Ida[65] – though the way one annalist observes that Alhred was said by some to be of the lineage of Ida[66] implies that he was regarded by others as an intruder into the kingship (see Appendix, Fig. 9). The claim to descent from Ida, nevertheless, suggests that it was a Bernician family which intervened at this point. Alhred's power-base may have been in the lower Tyne, for the body of his son, Osred, was carried to Tynemouth to be buried in the monastery there.[67]

In 768 Alhred married Osgifu, daughter of King Oswulf (758–9),[68] presumably an attempt to strengthen the dynastic aspirations of both families by a judicious alliance, and the indications are that he made an effort to behave in a way appropriate to his new position. He minted coins[69] and his patronage of continental missionary activity is a noticeable feature of his reign. Aluberht was consecrated bishop of the Old Saxons at York in 767,[70] and Alhred presided over the council which sent Willehad to the Frisian mission field *c.* 770.[71] He sought the friendship of Charles, king of the Franks (Charlemagne). In a letter to Lul, archbishop of Mainz in 773, Alhred and Osgifu expressed the hope that Lul would help the Northumbrian envoys in Gaul to establish peace and friendship between the Northumbrian and Frankish courts. But the letter also refers to disturbances in the Northumbrian Church and among the Northumbrian people.[72] The Frisian, Liudger, later bishop of Münster, was studying at York under Alcuin when civil disturbances at York, involving Frisians and presaging perhaps the eventual overthrow of Alhred, obliged Alcuin to send him back to Frisia.[73] This evidence sheds valuable light, therefore, not only on the first recorded Northumbrian royal overtures to the Frankish court but also on the disturbed state of the kingdom on the eve of Alhred's expulsion in 774 when he was driven from York at Easter (*ASC* D, *s.a.* 774) into exile among the Picts.[74] Alhred's eclipse seems to have been total. He is said to have been deprived of the royal household and nobles with the counsel and consent of all his people, and to have fled from Bamburgh with only a few companions, which would suggest an almost outright rejection. The reference in the letter to Lul to disturbances in the Church and the fact that Alhred was dethroned in York may hold the key to part of the explanation – that Alhred did not perhaps enjoy the support of Aethelberht, archbishop of York, who had replaced his kinsman Ecgberht in 767.[75] A second factor must certainly have been the challenge to Alhred from Aethelred, son of Aethelwald Moll, who was crowned in Alhred's place 'with great honour'.[76] Alhred was clearly extremely vulnerable in Deira to a Deiran rival and Aethelred's acquisition of the kingship at this point indicates the residual power of his family, notwithstanding his father's deposition. If Aethelwald and Aethelred do represent a revival of Deiran royalty, it may be no coincidence that Archbishop Aethelberht (though at an unspecified date) constructed a new great altar in the minster at York on the spot where Eadwine was said to have been baptized.[77]

Aethelred's parents had been married in 762, so he will only have been about 11 when he became king on Alhred's expulsion and those around him must have exercised real power. Very little is recorded of his subsequent activities but on 22 March 778[78] he ordered three *duces* (ealdormen) to be slain by the nobles, Aethelbald and Heardberht – Ealdwulf, son of Bosa, at Coniscliffe and Cynewulf and Ecga at *Helathirnum* (*ASC* D, *s.a.* 778),[79] and this action may have weakened his position for in the following year he was driven out by Aelfwald, son of Oswulf (*ASC* D, *s.a.* 778).[80] Again, a substantial withdrawal of allegiance from Aethelred must have occurred. Archbishop Aethelberht is said not to have spared evil kings,[81] and there must be a possibility that he was soon as disenchanted with Aethelred's faction as he had been with Alhred's. Under Aelfwald the kingship passed back into the archbishop's own family – the descendants of Leodwald (see Appendix, Fig. 9), to whom Aethelberht, as a kinsman of Ecgberht, will have been related.

Aelfwald was certainly involved with Northumbrian ecclesiastical developments. He sent for a pallium for the new archbishop, Eanbald (I), in 780 or 781 (*ASC* D, *s.a.* 780)[82] and in 786 received the papal legate, George, bishop of Ostia, who had come to York to inquire into the state of the Northumbrian Church, at a council attended by all the chief men, ecclesiastical and lay, in the kingdom, when the legate pronounced on much that displeased him. The Northumbrians were instructed not to establish as king anyone who was illegitimate (a slighting reference perhaps to Aldfrith and his descendants, or, for all that we know to the contrary, to other rulers

152

– Aethelwald or Alhred) nor to conspire to kill a king who was the Lord's anointed, and any bishop or priest who was involved in such a crime was to be expelled from the Church and any layman excommunicated. The decrees of the council were confirmed by King Aelfwald, Archbishop Eanbald and the Northumbrian bishops, and the 'patrician' Sicga and two *duces* (ealdormen), Alric and Sigewulf.[83] Alric may have been a son of the Heardberht of 778 for an Alric, son of Heardberht, perished in 798 (*ASC* D, *s.a.* 798).

Subsequently, however, in the 790s in his letters of that time,[84] Alcuin detected a serious decline in the standards of Northumbrian life 'from the days of King Aelfwald' – that is to say, inclusive of the reign of Aelfwald[85] – with an increase in sexual offences, even against nuns, and law-breaking.[86] These somewhat standard indictments nevertheless came from a scholar who had grown up in the York school under Archbishop Ecgberht and gained maturity in the household of Archbishop Aethelberht as master of the school until he joined the court of Charlemagne in the early 780s.[87] By the early 790s, though still only a deacon, he was corresponding on behalf of Charlemagne and the Frankish court with Anglo-Saxon kings, abbots, bishops and archbishops, and was not given to mincing his words. His rather peremptory and often harshly critical letters sought to bring the diplomatic influence of the king of the Franks to bear on Anglo-Saxon political and ecclesiastical circles to act in accordance with Frankish desires.[88] Alcuin had become an instrument of Frankish policy. His criticism of Aelfwald, therefore, must be heeded. Moreover, he must have known Aelfwald personally for as Aelfwald's representative he accompanied George, bishop of Ostia and papal legate, south into Mercian territory in 786. On the other hand, what Alcuin has to say must be set beside the respect accorded Aelfwald's memory at Hexham where the king was buried (*ASC* D, *s.a.* 788),[89] which shows that the community at Hexham thought highly of him in the twelfth century and probably earlier. Aelfwald was residing in the far north of his kingdom when George arrived in Northumbria in 786[90] and this and the association of his cult with Hexham seem to locate this Bernician prince essentially outside Deira. His reign lacks recorded political incident. It began inauspiciously with the burning of Bearn, a 'patrician' of the king in *Seletun* by the *duces* (ealdormen) Osbald and Aethelheard on 25 December 780 (*ASC* D, *s.a* 779),[91] and it ended with the assassination of the king at *Scythlecester* (perhaps Chesters) near Hadrian's Wall on 23 September 788 after a conspiracy had been formed by Sicga, Aelfwald's 'patrician' and principal lay representative at the legatine council of 786 (*ASC* D, *s.a.* 788).[92] Aelfwald's sons, Oelf and Oelfwine, took sanctuary in the church of St Peter at York.[93] The intended beneficiary of this dynastic coup was Osred (II), the son of King Alhred by Osgifu, Aelfwald's sister, a youth of no more than 19 at the time, who reigned for a year but then fell a victim to further shifts of allegiance when in 789 he was taken prisoner, deprived of his kingdom, tonsured at York and expelled, and Aethelred, son of Aethelwald, resumed royal power (*ASC* D, *s.a.* 788, 789).[94]

Aethelred's recovery is impressive and testifies to the strength of his following. It came about almost certainly because of the division within Bernician royal circles and the (probably) Deiran support which Aethelred was able to rally. The tonsuring of Osred at York could suggest that he did not enjoy the support of Archbishop Eanbald, whereas the likelihood that Deira was the power-base of Aethelred receives strong support from the records for his second reign. In 792 he took a new wife, Aelfflaed (*ASC* D, *s.a.* 792), daughter of Offa, king of the Mercians, marrying her at Catterick where his own parents had been married.[95] This is not to say that Aethelred was without rivals, among whom was one with apparently Deiran connections. In 790 a Northumbrian nobleman, Eardwulf, was captured and brought to Ripon where orders were given by Aethelred for him to be put to death outside the gates of the monastery. Left for dead, the body was carried into the monastery by the monks and laid in a tent outside the church, but after midnight Eardwulf was found in the church alive.[96] There is a possibility that Aethelred was seeking to make an example of Eardwulf in Eardwulf's own territory and that the attempted assassination was frustrated by Eardwulf's supporters. Nothing is known of Eardwulf's ancestry except that he was a son of an Eardwulf,[97] but that he belonged to a family with strong Ripon associations is probable. Eardwulf escaped into exile. Others were not so fortunate. The sons of Aelfwald, still in sanctuary in York minster, were persuaded in 791 to leave the church by what are said to have been false promises and then killed, presumably drowned, by Aethelred in *Wonwaldremere*.[98] Such an act may well have provoked strong reaction in both ecclesiastical and lay circles, and Osred, exiled son of Alhred, was tempted back the following year from exile on the Isle of Man by the oaths of certain Northumbrian nobles; but his supporters then deserted him and he was captured by King Aethelred and killed at *Aynburg* on 14 September 792.[99]

Alcuin was resident among the Northumbrians in 790 and remained there for some time in the hope of influencing Aethelred, whose accession he welcomed,[100] though evidently to no avail for shortly after he declared that he was working against injustice and that Aethelred's attitude was not as he had hoped.[101] Alcuin wrote to Aethelred, probably in 791, expressing affection for him and urging him to display kindness not cruelty and reason not anger in his deeds, and to speak truth not falsehood,[102] but the sack of Lindisfarne by Vikings in June 793 (*ASC* D, *s.a.* 793)[103] provided a shocked and outraged Alcuin with an opportunity to declaim against the evils of Northumbrian society, as he saw them, and the shortcomings of the king himself in a letter to Aethelred and his nobles.[104] He denounced the immoralities which had prevailed in Northumbrian society since the days of King Aelfwald and contrasted the adornments of dress and hair and the luxurious standard of living of Aethelred's court-circle with an absence of concern for the poor and the starving. In a subsequent letter to Aethelred, the 'patrician' Osbald (possibly to be identified with the *dux* (ealdorman) Osbald of 780), and another Northumbrian lord, Osberht, Alcuin warned against worldly ambition, the pursuit of pleasure, and lust for revenge. He reminded them of how their predecessors had been punished for their wickedness and repeatedly urged obedience to the commands of the Church.[105] Though these letters, in common with other hortatory epistles of Alcuin, mirror an ideal standard of kingship and moralize within the framework of conventional Carolingian political thinking on kingship and its obligations and responsibilities,[106] the image conveyed by Alcuin is of a somewhat vainglorious, quarrelsome and vindictive, even ill-advised aristocracy rent by the consequences of faction and vendetta.

Nevertheless, the Frankish court, where Alcuin now resided, was favourably disposed towards Aethelred and it may be that Frankish support was what enabled a prolongation of his rule. Charlemagne sent gifts to him in late 795 or early 796, but when Aethelred was killed in 796 and the Frankish envoys returned to Gaul with the news, Charles recalled his gifts, furious that the Northumbrians should murder their lord and holding them worse than pagans;[107] and this sudden loss of his Northumbrian protégé may well have endangered the delicate balance Charlemagne was seeking to maintain in England to circumscribe the power of Offa of Mercia (see below, p. 176 ff.). Aethelred was assassinated on 18 April 796, perhaps at Corbridge,[108] by a group of conspirators which included the ealdormen Ealdred and Wada, and the kingdom plunged into confusion.[109] Ealdorman Torhtmund, a loyal servant of Aethelred, who slew Ealdred in vengeance for his lord in 799,[110] was warmly recommended by Alcuin to Charlemagne in 801 when he visited the Frankish court.[111]

The immediate choice of king by those Northumbrians responsible for the murder of Aethelred was the 'patrician', Osbald, but others recalled Eardwulf, son of Eardwulf, from exile and after only twenty-seven days the royal household and nobles deserted Osbald and he was forced to flee, sailing from Lindisfarne to the kingdom of the Picts[112] as Alhred had done from Bamburgh before him. There is no record of Osbald's parentage but a Bernician extraction seems highly probable. He is almost certainly to be identified with the Osbald of Alcuin's letter to Aethelred and perhaps with the Osbald who burnt a 'patrician' of King Aelfwald in 780.[113] The indications are that Aethelred needed to involve leading members of the Bernician aristocracy with his court, which may have been an element in his undoing. When Charlemagne gave his support and patronage to Aethelred, he was honouring only one of at least four princely lines – Osred's, Osbald's, Aethelred's and Eardwulf's – and even with Frankish blessing Aethelred was unable in these circumstances to establish a long-lasting regime. Nor was Osbald any better placed. When Alcuin wrote to him in exile, probably in 798, he reminded him of how much blood of kings, princes and people had been shed by him and his family.[114]

Northumbrian regnal tradition gave a reign of ten years to Eardwulf,[115] who returned from exile and was acclaimed king of Northumbria on 14 May 796 and consecrated on 26 May at York by Archbishop Eanbald and the three Northumbrian bishops of Hexham, Whithorn and Lindisfarne (*ASC* D, *s.a* 796).[116] The impression is of a king who at his accession was thoroughly acceptable to the Church but the persistence of dynastic in-fighting demonstrates that he was by no means universally popular among the lay nobility. Eardwulf met and countered a succession of threats from rival aethelings in the first years of his reign. In 798 those who had plotted against King Aethelred now came together again, probably with the intention of restoring Osbald, for Alcuin wrote to Osbald evidently seeking to deter him from renewed intervention in Northumbrian affairs.[117] This letter was written to Osbald in exile, two years after he had failed to take Alcuin's advice and enter a monastery. Its most likely date, therefore, is 798. The conspirators were led by Ealdorman Wada but were defeated in battle on Billington Moor, near Whalley in Lancashire, on 2 April 798 and put to flight. Amongst the slain was Alric, son of Heardberht, though it is not clear on which side he was fighting (*ASC* D, *s.a.* 798).[118] Osbald died a year later in 799 as an abbot and was buried in York.[119] Other challenges to Eardwulf were also countered. In 799 Ealdorman Moll, whose name may have family associations, was killed by the urgent orders of King Eardwulf;[120] and Ealhmund, said by some to have been a son of King Alhred, was seized by Eardwulf's men and put to death in 800.[121]

Among those not wholly enamoured of Eardwulf was Alcuin. In 797 he wrote to the people of Kent lamenting that scarcely any ruler was now to be found of the old stock of kings.[122] It is not quite clear what he meant by this; the point may well be not that the new kings – Eardwulf in Northumbria, and Coenwulf in Mercia – were of non-royal stock but that they were not of the lineage, respectively, of Aethelred and Offa – but it could easily be construed as a slur. Certainly, however, Alcuin was greatly concerned for the safety of Eardwulf. Personal sins, he warned him as early as 796, could lose him his kingdom, for of his predecessors who had lost life and kingdom God condemned the perjury of some, the adultery of others, the avarice and fraud of others, and the unjust deeds of the rest.[123] Specifically relevant to Eardwulf was adultery for, according to Alcuin, the king had dismissed his wife and publicly taken a concubine and Alcuin feared that this affront to God would soon cost him his throne.[124]

Eardwulf's adultery was in fact potentially serious because he became estranged from Eanbald (II), archbishop of York, who succeeded his namesake in 796. According to Alcuin the oppression of the Church by the secular power had been for some time a feature of Northumbrian political and ecclesiastical life,[125] but the problem now was that Eanbald was said to be accompanied on his journeys through Northumbria by a retinue more numerous than any which had attended on his predecessors and inclusive of low-born soldiers, and Alcuin affected to be at a loss as to why he needed so large a force.[126] In Alcuin's opinion, part of Eanbald's trouble arose because he received the king's enemies and protected their possessions and because he was involved in seizing the lands of others. The dispute between Eardwulf and Eanbald, therefore, also concerned property and conflicts of landed interest and probably some support for rival aethelings. The alienation of king and archbishop gave added significance to long-standing grievances at a time when by protecting Eardwulf's enemies the archbishop was allying himself against the king. In addition, this was at a time when Coenwulf, king of the Mercians, was also giving protection to opponents of Eardwulf. It cannot be without significance that Ealhmund, slain by Eardwulf's men in 800, was buried at Derby and venerated as a saint in Mercia.[127] In 801 Eardwulf responded by leading an army against the Mercians. After a long campaign a firm peace was made by the advice of the nobles and bishops on both sides which the kings confirmed with an oath.[128] The relatively detailed information in the annals and in the correspondence of Alcuin for this phase of the reign of Eardwulf enables us to perceive more clearly than is usually the case the way in which an attempt to challenge a Northumbrian king could embrace both internal dissent and external interference.

Alcuin's worst fears were not fulfilled until 806. The sequence of eighth-century Northumbrian annals is lost after 801 but the sparse fragments of a former continuation which are preserved in the *Anglo-Saxon Chronicle* terminate in 806 with a note of the expulsion of King Eardwulf (*ASC* D, *s.a.* 806). According to Roger of Wendover's *Flores Historiarum*[129] he was expelled by a certain Aelfwald (II),[130] who was accorded a reign of two years (806–8) in Northumbrian regnal tradition.[131] It is the sequel, however, which is particularly revealing. Frankish annals record that Eardwulf visited Charlemagne and Pope Leo III and that he was escorted back by imperial and papal envoys and re-established in his kingdom in 808.[132] How long he survived his restoration is not certainly known for Northumbrian regnal tradition retained no memory of Eardwulf's second reign, but there is a possibility that it lasted some three or four years (see below, p. 196). Despite Alcuin's reservations about Eardwulf, the king must have stepped into the shoes of the slain Aethelred as a recipient of Carolingian favours and may even have married a kinswoman of Charlemagne.[133] It would be difficult to demonstrate more dramatically the value of Frankish support for a Northumbrian ruler.

It should not be assumed that the royal and princely feuds of this period necessarily brought the Northumbrian kingdom into serious governmental disarray.[134] Some of the Northumbrian noblemen who were styled 'patrician' were clearly very powerful men,[135] even potentially over-mighty subjects, but they were not peculiar to Northumbria. The monetary system remained intact[136] in Aethelred's first reign and under Aelfwald, and in Aethelred's second reign a coinage with a higher silver content was even introduced.[137] Thereafter, however, there was monetary breakdown. Aethelred's new coinage failed in the early 790s and no new coins were minted under Eardwulf. When a coinage did reappear in the reign of the Northumbrian king, Eanred, in the early ninth century it did so at a lower silver standard which continued to decline.[138] There would seem to have been a shortage of silver in Northumbria from the 790s on, certainly for minting purposes. It may be that a variety of non-Northumbrian factors also played a part here – not least the early Viking raids, the likely disruption of shipping routes and Anglo-Frankish trading disputes – but the cessation of minting during Aethelred's second reign is in such striking contrast to what happened in southern England[139] that essentially it remains a mystery. There may, however, have been a diminution in tribute and revenues from possibly less securely held border regions and it would be surprising if the political problems of this period were not at least a factor in what has been called a 'drastic economic collapse'.[140]

Notes

1 D. P. Kirby, 'Bede and the Pictish Church', *Innes Review*, vol. 24 (1973), pp. 6–25 (pp. 10–11).

2 F. T. Wainwright, 'The Picts and the Problem', in F. T. Wainwright (ed.), *The Problem of the Picts* (Edinburgh and London, 1955), pp. 1–53 (p. 8). See also idem, 'Nechtanesmere', *Antiquity*, vol. 22 (1948), pp. 82–97.

3 Cf., recently, C. L. Neuman de Vegvar, *The Northumbrian Renaissance: A Study in the Transmission of Style* (London and Toronto, 1987).

4 Cf., P. H. Sawyer, *From Roman Britain to Norman England* (London, 1978), pp. 107–8.

5 *Two Lives of St Cuthbert*, ed. and trans. B. Colgrave (Cambridge, 1940), pp. 238–9.

6 F. J. Byrne, *Irish Kings and High Kings* (London, 1973), p. 104.

7 Aldfrith and Aldhelm, abbot of Malmesbury and subsequently bishop of Sherborne, who died in 709, were approximately the same age, but William of Malmesbury's statement that Aldhelm was at least 70 when he died may be conjectural: M. Lapidge and M. Herren, *Aldhelm: The Prose Works* (Ipswich, 1979), p. 12.

8 *Two Lives of St Cuthbert*, Colgrave, pp. 104–5.

9 ibid., pp. 236–7.

10 *The Life of Bishop Wilfrid by Eddius Stephanus*, ed. and trans. B. Colgrave (Cambridge, 1927).

11 Cf., A. P. Smyth, *Celtic Leinster* (Black Rock, Ark., 1982), pp. 118–22.

12 *Alcuin: The Bishops, Kings and Saints of York*, ed. P. Godman (Oxford, 1982), ll. 844–6 (pp. 70–1).

13 *Aldhelmi Opera Omnia*, ed. P. Ehwald, *MGH Auctores Antiq.*, Vol. XV (Berlin, 1919), pp. 486 ff. and for a translation, Lapidge and Herren, *Aldhelm: The Prose Works*, pp. 34 ff.

14 *Two Lives of St Cuthbert*, Colgrave, pp. 104–5, 236–7.

15 Cf., J. M. Wallace-Hadrill, *Bede's Ecclesiastical History of the English People* (Oxford, 1988), pp. 232–3.

16 H. Moisl, 'The Bernician royal dynasty and the Irish in the seventh century', *Peritia*, vol. 2 (1983), pp. 103–26 (pp. 120 ff.) (but that the Pictish offensive of 685 was mounted with Uí Néill help, specifically to establish Aldfrith on the Northumbrian throne, as Moisl suggests, art.cit., p. 123, is less certain).

17 *Adomnan's Life of Columba*, ed. and trans. A. O. and M. O. Anderson (Edinburgh and London, 1961), II, 46; J. M. Picard, 'The purpose of Adomnán's *Vita Columbae*', *Peritia*, vol. I (1982), pp. 160–77 (p. 161 and notes).

18 H. Vollrath explores the tension between Aldfrith and Wilfrid: *Die Synoden Englands bis 1066* (Paderborn, 1985), pp. 107–9.

19 On which see, W. Levison, *England and the Continent in the Eighth Century* (Oxford, 1946), pp. 24–5.

20 Vollrath, *Die Synoden Englands*, pp. 116–18, argues that Wilfrid's proposed resignation of his see at York was without prejudice to its metropolitan status.

21 *Symeonis Monachi Opera Omnia*, ed. T. Arnold, 2 vols (Rolls series: London, 1882, 1885), Vol. II, p. 38.

22 P. Hunter Blair, 'The *Moore Memoranda* on Northumbrian history', in C. Fox and B. Dickins (eds), *The Early Cultures of North-West Europe* (Cambridge, 1950), pp. 245–57 (p. 246) (reprinted in Blair, *Anglo-Saxon Northumbria*, ed. M. Lapidge and P. H. Blair (London, 1984); D. N. Dumville, 'The Anglian collection of royal genealogies and regnal lists', *Anglo-Saxon England*, vol. 5 (1976), pp. 23–50 (pp. 32, 36).

23 K. Harrison, *The Framework of Anglo-Saxon History to A.D. 900* (Cambridge, 1976), pp. 89–90.

24 If Bede really did regard the first full calendar year a king reigned as his first year (see above, p. 98) it would have been impossible for him to regard Aldfrith, nearly having completed twenty years, as dying on 14 December 704 for otherwise he would have predeceased the beginning of his twentieth year. The likelihood, however, that Aldfrith died on 14 December 704 re-emphasizes the point that Bedan dates, in whatever way devised, should not necessarily be allowed to dictate in all matters of seventh-century Anglo-Saxon chronology.

25 P. Grierson and M. Blackburn, *Medieval European Coinage*, Vol. I: *The Early Middle Ages* (Cambridge, 1986), p. 166.

26 Vollrath, *Die Synoden Englands*, pp. 119–20.

27 D. P. Kirby, 'Bede, Eddius Stephanus and the "Life of Wilfrid"', *English Historical Review*, vol. 98 (1983), pp. 101–14 (p. 113).

28 'Bedas metrische Vita sancti Cuthberti', ed. W. Jaager, *Palaestra* 198 (Leipzig, 1935), p. 100 (l. 554).

29 C. Plummer, *Venerabilis Baedae Opera Historica*, 2 vols (Oxford, 1892, 1896), Vol. I, p. 416.

30 J. Raine (ed.), *Historians of the Church of York*, 3 vols (Rolls series: London, 1879–94), Vol. I, p. 254.

31 *Aethelwulf De Abbatibus*, ed. and trans. A. Campbell (Oxford, 1967), pp. 4–7.

32 Dumville, 'The Anglian collection of royal genealogies', pp. 30, 32, 35.

33 He is called 'filius Alfridi': *Symeonis Monachi Opera Omnia*, Vol. I, p. 39, and on Alfrid's identity, see Plummer, *Venerabilis Baedae Opera Historica*, Vol. II, pp. 337–8 (though Plummer perhaps exaggerates the unlikelihood of Osric as a son of Ealhfrith).

34 Dumville, 'The Anglian collection of royal genealogies', pp. 30, 32, 35.

35 *Symeonis Monachi Opera Omnia*, Vol. II, p. 42.

36 It is incorrect to say that Ceolwulf was also known to the Irish as Eochaid: *AU s.a.* 730 has two separate references, one to a certain Eochaid and the other to Cuthwine's son – not one reference to Eochaid, Cuthwine's son as in *AT* p. 235. Eochaid was Eochaid, son of Eochaid, king of the Dalriadic Scots, on whom see M. O. Anderson, *Kings and Kingship in Early Scotland* (Edinburgh, 1973), pp. 181–2.

37 Plummer, *Venerabilis Baedae Opera Historica*, Vol. I, p. 412.

38 *Bede's Ecclesiastical History of the English People*, ed. and trans. B. Colgrave and R. A. B. Mynors (Oxford, 1969) pp. 572–3. W. Goffart comments, *The Narrators of Barbarian History* (Princeton, NJ, 1988), p. 274, n. 181.

39 C. Plummer, *Venerabilis Baedae Opera Historica*, Vol. I, p. 413 ff. (*EHD* I, no. 170 (pp. 739 ff.).) Vollrath comments, *Die Synoden Englands*, p. 121.

40 See further, A. P. Smyth, *Warlords and Holy Men: Scotland AD 80–1000* (London, 1984), pp. 132, 138–9, and M. Herbert, *Iona, Kells and Derry: The History and Hagiography of the Monastic Familia of Columba* (Oxford, 1988), pp. 58–9; and for earlier papers, D. P. Kirby, 'Bede and the Pictish Church', *Innes Review*, vol. 24 (1973), pp. 6–25, and A. A. M. Duncan, 'Bede, Iona and the Picts', in R. H. C. Davies and J. M. Wallace-Hadrill (eds), *The Writing of History in the Middle Ages* (Oxford, 1981), pp. 1–42.

41 *Bede's Ecclesiastical History of the English People*, Colgrave and Mynors, pp. 572–3.

42 ibid.

43 ibid. and *Symeonis Monachi Opera Omnia*, Vol. I, p. 47; Vol. II, p. 32.

44 *Symeonis Monachi Opera Omnia*, Vol. I, pp. 47, 52, 201.

45 Dumville, 'The Anglian collection of royal genealogies', pp. 30, 32, 35.

46 *Symeonis Monachi Opera Omnia*, Vol. II, p. 40.

47 ibid.

48 ibid., p. 41.

49 *Alcuin: The Bishops, Kings and Saints of York*, Godman, ll. 1276–7 (pp. 100–1).

50 *Bede's Ecclesiastical History of the English People*, Colgrave and Mynors, pp. 574–5.

51 ibid., pp. 572–5.

52 *Symeonis Monachi Opera Omnia*, Vol. II, pp. 40–1.

53 G. R. Gilmore and D. M. Metcalf, 'The alloy of the Northumbrian coinage in the mid-ninth century', *Metallurgy in Numismatics*, vol. 1 (1980), pp. 83–98 (p. 85).

54 Grierson and Blackburn, *Medieval European Coinage*, Vol. I, p. 173.

55 *Bede's Ecclesiastical History of the English People*, Colgrave and Mynors, pp. 574–5: *Symeonis Monachi Opera Omnia*, Vol. II, pp. 39–40.

56 *Symeonis Monachi Opera Omnia*, Vol. II, p. 44.

57 *Bede's Ecclesiastical History of the English People*, Colgrave and Mynors, pp. 574–5: *Symeonis Monachi Opera Omnia*, Vol. II, p. 44.

58 *Councils and Ecclesiastical Documents of Great Britain and Ireland*, ed. A. W. Haddan and W. Stubbs, 3 vols (Oxford, 1869–71), Vol. III, pp. 394–6.

59 *Symeonis Monachi Opera Omnia*, Vol. II, p. 42.

60 Gilmore and Metcalf, 'The alloy of the Northumbrian coinage', p. 86.

61 J. Booth, 'Coinage and Northumbrian history: *c*.790–*c*.810', in D. M. Metcalf (ed.), *Coinage in Ninth-Century Northumbria* (BAR British Series 180, 1987), pp. 57–85 (p. 73).

62 *Symeonis Monachi Opera Omnia*, Vol. II, p. 41.

63 ibid., p. 43.

64 ibid., pp. 51, 59.

65 Dumville, 'The Anglian collection of royal genealogies', pp. 30, 32, 35.

66 *Symeonis Monachi Opera Omnia*, Vol. II, p. 43'; cf., D. N. Dumville, 'The aetheling: a study in Anglo-Saxon constitutional history', *Anglo-Saxon England*, vol. 8 (1979), pp. 1–33 (p. 16, n. 4).

67 *Symeonis Monachi Opera Omnia*, Vol. II, p. 54.

68 ibid., pp. 44, 52; a son of this marriage is described as a nephew of Aelfwald, son of Oswulf: ibid., p. 52.

69 J. Booth, 'Sceattas in Northumbria', in D. Hill and D. M. Metcalf (eds), *Sceattas in England and on the Continent* (BAR British Series 128, 1984), pp. 71–112 (pp. 81 ff.); Grierson and Blackburn, *Medieval European Coinage*, Vol. I, p. 297.

70 *Symeonis Monachi Opera Omnia*, Vol. II, p. 43.

71 *MGH Scriptores*, Vol. II, ed. G. Pertz (Hanover, 1829), p. 380. Cf., Levison, *England and the Continent in the Eighth Century*, pp. 109–10.

72 *Epistolae Selectae*, Vol. I, ed. M. Tangl (Berlin, 1955), no. 121 (*EHD* Vol. I, no. 187).

73 *MGH Scriptores*, Vol. II, p. 407 (*EHD* Vol. I, no. 160). Cf., D. A. Bullough, 'History as patriotism: Alcuin's "York poem" and the early Northumbrian "vitae sanctorum"', *Hagiographie cultures et sociétés IVᵉ–XIIᵉ siècles* (Actes du Colloque organisé à Nanterre et à Paris, 1979) (Paris, 1981), pp. 339–59 (pp. 350–1).

74 *Symeonis Monachi Opera Omnia*, Vol. II, p. 45.

75 Alcuin records that Aethelberht was related to Archbishop Ecgberht: *Alcuin: The Bishops, Kings and Saints of York*, Godman, l. 1429 (pp. 112–13).

76 *Symeonis Monachi Opera Omnia*, Vol. II, p. 45.

77 *Alcuin: The Bishops, Kings and Saints of York*, Godman, ll. 1490 ff. (pp. 118–19).

78 This date (*ASC* D, *s.a.* 778) may be preferable to the 29 September of the *Historia Regum* (*Symeonis Monachi Opera Omnia*, Vol. II, p. 46), for Aethelred is said to have been in his fourth year, which, if he succeeded at Easter 774, he would not have been on 29 September 778.

79 *Symeonis Monachi Opera Omnia*, Vol. II, p. 46.

80 ibid., pp. 46–7.

81 *Alcuin: The Bishops, Kings and Saints of York*, Godman, l. 1479 (pp. 116–17).

82 *Symeonis Monachi Opera Omnia*, Vol. II, p. 47.

83 *Councils and Ecclesiastical Documents*, Haddan and Stubbs, Vol. III, pp. 459–60. Vollrath discusses the Northumbrian gathering: *Die Synoden Englands*, pp. 165 ff.

84 *Epistolae Karol. Aevi*, Vol. II, ed. E. Dümmler, *MGH Epistolae*, Vol. IV (Berlin, 1895) (the letters of Alcuin are translated by S. Allott, *Alcuin of York* (York, 1974)).

85 Dumville, 'The aetheling', p. 26, n. 4.

86 *Epistolae Karol. Aevi*, Vol. II, no. 16 (*EHD* Vol. I, no. 193).

87 On Alcuin's role at the court of Charlemagne, see, for example, D. A. Bullough 'Alcuin and the Kingdom of Heaven: liturgy, theology and the Carolingian age', in U.-R. Blumenthal (ed.), *Carolingian Essays* (Washington, DC, 1983), pp. 1–70, and idem, 'Albuinus deliciosus Karoli regis: Alcuin of York and the shaping of the early Carolingian court', in L. Fenske (ed.), *Institutionen, Kultur und Gesellschaft im Mittelalter* (Sigmaringen, 1984), pp. 73–92.

88 Cf., J. M. Wallace-Hadrill, 'Charlemagne and England', *Early Medieval History* (Oxford, 1975), pp. 155–80 (p. 157) and *The Frankish Church* (Oxford, 1983), pp. 196–7, 205 ff.

89 *Symeonis Monachi Opera Omnia*, Vol. II, p. 52.

90 *Epistolae Karol. Aevi*, Vol. II, no. 3.

91 *Symeonis Monachi Opera Omnia*, Vol. II, p. 47.

92 ibid., p. 52.

93 ibid., p. 53.

94 ibid., p. 52.

95 ibid., p. 54.

96 ibid., p. 52.

97 ibid., p. 57.

98 ibid., p. 53.

99 ibid., p. 54.

100 *Epistolae Karol. Aevi*, Vol. II, no. 8.

101 ibid., no. 9.

102 ibid., no. 30.

103 *Symeonis Monachi Opera Omnia*, Vol. II, p. 54.

104 *Epistolae Karol. Aevi*, Vol. II, no. 16 (*EHD* Vol. I, no. 193).

105 *Epistolae Karol. Aevi*. Vol. II, no. 18.

106 L. Wallach, *Alcuin and Charlemagne* (Ithaca, NY, 1959): cf., L. K. Born, 'The specula principis of the Carolingian Renaissance', *Revue Belge de Philologie et d'Histoire*, vol. 12 (1933), pp. 583–612 (pp. 589–92).

107 *Epistolae Karol. Aevi*, Vol. II, nos 100 (*EHD* Vol. I, no. 197), 101 (*EHD* Vol. I, no. 198).

108 *Symeonis Monachi Opera Omnia*, Vol. II, p. 376.

109 ibid., pp. 57, 59, 62.

110 ibid., p. 62.

111 *Epistolae Karol. Aevi*, Vol. II, no. 231 (*EHD* Vol. I, no. 206).

112 *Symeonis Monachi Opera Omnia*, Vol. II, p. 57.

113 ibid., p. 47.

114 *Epistolae Karol. Aevi*, Vol. II, no. 109 (*EHD* Vol. I, no. 200).

115 *Symeonis Monachi Opera Omnia*, Vol. II, pp. 376, 391.

116 ibid., p. 58.

117 *Epistolae Karol. Aevi*, Vol. II, no. 109 (*EHD* Vol. I, no. 200).
118 *Symeonis Monachi Opera Omnia*, Vol. II, p. 59.
119 ibid., p. 62.
120 ibid.
121 ibid., p. 63.
122 *Epistolae Karol. Aevi*, Vol. II, no. 129.
123 ibid., Vol. II, no. 108 (*EHD* Vol. I, no. 199).
124 ibid., Vol. II, no. 122 (*EHD* Vol. I. no. 202).
125 ibid., Vol. II, nos 209, 232 (*EHD* Vol. I, no. 207).
126 ibid., Vol. II, no. 233 (*EHD* Vol. I, no. 208).
127 D. W. Rollason, 'The cults of murdered royal saints', *Anglo-Saxon England*, vol. 11 (1983), pp. 1–22 (p. 20). Cf., R. A. Hall, 'The Five Boroughs of the Danelaw: a review of present knowledge', *Anglo-Saxon England*, vol. 18 (1989), pp. 149–206 (pp. 156–7).
128 *Symeonis Monachi Opera Omnia*, Vol. II, p. 65.
129 *Roger de Wendover Chronica sive Flores Historiarum*, ed. H. O. Coxe, 4 vols (London, 1841–2), Vol. I (trans. J. A. Giles, *Roger of Wendover's Flowers of History*, 2 vols (London, 1849)).
130 *Roger de Wemdover*, Vol. I, p. 270 (*EHD* Vol. I, no. 4).
131 *Symeonis Monachi Opera Omnia*, Vol. II, pp. 376, 391.
132 *Annales Regni Francorum*, ed. F. Kurze, *Scriptores Regum Germanicarum in Usum Scholarum ex Monumenta Germaniae Historicis* (Hanover, 1895), p. 126 (*EHD* Vol. I, no. 21). See also *Councils and Ecclesiastical Documents*, Haddan and Stubbs, Vol. III, p. 566.
133 See the observations of Wallace-Hadrill, 'Charlemagne and England', p. 170.
134 See J. Campbell, 'Elements in the background to the life of St Cuthbert and his early cults', in G. Bonner, D. Rollason and C. Stancliffe (eds), *St Cuthbert, his Cult and his Community to AD 1200* (Woodbridge, 1989), pp. 3–20 (p. 7).
135 A. T. Thacker, 'Some terms for noblemen in Anglo-Saxon England, *c.* 650–900', *Anglo-Saxon Studies in Archaeology and History*, no. 2, ed. D. Brown, J. Campbell and S. C. Hawkes (BAR British Series 92, 1981), pp. 201–36 (pp. 215 ff.).
136 Booth, 'Coinage and Northumbrian history: *c.*790–*c.*810', p. 67.
137 Gilmore and Metcalf, 'The alloy of the Northumbrian coinage', p. 86.
138 ibid., pp. 86, 93 ff.
139 Booth, 'Coinage and Northumbrian history: *c.*790–*c.*810', pp. 74–6, and cf., 'Discussion', pp. 84–5.
140 Booth, 'Coinage and Northumbrian history', p. 73.

8 Offa

According to the Anglian genealogies, Offa, son of Thingfrith, son of Eanwulf, was a descendent of Eowa, the brother of Penda (see Appendix, Fig. 8).[1] If the genealogical information is correct, Eanwulf was Aethelbald's cousin, and he received from Aethelbald land at Westbury and Henbury in the territory of the Hwicce (CS 272, 273: S 146). Indeed, Eanwulf's connections with Hwiccian territory appear to have been considerable, for he founded the monastery of Bredon in Worcestershire, of which Offa was subsequently a patron (CS 234, 847: S 117; CS 236: S 116)[2] but Offa's family is not certainly known to have been related to the princes of the Hwicce. There has been a suggestion that Aethelburh, kinswoman of Ealdred, sub-king of the Hwicce, and abbess of Fladbury in Worcestershire (CS 238: S 62), was Offa's daughter of the same name who was also an abbess (CS 251: S 127),[3] but there were clearly several prominent women of this name. Ealdred's kinswoman could have been Abbess Aethelburh, daughter of a local lord, Aelfred, who was given Withington in Gloucestershire in the 770s (CS 217: S 1255). None of Offa's immediate forebears had been king of the Mercians and Offa himself is another example (like Aethelbald) of an aetheling competing successfully for the kingship from outside the innermost core of royal power. According to the *Anglo-Saxon Chronicle* A (*s.a.* 755) Beornred succeeded to the kingdom on the death of Aethelbald but held it only for a short time and unhappily. It is not known how he was related to former kings of Mercia, but it is possible that he represented a line claiming descent from Penda. Northumbrian annals record that Offa put him to flight (perhaps with Hwiccian help)[4] and took the Mercian kingship.[5] A record of the settlement of a dispute involving the bishop of Worcester in 789, which refers to Offa as then in his thirty-first year as king (CS 256: S 1430), means that Offa cannot have become king before 758.

Within Mercia and among its traditional dependencies, it is difficult to judge the impact of the assassination of Aethelbald and the civil war of 757–8.[6] The evidence indicates an immediate confirmation of Mercian overlordship in the territory of the Hwicce, when at the beginning of his reign Offa defined the relationship of Eanberht and his brothers, Uhtred and Ealdred, rulers of the Hwicce, to himself as that of *reguli*, kinglets (CS 183: S 55; CS 107: S 56), but Offa's position may have been more secure here than elsewhere. Aldfrith, king probably of Lindsey, only witnesses one of Offa's charters and that after *c.* 789 (CS 262: S 1183), but whether Lindsey detached itself from Mercian control in 757–8 and, if so, how long an interval elapsed before Offa reasserted himself is unknown.[7] Similarly, the history of the

East Saxon kingdom under the successive kings, Swithred and Sigeric (I) (see Appendix, Fig. 2),[8] in the time of Offa is quite unknown. Offa must certainly have been concerned from the earliest years of his reign to secure Mercian control of Middle Saxon territory (*CS* 201: S 106) and London. In response to Frankish currency reform he began to mint new silver pennies in the 760s and 770s, when London emerges as an important royal Mercian minting centre, if not Offa's principal mint; it may have been here that his first coins were produced.[9] What the evidence does show is that, even in an area where a traditional Mercian involvement was sustained, relations with Offa were not hostile and Mercian influence not at first particularly oppressive. Offa's description of Ealdred as 'my *subregulus, dux*, that is, of his own people, the Hwicce' (*CS* 223: S 113), which reveals *dux* becoming an acceptable term for a sub-king, dates to as late as 778, twenty years after Offa's accession. Thereafter Offa assumed direct rule of Hwiccian territory in the 780s,[10] and by the 790s the province was under the command of an individual known simply as *dux* (*CS* 272, 273: S 146), but it is worth emphasizing how long this process took.

Beyond the traditional Mercian heartland there are signs that Aethelbald's *imperium* had disintegrated and that 'the Mercian polity . . . was in disarray'.[11] Cynewulf, king of the West Saxons, having successfully vanquished his rival, Sigeberht (*ASC* A, *s.a.* 755), was clearly in a strong enough position to advance into Berkshire, an area previously controlled by Aethelbald. His seizure of the monastery of Cookham, which Aethelbald had given to Christ Church, Canterbury (and the purloining from Canterbury of its Cookham charters *c.* 760), reveals him as a presence in what Stenton called 'the debatable land' along the Thames (*CS* 291: S 1258). In East Anglia, where Beonna probably became king *c.* 758, the trading centre at Ipswich may have been expanding and the first attempt to restore a southern coinage was made, predating Offa's first issues and suggesting an impressive degree of independence on Beonna's part.[12] The western marches of Offa's kingdom may have been experiencing renewed British harassment. It is evident from the massive character of the great border dyke which Asser in his *Life of Alfred* in the late ninth century[13] attributes to Offa (*Life of King Alfred*, ch. 14), running from Sedbury Cliffs near Chepstow to Treuddyn to link up with Wat's Dyke which ends at Basingwerk in north Wales, that considerable energy and manpower must have been devoted to the delineation, construction and maintenance of this frontier line.[14] Military vicissitudes were a feature of border life at this time. Cyngen ap Cadell, king of Powys in the mid-ninth century, erected a monument, Eliseg's Pillar, to his great-grandfather, Eliseg, who is said to have annexed the inheritance of Powys from the power of the Angles.[15] Eliseg is probably to be dated approximately to the mid-eighth century. On this evidence the loss of previous territorial gains by the Mercians would seem to have characterized Mercian–Welsh relations in the period before the building of

Offa's Dyke. The Welsh annals record a battle at Hereford between Britons and Saxons in 760 (*AC, ByT s.a.* 760), the harrying of men of south Wales by Offa in 777 or 778 (*AC s.a.* 778: *ByT s.a.* 777), and a further harrying of the Britons by Offa in 783 or 784 (*AC s.a.* 784: *ByT s.a.* 783). In 786 the papal legate Theophylact, bishop of Todi, visited the territories of Offa, including 'parts of Britain'.[16] The indications are, therefore, that Offa was engaged fairly intensively against the Welsh across the first twenty-five or so years of his reign and this may have prevented him from pursuing Mercian interests in eastern and south-eastern England too vigorously before the mid-780s.

During Offa's first years as king the southern kingdoms were relatively stable. The first signs of instability appeared in the south-east in Kent. When Aethelberht, king of Kent, died in 762 (*ASC* A, *s.a.* 760), the position of his co-ruler, Eadberht, was immediately threatened. Eadberht last appears in 762 as a witness to a grant of land at Rochester to the bishop of Rochester by Sigered, king of Kent (*CS* 193: S 32), the name suggesting a possible East Saxon origin. Sigered was styled very soon after in 763–4, however, only 'king of half Kent' (presumably west Kent) when he granted land, again to Rochester, subject to the confirmation of a new co-ruler, Eanmund (*CS* 194: S 33), possibly in east Kent.[17] This sequence of events resulted in the intervention of Offa. In 764 Heahberht, who had witnessed Sigered's grant of land to Rochester in 762, appears as king of Kent in the company of Offa and members of the Mercian nobility in Canterbury when Offa granted land to the bishop of Rochester in Kent in his own name (*CS* 195: S 105), the first occasion on which a Mercian king is known to have done so, and the same land which had only recently been granted to Rochester by Sigered and Eanmund.[18] The evidence would suggest at least that Heahberht was established and secured in power in Kent through Offa's intervention and support.

In the course of the following year, however, Offa confirmed at Peterborough a grant of land in Rochester by Ecgberht, king of Kent, to the bishop of Rochester which King Heahberht also witnessed (*CS* 196: S 34). Ecgberht may have received wide support in Kent and cannot necessarily be regarded as wholly dependent on Offa for his kingship. In 776 the *Anglo-Saxon Chronicle* A (*s.a.* 773) records that the Mercians and the men of Kent fought at Otford but does not state the outcome. Stenton believed that Offa dominated Kent down to 776 but that the Mercians were defeated at Otford and Mercian authority not re-established in Kent until 785 when Offa again granted land in Kent in his own name (*CS* 247: S 123).[19] If there is no certain indication that Offa was able to establish his authority in Kent in the aftermath of Otford, however, there is no substantial indication either that he continued to be a political presence in Kent after 765. A grant of land by Offa to St Augustine's, Canterbury (*CS* 207: S 140), for which the date 772 has been proposed,[20] could, even if genuine, be much later. Two other records of grants of land in Kent by Offa to Archbishop Jaenberht, dated 774 (*CS* 213: S 110; *CS* 214, 215: S 111), are of doubtful authenticity.[21] Moreover, some time in or after 765 King Heahberht witnessed a charter by which King Ecgberht granted land to the bishop of Rochester without any reference to Offa (*CS* 260: S 37). The indications are, therefore, that Offa's involvement in Kentish affairs in 764–5 was shortlived, either a response to or an attempt to take advantage of a particular crisis – almost certainly the emergence of so many rival rulers in Kent in the immediately preceding period – and that the advent of Ecgberht terminated it. It is not certain how long Heahberht survived Offa's withdrawal. He was secure enough to mint his own silver pennies, which must have been among the first of the new coins to be produced and an indication of the economic vitality and continuing independence of his kingdom. Ecgberht also minted his own coins and was doing so by the early 770s at the latest if one of them, as has been suggested, served as a prototype for one of Charlemagne's which must date to before *c*. 772, if not before *c*. 770.[22] It was Ecgberht who ruled in Kent across the 770s. He was still king in 779 when he granted land to the bishop of Rochester (*CS* 228: S 36) and it is not until 784 that a new king, Ealhmund, appears, granting land to the abbot of Reculver (*CS* 243: S38). Ecgberht enjoyed good relations with Archbishop Jaenberht, whom he described as dear to him in all things (*CS* 196: S 34), and the archbishop's kinsman, Ealdhun, was his reeve (*CS* 332: S 1264; *CS* 319, 320: S 1259). He was a generous patron of Christ Church, Canterbury, and *c*. 780 Ealdhun also gave lands which Ecgberht had given him to the *familia* of Christ Church (*CS* 293: S 155; cf., *CS* 319, 320: S 1259 and *CS* 332: S 1264).[23] Whether the battle of Otford in 776 was fought in the aftermath of the death of Heahberht or as a consequence of some other matter in dispute between Ecgberht and the Mercians, after 765 there is no certain evidence that Ecgberht was for long, if at all, 'a mere dependant'[24] of Offa.[25]

One of the features of the years 765–85 may have been a closer involvement on Offa's part with the kingdom of the East Angles. East Anglian independence survived long enough for coins to be minted for Aethelberht, king of the East Angles, and it has been suggested that Offa's East Anglian coinage may not have begun much before *c*. 790.[26] That one of Beonna's moneyers, Wilred, went on to mint coins for Offa,[27] however, may imply a somewhat earlier date for some at least of Offa's East Anglian coins, and Offa's position in East Anglia was already secure enough for the East Anglian bishoprics of *Dommoc* and Elmham to be included in 787 in the new archdiocese of Lichfield (see below, p. 174). It may be that it was because he was so secure in East Anglia that Offa was subsequently able to involve himself so much more forcefully in the south-east.

A crucial stage in the reign of Offa was certainly reached in 784–5 when he intervened again in Kent, this time decisively. The death of Ecgberht and the emergence of a new king, Ealhmund, subsequently identified by a later Canterbury scribe (*ASC* F, *s.a.* 784) as the father of Ecgberht (*ASC* A, Preface; *s.a.* 855); (see Appendix, Fig. 3), king of the West Saxons (802–39), was probably what led to this renewed involvement, for nothing more is heard of Ealhmund nor did any successor to him appear in Kent, even as *subregulus*. Instead, Offa's direct personal participation in Kentish affairs is revealed in a series of documents across the years 785–9 (*CS* 247: S 123; *CS* 248: S 125; *CS* 254: S 128; *CS* 253: S 129; *CS* 257: S 130; *CS* 244: S 131), and in 792 it was Offa who confirmed the immunities from secular obligations of Kentish churches (*CS* 848: S 134). Furthermore, the donations of King Ecgberht and the reeve, Ealdhun, to Canterbury were revoked by Offa (*CS* 293: S 155; cf., *CS* 319, 320: S 1259 and *CS* 332: S 1264), who objected to the fact that his *minister* (thegn) had presumed to give land allotted to him by his lord into the power of another without his witness (*CS* 293: S 155). There is a possibility that *minister* here refers to Ealdhun and that Offa was angered because Ealdhun had given his lands to Christ Church, Canterbury, without King Ecgberht's permission,[28] but even if this were the case, it is clear that Offa's reaction was to the way in which Ecgberht also had made grants of land without his permission; he revoked both Ealdhun's donations and Ecgberht's, not only to Canterbury but to Rochester.[29] In a document of 811 Wulfred, archbishop of Canterbury, specifically declares that Offa had cancelled one of Ecgberht's charters on the grounds that Ecgberht had no right to grant land by charter in perpetuity (*CS* 332: S 1264). What was now involved here was more than the imposition of Offa's overlordship upon the rulers of Kent; it was the annexation of the province and the suppression of the native line. From 785, as Patrick Wormald observes, 'Offa was the rival, not the overlord, of Kentish kings'.[30]

It is disappointing that South Saxon charters for these years are frequently of doubtful authenticity, if not entirely spurious, but they hint at a sequence of events similar to those in Kent. A certain Osmund appears to have been king of the South Saxons until at least *c.* 770 (*CS* 206: S 49), evidently in association with three other kings, Ealdwulf, Aelfwald, and (?) Oslac (*CS* 197: S 50).[31] The names of Offa, his queen, Cynethryth, and his son, Ecgfrith, have subsequently[32] been attached to the witnesses of a grant of land by Ealdwulf (*CS* 197: S 50), but Offa appears to have consented to Osmund's grant of 770 (*CS* 206: S 49) and in 771 he gained a victory over the men of Hastings.[33] His intervention at this time, in the same way as his intervention in Kent in 764-5, was probably a response to political instability among the South Saxons. Furthermore, just as in Kent in 764–5, so in Sussex in 770–1, Offa's involvement appears to have been limited and shortlived. It must be stressed that if the record of a lease of land by Offa to Oswald, bishop of the South Saxons, in 772 (*CS* 208: S 108) is what Stenton called it – a 'patent forgery'[34] – there is no evidence for Offa's presence as a dominant factor in South Saxon affairs until the late

780s. Though Oslac, *dux* of the South Saxons, and Ealdwulf, also *dux* of the South Saxons, may be identical with the kings of these names *c.* 770, it was not until after *c.* 789 (when Wihthun was bishop of the South Saxons) that Offa confirmed their grants to South Saxon churches (*CS* 237, 1334: S 1184; *CS* 262: S 1183) (cf., Offa's consent to a further grant by Ealdwulf in 791, *CS* 261: S 1178). The first clear indication that Offa had gained control of the South Saxons, therefore, comes only *c.* 790, suggesting a Mercian annexation of the area in the late 780s. These developments closely parallel those in Kent.

The almost simultaneous involvement of Offa in both Kent and Sussex in the mid- to late 780s may suggest a connection at this time between the two. The central fact of the history of the south-east before 784 is the independent rule of Ecgberht, king of Kent, and it is not impossible that before the late 780s Sussex was more within his sphere of influence than Offa's. This may have been true also of part at least of Surrey and conceivably part at least of the kingdom of the East Saxons. The *Anglo-Saxon Chronicle* A was later to claim that Kent, Sussex, Essex and Surrey had been wrongfully forced away from the kindred of Ecgberht, son of Ealhmund, king of the West Saxons (*ASC* A, *s.a.* 823). A possible explanation of this is that Ecgberht was indeed regarded as Ealhmund's heir and that Ealhmund in turn inherited from King Ecgberht of Kent a local overlordship of south-eastern England which in varying forms had been a recurring feature of historical development in the area since the time of Aethelberht, son of Eormenric. For the kings of the East Saxons to have acknowledged a dependency on the king of Kent would have been in the oldest known tradition of Kentish–East Saxon relationships, and the same is true of Surrey. Though Offa granted land to Woking in Surrey (*CS* 275: S 144), he cannot be shown to have had influence here before 784–5. It may be that the battle of Otford was a Kentish response to Mercian interference in the mid-770s in areas that were regarded by Ecgberht as within a Kentish sphere of influence. A Kentish hegemony in south-east England at this time is not, therefore, wholly out of the question, and Offa's intention in intervening in 784–5 and thereafter may have been to gain mastery of it and contain it.

Moreover, Cynewulf, king of the West Saxons, is not found (apart from the unacceptable evidence of *CS* 208: S 108) in Offa's entourage, nor does Offa's confirmation of Cynewulf's grant of land at North Stoke, north of Bath (itself not above suspicion),[35] to the monastery of Bath in the territory of the Hwicce (*CS* 327: S 265) necessarily imply a position of dependence on Offa. Rather could Offa have been securing himself in territory only recently recovered from Cynewulf. Cynewulf's annexation of land bordering on the Thames in Berkshire in the early years of Offa's reign certainly appears to have been followed up by further action in the original Gewissian territory around Dorchester. It was not until 779 that Offa was able to defeat Cynewulf in battle and take Bensington, near Dorchester, from him (*ASC* A, *s.a.* 777) and begin the re-annexation of this territory. Only thereafter was he able to consolidate his position also in West Saxon land along the south bank of the Avon (*CS* 241: S 1257).[36] This does not give the impression of a Mercian king in control of the south-eastern provinces from the mid-760s. Cynewulf, remembered for his campaigns against the Britons (*ASC* A, *s.a.* 755), was probably a force to be reckoned with, and it is conceivable that Ecgberht, son of Ealhmund, took refuge with him in 785. Cynewulf was slain in 786 by a rival aetheling, Cyneheard, the brother of the former king, Sigeberht, whom he had been seeking to expel from Wessex (*ASC* A, *s.a.* 755), and succeeded by Beorhtric. It is interesting that Offa subsequently required the assistance of Beorhtric to effect the expulsion of Ecgberht from England (*ASC* A, *s.a.* 836). Offa's victory over Cynewulf in 779, therefore, would seem to have been a signal for intensified Mercian activity on Offa's southern border which may have been an essential prerequisite to any sustained involvement in the south-east. It was probably the deaths of Ecgberht in Kent *c.* 784 and of Cynewulf in Wessex in 786 which then enabled the political map of Kent and the adjacent territories to be redrawn.

It cannot be entirely coincidental that these years were a time of important new developments in both the Church and the Mercian kingdom. In 786, for the first time since the coming of Augustine, papal legates visited England to reaffirm papal authority and ensure conformity to the requirements of canonic law. In 787 the ecclesiastical province of Canterbury was divided to create a second metropolitan see at Lichfield in the heart of Offa's kingdom. The same year Offa's son, Ecgfrith, was consecrated king and associated in the kingship of the Mercians with his father.

At a time when what would seem to have been a 'Carolingian connection' can be identified in insular art, architecture and archaeology,[37] a Carolingian emphasis on the importance of increasing the number of metropolitans and re-establishing metropolitan authority is likely to have created a context by the mid-780s for consideration of the situation in the Anglo-Saxon Church where the archbishop of Canterbury presided over as many as twelve suffragans. A subdivision of so large a province may well have seemed desirable in purely pastoral terms. Unfortunately, there is no contemporary account of the setting up of the archdiocese of Lichfield. What evidence there is comes from partisan statements made in 798 after the death of Offa by Offa's successor, Coenwulf, and by Pope Leo III. It must be appreciated, therefore, that when Coenwulf maintained that Offa wished to diminish the dignity of Canterbury because of his hatred of Archbishop Jaenberht and the people of Kent,[38] whereas Pope Leo declared that it was because of the vastness of his lands and kingdom that Offa had desired it,[39] both were representing Offa's motives in ways which suited their immediate purposes. Coenwulf now wanted London to supersede both Lichfield and Canterbury as the single metropolitan see of the southern province in accordance with the plan of Pope Gregory I, and was therefore concerned to minimize any argument for more than one archbishopric based on territorial extent; Pope Leo, on the other hand, was anxious to disassociate the papacy and his predecessor, Hadrian I, from complicity with Offa in acting against Canterbury for so base a reason as Offa's antagonism to the people of Kent. Both Offa's dislike of the men of Kent and the extent of the territory now coming under his control may have been factors in the situation in the late 780s, but in 798 Coenwulf and Leo were deploying these arguments selectively and in a way which compromises their validity as single explanations of what was probably a complex situation.

It is disappointing that the report of the unique legatine mission to England in 786 of Theophylact, bishop of Todi, and George, bishop of Ostia, as emissaries of Pope Hadrian I, accompanied by Abbot Wigbod representing Charlemagne, contains no reference to this matter. The legates were first received by Archbishop Jaenberht at Canterbury, from whence they journeyed to the court of Offa, who received them most favourably, and Offa, together with Cynewulf, king of the West Saxons, came together in a council where papal letters directing attention to the need for reform in the Anglo-Saxon Church were consulted and promises of reform made. At this stage in the proceedings the papal party split up, Theophylact visiting Mercia and 'parts of Britain'; George went into Northumbria, where a council was held in the presence of King Aelfwald and Eanbald, archbishop of York, in which canons were passed to correct the erroneous ways into which the Northumbrian Church was thought to have fallen. George's return from Northumbria, in the company of Alcuin, a representative on this occasion of King Aelfwald, was followed by a great southern council, presided over by Archbishop Jaenberht and King Offa and attended by all the bishops of the southern province, at which reforming decrees were promulgated.[40] The report is unfortunately incomplete. It represents George's view of events[41] and retains a lengthy account of the proceedings of the Northumbrian council while doing less than justice to the southumbrian gatherings. Nothing is said of the progress of Theophylact in Mercia and 'parts of Britain'. There is no reference in the report to Offa's undertaking to Theophylact and George to send money every year to Rome for the support of the poor and provision of lights, the details of which are known only from Pope Leo's letter to Coenwulf in 798.[42] The absence of reference to a division of the southern province, therefore, is not altogether surprising. The matter was probably not one on which the legates were even required to report because it was a quite separate issue from the question of Church reform with which they were concerned.[43] This need not mean, however, that it was not discussed.

That there were issues important enough seriously to disturb Anglo-papal relations at this time is confirmed by a letter of Pope Hadrian I to Charlemagne which dates to between 784 and 791. The anxiety of the pope over a rumour concerning Offa's malice towards him is here very evident. Charlemagne had received information from certain persons that Offa was suggesting that the Frankish king should depose Hadrian and replace him with a new pope of Frankish extraction. Envoys of Offa, however, had arrived at the court of Charlemagne affirming that this rumour was the work of men who were enemies of both Charlemagne and Offa, and had gone on their way to Rome, accompanied by Frankish envoys, to reiterate Offa's denial of a plot against Hadrian before the pope himself. The pope remained torn between disbelief that Offa would ever have attempted to persuade Charlemagne to adopt such a course of action and lingering suspicion of the Mercian king, but he finally received Offa's representatives and seems to have accepted their assurances.[44] The identity of the enemies of Offa and Charlemagne is never clarified. It would be natural to assume that this attempt to create a rift between Offa and the papacy occurred before the visit of the legates in 786 and that the visit was part of a process of reconciliation, but this is not wholly justified for Hadrian's letter could date to the late rather than the mid-780s,[45] and reflect hostility to one or more of a number of Offa's actions.

Nevertheless, the letter shows clearly the intensity of feeling in England in this period, and the creation of a new archbishopric at Lichfield is certain to have been an extremely controversial matter. The legatine visitation would provide Offa with an opportunity to acquaint the pope with his plans and the thinking behind them, but there can be no question about the opposition to them at Canterbury. Those whose interests were prejudiced by the events of 787 are likely to have joined the ranks of Offa's enemies, and it was later believed that Archbishop Jaenberht even plotted with Charlemagne against Offa to guarantee him free entry into Kent if he should invade.[46] Though this is probably fanciful and certainly without basis in contemporary record, Jaenberht's alienation from Offa may have been very real, because of the suppression of Kentish independence after 784–5 and now the partition of his province. Alcuin's opinion in 796, as expressed in a letter to Archbishop Aethelheard following the death of Offa, was that the unity of the Church in England had been destroyed not by reasonable consideration but by lust for power;[47] and in 803, when Canterbury's rights were being restored at a council at *Clofesho*, Aethelheard pronounced that 'tyrannical power' had presumed to diminish Canterbury's honour, the pope having been deceived into granting a pallium to the bishop of Lichfield by deception and lies.[48] The *Anglo-Saxon Chronicle* A (*s.a.* 785) refers to the council of Chelsea in 787 as a contentious synod when Archbishop Jaenberht lost a part of his province and Hygeberht, bishop of Lichfield, was chosen to be archbishop of a second metropolitan see by King Offa. Even though Hygeberht received the pallium from Pope Hadrian,[49] his status as archbishop was not willingly recognized by the community at Canterbury (*CS* 254: S 128).[50]

Perhaps surprisingly, the indications are that Offa continued to hold Canterbury in high regard. Aethelheard, abbot of Louth in Lindsey, who became archbishop of Canterbury in 797, may have been seen in Kent as a 'symbol of Mercian rule',[51] but he appears to have obtained from Offa a confirmation of the immunity of Kentish churches (*CS* 848: S 134)[52] and he presided without Hygeberht over a synod at London attended by most of the bishops of southern England (*CS* 265: S 132).[53] Moreover, between 793 and 796 Aethelheard but not Hygeberht subscribed to a grant of land by Offa to the church of Worcester within the archdiocese of Lichfield (*CS* 272, 273: S 146), and in 796 to a grant of land also in Hwiccian territory by Ecgfrith, king of the Mercians, Offa's son and shortlived successor, again without Hygeberht (*CS* 277, 278: S 148). On the other hand, there is nothing here to show necessarily a diminution in Offa's enthusiasm for an archbishopric of Lichfield or lessening regard for Hygeberht. Indeed, Alcuin had advised Offa that it was in order for Aethelheard to be consecrated on 21 July 793 by Archbishop Hygeberht, now the senior metropolitan.[54]

Only in the political disarray which followed the deaths of Offa and Ecgfrith is there evidence of an eagerness to abandon Lichfield, when Coenwulf, king of the Mercians, proposed in a letter to Pope Leo in 797 and again in 798[55] the creation of an archiepiscopal see for a single southern province for Aethelheard at London to replace both Canterbury and Lichfield. There may always have been some in Mercia who did not approve of Offa's Lichfield policy and the realization that London would be the ideal centre for the southern provinces offered a neat solution to a tangled ecclesiastical and political situation. Coenwulf and his counsellors reminded Pope Leo that Gregory the Great had originally intended two metropolitan sees, one at York, the other at London, and blamed the decision about Lichfield on papal ineptitude – Pope Hadrian presuming to diminish the authority of Canterbury simply because of Offa's enmity towards Jaenberht and the men of Kent. The papacy did not respond well to this criticism of Hadrian, and Leo retaliated sharply in 798. First, the pope asserted that it was upon evidence presented by Offa that Hadrian had based his judgement, Offa testifying that it was the unanimous wish of all that a pallium be sent to the bishop of Lichfield. Second, he refused to transfer all metropolitan authority in the southern province to London on the grounds that whatever Gregory's original intentions, Canterbury now possessed the primacy by ancient right.[56] The pope made no direct statement about Lichfield at this time but Aethelheard visited Rome in 801 (*ASC* A, *s.a.* 799) and the pope wrote to him in January 802 (and to Coenwulf) conceding to Aethelheard and his successors authority over all the churches of the Anglo-Saxons (with reference specifically to the twelve bishoprics of the southern province).[57] The following year, on 12 October 803, at *Clofesho*, the restoration to Canterbury of all its rights and the declaration that never again should an archiepiscopal see be placed in Lichfield or anywhere else in the southern province other than Canterbury, completed the destruction of Lichfield's position.[58] But Hygeberht had been demoted some time before. Despite Alcuin's plea to Aethelheard that he not be stripped of his pallium during his lifetime,[59] it was only as bishop that Hygeberht attended the council of Chelsea in 801 (*CS* 302: S 158) and as abbot, that of *Clofesho* in 803. It is probable that his last act as archbishop was to consecrate as his successor as bishop of Lichfield, Ealdwulf, who witnesses as bishop from *c.* 800 (*CS* 201: S 106).[60]

Offa's plans for a metropolitan see at Lichfield, therefore, collapsed on his death. Why had he been so determined to create a second see of archiepiscopal rank in the southern province in the first place? Offa's choice of Lichfield, the principal Mercian see, as the recipient of the new honour would indicate that the scheme had a particular Mercian significance. The *Anglo-Saxon Chronicle* A (*s.a.* 785) records immediately after the appointment of Hygeberht as archbishop that Offa's son, Ecgfrith, was consecrated king, by implication by Hygeberht. It is generally assumed first, that this 'ceremonial recognition of his son as king in his own lifetime was something new'[61] (though Aethelred of Mercia, for example, is said to have appointed Coenred as his heir (*Vita Wilfridi*, ch. 57)), second, that it was the first royal anointing in England (though reservations have been expressed as to whether Ecgfrith was anointed or, if he was, whether he was the first),[62] and, third, that Offa was basing his action on the recent papal consecration in 781 of the Frankish princes, Pippin and Louis, sons of Charlemagne (though Byzantine precedents are also possible).[63] So the precise significance of what occurred in 787 is ambiguous. It is possible that Offa would have liked Ecgfrith to have been consecrated either by the pope or by the papal legates. It may be that Archbishop Jaenberht refused to consecrate him so that Offa was driven to establishing a metropolitan see at Lichfield in order to procure an archbishop who would perform the ceremony. On the other hand, Ecgfrith's consecration was a specifically Mercian matter for he was being consecrated as Offa's successor in Mercia, and it may be that Offa desired archiepiscopal status for the Mercian bishop who would officiate and whom he had always intended should do so. The correspondence of Alcuin reveals that there was opposition within Mercia to the succession of Ecgfrith, presumably from princes who felt in danger of being excluded from the succession, and Offa evidently embarked on what could be described as a purge of these opponents. In a well-known passage, Alciun laments the blood shed by Offa to secure the kingdom for Ecgfrith as the kingdom's ruination.[64] The consecration of Ecgfrith by Hygeberht as archbishop of Lichfield, therefore, was probably designed to enhance Ecgfrith's position as Offa's heir and consolidate support for him within Mercia. In other words, Offa may never have wished this to be anything other than a wholly Mercian ceremony.

There may have been an additional dimension to all this. The extent of Hygeberht's authority perhaps sheds light on Offa's principal area of interest. The suffragan sees of Lichfield were Worcester, Hereford, Leicester, Lindsey, *Dommoc* and Elmham; Canterbury retained Winchester, Sherborne, Rochester and London.[65] Hygeberht's archdiocese, therefore, embraced Mercia and its dependent border territories in the midlands and East Anglia. The pallium gave Hygeberht no jurisdiction in Saxon territories or in Kent but it did afford him metropolitan rights over all the Anglian peoples north of the Thames and south of the Humber, which may suggest that Offa was seeking not just an archbishop of the Mercians but a new ecclesiastical order for the Angles of midland and eastern England. So much evidence, relatively speaking, survives to illustrate Offa's dealings with the men of Kent and to a lesser extent with the South Saxons and so little to illuminate his relations with the Anglian groups of eastern England that the order of importance of these areas to Offa can easily be inverted.

It used to be thought that, when Offa was styled on occasion in the charters of the period *rex Anglorum*, this signified that he aspired to lordship over all the Anglo-Saxons[66] or at least to make himself the only king south of the Humber.[67] It is true that he gave one daughter, Eadburh, in marriage to Beorhtric, king of the West Saxons (*ASC* A, *s.a.* 787), and another, Aelfflaed, to Aethelred, king of Northumbria, in 792,[68] but the revival of a Northumbrian coinage at this time by Aethelred (see above, p. 158) and the inauguration of a new West Saxon coinage by Beorhtric at Winchester or Southampton testifies to their continuing independence.[69] It is not even certain that *rex Anglorum* is anything other than a later tenth- or eleventh-century interpolation in those charters of the reign in which it appears.[70] If it occurs anywhere in Offa's reign it does so as *Of Rx A* on a few of Offa's coins by the London moneyer, Alhmund.[71] It need not, however, have had the significance it acquired in tenth-century documents when it did come to express claims to a kingship of all Anglo-Saxons. The title *Rex Anglorum* had been adopted in early papal correspondence. The *Life of Guthlac*[72] uses it to describe Aethelred, king of the Mercians (ch. 1). *REX ANG* was used on some of his coins by Aethelstan, king of the East Angles, in the 830s and subsequently *REX AN* by Eadmund, king of the East Angles.[73] The creation of an Anglian archdiocese could have been primarily intended as an expression of a new southern Anglian political community. Its ecclesiastical centre was Lichfield, its principal trading emporia London and Ipswich.[74] What happened in Kent and Sussex can obscure the central fact of the reign, namely, that Mercia had changed from 'a confederation of peoples under Mercian overlordship to a vast kingdom comprising most of the English areas between the Thames and the Humber'.[75] Here the continued acceptance of a dependent relationship with the Mercians on the part of the East Angles was crucial. Without East Anglian acceptance of a subordinate role, Offa's Anglian empire would be of short duration. The greater the Mercian involvement in south-eastern England, particularly Kent, however attractive control of Kentish resources may have been or however militarily desirable the containment of a possibly unstable local hegemony, the more vulnerable was Offa's position in the face of hostile anti-Mercian sentiment south as well as north of the Thames. If to this is added the domestic tensions occasioned by Offa's determination to secure the succession of his son, Ecgfrith, it becomes clear how highly charged the political atmosphere must have been in Offa's last years.

The 790s are one of the best documented decades in Anglo-Saxon history and this enables the years of crisis which followed the establishment of Offa's dominant position to be comprehended in some detail. The Carolingians maintained close contact with Offa's court and Alcuin congratulated Offa in the late 780s on his eagerness to encourage learning in his kingdom,[76] sent greetings to Queen Cynethryth,[77] and urged Ecgfrith not to be unworthy of his noble birth.[78] In the early 790s Charlemagne is thought to have been anxious to secure Anglo-Saxon support against iconoclasm at the council of Frankfurt in 794.[79] A heavier penny coinage was introduced by Offa to conform with contemporary Carolingian developments.[80] In 796, at a time when the volume of long-distance trade was increasing, the two rulers were corresponding about their mutual commercial interests and reciprocal protection of merchants.[81] Not surprisingly, therefore, Sir Frank Stenton believed that Offa was able 'to deal on equal terms' with Charlemagne.[82] Perhaps the most conspicuous feature of the early 790s, however, was the often uneasy relations between the two rulers. Offa's increased power and prestige across the 780s evidently introduced a new factor into Anglo-Frankish relations and rendered them somewhat ambivalent. A proposal by Charlemagne *c.* 789–90 that his oldest son, Charles, should marry one of Offa's daughters may already have been more an attempt to 'patch up bad relations' than to give effect to good ones,[83] and, when acceptance of this extremely prestigious offer was made dependent by Offa on one of Charlemagne's daughters marrying Ecgfrith, so affronted was Charlemagne that he gave orders that no one from Britain and the Anglian race was to land on the sea-coast of Gaul for the sake of commerce.[84] The reality of this breakdown in relations is confirmed by letters written by Alcuin in 790 in which he reported a quarrel between Charlemagne and Offa so serious that on both sides traders were forbidden to sail.[85] Alcuin thought he might be employed in making peace,[86] but the fact that he found it necessary to protest that he had never been disloyal to Offa suggests that his allegiances were being called into question.[87] Gervold, abbot of St Wandrille, who had for some time supervised the exaction of tolls at various Channel ports (particularly Quentovic) and established cordial relations with Offa, evidently mollified

Charlemagne and a trade embargo was not maintained.[88] If Offa thought he could attempt 'to deal on equal terms' with Charlemagne, therefore, he was mistaken, and the likelihood is that the Frankish court had come to view his ascendancy in southern England with misgivings, destroying as it had done the traditional shape of political power in the south-east.

Carolingian involvement with kingdoms other than Mercia and with elements opposed to Offa certainly now becomes a feature of Anglo-Saxon political life. Welsh rulers, with whom Offa may have been at war and who possibly ruled in British territory subject to him, could have been among the kings of the Scots (Irish) who recognized the lordship of Charlemagne.[89] Among the Anglo-Saxons Charlemagne sought to establish good relations with Northumbria.[90] Alcuin was soon disappointed in the new king Aethelred, son of Aethelwald, and his disapproval of Aethelred and his court circle for excessive self-indulgence and immoral and unrighteous conduct was consistently sustained (see above, p. 154). Nevertheless, he vowed that he would never cease to give Aethelred advice,[91] and when Charlemagne was so enraged by the assassination of Aethelred in 796 that his Northumbrian gifts were recalled, threats of worse consequences were averted in Alcuin's view only by his intercession.[92] Alcuin was also critical of the new Northumbrian king, Eardwulf, but when Eardwulf was driven out of his kingdom in 806 he was restored two years later through the intervention of Charlemagne and the pope (see above, p. 157), a clear enough demonstration of the continued maintenance of Northumbria at this time as a Carolingian sphere of influence.

No volume of correspondence similar to Alcuin's survives to illustrate Charlemagne's dealings with other Anglo-Saxon kingdoms but the support Charlemagne is known to have given to Offa's enemies reveals widespread diplomatic activity around the borders of Mercia. In a letter to Archbishop Aethelheard and Ceolwulf, bishop of Lindsey, written 793–6, Charlemagne asked them to intercede with Offa for certain individuals who had gone into exile with their lord, Hringstan, who had now died.[93] Ceolwulf left England himself in 796 in the company of the bishop of London (*ASC* A, *s.a.* 794) but whether to go on pilgrimage or into exile is not known and he died the same year (*ASC* D, *s.a.* 796). In 796 Charlemagne was giving shelter to an important exile from England, the priest Odberht, almost certainly to be identified with the Eadberht Praen[94] who was accused of being an ex-priest[95] and who subsequently seized the Kentish kingdom on the death of Offa. Archbishop Aethelheard was at Rome seeking to secure the person of Odberht/Eadberht to answer charges brought against him by Offa, but Charlemagne had also sent Eadberht and others, who were in fear of death from Offa and had sought his protection, to Rome to defend themselves in person before the pope.[96] Another exile in Gaul was Ecgberht, son of Ealhmund, who had been driven out by Offa and Beorhtric, king of the West Saxons, and who sought refuge in Gaul (*ASC* A, *s.a.* 836) where, according to William of Malmesbury writing in a later age, he learnt the arts of government.[97] He certainly learnt that of survival.

The keynote for the last years of Offa, however, is sounded by an event much closer to home than the Carolingian court. In 794 Offa had Aethelberht, king of the East Angles, beheaded (*ASC* A, *s.a.* 792). Nothing further is known of the episode from contemporary sources. Aethelberht had evidently been left as king among the East Angles but whether as a *regulus* or *subregulus* is unknown in the absence of East Anglian charters. Certainly, he had been stopped from minting his own coins. His later *Lives* do not inspire great confidence in their historical details about a young king seeking the hand of Offa's daughter in marriage and falling a victim to the machinations of Queen Cynethryth, who alleged that Aethelberht's real intention was to reconnoitre the Mercian kingdom with a view to invading it,[98] and when the *Chronicon ex Chronicis* also claims that Aethelberht was put to death by Offa at the instigation of Queen Cynethryth[99] it is not necessarily independent of the legend. Nevertheless, however it came about, Offa's slaying of Aethelberht represented a serious blow to the realization of a peaceful union of south Anglian peoples under the overlordship of the Mercian king and augured more forceful compulsion.

Following this confrontation, a succession of crises seriously undermined the Mercian position further. The first was not so much Offa's death on 26 or 29 July 796[100] (*ASC* D, *s.a.* 796) as the death of Ecgfrith, his successor, 141 days later (*ASC* A, *s.a.* 755) which threatened all that Offa had struggled to achieve within Mercia and created dynastic uncertainty at the centre of the Mercian polity as royal power was assumed by Coenwulf, a prince claiming descent not from Eowa or Penda but from a certain Coenwealh, allegedly in the genealogies a brother of Eowa and Penda (see Appendix, Fig. 8).[101] Coenwulf had several brothers and would seem to have been a member of a very powerful kindred, some of whose landed estates were centred on the region of Winchcombe,[102] but none of his forebears had reigned as kings and Alcuin's observations in a letter to the people of Kent in 797 that scarcely anyone was to be found now of the old stock of kings and the more obscure their origin, the less their courage, could certainly be construed as a slight on Coenwulf.[103] It was not at all clear at his accession how far the new king would pursue Offa's policies nor how he would deal with the Carolingians. Alcuin was so far from being certain of his standing with Coenwulf that he asked a Mercian patrician - probably the senior Mercian ealdorman Brorda[104] - to greet the king peaceably 'if it is possible to do so'.[105] Alcuin regarded the dynastic purges of Offa's reign as an unmitigated evil, for which the premature death of Ecgfrith represented divine retribution. Nevertheless, he viewed Coenwulf as a tyrant,[106] who had compounded his deficiencies by putting away his wife and taking another (as Eardwulf had done in Northumbria), and urged the Mercian patrician to advise the Mercian people to observe what he referred to as the good and chaste customs of Offa. When he did feel able to write to Coenwulf he reminded him of his humble origins (but avoided reference to his matrimonial difficulties) and exhorted him to remember always the very best features of Offa's reign, avoiding Offa's displays of greed and cruelty.[107] No other material illustrates more vividly the political consternation and diplomatic uncertainty attendant on the accession of a new king.

Moreover, at some point – probably on Ecgfrith's death – Eadberht Praen, recently an exile at the court of Charlemagne, returned to England and established himself as king in Kent (*ASC* A, *s.a.* 794),[108] his grip on the kingdom underlined by the minting of his own coins at Canterbury.[109] The implication must be that Eadberht denied that he had previously taken holy orders and affirmed the legitimacy of his claim, but Archbishop Aethelheard fled[110] and Christ Church, Canterbury, was probably sacked.[111] The minting of coins, possibly simultaneously, in East Anglia in the name of a king, Eadwald, indicates that the East Angles also emancipated themselves from Mercian control.[112] At the same time a breakdown in the relations between the Mercians and the West Saxons left the Mercians temporarily friendless and isolated in southern England (see below, p. 179).

Alcuin was furious with Archbishop Aethelheard for fleeing but there must be a possibility, representing Carolingian interests as he did, that Alcuin was more disturbed by Aethelheard's refusal to accept as king the Carolingian protégé, Eadberht Praen. That Aethelheard's flight was not generally seen as discreditable is clear from Leo III's subsequent praise of him for endangering his life against 'Julian the Apostate', as the pope described Eadberht,[113] but Alcuin gave Aethelheard no such credit and remained highly critical of him for allegedly neglecting his Christian duty[114] and it is possible that in his absence the Kentish leaders were considering the election of another archbishop.[115] It is clear that Coenwulf did not dare to risk ecclesiastical sanction by proceeding against Eadberht until the papal position on the matter was made quite clear. In his reply to Coenwulf, the pope refused to countenance the removal of the archbishop of Canterbury to London, but the impact of this papal prohibition was offset by the papal recognition of Eadberht's earlier ordination and consequent ineligibility for the kingship and permission was given to proceed against him as a pretender to royal power. The Church had no alternative but to condemn him, excommunicate and reject him, as Pope Leo put it, 'having regard to the safety of his soul', the pope expressing the hope that in return Coenwulf would be more generous to the Church of St Peter than Offa had been.[116]

The failure of the pope to pronounce on this matter until 798 meant a dangerous delay for Coenwulf and was probably a factor in his desire for an archbishopric at London, but the papal judgement when it came gave him a free hand and made London as an archiepiscopal see dispensable. Coenwulf vigorously crushed the revolt in Kent and captured Eadberht, who was blinded and mutilated and taken in chains into Mercia (*ASC* A, F, *s.a.* 796)[117] where he was imprisoned for some years at Winchcombe.[118] Aethelheard returned to Canterbury and set about imposing his authority anew on the bishops of the southern province,[119] and by 801 at the latest Coenwulf had installed one of his brothers, Cuthred, as king in Kent, to govern the territory more securely (*CS* 303: S 157). What happened in East Anglia is obscure but Eadwald disappeared and *c.* 805[120] Coenwulf resumed the minting of coins in East Anglia in his own name.[121] It seems probable that rebellion in East Anglia was as rigorously suppressed as in Kent. By 799 Coenwulf was also in a position to conclude a new treaty of peace with the West Saxons, which seems to have terminated a period of temporary estrangement (*CS* 295: S 154).[122] In that year Coenwulf allowed himself the luxury of the elaborate royal style *rector et imperator Merciorum regni* (*CS* 289: S 153), 'the first time a western ruler had called himself "emperor" in an official record since the Roman Empire'.[123] He had survived the crisis of 796–8 remarkably well. His plan for a metropolitan see at London had been stillborn but he had rid himself of the problem of Lichfield (a process completed by 803), successfully confounded his enemies and consolidated the position Offa had established at the height of his power.

Offa had been a powerful king whose interventionist rule was no more acceptable to those outside the Mercian kingdom and its traditional dependencies than that of previous overlords. It is probably anachronistic to imagine that Offa intended to create a single southern Anglo-Saxon kingdom under one ruler. What he aspired to was the union of southern Anglian peoples under the leadership of a Mercian king and a Mercian archbishop. He displayed no desire to interfere militarily in Wessex or Northumbria though his response to what was probably a local Kentish hegemony in the south-east after 784/5 reveals his potential for aggression. The skill with which Coenwulf conserved Offa's *imperium*, however, can obscure some fundamental shifts of emphasis. First, the abandonment of a Mercian archbishopric implied a renunciation of the idea of a southern Anglian realm as a distinct political entity. Second, the Mercian grip on Kent and the south-east tightened. Offa's still rather distant control had been replaced by a permanent Mercian royal presence. Third, the diplomatic accord which the Carolingians had earlier enjoyed with Offa in Mercia had been destroyed (see below, pp. 185 ff.). Though Coenwulf's 'empire' may look like Offa's, therefore, the crisis of 796–8 had helped to establish possibly a less flexible regime and certainly one more insular in outlook. The degree of stability to which it could attain remained to be seen.

Notes

1   D. N. Dumville, 'The Anglian collection of royal genealogies and regnal lists', *Anglo-Saxon England*, vol. 5 (1976), pp. 23–50 (pp. 31, 33, 36).
2   On these documents, see A. Scharer, *Die angelsächsische Königsurkunde im 7. und 8. Jahrhundert* (Vienna, 1982), pp. 247 ff. Cf., S. Bassett's comments in idem, *The Origins of Anglo-Saxon Kingdoms* (Leicester, 1989), p. 241 (n. 35).
3   W. Levison, *England and the Continent in the Eighth Century* (Oxford, 1946), p. 251.
4   For this suggestion, see Scharer, *Die angelsächsische Königsurkunde*, p. 215.
5   *Bede's Ecclesiastical History of the English People*, ed. and trans. B. Colgrave and R. A. B. Mynors (Oxford, 1969), pp. 574–5.
6   *Symeonis Monachi Opera Omnia*, ed. T. Arnold, 2 vols (Rolls series: London, 1882, 1885), Vol. II, p. 41.
7   On Aldfrith, see F. M. Stenton, 'Lindsey and its kings', in D. M. Stenton (ed.), *Preparatory to Anglo-Saxon England* (Oxford, 1971), pp. 127–35 (pp. 129–30). Offa gave generously to the shrine of King Oswald at Bardney; *Alcuin: The Bishops, Kings and Saints of York*, ed. and trans. P. Godman (Oxford, 1982), ll. 388–90 (pp. 34–5).
8   B. E. A. Yorke, 'The kingdom of the East Saxons', *Anglo-Saxon England*, vol. 14 (1985), pp. 1–36 (pp. 23–4).
9   I. Stewart, 'The London mint and the coinage of Offa', in M. Blackburn (ed.), *Anglo-Saxon Monetary History* (Leicester, 1986), pp. 27–43. Of the substantial literature on Offa's pennies, see C. E. Blunt, 'The coinage of Offa', in R. H. M. Dolley (ed.), *Anglo-Saxon Coins* (London, 1961), pp. 39–62; F. M. Stenton, 'The Anglo-Saxon coinage and the historian', in Stenton, *Preparatory to Anglo-Saxon England*, pp. 371–82 (pp.379 ff.); C. S. S. Lyon, 'Historical problems of Anglo-Saxon coinage', *British Numismatic Journal*, 36 (1967), pp. 215–21; and the review by D. M. Metcalf, 'Monetary expansion and recession: interpreting the distribution-pattern of seventh- and eighth-century coins', in J. Casey and R. Reece (eds), *Coins and the Archaeologist* (BAR 4, 1974), pp. 206–23 (reprinted and revised in the 2nd edn (London, 1988), pp. 230–53), and P. Grierson and M. Blackburn, *Medieval European Coinage*, Vol. I: *The Early Middle Ages* (Cambridge, 1986), pp. 270 ff.
10 Scharer, *Die angelsächsische Königsurkunde*, p. 258.
11 R. Hodges, *The Anglo-Saxon Achievement: Archaeology and the Beginnings of English Society* (London, 1989), p. 101.
12 Grierson and Blackburn, *Medieval European Coinage*, Vol. I, p. 277; Hodges, *The Anglo-Saxon Achievement*, p. 101. *Florentii Wigorniensis monachi Chronicon ex Chronicis*, ed. B. Thorpe, 2 vols (London, 1848), Vol. I, p. 57, places Beonna *c.* 758 (see above p. 140, n. 100).
13 *Asser's Life of King Alfred*, ed. W. H. Stevenson (rev. edn, Oxford, 1959). For a translation of the *Life* and other documents, see S. Keynes and M. Lapidge, *Alfred the Great: Asser's Life of Alfred and Other Contemporary Sources* (Harmondsworth, 1983).
14 C. Fox, *Offa's Dyke* (London, 1955) is being superseded by a more recent study by D. Hill, 'Offa's and Wat's Dykes - some exploratory work on the frontier between Celt and Saxon', in T. Rowley (ed.), *Anglo-Saxon Settlement and Landscape* (BAR 6, 1974), pp. 102–7; idem, 'The inter-relation of Offa's and Wat's Dykes', *Antiquity*, vol. 48 (1974), pp. 309–12; and idem, 'Offa's and Wat's Dykes: some aspects of recent work', *Transactions of the Lancashire and Cheshire Antiquarian Society*, vol. 79 (1977), pp. 21–33. Cf., also, F. Noble, *Offa's Dyke Path* (London, 1969) and C. J. Wright, *A Guide to Offa's Dyke Path* (London, 1975). M. Worthington comments on the Offa's Dyke project in *Archaeology in Wales*, vol. 25 (1985), pp. 9–10. See also P. Wormald, 'Offa's Dyke', in J. Campbell (ed.), *The Anglo-Saxons* (Oxford, 1982), pp. 120–1.
15 P. C. Bartrum (ed.), *Early Welsh Genealogical Tracts* (Cardiff, 1966), pp. 1–3.
16 *Epistolae Karol. Aevi*, Vol. II, ed. E. Dümmler, *MGH Epistolae*, Vol. IV (Berlin, 1895), no.3.
17 Cf., B. E. A. Yorke, 'Joint kingship in Kent', *Archaeologia Cantiana*, vol. 99 (1983), pp. 1–19 (p. 11).
18 Cf., N. Brooks, *The Early History of the Church of Canterbury* (Leicester, 1984), p. 112 and K. P. Witney, *The Kingdom of Kent* (London and Chichester, 1982), p. 201.

Stenton was uneasy about *CS* 195: S 105 but felt there was no obvious motive for fabrication (*Preparatory to Anglo-Saxon England*, p. 62, n. 1), and see also now Scharer, *Die angelsächsische Königsurkunde*, pp. 217 ff. The charters of Rochester have been separately edited by A. Campbell, *Charters of Rochester* (London, 1973).

19 F. M. Stenton, 'The supremacy of the Mercian kings' in Stenton, *Preparatory to Anglo-Saxon England*, pp. 48–62 (p. 62), and cf., idem, 'The Anglo-Saxon coinage and the historian', ibid., pp. 371–82 (p. 379); idem, *Anglo-Saxon England* (3rd edn, Oxford, 1971), p. 207.

20 Cf., Brooks, *The Early History of the Church of Canterbury*, p. 319.

21 ibid., pp. 319–20. Cf. Scharer, *Die angelsächsische Königsurkunde*, pp. 228 ff., and P. Wormald, 'Bede, the *bretwaldas* and the origins of the *Gens Anglorum*', in P. Wormald, D. Bullough and R. Collins (eds), *Ideal and Reality in Frankish and Anglo-Saxon Society* (Oxford, 1983), pp. 99–129 (p. 110).

22 Metcalf, 'Monetary expansion and recession', p. 240.

23 Cf., Brooks, *The Early History of the Church of Canterbury*, pp. 115, 158.

24 Stenton, *Anglo-Saxon England*, p. 207.

25 Cf., Scharer, *Die angelsächsische Königsurkunde*, p. 226.

26 Blunt, 'The coinage of Offa', p. 50; Metcalf, 'Monetary expansion and recession', p. 243.

27 Stewart, 'The London mint and the coinage of Offa', p. 31; Grierson and Blackburn, *Medieval European Coinage*, Vol. I, pp. 277–8.

28 H. Vollrath-Reichelt, *Königsgedanke und Königtum bei den Angelsachsen* (Cologne, 1971), pp. 163 ff.

29 Cf., Brooks, *The Early History of the Church of Canterbury*, p. 115 (and nn. 21, 23), and pp. 321–2.

30 Wormald, 'Bede, the *Bretwaldas* and the origins of the *Gens Anglorum*', p. 113; cf., Vollrath-Reichelt, *Königsgedanke und Königtum*, pp. 173 ff., and Scharer, *Die angelsächsische Königsurkunde*, pp. 216, 268.

31 Cf., Scharer, *Die angelsächsische Königsurkunde*, p. 260. M. Welsh, 'The kingdom of the South Saxons: the origins', in Bassett, *The Origins of Anglo-Saxon Kingdoms*, pp. 75–83, suggests a division of the kingdom, perhaps between two rival royal families (p. 80). For 'A preliminary study of the seventh- and eighth-century South Saxon charters', see idem, *Early Anglo-Saxon Sussex*, vol. ii (BAR British Series 112 (ii), 1983), pp. 323–31.

32 Stenton, *Anglo-Saxon England*, p. 208 (n. 3).

33 *Symeonis Monachi Opera Omnia*, Vol. II, p. 44.

34 *Preparatory to Anglo-Saxon England*, Stenton, p. 62 (n. 2). He took a less severe view subsequently - *Anglo-Saxon England*, p. 208 (n. 5): but the untypical witness-list as it stands is surely highly suspect; cf., Scharer, *Die angelsächsische Königsurkunde*, p. 261. M. G. Welch comments, *Early Anglo-Saxon Sussex*, vol. i (BAR British Series, 112 (i) 1983), p. 274.

35 Scharer, *Die angelsächsische Königsurkunde*, p. 214.

36 P. Sims-Williams, 'Continental influence at Bath monastery in the seventh century', *Anglo-Saxon England*, vol. 4 (1975), pp. 1–10 (p. 9).

37 Hodges, *The Anglo-Saxon Achievement*, pp. 116 ff.

38 *Councils and Ecclesiastical Documents*, ed. A. W. Haddan and W. Stubbs, 3 vols (Oxford, 1869–71), Vol. III, pp. 521–3 (p. 522) (*EHD* Vol. I, no. 204).

39 *Epistolae Karol. Aevi*, Vol. II, no. 127 (*EHD* Vol. I, no. 205).

40 ibid., no. 3 (*EHD* Vol. I, no. 191). P. Wormald, 'The age of Offa and Alcuin', in Campbell, *The Anglo-Saxons*, pp. 101–31 (p. 125), suggests that the laws of Offa, to which the laws of Alfred refer, were these decrees.

41 Cf., Levison, *England and the Continent in the Eighth Century*, pp. 127 ff.; H. Vollrath, *Die Synoden Englands bis 1066* (Paderborn, 1985), p. 163.

42 *Epistolae Karol. Aevi*, Vol. II, no. 127 (*EHD* Vol. I, no. 205).

43 See Vollrath, *Die Synoden Englands*, pp. 172–3.

44 *Councils and Ecclesiastical Documents*, Haddan and Stubbs, Vol. III, pp. 440–2 (trans. H. R. Loyn and J. Percival, *The Reign of Charlemagne* (London, 1975), no. 39).

45 Brooks, *The Early History of the Church of Canterbury*, p. 350 (n. 29).

46 ibid., pp. 115–16.
47 *Epistolae Karol. Aevi*, Vol. II, no. 128 (*EHD* Vol. I, no. 203).
48 *Councils and Ecclesiastical Documents*, Haddan and Stubbs, Vol. III, pp. 542–4 (*EHD* Vol. I, no. 210).
49 ibid., Vol. III, p. 543.
50 Cf., Brooks, *The Early History of the Church of Canterbury*, p. 119.
51 ibid., pp. 120–1.
52 ibid., p. 120 and cf., N. Brooks, 'The development of military obligations in eighth- and ninth-century England', in P. Clemoes and K. Hughes (eds), *England before the Norman Conquest* (Cambridge, 1971), pp. 69–84 (pp. 79–80).
53 Brooks, *The Early History of the Church of Canterbury*, pp. 120–1, 320–1.
54 Levison, *England and the Continent in the Eighth Century*, pp. 244–6: cf., Brooks, *The Early History of the Church of Canterbury*, p. 120.
55 *Councils and Ecclesiastical Documents*, Haddan and Stubbs, Vol. III, pp. 521–3 (*EHD* Vol. I, no. 204).
56 *Epistolae Karol. Aevi*, Vol. II, no. 127 (*EHD* Vol. I, no. 205). See Vollrath, *Die Synoden Englands*, pp. 163 ff., 181 ff.
57 *Councils and Ecclesiastical Documents*, Haddan and Stubbs, Vol. III, pp. 536–7 (*EHD* Vol. I, no. 209), pp. 538–9.
58 ibid., Vol. III, pp. 522–4 (*EHD* Vol. I, no. 210).
59 *Epistolae Karol. Aevi*, Vol. II, no. 128 (*EHD* Vol. I, no. 203).
60 Cf., J. W. Lamb, *The Archbishopric of Lichfield 787–803* (London, 1964), pp. 36–7.
61 E. John, *Orbis Britanniae and Other Studies* (Leicester, 1966), p. 34.
62 J. L. Nelson, *Politics and Ritual in Early Medieval Europe* (London, 1986), pp. 285, 324.
63 ibid., p. 319, n. 4. This was at about the time when a unique coinage was issued in the name of Offa's queen, Cynethryth, based on the example of Byzantine coins of the Empress Irene: Grierson and Blackburn, *Medieval European Coinage*, Vol. I, pp. 279–80.
64 *Epistolae Karol. Aevi*, Vol. II, no. 122 (*EHD* Vol. I, no. 202).
65 *Willelmi Malmesbiriensis Gesta Pontificum Anglorum*, ed. N. E. S. A. Hamilton (Rolls series: London, 1870), p. 16.
66 Stenton, *Anglo-Saxon England*, p. 211 (cf., idem, 'The supremacy of the Mercian kings', in Stenton, *Preparatory to Anglo-Saxon England*, p. 63).
67 John, *Orbis Britanniae*, p. 26.
68 *Symeonis Monachi Opera Omnia*, Vol. II, p. 54.
69 Grierson and Blackburn, *Medieval European Coinage*, Vol. I, pp. 294, 298.
70 Scharer, *Die angelsächsische Königsurkunde*, p. 228, n. 6; Wormald, 'Bede, the *bretwaldas* and the origins of the *Gens Anglorum*', pp. 110–11. Though Scharer, op. cit., p. 228, n. 6, considers that the implication of *CS* 274: S 139 (in which Offa is 'made king by the King of Kings') is that Offa was regarded as the only Anglo-Saxon king entitled to use the title *rex* (cf., p. 278), this seems very fanciful.
71 D. M. Metcalf, 'Offa's pence reconsidered', *Cunobelin*, vol. 9 (1963), pp. 37–52 (p. 41).
72 *Felix's Life of Saint Guthlac*, ed. B. Colgrave (Cambridge, 1956).
73 H. E. Pagan, 'The coinage of the East Anglian kingdom', *British Numismatic Journal*, vol. 52 (1982), pp.41–83 (pp. 43–6, 49, 65–6, 71 ff.): Grierson and Blackburn, *Medieval European Coinage*, Vol. I, p. 294.
74 On these emporia, see Hodges, *The Anglo-Saxon Achievement*, pp. 134–5.
75 B. E. A. Yorke, *Kings and Kingdoms in Early Anglo-Saxon England* (London, 1990 [forthcoming]), Chap. 6.
76 *Epistolae Karol. Aevi*, Vol. II, no. 64 (*EHD* Vol. I, no. 195).
77 ibid., no. 62.
78 ibid., no. 61.
79 Vollrath, *Die Synoden Englands*, pp. 179 ff. Cf., also the comments of J. M. Wallace-Hadrill, 'Charlemagne and England', *Early Medieval History* (Oxford, 1975), pp. 155–80 (p. 164), and idem, *Early Germanic Kingship in England and on the Continent* (Oxford, 1971), p. 118.

80 Blunt, 'The coinage of Offa', p. 53: Grierson and Blackburn, *Medieval European Coinage*, Vol. I, p. 280.
81 *Epistolae Karol. Aevi*, Vol. II, no. 100 (*EHD* Vol. I, no. 197); Hodges, *The Anglo-Saxon Achievement*, p. 119.
82 Stenton, *Anglo-Saxon England*, p. 215.
83 Wallace-Hadrill, *Early Germanic Kingship in England and on the Continent*, p. 115; cf., idem, 'Charlemagne and England', pp. 161–2. Note, however, that in 790, so far as Alcuin was concerned, Offa and Charlemagne were 'former friends' (*Epistolae Karol. Aevi*, Vol. II, no. 9). There is no hint here of previous estrangements.
84 *Gesta sanctorum patrum Fontanellensis coenobii*, ed. F. Lohier and R. P. J. Laporte (Société de l'histoire de Normandie; Rouen and Paris, 1936), p. 87 (*EHD* Vol. I, no. 20).
85 *Epistolae Karol. Aevi*, Vol. II, no. 7 (*EHD* Vol. I, no. 192).
86 *Epistolae Karol. Aevi*, Vol. II, nos 7, 9.
87 ibid., no. 82.
88 *Gesta sanctorum patrum Fontanellensis coenobii*, pp. 86–7 (*EHD* Vol. I, no. 20).
89 Wallace-Hadrill, 'Charlemagne and England', p. 172.
90 ibid., p. 165.
91 *Epistolae Karol. Aevi*, Vol. II, no.30.
92 ibid., no. 101 (*EHD* Vol. I, no. 198).
93 ibid., no. 85 (*EHD* Vol. I, no. 196).
94 Brooks, *The Early History of the Church of Canterbury*, p. 114.
95 *Epistolae Karol. Aevi*, Vol. II, no. 127 (*EHD* Vol. I, no. 205).
96 ibid., no. 100 (*EHD* Vol. I, no. 197).
97 *Willelmi Malmesbiriensis monachi De Gestis Regum Anglorum*, ed. W. Stubbs, 2 vols (Rolls series: London, 1887, 1889), Vol. I, p. 105.
98 M. R. James, 'Two Lives of St Ethelberht, king and martyr', *English Historical Review*, vol. 32 (1917), pp. 214–44.
99 *Florentii Wigorniensis monachi Chronicon ex Chronicis*, ed. B. Thorpe, 2 vols (London, 1848), Vol. I, pp. 62–3.
100 *Symeonis Monachi Opera Omnia*, Vol. II, p. 58.
101 Dumville, 'The Anglian collection of royal genealogies', pp. 32, 33, 37.
102 Cf., Levison, *England and the Continent in the Eighth Century*, pp. 249 'f., H. P. R. Finberg, 'The ancient shire of Winchcombe', *The Early Charters of the West Midlands* (Leicester, 1961), pp. 228–35, and S. Bassett, 'In search of the origins of Anglo-Saxon kingdoms', in Bassett, *The Origins of Anglo-Saxon Kingdoms*, pp. 3–27 (pp. 8 ff.) (who regards Coenwulf (n. 29) as of possibly Hwiccian descent).
103 *Epistolae Karol. Aevi*, Vol. II, no. 129.
104 On his identity, see A. T. Thacker, 'Some terms for noblemen in Anglo-Saxon England, *c.* 650–900', in D. Brown, J. Campbell and S. C. Hawkes (eds), *Anglo-Saxon Studies in Archaeology and History*, no. 2 (BAR British Series 92, 1981), pp. 201–36 (pp. 218–20).
105 *Epistolae Karol. Aevi*, Vol. II, no. 122 (*EHD* Vol. I, no. 202).
106 ibid., no. 300.
107 ibid., no. 123.
108 Brooks, *The Early History of the Church of Canterbury*, p. 122, thinks that Eadberht established himself in Kent while Ecgfrith was alive, but Frankish support for his venture is more likely to have been forthcoming on Ecgfrith's death.
109 Blunt, 'The coinage of Offa', pp. 50, 55; C. E. Blunt, C. S. S. Lyon and B. H. I. H. Stewart, 'The coinage of southern England 791–840', *British Numismatic Journal*, vol. 32 (1963), pp. 1–74 (pp. 5, 7).
110 *Epistolae Karol. Aevi*, Vol. II, no. 128 (*EHD* Vol. I, no. 203).
111 Brooks, *The Early History of the Church of Canterbury*, p. 121.
112 Blunt, 'The coinage of Offa', pp. 50, 54; Blunt, Lyon and Stewart, 'The coinage of southern England', pp. 26, 27.
113 *Epistolae Karol. Aevi*, Vol. II, no. 127 (*EHD* Vol. I, no. 205).
114 ibid., no. 128 (*EHD* Vol. I, no. 203).
115 ibid., no. 129. Alcuin remained critical of Aethelheard even during the archbishop's visit to Rome in 801 (ibid., no. 230).

116   *Councils and Ecclesiastical Documents*, Vol. III, p. 524.
117   *Symeonis Monachi Opera Omnia*, Vol. II, p. 59.
118   Cf., Brooks, *The Early History of the Church of Canterbury*, pp. 124–5.
119   ibid., p. 125.
120   Grierson and Blackburn, *Medieval European Coinage*, Vol. I, p. 293.
121   Blunt, Lyon and Stewart, 'The coinage of southern England', pp. 26, 40.
122   The date of this document seems to be acceptable – the seventh indiction and the year 799 – but friendship was not confirmed between the kings, Coenwulf and Ecgberht, but between Coenwulf and Beorhtric, for whose name Ecgberht's has been erroneously substituted.
123   John, *Orbis Britanniae*, p. 21: cf., Wallace-Hadrill, 'Charlemagne and England', pp. 168–9.

9 The Anglo-Saxon kingdoms in the first three-quarters of the ninth century

When Coenwulf, king of the Mercians, died in 821 he had reigned for a quarter of a century. His brother and successor, Ceolwulf, however, was deposed after two years. Two years after that Ceolwulf's successor, Beornwulf, was defeated by Ecgberht, king of the West Saxons, and subsequently fell in battle against the East Angles, as did his successor, Ludeca, a year later. In 829 Wiglaf, king of the Mercians, was driven out by Ecgberht who conquered the Mercian kingdom and 'everything south of the Humber' (*ASC* A, *s.a.* 819, 821, 823, 825, 827). This sequence of domestic and military disasters across the years 821–9 is in striking contrast to the preceding period of apparent stability between 798 and 821. Nor, in the face of a resilient East Anglia and a mightier Wessex under the dynasty of Ecgberht, were subsequent Mercian kings ever wholly able to redress the new balance of power. The political map of the Anglo-Saxon kingdoms south of the Humber was being redrawn in these years as Mercian strength proved inadequate to the maintenance of the position established by Offa and redefined by Coenwulf. To what extent the territorial integrity of Northumbria was maintained until the Danish capture of York in 866[1] is unknown, but it would be surprising if Northumbrian kings did not face problems similar to those confronting their Mercian counterparts in southern England.

The Mercian successors of Offa

Coenwulf's reign had itself begun in a thoroughly inauspicious manner; the intrusion into Kent of the exile, Eadberht Praen, almost certainly with Carolingian support, and the papal rebuff of Coenwulf's plan for the establishment of London as the southern metropolitan see, demonstrated quite clearly that papal and Carolingian interests were not necessarily compatible with Mercian. The successful restoration, probably by 799, of Mercian authority over the territories formerly subject to Offa was an impressive achievement but as the reign of Coenwulf progressed the alienation of the Mercian king from emperor and pope came into sharper focus.

185

In Northumbria, Alcuin was striving, on behalf of the Carolingian court, for an accommodation with King Eardwulf while Coenwulf was giving shelter to Eardwulf's enemies, yet so well-established in imperial and papal regard did Eardwulf become that Charlemagne and Leo supported his restoration to his kingdom in 808 two years after his expulsion (see above, p. 157). A few years before, on the death of Beorhtric, king of the West Saxons in 802, the accession of Ecgberht, son of Ealhmund, following his return from exile in Gaul (*ASC* A, *s.a.* 8700, 836), was also probably a consequence of Carolingian and possibly even papal influence, exerted on this occasion on behalf of a southern-based family which had no love for Offa who had driven Ecgberht out of England with Beorhtric's help.[2] For Asser in his *Life of King Alfred*, written in the early 890s,[3] Offa was a tyrant who terrified all his neighbouring kings and provinces (ch. 14), and Alfred, Ecgberht's grandson, evidently enjoyed narrating quite malicious stories about Offa's daughter, Eadburh, the queen of Beorhtric (chs 14–15). Ecgberht claimed direct male descent from Ingild, the brother of Ine (*ASC* A, *s.a.* 855) (see Appendix, Fig. 3),[4] but if the chronicler's statement that the men of Kent, Sussex, Surrey and Essex had been forced away from Ecgberht's kindred (by Offa) (*ASC* A, *s.a.* 823) has any validity, it may imply that he had an important secondary association through his father, Ealhmund, with Kent and south-east England (see above, p. 168). The Mercians, not surprisingly, continued to be opposed to him. On the same day that Ecgberht became king of the West Saxons, Aethelmund, *dux* (*CS* 272, 273: S 146), or as the *Anglo-Saxon Chronicle* calls him ealdorman, of the Hwicce, led an expedition into West Saxon territory. He was defeated by Weohstan, ealdorman of Wiltshire (*ASC* A, *s.a.* 800), soon to be, if not already, Ecgberht's brother-in-law.[5]

At Canterbury Coenwulf became estranged from Aethelheard's successor as archbishop, Wulfred, a Mercian or Middle Saxon, who was elected and consecrated in 805.[6] Though the freedom given to Wulfred to mint coins without naming the Mercian king on the reverse[7] is generally taken to be a sign of Coenwulf's good will, it may also signify a weakening of Mercian influence at Christ Church in the immediate aftermath of the restoration of Canterbury's metropolitan authority in 803 and certainly by 808 a rift of some standing between Coenwulf and Wulfred was common knowledge in political and ecclesiastical circles on the continent when the pope informed Charlemagne that Coenwulf had not yet made peace with his archbishop.[8]

From 809 to 815 a period of better relations seems to have prevailed, during which Coenwulf made generous grants to Christ Church, but in 814 Wulfred went to Rome with Wigberht, bishop of Sherborne, returning with Pope Leo's blessing (*ASC* A, *s.a.* 812), and in 816 the council of Chelsea, presided over by the archbishop, mounted a serious attack on lay control of religious houses and the secularization of ecclesiastical land.[9]

This council directly challenged the right of Coenwulf to appoint to vacant nunneries and monasteries, despite earlier papal privileges of Hadrian I and Leo III to Offa and Coenwulf permitting them to do so.[10] Among the latest such appointments in the diocese of Canterbury, Cwoenthryth, Coenwulf's daughter, was the recently appointed abbess of Minster-in-Thanet. It was perhaps fortunate for Coenwulf that the new pope, Paschal I, proved more conciliatory and he was able to obtain from the pope confirmation of these earlier privileges in 817 (*CS* 363),[11] but the matter did not end there. King and archbishop contested each other's rights in respect of the estates and probably the revenues of Kentish churches. According to an account from Canterbury concerning specifically a quarrel over the monasteries of Reculver and Minster-in-Thanet, the king 'deprived' the archbishop of his authority and the ministry of baptism was suspended for six years (*CS* 384, 385: S 1436). Wulfred was witnessing as archbishop as late as 817 (*CS* 359: S 182; *CS* 360: S 181) and on 17 September 822 he officiated at the consecration of King Ceolwulf (*CS* 370: S 186). The suspension of Wulfred, therefore, was probably lifted in the course of 822, when the quarrel was in its sixth year. The controversy was certainly still raging at the close of Coenwulf's reign when, probably in 821, at a council in London Coenwulf threatened to despoil and exile his archbishop unless he capitulated and surrendered estates which were in dispute and paid money to the king. Wulfred is said to have given way but it was not until the councils of *Clofesho* in 824 and 825 that an agreement was made and even then not until 'the second year after' (presumably 826–7) that a settlement between Wulfred and Abbess Cwoenthryth was finally implemented (*CS* 378: S 1434; *CS* 384: S 1436).[12] The absence of additional documentary evidence prevents a detailed analysis of changing attitudes across this evidently divisive and wide-ranging dispute but the intensity of it and its prolongation must have exposed Coenwulf to external pressure to reach a settlement with his archbishop. Coenwulf's declaration at the council in London that he would not allow Wulfred to re-enter England once he had been exiled whether at the intercession of pope or emperor conveys an impression of a king increasingly estranged from the political community of Frankish Europe.[13] Nor, indeed, is there any suggestion of papal mediation in the final settlement.

There is no indication that Mercian military might was significantly diminished across these years. Coenwulf successfully overcame the crisis which faced him on his accession in East Anglia and the south-east. Simultaneously he confronted the Welsh on his western frontier, who were not to know when they engaged Mercian forces at Rhuddlan in 796 or 797 (*AC s.a.* 797: *ByT s.a.* 796) that Coenwulf would so quickly reassert Mercian power in England as to be in a position to invade in 798 and slay Caradog ap Meirion, king of Gwynedd, a prince of the maritime province of Rhos between the Clwyd and the Conwy (its eastern border marching against Rhuddlan). Nearly twenty years later, when Cynan ap Rhodri, king of Gwynedd, died in 816 or 817 and Hywel ap Caradog succeeded after three years of civil war, the Mercians ravaged the mountains of Eyri (Snowdonia) and took Rhufuniog, an inland principality immediately to the south of Rhos (*AC s.a.* 816: *By T s.a.* 817). They may have been involved in the battle of Llan-faes on Môn (Anglesey) in 817 or 818 (*AC s.a.* 817: *By T s.a.* 818) and certainly in 818 or 819 Coenwulf devastated Dyfed, taking his army into the most south-westerly of the British kingdoms of Wales (*AC s.a.* 818: *By T s.a.* 819). It is possible that Coenwulf was involved at least in planning a further campaign when he died at Basingwerk at the northern end of Wat's Dyke in 821,[14] for a Mercian offensive in either 822 or 823 resulted in the destruction of the fortress of Degannwy in Gwynedd and a Mercian conquest of the kingdom of Powys (*AC s.a.* 822: *By T s.a.* 823).

On the death of Coenwulf dynastic discord re-emerged as a powerful force in Mercian political life. Coenwulf's brother,[15] Ceolwulf (see Appendix, Fig. 8), took the kingship (*ASC* A, *s.a.* 819), against a background – if the legend of Cynehelm has any historical value – of the murder of Cynehelm, son of Coenwulf,[16] only to be deposed in 823 (*ASC* A, *s.a.* 821) and replaced by Beornwulf whose antecedents are unknown but who almost certainly represented another lineage, either a royal lineage or one with aspirations to royalty. It is unfortunate that the conquest of Powys cannot be dated more precisely, for there are two alternative contexts in Mercian history in which it can be placed. It could belong in the reign of Ceolwulf, who was king as late as 26 May 823 (*CS* 373, 374: S 187), but it seems unlikely that he would have faced deposition in the aftermath of such a military success. Even if challenged by a party opposed to that degree of military involvement beyond Offa's Dyke, he would presumably have continued to enjoy the support of his army. Alternatively, the attack could have taken place in 823 in the early months of the reign of Beornwulf. Beornwulf is known to have been a vigorous ruler. He attacked Ecgberht, king of the West Saxons, in 825 and the East Angles in 826 (see below, pp. 189–91). Beornwulf appears as a man of action, more likely to have been responsible for so extended a campaign in Wales than the more obscure Ceolwulf whose reign ended in deposition. So far as can be seen Ceolwulf's reign was a time of general disorder. A document issued at *Clofesho* in 825 concerning the restoration of estates to the church of Selsey declares that after the death of Coenwulf 'much discord and innumerable disagreements arose between various kings, nobles, bishops and ministers of the Church of God on very many matters of secular business' (*CS* 387: S 1435). An anonymous issue of coins at Canterbury *c.* 821–3 suggests 'a phase of political uncertainty at Canterbury' during which the Canterbury moneyers were in doubt as to whose authority they should respect.[17] Though the king and his archbishop came to a sufficient accord for Wulfred to consecrate

Ceolwulf, the ceremony was not performed until September 822 and did not in itself signify the resolution of the dispute between the Church and the Mercian royal family. It was Beornwulf who effected a reconciliation with Wulfred. Moreover, the appointment, probably by Beornwulf, of a sub-king, Bealdred, to rule in Kent - and Bealdred may not even at first have been in control of the whole of Kent[18] - suggests that under Ceolwulf the south-eastern provinces had been showing further signs of unrest. None of this creates the image of Ceolwulf as a king able to embark on the conquest of Powys and the invasion of Gwynedd. The balance of probability is that it was Beornwulf who began his reign with a vivid demonstration of Mercian power in north-east Wales beyond Offa's Dyke before turning to the resolution of problems inherited from Ceolwulf in southern England.

Mercian military strength, therefore, was still impressive. Furthermore, the apparent unrest in south-east England seems to have been contained in accordance with Coenwulf's earlier policy of imposing a Mercian candidate on Kent to govern the province directly. In view of Beornwulf's attack on Wessex two years after his accession, however, there must be more than a suspicion of a connection between Ecgberht, son of Ealhmund, and recent unease in the south-east.

Ecgberht, King of Wessex

So little is known of Ecgberht's activities between 802 and 825 that it is easy to imagine him reigning unobtrusively in Wessex across those years, but in 815 he ravaged the Britons of Dumnonia from east to west (*ASC* A, *s.a.* 813) and on 19 August 825, perhaps in the aftermath of a battle at Galford between the men of Devon and the Cornish Britons (*ASC* A, *s.a.* 823), he was engaged on a further campaign against them (*CS* 389: S 273).[19] The impression of quiescence is illusory.

Certainly Beornwulf was roused to attack him. There can be little doubt that it was Beornwulf who was the aggressor, perhaps taking advantage of West Saxon involvement in Dumnonia, when he marched on Ecgberht in 825 only to encounter him at *Ellendun* (Wroughton), on the approach to the Wiltshire Downs, where the Mercians were defeated (*ASC* A, *s.a.* 823). Moreover, the sequel to this defeat makes Ecgberht's connection with unrest in the south-east absolutely clear. The *Chronicle* declares that from the army - that is, in the immediate aftermath of *Ellendun* – Ecgberht sent his son, Aethelwulf, with Ealhstan, bishop of Sherborne, and Ealdorman Wulfheard with a large force into Kent; King Bealdred was driven out and, according to the *Chronicle*, 'the people of Kent and of Surrey and the South Saxons and the East Saxons submitted to him [Ecgberht] because they had been wrongfully forced away from his kinsmen' (*ASC* A, *s.a.*

823). The expulsion of Bealdred was not accomplished as swiftly as the *Chronicle* implies. A Kentish document of March 826 is dated by the third year of King Beornwulf (*CS* 1337: S 1267), which indicates continuing recognition of Beornwulf's authority in Kent at this date.[20] It seems probable, therefore, that Bealdred was not driven out of Kent until 826. His expulsion was followed at an uncertain date by that of Sigered, king of the East Saxons (see Appendix, Fig. 2), Roger of Wendover associating this with Ecgberht's campaign against Wiglaf, king of Mercia, in 829.[21] By 838 Ecgberht had entrusted the south-eastern provinces as a sub-kingdom to Aethelwulf (*CS* 418: S 280; *CS* 419, 420: S 286). If the testimony of the Alfredian chronicler can be accepted, Ecgberht and his family were establishing their authority over territory which they had a claim to rule by virtue of ties of kinship. Ecgberht's ability to annex the south-eastern territories may be explained by regarding him not only as a royal heir to the kingdom of Kent but as the heir also to a local Kentish south-eastern hegemony which went back intermittently into the sixth century but which was also recent enough to have retained political significance into the 780s. Against the possible background of a Kentish kingdom still able to dominate its immediate neighbours in the central years of Offa's reign (see above, p. 168), Mercian hostility to Ecgberht acquires an additional dimension and the threat he represented to the Mercians a greater reality. This is why Beornwulf attacked him in 825.

Ecgberht's apparent claim to the territories of the south-east and the successful invasion of Kent and the surrounding area in 826 created a new situation in the political affairs of southern England. No king of the western Saxons since Caedwalla had so successfully intruded himself into these regions, nor had any ever claimed, so far as is known, Ecgberht's degree of kinship with the local communities there. Ecgberht now began to mint coins at Canterbury and Rochester and then at Winchester or Southampton.[22] The West Saxon presence in Kent and the south-east, however, was not necessarily welcome to all. The seizure of an estate at Malling, which Bealdred granted to Christ Church while in flight before the advancing West Saxon army (*CS* 421, 422: S 1438), and Ecgberht's termination of Wulfred's coinage can hardly have been well-received at Canterbury by the archbishop and his kinsmen.[23] The Mercians may have hoped for a military recovery in Kent in association with such discontented elements, but the subsequent confrontations with the East Angles proved particularly catastrophic for the Mercians and confirmed the West Saxons in control of the south-east. The East Angles had been under Mercian domination since the reign of Offa as an integral component of a Mercian south-Anglian political community, the revolt of 796 having been suppressed by Coenwulf and a brief moment of independence extinguished. The *Anglo-Saxon Chronicle* A (*s.a.* 823) records that the East Angles appealed to Ecgberht for protection, because of their fear of the Mercians, placing this appeal in the same year as the defeat of Beornwulf at *Ellendun* and the invasion of the south-eastern provinces by Aethelwulf; but, whether the appeal came in 825 immediately on Ecgberht's victory at *Ellendun* or, more likely, on Aethelwulf's advance into Kent in 825–6, it will have been in 826 that Beornwulf marched on the East Angles, only to perish on campaign (*ASC* A, *s.a* 823).[24] The following year Ludeca, Beornwulf's successor and kinsman, seeking no doubt to regain control of the situation, also invaded East Anglia where he too fell in battle[25] and, the *Chronicle* adds, 'his five ealdormen with him' (*ASC* A, *s.a.* 825).

The impact of these two successive defeats on the stability of the Mercian kingdom must have been enormous. Within Mercia royal power passed to Wiglaf, whose grandson, Wigstan, son of Wiglaf's son, Wigmund, and Aelfflaed, daughter of Ceolwulf (I), was remembered at Evesham as a descendant of Coenred, king of the Mercians, founder of Evesham and grandson of Penda.[26] Whether this means that Wiglaf was of Penda's line is uncertain. The connection might have been through Wiglaf's queen, Cynethryth, and both Wiglaf and Wigstan were buried at Repton[27] which could suggest a kinship with the family of Aethelbald, who was also buried there. Two years later in 829 Ecgberht invaded Mercia and drove Wiglaf out (*ASC*, *s.a.* 827). This gave Ecgberht control of the London mint and he issued coins as king of the Mercians.[28] So great now was Ecgberht's authority south of the Humber that the Alfredian chronicler described him as *bretwalda* ('ruler of Britain') (*ASC* A, *s.a* 827) or – more correctly – *brytenwealda* ('wide ruler') (*ASC* BCDE, *s.a.* 827) (see above, p. 18) and associated him with Bede's list of seven kings who had ruled all the Anglo-Saxon kingdoms south of the Humber (*ASC* A, *s.a.* 827). He certainly advanced in 829 as far as the Mercian border with Northumbria. He may even, if Roger of Wendover is to be believed, have invaded Northumbrian territory and ravaged it.[29] Thereafter at Dore, near Sheffield, he received the submission of the Northumbrians (*ASC* A, *s.a.* 827). Ecgberht's subsequent campaign in 830 against the Welsh is said to have resulted in their subjection also (*ASC* A, *s.a.* 828) and there can be little doubt that Ecgberht was here seeking to carry West Saxon involvement across Offa's Dyke into what had been hitherto a Mercian sphere of influence, but the success of this campaign must have been overshadowed by Wiglaf's recovery of his kingdom later in the year (*ASC* A, *s.a.* 828) (*CS* 400, 401: S 188).

Ecgberht's ascendancy across the years 825–9 is undeniably impressive. It was then almost as dramatically checked and reversed. Wiglaf was restored in Mercia in 830 (*ASC* A, *s.a.* 828) and Ecgberht seems to have lost control of the London mint.[30] It may even be that Essex under King Sigeric (II) (see Appendix, Fig. 2) was re-established by Wiglaf as a Mercian satellite (S 1791).[31] Berkshire also passed in large measure at least under Mercian control either in Wiglaf's reign or in the early years of his successor, Berhtwulf, who was given land at Pangbourne on the Thames by Ceolred, bishop of Leicester, in 844 in return for a grant of liberties to certain monasteries including Abingdon, Berhtwulf then giving the land to Aethelwulf, ealdorman of the Berkshire area, who was himself of Mercian extraction (*CS* 443: S 1271).[32] The Welsh were also brought back into subjection to the Mercians by either Wiglaf or Berhtwulf, for by 853 they were in a state of rebellion against the Mercians (see below, p. 195). By 836 at Croft in Middle Anglian territory Wiglaf presided with Ceolnoth, Wulfred's successor as archbishop of Canterbury, over a council of leading churchmen from the whole of the southern province (*CS* 416: S 190), and must have been by then a ruler of prestige and influence. At the same time, Aethelstan, king of the East Angles, demonstrated a new-found independence by minting his own coins, possibly in 827[33] though *c.* 830 is perhaps more likely as Ecgberht's influence in Anglian territory probably began to wane when Wiglaf returned to power in Mercia. Aethelstan must have taken advantage of the rapidly changing political situation to emancipate himself from subjection to both Ecgberht and Wiglaf. As the king most probably responsible for the defeat first of Beornwulf and then of Ludeca, a position of subservience to Ecgberht is not likely to have been tolerated for long.

But the problem remains. How was it that Ecgberht, strong enough to master the whole of England south of the Humber in the four years between 825 and 829, then lost this predominant position? Various arguments for Ecgberht's ascendancy have been advanced – for example, that Wessex was particularly resilient because of its natural frontiers, mixed Saxon and Celtic population and the precocity of its administration – none of them convincing, [34] or that it had developed a more stable tributary system. [35] It is difficult to demonstrate, in view of the general paucity of comparative evidence, any significant difference between Wessex and Mercia at this time. [36]

It is not impossible that the key to Ecgberht's fluctuating fortunes lies in variable Carolingian influence and support. Ecgberht had been an exile at the court of Charlemagne. It is likely that Frankish support helped to put him on the West Saxon throne in 802 in the first place, just as it helped to restore Eardwulf to his Northumbrian kingdom in 808. Ecgberht was in touch with the Emperor Louis the Pious at Easter 839 and was anxious to arrange a safe passage through Gaul to Rome,[37] intending either a prestigious visit overseas to pope and emperor or to conclude his reign by going to Rome to die in imitation of Caedwalla and Ine, his predecessors and reputed forebears. A relationship with the Carolingians, therefore, appears as a constant factor of West Saxon political and diplomatic life across these years. It is difficult not to suspect that Ecgberht was maintained among the West Saxons by Carolingian support and that Carolingian backing was the crucial factor which enabled him to make the political and military advances which characterize West Saxon history in the first half of the ninth century. It seems likely, however, that the economic life of southern England was adversely affected in the early ninth century (after *c.* 820/30) by the collapse, as it has been described, of the Rhenish and Frankish commercial networks on which it was to a considerable extent dependent.[38] It was, moreover, in February 830 that revolt broke out in Gaul against Louis the Pious, the first in a series of disputes between the emperor and his sons which intermittently divided the Frankish world until the death of Louis in July 840 and persisted between Charles the Bald and his brothers until the treaty of Verdun in August 843, so that thereafter Charles, as ruler only of the West Frankish kingdom, threatened by internal rebellion and the possibility of invasion, attacked by Vikings and unable to secure the imperial title until 877, was a far less powerful and prestigious figure than his father.[39] Consequently, from February 830 or soon after imperial attention is likely to have been diverted from any far-flung Anglo-Saxon involvement and concentrated on more immediate matters closer to home. There may also have been some concern by 829–30 that Ecgberht's ascendancy was as damaging to traditional power structures as Offa's and Coenwulf's had been. Nothing would better explain the change which comes over the West Saxon military advance after 830 than a relatively sudden withdrawal of Frankish support. Such a weakening of the West Saxon position could have allowed Wiglaf his recovery in Mercia and enabled Aethelstan to assert his independence in East Anglia. In the absence of any further Frankish aid and support, as the Carolingian domestic scene deteriorated rather than improved, the three surviving Anglo-Saxon kingdoms in southern England – the Mercian, East Anglian and West Saxon – will have been left to find their own level of influence so that a more natural equilibrium established itself from the mid-830s onwards.

Despite the Mercian recovery under Wiglaf, Ecgberht had retained control of the south-eastern provinces and his success in so doing created a completely transformed political situation. Wiglaf's recovery was contained. Impressive though it was, he regained control neither of the south-east (except perhaps for Essex) nor East Anglia and minted few coins across his remaining years as king.[40] Nor were there any further ecclesiastical gatherings of the whole southern province in Wiglaf's territory. Nevertheless, it may well be that Ecgberht continued to fear a Mercian revival, and the estates which his son, Aethelwulf, gave as king of Kent to Christ Church, Canterbury, were presumably intended to counter residual Mercian influence. Ecgberht was probably also anxious to render conditions stable enough at home to make possible a pilgrimage to Rome in 839. At the council of Kingston-on-Thames in 838 he restored Malling to Christ Church, Canterbury, in return for recognition of Aethelwulf as his heir. Ecgberht and Aethelwulf were accepted by Archbishop Ceolnoth as the lords and protectors of the monasteries under their control, Aethelwulf subsequently conceding liberty of elections in those monasteries, though only after his lifetime. These agreements then received confirmation after Ecgberht's death at the councils of Wilton and *aet Astran* in 839 (*CS* 421: S 1438).[41] This suggests that the church of Canterbury had come to accept the authority of Ecgberht and Aethelwulf as a new political force in the south of England with which it must necessarily come to terms. Similar agreements may have been made with other churches, for land was also granted to Winchester at the council of Kingston in return for recognition of Aethelwulf as Ecgberht's heir and confirmed at *aet Astran* (*CS* 423: S 281). Ecgberht was securing Aethelwulf's position not only in the south-east but in the heart of Wessex. In the south-west Ecgberht's authority was consolidated by a defeat of a British and Viking force at Hingston Down in 838 (*ASC* A, *s.a.* 835). Though this victory did not lead to the suppression of the native Dumnonian royal line, it placed the West Saxon king in command of the Cornish peninsula.[42] The years 836–9, therefore, witnessed no further extension of a West Saxon *imperium* but certainly a dramatic consolidation of the position of Ecgberht and Aethelwulf south of the Thames. When Aethelwulf became king of the West Saxons in 839 he established his son, Aethelstan, as king over Kent and the south-eastern provinces (*ASC* B, *s.a* 836).

The threat of a revival of Mercian fortunes never did materialize and a further factor here could have been the death of Wiglaf and continuing Mercian dynastic tension. The date of Wiglaf's death can be inferred from regnal chronology; Burgred, king of the Mercians, was driven out by Vikings in 874 after reigning twenty-two years (*ASC* A, *s.a.* 874) and two of Burgred's charters indicate that he succeeded before 25 July (*CS* 509: S 210) in the year 852 (*CS* 524: S 214). A Mercian regnal list gives his predecessor, Berhtwulf, a reign of thirteen years,[43] and a date for his accession in 839 seems to be confirmed by regnal references in his charters (e.g. *CS* 432: S 196); Wiglaf, therefore, appears to have died in 839 and could have been in failing health for some time. His successor, Berhtwulf, is of unknown extraction – unless the alliteration' in the name reveals him as a kinsman of Beornwulf – and his accession may represent a further shift of royal power from one noble family to another. According to Evesham tradition Berhtfrith, son of Berhtwulf,[44] was a kinsman of Wiglaf's grandson, Wigstan, son of Wigmund, and sought to marry Aelfflaed, daughter of Ceolwulf (I) and widow of Wigmund, so that he might succeed King Wigmund; when Wigstan opposed this union, Berhtfrith, who was his godfather, slew him in 849 during a council at *Wistanstowe*.[45] There is no other evidence that Wiglaf's son, Wigmund, reigned as king of the Mercians, and this detail must necessarily be suspect, but his royal descent invests this family squabble with dynastic significance and conveys the impression of serious dissension within the Mercian court in the third and fourth decade of the ninth century.[46] By contrast, West Saxon dynastic stability at this time is an impressive tribute to the achievement not only of Ecgberht but also of Aethelwulf, who fathered four sons - Aethelbald, Aethelberht, Aethelred and Aelfred (Alfred) (see Appendix, Fig. 10) - in addition to Aethelstan, who died in or soon after 851, all of whom became successively kings of the West Saxons, yet managed to preserve family solidarity into the mid-850s.

The new balance between the Mercians and the West Saxons appears to have been refined further in the period 839–51. Aethelwulf must have successfully extended his influence into Berkshire, for Asser's *Life of King Alfred* places the birth of his son, Alfred, at Wantage in 849 (*Life of King Alfred*, ch. 1), though the Mercian, Aethelwulf, remained as ealdorman.[47] Berhtwulf, on the other hand, had revived Mercian coinage at the London mint by *c.* 841–2.[48] A coin with a portrait of Berhtwulf, king of the Mercians, on the reverse, coupled with an obverse design and the name of Aethelwulf, king of the West Saxons, has been seen as evidence for an alliance between the two rulers, possibly even a commemoration of a peaceful surrender of Berkshire by Berhtwulf in return for minting rights in Kent,[49] but it may be rather an irregular and imitative issue;[50] and, though Rochester dies were used by Berhtwulf, Berhtwulf's coins were probably minted not at Rochester but at London.[51]

Nevertheless, alliances were possible. In 853 Berhtwulf's successor as king of the Mercians, Burgred, is said to have asked Aethelwulf to help bring the Welsh, or the Middle Britons as Asser calls them, back into subjection to him. Aethelwulf responded by taking his army across Mercia and into Wales in support of the Mercian king (*ASC* A, *s.a.* 853). It may well be that this campaign led directly to the departure of Cyngen ap Cadell, king of Powys, who died in Rome *c.* 855 (*AC s.a.* 854: *ByT s.a.* 856). The pillar of Eliseg, which Cyngen raised to the memory of his great-grandfather's reconquest of Powysian territory from the Anglo-Saxons, also testifies to his own military success,[52] and it is possible that it was this which provoked the combined Mercian-West Saxon attack of 853, for Asser reports that the Britons had been struggling against Burgred with unusual vigour (*Life of King Alfred*, ch. 7). For as long as the Mercians and the West Saxons could respect independent spheres of influence for each other, harmonious arrangements of this kind could be entered into and the joint Mercian and West Saxon campaign against the Welsh was complemented in 853 by the marriage of Burgred at Easter to Aethelwulf's daughter, Aethelswith, at Chippenham (*ASC* A, *s.a.* 853, 888; *Life of King Alfred*, ch. 9). There is no evidence for Mercian military action against the East Angles, among whom Aethelstan's apparent successor as king, Aethelweard (*c.* 848– *c.* 854), continued to mint his own coins,[53] and was succeeded on Christmas Day 854 by the 14-year-old Eadmund (*ASC* St Neots, *s.a.* 855). Nor is there any hint of a West Saxon relationship at this time with the East Angles.

Northumbria

Beyond the Humber the abandonment of even a semblance of a silver coinage by the Northumbrians and its replacement in mid-century by largely brass coins,[54] while south of the Humber a silver coinage persisted, albeit increasingly debased, across the 860s, serve to heighten the impression of an isolated Northumbrian kingdom. The problem is that so little evidence survives to illuminate ninth-century Northumbrian history after 808 that even the regnal chronology of the period is unresolved. It is relatively clear what later Northumbrian tradition was. King Aella was said to have been in his fifth year on 1 November 866,[55] so that he succeeded in 861 or 862, having deposed his predecessor, Osberht, who is given a reign of thirteen years in Northumbrian regnal tradition[56] but eighteen in the *Flores Historiarum*,[57] Aella's regnal years presumably being included here and Osberht's reign not regarded as interrupted by Aella's. Indeed, the *Anglo-Saxon Chronicle* A (*s.a.* 867) also seems to have regarded Osberht as still king at the time of his death in 867. These figures (reckoning back from the deaths of Osberht and Aelle in 867) indicate 849 for Osberht's accession. Osberht's predecessor, Aethelred, is given a reign of nine years in Northumbrian regnal tradition;[58] and though he is only accorded seven in the *Flores Historiarum*,[59] his accession is there placed in 840 and his assassination in 848. Aethelred's father, Eanred, son of Eardwulf, is credited with a reign of thirty-two[60] or thirty-three[61] years, which represents a period evidently thought of as extending from 808 to 840/1.

Two pieces of evidence suggest, however, that this chronological scheme requires some readjustment. First, it takes no cognizance of a second reign for Eardwulf, restored with the support of Charlemagne and the pope in 808. Second, according to one Northumbrian source, the *Historia de Sancto Cuthberto*, a mid-eleventh-century record but possibly with a tenth-century nucleus,[62] Osberht lost his kingdom and his life in 867 within a year from his seizure, while he was still king, of certain estates of the church of Lindisfarne.[63] This could imply that he was challenged by Aella only months before he was slain, that is, in 866, not 861 or 862, and that Aella was king for less than a year. If so, Osberht could have become king in 853. This would mean that Aethelred succeeded in 844 and Eanred's reign began in 811 or 812 (depending on whether he reigned thirty-two or thiry-three years), leaving the years from 808 to 811/12 for the second reign of Eardwulf. It may be that it was the failure to integrate a second reign for Eardwulf of three or four years into the Northumbrian regnal tradition which occasioned some difficulty for subsequent Northumbrian historians, leaving a period in the 860s which could only be accounted for on the assumption that Aella reigned four or five years instead of one or Osberht eighteen instead of thirteen.[64]

One or two observations on Northumbrian political history in the ninth century are possible. The long reign of Eanred, son of Eardwulf, implies a degree of dynastic stability in some contrast to the immediately preceding period of Northumbrian history. It is evident that Eardwulf, despite the troubles of his reign, created a resilient enough power-base for his son and grandson effectively to dominate the Northumbrian kingship across the first half of the ninth century. Seen in this perspective, the seizure of royal power in the reign of Aethelred by a certain Raedwulf, who perished within the year fighting pagans (Vikings),[65] and Aethelred's eventual assassination[66] mark attempts, which may reflect dynastic tensions going far back in Northumbrian history, to displace a powerfully entrenched family. Unfortunately, the relationship of these princes to one another is unknown but Aella is described as Osberht's brother in the *Historia de Sancto Cuthberto*[67] and these dynastic conflicts could have been waged between no more than two rival lineages (if Raedwulf was a kinsman of Osberht and Aella) or three (if he were not).

It is certainly not correct to assume that throughout this period Northumbria existed in a state of political isolation. The contacts and connections which secured for Eardwulf Carolingian and papal support in 808 are unlikely to have been suddenly extinguished and may well have helped to create the stable conditions of Eanred's reign. Such external influences are likely to have persisted, as in the south, to *c.* 830. It is not clear, however, how well the Northumbrians were able thereafter to respond to external developments which impinged on them. Later Scottish tradition maintained that the last kings of the Picts were given military assistance against the Scots by the Northumbrians in the 840s, though to no avail,[68] and the Scottish king, Cináedh mac Ailpín, is said in a late source to have invaded Northumbria as many as six times, burning Dunbar and Melrose, before his death in 858.[69] The Viking raids were first experienced along the Northumbrian coast in the 790s and Raedwulf's death in battle with pagans (the *Flores Historiarum* places it in 844 but if Aethelred's reign is to be dated 844–53 Raedwulf's usurpation must be later than 844, though how much later is not clear)[70] suggests a major and disastrous confrontation. Though nothing is known of Northumbrian dealings with the Mercians in these years, it is unlikely that Coenwulf, king of Mercia, ceased to give aid to Eardwulf's enemies in 808 and it may well be that Raedwulf, Osberht and even Aella received Mercian support in the pursuit of their dynastic and personal ambitions. West Saxon influence was certainly brought to bear on Northumbria in 829 when Ecgberht received the submission, presumably of Eanred, at Dore (*ASC* A, *s.a.* 827), but is generally thought to have been shortlived, the recovery of Mercia under Wiglaf and the creation of an independent East Anglia under Aethelstan precluding further West Saxon involvement north of the Humber. That channels of communication did not entirely break down, however, is indicated by the relatively detailed account in the *Chronicle* of the capture of York by the Vikings in 866 and the subsequent battle for York in 867 (*ASC* A, *s.a.* 867).

There remains, moreover, the enigma of the unique EANRED REX silver penny, found in the hoard from Trewhiddle, Cornwall. Its stylistic affinities are with coins of Aethelwulf and Berhtwulf no earlier than *c.* 850,[71] whereas Eanred, king of Northumbria, died in 840/1 or 844. No other King Eanred is recorded and attempts to argue for the existence of an otherwise unknown Eanred as king in Kent *c.* 851 or as a successor for a brief period to Berhtwulf in Mercia *c.* 852 have been described as verging on 'special pleading', especially given that in some respects (in the character of its inscriptions and the apparent failure to include the moneyer's name) the Eanred penny is quite untypical of southern coins.[72] It is this penny, therefore, which could make necessary a further and more substantial readjustment of Northumbrian regnal chronology;[73] whether it will or not has yet to be resolved. However the coin is to be interpreted, it may hint at a closer relationship between Eanred, king of Northumbria, and either the Mercians or the West Saxons than would otherwise have been suspected.

King Aethelwulf and his sons

There is no doubt that the Northumbrians were in touch with the continent in the mid-ninth century as were the West Saxons. In 852 Lupus, abbot of Ferrières, wrote to Wigmund, archbishop of York,[74] Ealdsige, abbot of York,[75] Aethelwulf, king of the West Saxons,[76] and Felix, a Frankish scribe in the employ of Aethelwulf,[77] renewing old friendships, inviting prayers, borrowing books and soliciting gifts.[78] Felix was probably an important source of information about the West Saxons.[79] There were other transcontinental contacts. Pope Leo IV corresponded with Berhtwulf, king of the Mercians, and Archbishop Ceolnoth,[80] and in 855–6 King Aethelwulf travelled across Europe and was received by Leo's successor Benedict III.[81]

Aethelwulf's journey to Rome is of great interest for it did not signify abdication and a retreat from the world as their journeys to Rome had done for Caedwalla and Ine and other Anglo-Saxon kings. It was more a display of the king's international standing and a demonstration of the prestige his dynasty enjoyed in Frankish and papal circles. The *Chronicle* A (*s.a.* 853) records that in 853, two years before his own departure, Aethelwulf sent his youngest son, Alfred, to Rome and that the pope consecrated Alfred king and stood sponsor to him at confirmation. A letter purporting to be from Leo IV to Aethelwulf, in which the pope informs the king that he had received Alfred as a spiritual son and invested him with the consulate,[82] has been dismissed, however, as an eleventh-century forgery.[83] The historicity of Alfred's visit to Rome in 853 has also been called into question on the grounds, first, that Asser says that Alfred accompanied Aethelwulf in 855–6 (*Life of King Alfred*, ch. 11), and two visits to Rome by Alfred so close together seem unlikely, and, second, that Alfred's court circle had to introduce a visit by Alfred to Rome before 855 if he was to be represented as having been consecrated by a pope with the significant papal name of Leo (the name of the pope who crowned Charlemagne emperor) rather than the insignificant one of Benedict.[84] If anything, however, the reference in the *Chronicle* to Alfred's journey to Rome in 853, already part of the text of the annals which Asser used, has priority over Asser's introduction of Alfred into the account of Aethelwulf's visit in 855–6. What does seem beyond question is that if Alfred received consecration at papal hands, whether in 853 or 856, it can hardly have been a royal anointing (for Alfred had three older brothers still living) and must have been a confirmation-anointing, subsequently interpreted by Alfred's court circle as a royal anointing.[85] It is unlikely that Alfred had any exact memory of the ceremony and such a gloss on what occurred would certainly have appealed to his advisers *c.* 890. Asser's statement that Aethelwulf took Alfred with him in 855–6 because he loved him more than his other sons may be true but is typical of Asser's panegyrical approach and a theme he develops more than once.[86] It seems conceivable that Aethelwulf intended that his youngest son should have a career in the Church, and that Alfred's papal confirmation and early visit (or visits) to Rome were intended to mark him out for holy orders.[87] If Alfred was sent to Rome in 853, he will not, of course, have gone unaccompanied, and Aethelwulf may simply have taken advantage in 853 of a dispatch of West Saxon envoys to Rome in connection with his own forthcoming visit in 855–6 to send Alfred also. Aethelwulf's arrival on the continent in 855 is not likely to have been unplanned and the amount of diplomatic cross-Channel activity generated by it both before and after 855–6 should not be underestimated.

Charles the Bald was seriously threatened in 855–6 first by unrest among the Aquitainians and the western Franks and second by Vikings in the valley of the Seine.[88] Nevertheless, he provided Aethelwulf with all that he needed for his journey across Gaul, including an escort to the frontiers of his kingdom, and in July 856 permitted Aethelwulf's betrothal to his 12- or 13-year-old daughter, Judith, the marriage solemnized at Verberie on 1 October.[89] So unusual was it for Carolingian princesses to marry foreign princes[90] that Charles's consent to this union must reflect a long-standing regard for the West Saxon dynasty. It was also no doubt a reflection of Aethelwulf's military successes against the Vikings in 851 (see below, p. 211) and the relevance of this to a shared Anglo-Frankish concern with Viking activity in the Channel,[91] conceivably also of a desire on Aethelwulf's part to renew the close association with the Franks which had probably characterized Ecgberht's early years as king (see above, p. 192). Moreover, Judith was crowned queen by Hincmar, archbishop of

Rheims, even though both the Frankish annals and Asser affirm that it had not been customary hitherto with Aethelwulf and his people to call the king's wife queen and that this was contrary to West Saxon practice (*Life of King Alfred*, ch. 13). She was also, most unusually, anointed, a charismatic sanctification which enhanced her status, blessed her womb and conferred additional throne-worthiness on her male offspring.[92] The implication that a son by this marriage was intended to succeed, if not to the whole of Aethelwulf's kingdom, at least to part of it, seems clear. The analogy of Charles's daughter, Judith, marrying an older king and father of grown-up sons with Charles's mother, Judith of Bavaria, marrying an older king-emperor with grown-up sons and yet still securing a royal inheritance for her son, is unlikely to have been missed by contemporaries.[93] Charles the Bald must have hoped for a grandson who would rule territory among the Anglo-Saxons. There is no reason to assume that Aethelwulf was in his fifties at the time of the marriage. He need have been no more than 15 or so in 825 at the time of *Ellendun*, by 856 a man of about 46 or 47 with a reasonable expectation of another ten years of life, possibly more. Certainly, in the aftermath of the victories of 851, Aethelwulf's state visit to the pope and to Charles the Bald and the marriage to Judith would seem to indicate some major redirection within the West Saxon polity at this time.

Before Aethelwulf left for the continent in 855 he made generous concessions to his thegns, intended, it would seem, ultimately to benefit also the Church in his kingdom,[94] but most immediately perhaps to consolidate his leading men, both lay and ecclesiastic, behind the West Saxon monarchy on the eve of his departure. Aethelwulf's journey occasioned a number of unorthodox policy-decisions. Whereas under normal conditions after the death of Aethelstan, Aethelwulf might have been expected to establish Aethelbald, evidently by now his oldest surviving son, as king of the south-eastern provinces, instead he associated both of his two older sons in the kingship, Aethelbald in Wessex[95] and Aethelberht in the south-eastern provinces.[96] What he found when he returned home is uncertain. According to Asser, during the time that Aethelwulf was away Aethelbald, with the support of Ealhstan, bishop of Sherborne, and Eanwulf, ealdorman of Somerset, plotted that he would not be received back into his kingdom (*Life of King Alfred*, ch. 12). This action has been seen as a rebellion against an unpopular king whose martial qualities were few and whose excessive piety took him to Rome at a time of Viking danger at home; pictured in this light, Aethelwulf's marriage to Judith was a response to rebellion at home.[97] Aethelwulf, however, whose entry as a young man into minor orders is hagiographical legend,[98] was a military leader who had distinguished himself against the Vikings in 851 (see below, p. 211) and his journey to Rome and back was a prestige-enhancing diplomatic success.[99] It is also barely conceivable that Charles the Bald would have sent his daughter as an anointed queen, with all that implied, into an overseas kingdom already known to be in revolt against her new husband. What is more likely is that Aethelbald's rebellion occurred after the marriage.

According to Asser, to avoid civil war Aethelwulf was obliged to surrender the western districts of his kingdom to Aethelbald, confining his own royal authority to the eastern, Asser's implication being that Aethelbald continued to rule in Wessex, with Aethelwulf as king only of the eastern provinces but leaving quite ambiguous how Aethelberht's position was thereby affected.[100] This cannot be right. The Frankish annals report that Aethelwulf returned to the control of his kingdom[101] and the *Anglo-Saxon Chronicle* A (*s.a.* 855) claims that his people were glad to see him. Even Asser acknowledges that Aethelwulf was able to insist that Judith sit beside him on the royal throne (by implication the West Saxon royal throne) as his queen (*Life of King Alfred*, ch. 13). In 856 he was still in a position to grant land in Berkshire (*CS* 491: S 317). What the evidence suggests, therefore, is that, if there was a division of the kingdom, it was West Saxon territory itself which Aethelwulf partitioned with Aethelbald, Aethelbald continuing to reign in west Wessex, beyond Selwood perhaps, while Aethelwulf ruled east and central Wessex,[102] leaving Aethelberht in Kent; in other words, a territory and position comparable to Aethelberht's in the south-east was carved out for Aethelbald in the south-west. This situation was probably a direct result of the unusual arrangements made for the kingdom during Aethelwulf's absence. If Aethelberht were to assume responsibility for Aethelstan's former territory, another sphere of influence would have to be created for Aethelbald, if the oldest son was not to be disadvantaged by a younger brother. It may be that Aethelbald was additionally anxious to secure territorial concessions from his father, if the possibility that a son by Judith would also need to be provided with a royal inheritance was fully appreciated at the time in Aethelbald's circle. Aethelwulf and Judith had no son and heir, however, and Aethelwulf's death less than two years after his return, probably unexpectedly, placed Aethelbald not only on his father's throne as king of the West Saxons but also in his father's bed as Judith's second husband,[103] contrary to Church law, as Asser observed (*Life of King Alfred*, ch. 17), but thereby securing this anointed queen as a potential mother of his own sons. The likelihood of Aethelred or Alfred, Aethelwulf's younger sons, succeeding must have seemed remote.

Aethelwulf anticipated that his sons might quarrel amongst themselves and made a will after his return from Gaul (*Life of King Alfred*, ch. 16). This will does not survive but Alfred's does, dating to 872–8,[104] which to a degree makes possible a reconstruction of Aethelwulf's. It has been argued that Aethelwulf set out to control the descent of the bulk of royal property through his sons to whichever of them should live the longest, with a presumption in favour of this being Alfred, the kingship following the same line of descent, so that land and kingship devolved together. The effect of this would be 'to preserve the union between the West Saxon royal property and the West Saxon kingship', but at the cost of disinheriting the sons of the brothers who died first.[105] Such an arrangement would have led to fratricidal strife. With three older brothers, Alfred's chances of reaching adulthood would, one feels, have been minimal.

It is important to bear in mind at the outset that Alfred's will is an *ex parte* statement. It was a response to a situation in which he was being accused of failing to observe the terms of an agreement with his brother, Aethelred, and thereby wronging his younger kinsmen, who would include not only Aethelwald and Aethelhelm, the sons of Aethelred, but possibly also a certain Osweald, who may have been a son of any one of Alfred's brothers.[106] Alfred was aware that the terms of his grandfather's will exercised a controlling influence on his own and his father's testamentary dispositions. In his own will, however, it was Aethelwulf's bequests which were the principal focus of his attention because of their relevance to the agreement with Aethelred, specifically 'the inheritance which my father, King Aethelwulf, bequeathed to us three brothers - Aethelbald, Aethelred and myself – that whichever of us should live longest was to succeed to the whole'.[107] Nevertheless, Asser makes it clear that Aethelwulf drew a distinction between the kingdom and his 'own inheritance' (*propria hereditas*). He partitioned the kingdom between his two eldest sons – that is, he confirmed the arrangement of 855 by which Aethelbald ruled in Wessex and Aethelberht in the south-eastern provinces, and divided his 'own inheritance' between his sons, daughter and kinsmen, part of his personal treasure being used to provide for prayers for his soul and part being divided between his sons and his nobles (*Life of King Alfred*, ch. 16). Alfred's will is only concerned with the second of these dispositions. The first makes it clear that Aethelwulf was not concerned to preserve his kingdom as a single entity. His arrangements transcend those which had prevailed hitherto. The south-eastern provinces pass to Aethelberht (and, by implication, to his descendants) and Wessex to Aethelbald (and his). That Aethelberht is not included with 'us three brothers' in Alfred's will suggests that a separate provision was made for him in respect of Aethelwulf's 'own inheritance'. Alfred records in his will that when, however, Aethelberht became king in Wessex as well as the south-east in 860 (*ASC* A, *s.a.* 860), he and Aethelred entrusted their shares in Aethelwulf's 'own inheritance' to Aethelberht; but when Aethelberht died and Aethelred succeeded in 865 (*ASC* A, *s.a.* 866), Aethelred told Alfred that he could not let Alfred have his share 'of our joint property' because, though he had tried, he could not divide the inheritance. What Aethelred also said was that after his death he would leave to no one in preference to Alfred whatever he held which belonged to them jointly and whatever he had personally acquired (just as he and Alfred had inherited from Aethelberht whatever he had personally acquired). This understanding was soon modified. When the Danish wars intensified Aethelred and Alfred made an agreement to provide for their children if anything should happen to either of them. It is at the point of describing the arrangements they then made at an assembly at *Swinbeorg* that Alfred's will makes clear just how many were the different parcels of land involved in these transactions. Aethelred and Alfred agreed that whichever of them lived the longest would give to the other's children (a) the lands which the deceased brother had personally acquired in his own lifetime, and (b) the lands which King Aethelwulf had given him. What would not be given, however, were (c) the lands which Aethelwulf bequeathed 'to us three brothers'. It is important to appreciate, therefore, that this last item does not represent the whole of the land which had been inherited from Aethelwulf.

Alfred says in his will that at the time of Aethelred's death (in 871 (*ASC* A, *s.a.* 871)) no one made known to him that the agreement at *Swinbeorg* had been superseded or modified, but because there had been so many disputes about the inheritance an assembly at *Langanden* reviewed the matter only to find that Alfred had not wronged his kinsfolk and there was no more just title to the lands in dispute than his. The matter was clearly an extremely contentious one. Moreover, Aethelwald, son of Aethelred, subsequently challenged the succession of Alfred's son, the aetheling Eadweard (Edward), in 899 in a war which imperilled the legacy of Alfred in southern England (*ASC* A, *s.a.* 900). But the quarrel over Aethelwulf's will and the war of succession after 899 should not be confused. The former was only one element in the dynastic crisis on Alfred's death. What was in dispute between Alfred and his kinsmen at *Langanden* was whether or not the lands bequeathed by Aethelwulf to 'us three brothers' really should pass to the surviving brother. Alfred's case was that they should. The basis of the kinsmen's case was almost certainly that they should not. It cannot even be assumed that these contested lands constituted the greater part of the royal estates.

Neither in Alfred's will, therefore, nor in Aethelwulf's partition of his kingdom is an intention evident on Aethelwulf's part to transmit the entire royal inheritance to whichever of his sons lived the longest. The kingdom was partitioned and there was a complex series of separate arrangements to control the distribution of property. In 858 Aethelbald's marriage to Judith, whose sons could have had a special entitlement to rule by virtue of her anointing, must have threatened to disinherit all his younger brothers from the kingship in Wessex permanently, while the south-eastern provinces were under the control of Aethelberht and his descendants. On Aethelbald's death in 860 (*ASC* A, *s.a.* 860), perhaps because of the youthfulness of Aethelred, Aethelberht succeeded to the whole kingdom, that is, he acquired Wessex (*ASC* A, *s.a.* 860) creating what David Dumville has called 'Greater Wessex'.[108] The death of Aethelbald witnessed a consolidation of royal power in the hands of only one of Aethelwulf's sons and no younger brother was installed in the south-eastern provinces even in subordination to Aethelberht. Judith left Wessex for the continent (where she eloped with Baldwin (I), count of Flanders, and her son, Baldwin (II), subsequently married Alfred's daughter, Aelfthryth). It may be that, with Judith's arrival back in Gaul, Frankish interest in England rapidly waned. Griffo, port-reeve of Quentovic, went on a mission on behalf of Charles the Bald to the kings of the Angles between 858 and 866,[109] but, whether because they were no longer being written at court[110] or for some other reason, the Frankish annals cease to notice Anglo-Saxon affairs after 860. A breakdown in Anglo-Saxon and Frankish communications appears to have been a phenomenon of these years.[111]

When Aethelred succeeded Aethelberht in 865 (*ASC* A, *s.a.* 866),[112] there would seem to have been a further consolidation of royal power in Wessex judging by Alfred's failure to secure control of a share of his inheritance, and it was probably only the seriousness of the Viking attack which obliged Aethelred to make any further arrangements with Alfred. Aethelred had two sons, Aethelwald and Aethelhelm, to whom Alfred makes reference in his will, and their existence introduced a critical new dimension into the dynastic situation. If Aethelred had lived until his sons were adult, the likelihood would have been that Alfred would never have become king and, indeed, what proportion even of the property to which he believed himself entitled under the terms of Aethelwulf's will he would have acquired it is impossible to say, but the suspicion must be not a great deal. Aethelred's death just after Easter 871, therefore, completely transformed the dynastic situation in Wessex. Alfred's accession in that year placed on the throne of Wessex perhaps the most remarkable of Anglo-Saxon rulers. His advent to royal power, however, was the consequence of a most amazing mortality of princes between 858 and 871 and could not have been foreseen by Aethelwulf when he drew up his will fourteen or fifteen years before.

Notes

1 As P. H. Sawyer suggests, *From Roman Britain to Norman England* (London, 1978), pp. 107–8.
2 Cf., J. M. Wallace-Hadrill – remarking that Coenwulf 'cannot have felt altogether happy about Charlemagne' – 'Charlemagne and England', *Early Medieval History* (Oxford, 1975), pp. 155–80 (p. 170).
3 Asser's *Life of King Alfred*, ed. W. H. Stevenson (rev. edn, Oxford, 1959). For a translation, see S. Keynes and M. Lapidge, *Alfred the Great: Asser's Life of King Alfred and Other Contemporary Sources* (Harmondsworth, 1983).
4 D. N. Dumville, 'The West Saxon Genealogical Regnal List: manuscripts and texts', *Anglia*, vol. 104 (1986), pp. 1–32 (p. 24).
5 *S. Editha sive Chronica Vilodunense*, ed. C. Horstmann (Heillbronn, 1853), p. 4.
6 N. Brooks, *The Early History of the Church of Canterbury* (Leicester, 1984), p. 132.
7 C. E. Blunt, C. S. S. Lyon and B. H. I. H. Stewart, 'The coinage of southern England', *British Numismatic Journal*, vol. 32 (1963), pp. 1–74 (pp. 19 ff., 69).

8   *Councils and Ecclesiastical Documents*, ed. A. W. Haddan and W. Stubbs, 3 vols (Oxford, 1869–71), Vol. III, p. 563.

9   ibid., Vol. III, pp. 579–85. Cf., H. Vollrath, *Die Synoden Englands bis 1066* (Paderborn, 1985), pp. 184 ff.

10 Brooks, *The Early History of the Church of Canterbury*, pp. 134 ff., 175 ff., reconstructs the course and significance of this quarrel between Coenwulf and Archbishop Wulfred.

11 W. Levison, *England and the Continent in the Eighth Century* (Oxford, 1946), pp. 255–7; Brooks, *The Early History of the Church of Canterbury*, pp. 185–6.

12 Cf., Vollrath, *Die Synoden Englands*, pp. 196 ff., 201 ff.

13 Cf., Wallace-Hadrill, 'Charlemagne and England', pp. 171–2.

14 *Gaimar L'Estoire des Engleis*, ed. A. Bell (Anglo-Norman Text Society, vols 14–16: 1960), l. 2236: cf., F. M. Stenton, *Anglo-Saxon England* (3rd edn, London, 1971), p. 230, n. 3

15 *Florentii Wigorniensis monachi Chronicon ex Chronicis*, ed. B. Thorpe, 2 vols (London, 1848), Vol. I, pp. 65, 266.

16 ibid., Vol. I, pp. 65, 266; see D. W. Rollason, 'Cults of murdered royal saints in Anglo-Saxon England', *Anglo Saxon England*, vol. 11 (1983), pp. 1–22 (pp.9–10), and A. Thacker, 'Kings, saints and monasteries in pre-Viking Mercia', *Midland History*, vol. 10 (1985), pp. 1–25 (pp. 8 ff.).

17 Blunt, Lyon and Stewart, 'The coinage of southern England', pp. 37, 42.

18 ibid., pp. 24, 41.

19 H. Edwards, *The Charters of the Early West Saxon Kingdom* (BAR British Series 198, 1988), pp. 150–3. Note that all the charters which are dated to 826 and refer to Ecgberht as then in the fourteenth year of his *ducatus* are fabrications; ibid., pp. 148, 153, 156.

20 Cf., Brooks, *The Early History of the Church of Canterbury*, p. 136.

21 B. E. A. Yorke, 'The kingdom of the East Saxons', *Anglo-Saxon England*, vol. 14 (1985), pp. 1–36 (pp. 9, 24); *Roger de Wendover sive Flores Historiarum*, ed. H. O. Coxe, 2 vols (London, 1849), Vol. I, p. 276.

22 P. Grierson and M. Blackburn, *Medieval European Coinage*, Vol. I: *The Early Middle Ages* (Cambridge, 1986), pp. 289, 294–5; cf., C. E. Blunt, 'The coinage of Ecgberht, king of Wessex, 802–39', *British Numismatic Journal*, vol. 28 (1957), pp. 467–76.

23 Brooks, *The Early History of the Church of Canterbury*, pp. 137, 198; Blunt, Lyon and Stewart, 'The coinage of southern England', p. 42.

24 A Mercian king-list gives Beornwulf a reign of three years – that is, 823–6; *Hemingi Chartularium Ecclesiae Wigorniensis*, ed. T. Hearne (Oxford, 1723), Vol. I, p. 242.

25 *Florentii Wigorniensis monachi Chronicon ex Chronicis*, Vol. I, pp. 66, 266.

26 *Chronicon Abbatiae de Evesham*, ed. W. D. Macray (Rolls series: London, 1863), pp. 325–6.

27 Cf., on these burials at Repton, M. Biddle, 'Archaeology, architecture and the cult of saints', in L. A. S. Butler and R. K. Morris (eds), *The Anglo-Saxon Church* (CBA Research Report, no. 60, 1986), pp. 1–31 (pp. 16–22).

28 Blunt, 'The coinage of Ecgberht, king of Wessex, 802–39', pp. 472–3; cf., Blunt, Lyon and Stewart, 'The coinage of southern England', p. 34.

29 *Flores Historiarum*, Vol. I, pp. 276–7 (*EHD* Vol. I, no.4).

30 H. E. Pagan, 'Coinage in southern England, 796–874', in M. Blackburn (ed.), *Anglo-Saxon Monetary History* (Leicester, 1986), pp. 45–65 (p. 47).

31 Yorke, 'The kingdom of the East Saxons', p. 24.

32 F. M. Stenton, *The Early History of the Abbey of Abingdon* (Reading, 1913), pp. 25–7; idem, *Anglo-Saxon England*, pp. 234–5.

33 H. E. Pagan, 'The coinage of the East Anglian kingdom', *British Numismatic Journal*, vol. 52 (1982), pp. 41–83 (p. 43).

34 R. H. Hodgkin discusses these points in *A History of the Anglo-Saxons*, 2 vols (2nd edn, Oxford, 1939), Vol. II, pp. 409 ff.

35 R. Hodges, *The Anglo-Saxon Achievement: Archaeology and the Beginnings of English Society* (London, 1989), p. 142.

36 Cf., N. Brooks, 'England in the ninth century: the crucible of defeat', *Transactions of the Royal Historical Society*, vol. 29 (1979), pp. 1–20 (pp. 1–2).

37 *Annales de Saint-Bertin*, ed. F. Grat, J. Vielliard and S. Clemencet (Paris, 1964), p. 28 (*EHD* Vol. I, no. 23). The 'king of the Angles' to whom these annals refer was almost certainly a king of the West Saxons and not a king of the East Angles – Aethelwulf is called king of the Angles in the annal for 855 (p. 70) – and has been taken to be Aethelwulf because it was at one time erroneously thought that Aethelwulf became king of the West Saxons in 836, the year under which the *Chronicle* A enters Ecgberht's death; but Ecgberht, who became king in 802, reigned for thirty-seven years and seven months (Dumville, 'The West Saxon Genealogical Regnal List: manuscripts and texts', p. 24) and will have lived, therefore, at least until the end of July 839. Interestingly, Ine went to Rome after reigning thirty-seven years.

38 R. Hodges, 'Trade and market origins in the ninth century: an archaeological perspective of Anglo-Carolingian relations', in M. Gibson and J. Nelson (eds), *Charles the Bald: Court and Kingdom* (BAR International Series 101, 1981), pp. 213–33. Cf., R. Hodges and D. Whitehouse, *Mohammed, Charlemagne and the Origins of Europe* (London, 1983), pp. 160 ff., and Hodges, *The Anglo-Saxon Achievement*, pp. 147–9.

39 R. McKitterick, *The Frankish Kingdoms under the Carolingians* (London, 1983), pp. 170 ff.

40 Grierson and Blackburn, *Medieval European Coinage*, Vol. I, p. 292.

41 Brooks, *The Early History of the Church of Canterbury*, pp. 145 ff., 197 ff., 323 ff. Cf., Vollrath, *Die Synoden Englands*, pp. 207 ff.

42 H. P. R. Finberg, 'Sherborne, Glastonbury and the expansion of Wessex', *Transactions of the Royal Historical Society*, vol. 3 (1953), pp. 101–24 (pp. 111 ff.) (reprinted in H. P. R. Finberg, *Lucerna* (London, 1964), pp. 95–115).

43 *Hemingi Chartularium Ecclesiae Wigorniensis*, Vol. I, p. 242: cf., *Florentii Wigorniensis monachi Chronicon ex Chronicis*, Vol. I, p. 267.

44 *Florentii Wigorniensis monachi Chronicon ex Chronicis*, Vol. I, pp. 72, 266–7.

45 *Chronicon Abbatiae de Evesham*, pp. 325–7; see Rollason, 'The cults of murdered royal saints', pp. 5 ff., and idem, *The Search for St Wigstan* (Leicester University Press, Vaughan Paper no. 27, 1981), and Thacker, 'Kings, saints and monasteries in pre-Viking Mercia', pp. 12 ff.

46 Cf., Rollason, 'The cults of murdered royal saints', p. 20, and Thacker, 'Kings, saints and monasteries in pre-Viking Mercia', p. 13.

47 The burial of Ealdorman Aethelwulf in 871 at Derby (*The Chronicle of Aethelweard*, ed. A. Campbell (Edinburgh and London, 1962), p. 37) suggests that he was of Mercian extraction. See also R. A. Hall, 'The Five Boroughs of the Danelaw: a review of present knowledge', *Anglo-Saxon England*, vol. 18 (1989), pp. 149–200 (pp. 155–6).

48 Grierson and Blackburn, *Medieval European Coinage*, Vol. I, p. 292.

49 C. S. Lyon, 'Historical problems of Anglo-Saxon coinage – (2) The ninth century – Offa to Alfred', *British Numismatic Journal*, vol. 37 (1968), pp. 216–38 (p. 229 and n. 2).

50 Pagan, 'Coinage in southern England, 796–874', p. 56; Grierson and Blackburn, *Medieval European Coinage*, Vol. I, p. 293.

51 Pagan, 'Coinage in southern England, 796–874', p. 55–6; Grierson and Blackburn, *Medieval European Coinage*, Vol. I, p. 293.

52 *Early Genealogical Tracts*, ed. P. C. Bartrum (Cardiff, 1966), pp. 1–3.

53 Pagan, 'The coinage of the East Anglian kingdom', pp. 46 ff.

54 See G. R. Gilmore and D. M. Metcalf, 'The alloy of the Northumbrian coinage in the mid-ninth century', *Metallurgy in Numismatics*, Vol. 1 (1980), pp. 83–98, and also now *Coinage in Ninth-Century Northumbria*, ed. D. M. Metcalf (BAR British Series 180, 1987).

55 *Symeonis Monachi Opera Omnia*, ed. T. Arnold, 2 vols (Rolls series: London, 1882, 1885), Vol. I, p. 54; cf., his reign of four years in the twelfth-century annals of Lindisfarne: *MGH Scriptores*, Vol. XIX, ed. G. H. Pertz (Hanover, 1866), p. 506.

56 *Symeonis Monachi Opera Omnia*, Vol. II, pp. 377, 391.

57 *Flores Historiarum*, Vol. I, p. 284.
58 *Symeonis Monachi Opera Omnia*, Vol. II, pp. 377, 391.
59 *Flores Historiarum*, Vol. I, p. 281.
60 *Symeonis Monachi Opera Omnia*, Vol. I, p. 52: Vol. II, p. 391.
61 ibid., Vol. II, p. 377: *Flores Historiarum*, Vol. I, p. 271.
62 Cf., P. H. Sawyer, 'Some sources for the history of Viking Northumbria', in R. A. Hall (ed.), *Viking-Age York and the North* (CBA Research Report no. 27: 1978), pp. 3–7 (p. 4).
63 *Symeonis Monachi Opera Omnia*, Vol. I, p. 201.
64 Cf., D. P. Kirby, 'Northumbria in the ninth century', in Metcalf (ed.), *Coinage in Ninth-Century Northumbria*, pp. 11–25 (pp. 16–17).
65 *Flores Historiarum*, Vol. I, pp. 282–3.
66 ibid., p. 283.
67 *Symeonis Monachi Opera Omnia*, Vol. I, p. 202.
68 *Johannis de Fordun Chronica Gentis Scotorum*, Historians of Scotland, Vol. I, ed. W. F. Skene (Edinburgh, 1861), pp. 147, 157, and Historians of Scotland Vol. IV, trans. F. J. H. Skene (Edinburgh, 1872), pp. 138, 147.
69 M. O. Anderson, *Kings and Kingship in Early Scotland* (Edinburgh, 1973), p. 250.
70 E. J. E. Pirie, 'Phases and groups within the styca coinage of Northumbria', in Metcalf (ed.), *Coinage in Ninth-Century Northumbria*, pp. 103–34 (p. 12).
71 D. M. Wilson and C. E. Blunt, 'The Trewhiddle Hoard', *Archaeologia*, vol. 98 (1961), pp. 75–122 (pp. 113–16); cf., Grierson and Blackburn, *Medieval European Coinage*, Vol. I, p. 301.
72 D. M. Metcalf, 'The Eanred penny', in Metcalf (ed.), *Coinage in Ninth-Century Northumbria*, pp. 36–8 (p. 37); cf. D. N. Dumville, 'Textual archaeology and Northumbrian history subsequent to Bede', in ibid., pp. 43–55, pointing out that an Eanred who succeeded Berhtwulf, however fleetingly, might still have been expected to appear in the Mercian regnal list and does not (p. 54).
73 As H. E. Pagan stressed in 'Northumbrian numismatic chronology in the ninth century', *British Numismatic Journal*, vol. 38 (1969), pp. 1–15 (p. 12).
74 *Loup de Ferrières Correspondence*, ed. L. Levillain (Les Classiques de l'histoire de France au moyen age), Vol. II (Paris, 1935), no. 86 (there is an English translation of *The Letters of Lupus of Ferrières* by W. Regenos (The Hague, 1966)).
75 ibid., p. 87.
76 ibid., p. 84.
77 ibid., p. 85.
78 See further, P. Stafford, 'Charles the Bald, Judith and England', in Gibson and Nelson (eds), *Charles the Bald: Court and Kingdom*, pp. 137–8.
79 ibid., pp. 138–9.
80 *MGH Epistolae Karol. Aevi*, Vol. III, ed. A. de Hirsch-Gereuth (Berlin, 1898), p. 592.
81 *Liber Pontificalis*, ed. L. Duchesne, Vol. II (Paris, 1892), p. 148.
82 *MGH Epistolae Karol. Aevi*, Vol. III, p. 602.
83 J. L. Nelson, 'The Problem of King Alfred's royal anointing', *Journal of Ecclesiastical History*, vol. 18 (1967), pp. 145–63 (reprinted in Nelson, *Politics and Ritual in Early Medieval Europe* (London and Ronceverte, 1986), pp. 309–27).
84 ibid., pp. 159 ff.
85 ibid., pp. 156 ff.
86 D. P. Kirby, 'Asser and his Life of King Alfred', *Studia Celtica*, vol. VI (1971), pp. 12–35 (p. 27). Cf., also now, J. Campbell, 'Asser's *Life of Alfred*' in C. J. Holdsworth and T. P. Wiseman (eds), *The Inheritance of Historiography 350–900* (Exeter Studies in History; Exeter, 1986), pp. 115–35.
87 Alfred's youngest son, Aethelweard, though he did not enter the Church, seems to have been educated for it, reading books in Latin as well as in English in the palace school (*Life of King Alfred*, ch. 75), a course of instruction intended for those destined for the priesthood (*King Alfred's West-Saxon Version of Gregory's Pastoral Care*, ed. H. Sweet (Early English Text Society, vol. 45; 1871), p. 7).
88 See McKitterick, *The Frankish Kingdoms under the Carolingians*, pp. 175 ff., 234.

89   *Annales de Saint-Bertin*, pp. 70, 73.

90   P. Stafford, 'Charles the Bald, Judith and England', p. 140; idem, *Queens, Concubines, and Dowagers: The King's Wife in the Early Middle Ages* (Athens, Georgia, 1983), p. 46.

91   Stafford, 'Charles the Bald, Judith and England', pp. 137, 139, and idem, *Queens, Concubines, and Dowagers*, p. 48. M. J. Enright, 'Charles the Bald and Aethelwulf of Wessex: the alliance of 856 and strategies of royal succession', *Journal of Medieval History* , vol. 5 (1979), pp. 291–302 is critical of the idea of an alliance between the two kings to combat the Vikings, but it seems probable that Charles and Aethelwulf displayed a mutual awareness of a shared problem.

92   *Annales de Saint-Bertin*, p. 73; *MGH Capitularia Regum Francorum*, Vol. II, ed. A. Boretius and V. Krause (Hanover, 1897), pp. 425–7. See J. L. Nelson, 'The earliest surviving royal *Ordo*: some liturgical and historical aspects', in B. Tierney and P. Lineham (eds), *Authority and Power: Studies in Medieval Law and Government* (Cambridge, 1980), pp. 29–48 (pp. 39–41) (reprinted in Nelson, *Politics and Ritual*, pp. 341–60).

93   Stafford, 'Charles the Bald, Judith and England', pp. 140 ff., and idem, *Queens, Concubines, and Dowagers*, p. 131; cf., Enright, 'Charles the Bald and Aethelwulf of Wessex', pp. 297 ff.

94   See Keynes and Lapidge, *Alfred the Great: Asser's Life of Alfred and Other Contemporary Sources*, pp. 232–4.

95   This is the implication of the *Life of King Alfred*, ch. 12, and Aethelbald, who died in 860, was accorded a five-year reign in the West Saxon regnal list (Dumville, 'The West Saxon Genealogical Regnal List: manuscripts and texts', p. 25).

96   Again, this is the implication of *CS* 486: S 315, and was certainly the situation on Aethelwulf's death in 858 (*ASC* A, *s.a.* 855).

97   Enright, 'Charles the Bald and Aethelwulf of Wessex', pp. 295–6.

98   Cf., Plummer's notes in *Two of the Saxon Chronicles Parallel*, 2 vols (Oxford, 1892, 1899) Vol. II, p. 75; cf., B. E. A. Yorke, 'The bishops of Winchester, the kings of Wessex and the development of Winchester in the ninth and early tenth centuries', *Proceedings of the Hampshire Field Club and Archaeological Society*, vol. 40 (1984), pp. 61–70 (pp. 62–3).

99   Cf., R. H. M. Dolley and K. Skaare, 'The coinage of Aethelwulf, king of the West Saxons, 839–58', in R. H. M. Dolley (ed.), *Anglo-Saxon Coins* (London, 1961), pp. 63–76 - 'History has scarcely done justice to Aethelwulf' (p. 63); H. P. R. Finberg, *The Early Charters of Wessex* (Leicester, 1964), characterized the king as a 'devout warrior' (p. 187).

100   Cf., D. N. Dumville, 'The aetheling: a study in Anglo-Saxon constitutional history', *Anglo-Saxon England*, vol. 8 (1979), pp. 1–33 (p. 23).

101   *Annales de Saint-Bertin*, p. 73.

102   Cf., Stafford, 'Charles the Bald, Judith and England', p. 143.

103   *Annales de Saint-Bertin*, p. 76.

104   F. E. Harmer (ed.), *Select English Historical Documents of the Ninth and Tenth Centuries* (Cambridge, 1914), pp. 15 ff. (Cf., *EHD* Vol. I, no. 96).

105   E. John, *Orbis Britanniae and Other Studies* (Leicester, 1966), pp. 36 ff. (p. 40); cf., A. Williams, 'Some notes and considerations on problems connected with the English royal succession, 860–1066', *Proceedings of the Battle Conference on Anglo-Norman Studies*, Vol. I (1978), pp. 144–67 (pp. 145 ff., pp. 153–4). Dumville comments in 'The aetheling', pp. 21 ff.

106   On Osweald, see Dumville, 'The aetheling', p. 11. If Osweald were a son of Aethelstan, however, he might not have been relevant to the agreements which are the concern of Alfred's will.

107   *EHD* Vol. I, no. 96 (p. 492).

108   Dumville, 'The aetheling', pp. 22 ff.

109   *MGH Scriptores*, Vol. XV (pt 1), ed. O. Holder-Egger (Hanover, 1887), pp. 408–9.

110   See J. L. Nelson, 'The Annals of St. Bertin', in Gibson and Nelson (eds), *Charles the Bald: Court and Kingdom*, pp. 15–36. Cf., Hodges and Whitehouse, *Mohammed, Charlemagne and the Origins of Europe*, p. 163.

111 Cf., on a narrowing of Frankish horizons, J. L. Nelson, '"A king across the sea":
Alfred in continental perspective', *Transactions of the Royal Historical Society*, vol. 36
(1986), pp. 45–68 (p. 47).

112 In most of the entries for 851–912 the year in the *Chronicle* begins with the Caesarean
indiction on 24 September, so that many events in the autumn of a year are placed in
the next calendar year; M. R. L. Beaven, 'The beginning of the year in the Alfredian
Chronicle', *English Historical Review*, vol. 32 (1918), pp. 331–42 and cf., D. Whitelock,
'On the commencement of the year in the Saxon chronicles', in the 1952 reprint of
Two Saxon Chronicles Parallel, ed. C. Plummer, Vol. II, pp. cxl–cxli.

10   The coming of the Vikings

The movements of Alfred's older brothers across Wessex – in so far as they can be reconstructed from the evidence of royal diplomas (from Somerton, for example, to Dorchester, to Sherborne), communicate the appearance of leisurely, pastoral tranquillity, of a quiet and uneventful perambulation through the *scirs* (shires), unhurried by military concerns and untroubled by political disturbance. Nothing could be further from the truth. The will of Alfred exposes the personal and dynastic tensions lying just beneath the surface of royal family relationships. Even more serious than these was the threat of attack from the still-pagan Scandinavians, the Vikings.

The *Anglo-Saxon Chronicle* provides an incomplete record of Viking activities. England had been subject to Viking raids since at least 793 but the 'heathen' are only mentioned for the first time in southern England as ravaging Sheppey in 835 (*ASC* A, *s.a* 832), despite the fact that the community of Lyminge in Kent had acquired a refuge within the walls of Canterbury as early as 804 (*CS* 317: S 160) and Viking armies had been active in Kent before 811, even building fortresses (*CS* 332: S 1264).[1] On the land in Kent which King Ceolwulf granted to Archbishop Wulfred in 823 the king maintained an obligation to destroy fortresses built by the pagans (*CS* 370: S 186), and in a grant of privileges to the monastery of Hanbury in the territory of the Hwicce King Wiglaf excluded from the privilege the construction of ramparts (*CS* 416: S 190). Viking raids along the coast of Wessex were a dominant concern of the West Saxon kings from 835 onwards and in 841 the whole of the east coast from Lindsey to Kent was affected (*ASC* A, *s.a.* 841). In 842 *Hamwic* was plundered.[2] Such incidents were inducing a state of acute apprehension among the Anglo-Saxons. King Ecgberht informed Louis the Pious in 839 of an apocalyptic vision, following a series of poor harvests, which had struck terror into their hearts, foretelling that unless there was immediate repentence darkness would prevail for three days and an immense heathen fleet would ravage Christian lands.[3] Nevertheless, it was not, so far as can be seen, until 846 that West Saxon charters indicate a royal concern in Wessex to exempt military burdens from grants of immunities and possibly not until the late 850s that fortress-work as well as army service and bridge-building was officially similarly reserved.[4]

Some of the encounters of these years certainly transcend the activities of mere raiding parties. In 844 the Northmen are said to have been victorious in a three-day battle in the territory of the Anglo-Saxons.[5] In 851 a fleet of 350 ships entered the mouth of the Thames and stormed Canterbury and London. When Berhtwulf went to the aid of the Londoners he was defeated and put to flight, but when the Viking army moved into Surrey Aethelwulf and his son, Aethelbald, crushed it at *Aclea*, and Aethelwulf's son, Aethelstan, ruler of Kent and the south-eastern provinces, defeated a Viking force in a naval engagement at Sandwich in Kent (*ASC* A, *s.a.* 851). This Viking attack in 851 appears to have had a considerable impact. Royal involvement in the minting of coins in Kent was interrupted and at London Mercian royal coinage was 'minimal' after 851.[6] A revival of West Saxon coinage only came in the last eighteen months of Aethelwulf's reign (after his return from the continent) with a *renovatio monetae* (a calling in of old coins and a restriking into new) and a large subsequent increase in volume from *c.* 860 onwards. Among the Mercians there was similarly a great increase in the number of moneyers between the mid-860s and the early 870s. This flurry of activity, however, cannot conceal a continuing and progressive debasement of West Saxon and Mercian coins from the closing stages of Aethelwulf's reign onwards.[7] So marked is the interruption of the coinage after 851 that in the south-east a loss of political control of Kent by the West Saxon royal house has been suggested; Aethelstan is not heard of again after 851 but Aethelwulf's son, Aethelberht, only appears as king of Kent in 855 (*CS* 486: S 315).[8] The record material is too uneven for confidence in this hypothesis. It is true that there are no West Saxon charters concerning land in Kent across 851–4 but there are no West Saxon diplomas at all for the years 851–3 (inclusive) or Mercian for the years 851–4 (inclusive). It is likely that both the Mercians and the West Saxons were shaken by the events of 851 but the successful confrontation of the military challenge at *Aclea* and Sandwich must have served, if anything, to consolidate the West Saxon rulers as the natural protectors of the south-eastern territories. The Alfredian chronicler says of *Aclea* that it was the greatest slaughter of a heathen army ever yet heard of (*ASC* A, *s.a.* 851), and the victory on which Lupus of Ferrières congratulated Aethelwulf was probably *Aclea*.[9] Nevertheless, the Vikings defeated the men of Kent in 853 (*ASC* A, *s.a.* 855).

The consequences of the Viking attacks were not necessarily wholly disastrous for the Anglo-Saxon dynasties. Evidence from Kent and Wessex reveals that with the displacement of monastic communities their estates passed under the control not only of the local nobility but also of the kings who must have been considerably enriched thereby.[10] The activities of new and larger Viking armies,[11] however, of which that of 851 and perhaps 844 were forerunners, were beginning seriously to threaten the defensive capabilities of the Anglo-Saxon kingdoms. The *Chronicle* A (*s.a.* 860) records the arrival of a great naval force – which crossed to England from the Somme[12] – and the storming of Winchester, followed by the defeat of the invaders by Osric, ealdorman of Hampshire, and the Mercian Aethelwulf, ealdorman of Berkshire. Aethelberht's accession to 'Greater

211

Wessex' may have been a response to this situation. Probably in late 864 'a heathen army' encamped on Thanet and ravaged the whole of east Kent despite the promise of money and peace by the men of Kent (*ASC* A, *s.a.* 865). The arrival of 'a great heathen army' in East Anglia in 865 (*ASC* A, *s.a.* 866), described by Aethelweard in the late tenth century as 'the fleets of the tyrant Ívarr',[13] was even more ominous. In 866 this army crossed the Humber estuary and, perhaps taking advantage of a continuing civil war among the Northumbrians between King Aella and his recently deposed brother, Osberht (see above, p. 196), captured York on 1 November. Wulfhere, archbishop of York, fled to Addingham in Wharfedale.[14] When Aella and Osberht combined forces to recover the city on 21 March 867, they were slain with eight leading noblemen (*ASC* A, *s.a.* 866: *AU s.a.* 866).[15] Under this impact the kingdom fractured. The Vikings secured themselves in possession of York and assumed direct control of Deira, appointing a puppet ruler, Ecgberht, beyond the Tyne.[16] From York the great army went into Mercia in late 867 and spent the winter of 867/8 in Nottingham (*ASC* A, *s.a.* 868).

Mercian military strength at this time should not be underestimated. In 865 the Mercians under Burgred had campaigned deep into Welsh territory, penetrating Gwynedd and reaching Môn (Anglesey) (*AU s.a.* 864).[17] The advent to royal power in 825 of Merfyn Frych ap Gwriad, a Powys prince with Manx connections, whose father had married a daughter of Cynan ap Rhodri, king of Gwynedd, established the second dynasty of Gwynedd.[18] Merfyn's marriage to Nest, sister of Cyngen ap Cadell, king of Powys, strengthened the Powysian associations of this second dynasty and either Merfyn's son, Rhodri Mawr, king of Gwynedd from the 850s into the 870s, or Rhodri's sons were able to annex the kingdom of Powys.[19] No details of the process are recorded and its chronology is uncertain, but it is likely to have been a long one and Burgred's campaign into Gwynedd in 865 suggests that it could have been already underway by then. The evident success of Burgred demonstrates that Mercian military strength in the mid-860s remained formidable. Nevertheless, against the Danes Burgred requested the assistance of Aethelred, king of the West Saxons, and Alfred, who joined with him in a siege of Nottingham in 868, only to find that the combined forces of Wessex and Mercia could not dislodge the Danes from their position, so that eventually the Mercians made peace and the Vikings withdrew back to York in the autumn of the year (*ASC* A, *s.a.* 868). This alliance of Burgred and Aethelred provides the immediate context in Asser's *Life of King Alfred*[20] for the marriage of Alfred in 868 to Ealhswith, the daughter of Aethelred Mucil, ealdorman of the Gaini among the Mercians (*Life of King Alfred*, ch. 29; *ASC* A, *s.a.* 902: BCD *s.a.* 903), and a descendant of King Coenwulf through her mother, Eadburh.[21] A reasonably prestigious match, it was, however, not unduly so. Alfred, although at least for the time being *secundarius* (second to the throne, the heir-apparent) (*Life of King Alfred*, chs 30, 38, 42),[22] was not given a king's daughter, as Burgred had been in 853 (which might have placed Wulfthryth, Aethelred's wife, in an invidious position)[23] but a minor princess appropriate to his status. Burgred may well have expected that this marriage would lead to further military co-operation with the West Saxons at any future moment of crisis.

In the autumn of 869 the leaders of the great heathen army, presumably leaving detachments behind at York and elsewhere, crossed Mercia into East Anglia and wintered at Thetford, during which time Eadmund, king of the East Angles, fought against them and was slain (*ASC* A, *s.a.* 870) on 20 November 869 (*ASC* St Neots, *s.a.* 870).[24] If Abbo of Fleury, writing his *Passion of Saint Eadmund* over a hundred years later, is to be believed, the Viking leader, Ívarr, sought to partition East Anglia with Eadmund as a subject king but his proposals were rejected.[25] A few coins of two kings, Aethelred and Oswald, which seem to be East Anglian and date to the period after the death of Eadmund,[26] may suggest that Ívarr did find pliant dependants who would accept his terms. Ívarr's death within a year of the killing of Eadmund,[27] that is in 869–70, or else his departure for Ireland,[28] did not deter the great army, again presumably leaving detachments behind in East Anglia, from advancing into West Saxon territory under the two kings, Bagsecg and Hálfdan[29] to Reading in late 870 or early 871. Aethelwulf, ealdorman of Berkshire, fought a detachment of the army at Englefield with some success, but when King Aethelred and Alfred encountered the whole army at Reading they were defeated and Aethelwulf killed (*ASC* A, *s.a.* 871). Despite the slaying of Bagsecg in a surprise victory over the whole Viking army at Ashdown, possibly in part due to the peculiar nature of the terrain (*Life of King Alfred*, ch. 39), Aethelred and Alfred experienced defeat thereafter. The arrival of a summer army had further augmented the great army at Reading when Aethelred died, and Alfred's forces were regularly overwhelmed before peace was made (*ASC* A, *s.a.* 871), on condition that the Vikings left Wessex (*Life of King Alfred*, ch. 43) (which implies the payment of geld). In late 871 the great army took up winter quarters at London and the Mercians also bought peace (*ASC* A, *s.a.* 872).[30] It is difficult to resist the conclusion that by now the West Saxons and the Mercians were experiencing such severe problems that further thoughts of going to each other's assistance had been abandoned.

A revolt in Northumbria in 872, in the course of which King Ecgberht and Wulfhere, archbishop of York, were driven out to seek refuge in Mercia and a certain Ricsige established himself as king,[31] took the great army back into Northumbria in 873 (*ASC* A, *s.a.* 873), where Archbishop Wulfhere was reinstated at York and Ricsige confined beyond the Tyne,[32] and in the autumn of that year the army returned south to winter first at Torksey near Lincoln (*ASC* A, *s.a.* 873) and then at Repton (*ASC* A, *s.a.* 874). Burgred was driven out of Mercia and subsequently died in exile in Rome, and the Vikings entrusted Mercia to Ceolwulf (II) (*Life of King Alfred*, ch. 43), who gave hostages and swore oaths, according to the *Anglo-Saxon Chronicle*, that the Vikings should have the kingdom whenever they wished and that he would be ready with all his followers to serve them (*ASC* A, *s.a.* 874). This achieved, in late 874 part of the army returned to Northumbria under Hálfdan's leadership. It wintered on the Tyne before launching an extensive campaign across north Britain in 875 (*ASC* A, *s.a.* 875) and then returning to share out land in Deira in 876 when, as the *Chronicle* puts it, 'they proceeded to plough and to support themselves' (*ASC* A, *s.a.* 876). It was during 875 that the community of St Cuthbert finally abandoned Lindisfarne and not until *c.* 880 that it was established at Chester-le-Street.[33] This must have resulted in a dislocation of diocesan life but politically the campaign of 875 appears, surprisingly, to have had little or no impact in Bernicia. Ricsige was succeeded beyond the Tyne in 876 by Ecgberht (II), not known to have been a Danish puppet, who certainly reigned for two years and possibly for twelve.[34]

That part of the great army which remained at Repton – for several divisions must have stayed behind in Mercia to garrison positions held there – went under its leaders, Guthrum, Oscetel and Anwend, to Cambridge in 874 (*ASC* A, *s.a.* 875). From there in 875–6 part at least sailed to Wareham where Alfred bought peace,[35] after which it traversed Wessex to Exeter before re-entering Mercia (*ASC* A, *s.a.* 876) and positioning itself at Gloucester.[36] Here it took part in a sharing out of the land, part of which was given to Ceolwulf (II) (*ASC* A, *s.a.* 877),[37] presumably west Mercia, south of Watling Street.[38] Guthrum's attack on Alfred in midwinter after Twelfth Night in the early days of January 878 was launched from Gloucester; the failure to capture Alfred at Chippenham (*ASC* A, *s.a.* 878), though from the Danish point of view unfortunate, was not necessarily disastrous, for a separate Viking force, which had wintered in Dyfed, crossed to effect a landing in Devon (*ASC* A, *s.a.* 878; *Life of King Alfred*, ch. 54), possibly so that Alfred, in his retreat on Athelney in the marshes of Somerset, could be trapped in a pincer movement of the two armies.[39] It was the destruction of this second army by the men of Devon at Countisbury (*Life of King Alfred*, ch. 54) which left Guthrum exposed, his lines of communication extended and vulnerable to a guerilla campaign by Alfred which culminated in the West Saxon king's mass-rally of his troops from the southern *scirs* at Ecgberht's Stone (somewhere near the edge of the Wiltshire Downs) and the defeat of Guthrum at the battle of Edington in May 878 (*ASC* A, *s.a.* 878).

Alfred had gained experience in dealing with these warriors in 877 at Wareham when he compelled them to give hostages and to swear oaths, one on their holy ring, that they would keep the peace (which, however, they violated) (*ASC* A, *s.a.* 877; *Life of King Alfred*, ch. 49), and again at

Exeter. Now he pursued Guthrum to Chippenham where he besieged him for a fortnight until the Danes again gave hostages and swore to leave his kingdom. Three weeks later Guthrum was baptized at Aller with Alfred as sponsor and eight days later his baptismal robes were removed in Alfred's presence at Wedmore (*ASC* A, *s.a.* 878). Through this enforced conversion Alfred probably hoped to be able to bind Guthrum to a recognizable code of Christian conduct – for example, in respect of oath-swearing and regard for Christian sanctuaries. In late 878 the Danish army withdrew into Mercia to Cirencester (*ASC* A, *s.a.* 879) and from there, probably in late 879, to East Anglia (*ASC* A, *s.a.* 880) where Guthrum, also known by his baptismal name of Aethelstan, reigned as king until his death in 890 (*ASC* A, *s.a.* 890), not always peacefully but presenting by himself no further menace. The Alfred and Guthrum treaty of 886 delineated the frontier between West Saxon and Danish territory in a balanced accord,[40] after which Guthrum may even have shared moneyers with Alfred 'near the border with the Danelaw'.[41]

Alfred is frequently thought of as 'the last surviving English king' by 878. This is not entirely true. Ceolwulf (II) reigned in part of Mercia, Ecgberht (II) may still have been reigning beyond the Tyne and Aethelred and Oswald in East Anglia. It must not be assumed that these men were not princes of the blood-royal. Ceolwulf (II) is caricatured by the Alfredian chronicler as 'a foolish king's thegn' (*ASC* A, *s.a.* 874) in the same way as Aella is described as of non-royal stock (*ASC* A, *s.a.* 867), although he is said elsewhere to have been a brother of Osberht who is not so described. Some of them were most probably discontented aethelings who sought the furtherance of their own interests through an alliance with the Vikings. This is exactly what Aethelwald, son of Aethelred, did after 899, when he joined forces with the Northumbrian Danes as their king (*ASC* A, *s.a.* 900). Nor were they necessarily politically negligible. There is no evidence that Hálfdan was able to destroy Ricsige or Ecgberht (II) north of the Tyne. Bernicia remained outside the immediate control of the Danes at York. It was probably the forces of Ceolwulf (II) which were responsible for the defeat and death of Rhodri Mawr in 878 (*AU s.a.* 877; *AC s.a.* 877: *ByT s.a.* 878). Ceolwulf shared moneyers with Alfred and participated in Alfred's restoration of a fine silver coinage which is hardly likely to date to before 878; the five-year reign for Ceolwulf in the Mercian regnal list,[42] which would indicate that he was king from 874 only to 879, may well be too short for this coinage and it seems probable that he reigned into the early 880s as *rex Merciorum*.[43] There is no evidence to show that Ceolwulf had been superseded by Aethelred, ealdorman of the Mercians, before 883 (*CS 551*: S 218). Nevertheless, it is true that by 878 only Alfred *rex Saxonum* ruled a kingdom which had not been conquered and partitioned by the Danes.

Faced with the advance of the great Viking army, the Northumbrian, East Anglian and Mercian kingdoms collapsed with surprising suddenness.

Despite an initial vigorous response, defeat followed swiftly. The Danish leaders were not necessarily seeking outright conquest. They appear to have been content to partition and to create conditions of dependency for subject native princes. Even so, the political world of Osberht and Aella, Eadmund and Burgred disappeared almost overnight[44] and the impression that 'the effects of Viking attack were very serious indeed'[45] is overwhelming. The ecclesiastical order was certainly disrupted across northern and eastern England and monastic and intellectual life appears to have passed into near-total eclipse. The contrast, therefore, between Alfred, who successfully resisted the Vikings and preserved the integrity of Wessex, and Aella and Osberht, Eadmund and Burgred who were defeated and slain or driven out and their kingdoms divided, or Ecgberht (I), Ceolwulf (II) and possibly Aethelred and Oswald who came to terms with the Danes, is a striking one which has never failed to impress.

Nor is it easy to explain. The lack of evidence for Northumbria, East Anglia and Mercia in the last decade or so of their existence makes comparisons impossible.[46] Alfred's military and naval reforms and his programme of *burh*-construction helped him to contain the Viking danger later in his reign but how did he survive the crisis of 871–8 before any such reorganization had been implemented? The Alfredian chronicler believed that Alfred succeeded as he did by virtue essentially of his own heroic personality, and historians, though they cannot quantify it, must not lose sight of this intangible dimension. Undoubtedly Alfred was a warrior-king of heroic proportions, evidently refusing to delay his engagement of the enemy at Ashdown while his brother said mass and fighting in the conflict 'like a wild boar' (*Life of King Alfred*, ch. 38). His subsequent reorganization of the West Saxon defences suggests an alert and intelligent military mind. Nevertheless, he faced desertion even by leading men among the West Saxons. Wulfhere, probably ealdorman of Wiltshire[47] and perhaps King Aethelred's brother-in-law,[48] certainly a nobleman of considerable standing, forsook Alfred at some point in the reign (possibly in 878) and his estates were subsequently confiscated (*CS* 595: S 362). Many fled overseas and those who remained – presumably those in some geographical proximity to Chippenham, Guthrum's principal base in Wessex – are said to have submitted to the Danes (*ASC* A, *s.a.* 878).[49] A familiar pattern was being repeated. It cannot be assumed that Alfred's martial qualities alone account for his survival.

In one other respect Alfred's achievement at this time must be qualified. The most central fact of these years is the geographical position of Wessex on the fringe of the activities of the great heathen army. The centre of gravity for the Danish forces lay in the oval of land bounded by York, Thetford, Reading and Repton. The Danes were no more able to establish a permanent presence of political significance in Bernicia or in west Mercia than they were in Wessex. Just as Alfred was able to secure West Saxon territory under his rule, so Ecgberht (II) and his successors, the ealdormen of Bamburgh, preserved the land beyond the Tyne as theirs, and first Ceolwulf (II) and then Ealdorman Aethelred the west midlands. The difference is one of degree and more is known about Alfred's activities than about those of other contemporary Anglo-Saxon rulers.

It is also clear that the great heathen army of 865 constituted an overwhelming military force. Burgred, fresh from a successful campaign against the Welsh, could achieve nothing against it, even with West Saxon assistance, in 868. Alfred, on the other hand, only encountered the united great army on West Saxon territory in 871 at Reading, and even by then probably quite sizeable detachments had been left behind in Northumbria and East Anglia. It is hardly surprising that the Alfredian chronicler could count nine major engagements south of the Thames fought in the course of that year, excluding minor expeditions (*ASC* A, *s.a.* 871). This will have been a time of genuine danger and, as Alfred's will shows, both Aethelred and Alfred were aware that they might lose their lives. What prevented the Vikings from pushing home their advantage in 871 is not certain, but the continued independent existence of Mercia, the readiness of the West Saxons to sue for peace, and perhaps intimations of unrest in Northumbria brought a cessation of hostilities and a withdrawal. The significant fact is that thereafter the great army never returned to Wessex. After the conquest of Mercia in 873–4 it broke up, some of the warriors no doubt anxious to adopt a settled life, others to go marauding elsewhere.[50] The bulk of the army went into Northumbria to York, with only a part moving southwards to Cambridge under Guthrum, Oscytel and Anwend, and the Vikings who attacked Chippenham in 878 probably represented only a part of the Cambridge force for nothing more is heard of Oscytel and Anwend. The possibility of further recruitment to these subdivisions of the great army remains,[51] and in 878 Guthrum was acting in concert in all probability with a quite separate Viking army from Dyfed, but the overwhelming impression is that it was a relatively minor challenge which nearly destroyed King Alfred in 878.[52]

In the midst of these upheavals Ceolwulf (II) still anticipated that degree of continuity which had characterized the past to prevail in the future. In 875 he acquired an estate from the bishop of Worcester which he was free to leave to three heirs, and after the lifetime of these heirs the land was to revert to Worcester 'for the soul of King Ceolwulf and his successors' (*CS* 540: S 215). Much did survive at grass-roots level. Even in territories under Danish rule 'important elements' in local government and hidage assessment survived.[53] But the great heathen army had torn apart the political fabric of the pre-Viking kingdoms of the heptarchy. The old ruling order had been destroyed and never would be re-created. Ceolwulf had no successors as king of the Mercians. So it was that Alfred was able to begin to extend his influence into Mercia to the extent that in 886 all the *Angelcyn* not under subjection to the Danes submitted to him (*ASC* A, *s.a.* 886). The political future now lay either with the leaders of the Danish armies in northern and eastern England or with Alfred and his successors in Wessex.[54]

Notes

1   N. Brooks, 'The development of military obligations in eighth- and ninth-century England', in P. Clemoes and K. Hughes (eds), *England before the Conquest* (Cambridge, 1971), pp. 69–84 (p. 80): cf., *The Early History of the Church of Canterbury* (Leicester, 1984), p. 201. If the evidence of *CS* 848: S 134 can be accepted, Offa was organizing military action in Kent and Sussex against the pagans by 792 (Brooks, 'The development of military obligations', p. 79). For the possibility that some of Offa's *burhs* had a defensive role, see J. Haslam, 'Market and fortress in England in the reign of Offa', *World Archaeology*, vol. 19 (1987), pp. 76–93.

2   *Nithard*, ed. Ph. Lauer (Les Classiques de l'histoire de France au moyen age: Paris, 1926), p. 125 (*EHD* Vol. I, no. 22).

3   *Annales de Saint-Bertin*, ed. F. Grat, J. Vielliard and S. Clemencet (Paris, 1964), pp. 29–30 (*EHD* Vol. I, no. 23).

4   Brooks, 'The development of military obligations', p. 81.

5   *Annales de Saint-Bertin*, p. 48.

6   H. E. Pagan, 'Coinage in southern England', in M. Blackburn (ed.), *Anglo-Saxon Monetary History* (Leicester, 1986), pp. 45–65 (p. 57).

7   P. Grierson and M. Blackburn, *Medieval European Coinage*, Vol. I: *The Early Middle Ages* (Cambridge, 1986), pp. 307 ff.

8   Pagan, 'Coinage in southern England', p. 57.

9   *Loup de Ferrières Correspondence*, ed. L. Levillain (Les Classiques de l'histoire de France au moyen age), Vol. II (Paris, 1935), no. 84 (and p. 71 and n. 4).

10 Brooks, *The Early History of the Church of Canterbury*, pp. 201 ff., and R. Fleming, 'Monastic lands and England's defence in the Viking Age', *English Historical Review*, vol. 100 (1985), pp. 247–65; J. L. Nelson, '"A king across the sea": Alfred in continental perspective', *Transactions of the Royal Historical Society*, vol. 36 (1986), pp. 45–68 (pp. 58–9, 61).

11 On the immediate Viking background, see A. P. Smyth, *Scandinavian Kings in the British Isles 850–880* (Oxford, 1977). On the possibility that the Viking armies came to be numbered in thousands, see N. Brooks, 'England in the ninth century: the crucible of defeat', *Transactions of the Royal Historical Society*, vol. 29 (1979), pp. 1–20.

12 *Annales de Saint-Bertin*, p. 83.

13 *The Chronicle of Aethelweard*, ed. A. Campbell (Edinburgh and London, 1962), p. 35.

14 *Symeonis Monachi Opera Omnia*, ed. T. Arnold, 2 vols (Rolls series: London, 1882, 1885), Vol. I, p. 225; see D. P. Kirby, 'Northumbria in the ninth century', in D. M. Metcalf (ed.), *Coinage in Ninth-Century Northumbria* (BAR British series 180, 1987), pp. 11–25 (p. 20, n. 93).

15 *Fragmentary Annals of Ireland*, ed. J. N. Radner (Dublin, 1978), pp. 128–9; *Symeonis Monachi Opera Omnia*, Vol. I, p. 55; *Roger de Wendover Chronica sive Flores Historiarum*, ed. H. O. Coxe, 2 vols (London, 1849), Vol. I, p. 298; cf., Smyth, *Scandinavian Kings in the British Isles*, pp. 179 ff.

16 Kirby, 'Northumbria in the ninth century', p. 19.

17 *Fragmentary Annals of Ireland*, pp. 116–17; cf., A. O. Anderson, *Early Sources of Scottish History*, 2 vols (Edinburgh, 1922), Vol. I, p. 295, n. 4.

18 J. E. Lloyd, *History of Wales from the Earliest Times to the Edwardian Conquest*, 2 vols (3rd edn, London, 1939), Vol. I, p. 323; N. K. Chadwick, 'Early culture and learning in North Wales', in N. K. Chadwick (ed.), *Studies in the Early British Church* (Cambridge, 1959), pp. 29–120 (pp. 79–80); D. P. Kirby, 'British Dynastic History in the pre-Viking period', *Bulletin of the Board of Celtic Studies*, vol. 27 (1976–8), pp.

81–114 (p. 97); cf., M. Miller, 'The Foundation-Legend of Gwynedd in the Latin Texts', *Bulletin of the Board of Celtic Studies*, vol. 27 (1976–8), pp. 515–32.

19 D. N. Dumville, 'The "six" sons of Rhodri Mawr: a problem in Asser's *Life of Alfred*', *Cambridge Medieval Celtic Studies*, vol. 4 (1982), pp. 5–18.

20 *Asser's Life of King Alfred*, ed. W. H. Stevenson (rev. edn, Oxford, 1959).

21 C. R. Hart, 'Athelstan "half-king" and his family', *Anglo-Saxon England*, vol. 2 (1973), pp. 115–44 (p. 116, n. 1).

22 D. N. Dumville, 'The aetheling: a study in Anglo-Saxon constitutional history', *Anglo-Saxon England*, vol. 8 (1979), pp. 1–33 (pp. 1–2, 24).

23 Her name appears in *CS* 520: S 340. There is no reason to suppose she was the daughter of a king and she may have been related to Aethelwulf's ealdorman, Wulfhere (see above, p. 216).

24 Smyth, *Scandinavian Kings in the British Isles*, pp. 201 ff; T. K. Derry, 'The martyrdom of St Edmund, A.D. 869', *Historisk Tidsskrift*, vol. 66 (1987), pp. 157–63. On the manner of the death of Eadmund (and Aella), see R. Frank, 'Viking atrocity and skaldic verse: the rite of the blood-eagle', *English Historical Review*, vol. 99 (1984), pp. 332–43.

25 *Memorials of St Edmund's Abbey*, ed. T. Arnold, 3 vols (Rolls series, London, 1890–6), Vol. I, pp. 11 ff.; cf., Smyth, *Scandinavian Kings in the British Isles*, pp. 206–9.

26 Grierson and Blackburn, *Medieval European Coinage*, Vol. I, p. 294.

27 *The Chronicle of Aethelweard*, p. 36.

28 Smyth, *Scandinavian Kings in the British Isles*, pp. 224 ff. Compare, however, the comments of R. W. McTurk, 'Ragnarr Lodbrók in the Irish Annals', *Proceedings of the Seventh Viking Congress*, ed. B. Almqvist and D. Greene (Dundalk, 1976), pp. 93–123 (pp. 117 ff.) and D. Ó Corráin, 'High-kings, Vikings and other kings', *Irish Historical Studies*, vol. 21 (1978–9), pp. 283–323 (pp. 314 ff.).

29 On the identity of Hálfdan, compare Smyth, *Scandinavian Kings in the British Isles*, pp. 225–7, 242–5, 255 ff. with McTurk, 'Ragnarr Lodbrók in the Irish Annals', pp. 117 ff., and Ó Corráin, 'High-kings, Vikings and other kings', pp. 320 ff.

30 See also *The Chronicle of Aethelweard*, p. 40 (and Smyth, *Scandinavian Kings in the British Isles*, p. 242).

31 *Symeonis Monachi Opera Omnia*, Vol. I, pp. 56, 225: Vol. II, pp. 110, 377, 397; *Flores Historiarum*, Vol. I, p. 325.

32 *Symeonis Monachi Opera Omnia*, Vol. I, p. 225: *Flores Historiarum*, Vol. I, p. 325. Ricsige has been the subject of different interpretations. Smyth, *Scandinavian Kings in the British Isles*, p. 242, following the *Historia Regum* and *Flores Historiarum*, sees Ricsige as appointed by the Danes in 873 in succession to Ecgberht, but according to Symeon of Durham the Northumbrians appointed Ricsige during the revolt (*Symeonis Monachi Opera Omnia*, Vol. I, p. 56) (cf., ibid., Vol. I, p. 225). F. M. Stenton, *Anglo-Saxon England* (3rd edn, Oxford, 1971), p. 251, thought that the Danes failed to re-establish control of York in 873 and that Ricsige continued to reign as king of the whole of Northumbria, but Hálfdan had certainly confined Ricsige north of the Tyne by 875 (*Symeonis Monachi Opera Omnia*, Vol. I, pp. 56, 202) and the likelihood is that this was the case before the Danes embarked on the conquest of Mercia. Ricsige is accorded a reign of three years in the Northumbrian regnal lists (*Symeonis Monachi Opera Omnia*, Vol. II, pp. 377, 397).

33 Smyth, *Scandinavian Kings in the British Isles*, pp. 255 ff.; Kirby, 'Northumbria in the ninth century', p. 19. On the community of St Cuthbert, Kirby, 'Northumbria in the ninth century', pp. 21–3, and D. Rollason, *Saints and Relics in Anglo-Saxon England* (Oxford, 1989), pp. 211–12.

34 *Symeonis Monachi Opera Omnia*, Vol. I, p. 225: Vol. II, pp. 111, 377, 391; *Flores Historiarum*, Vol. I, p. 327. The *Historia Regum* implies that Ecgberht was still alive in 883 (*Symeonis Monachi Opera Omnia*, Vol. II, p. 114).

35 *The Chronicle of Aethelweard*, p. 41.

36 ibid., p. 42.

37 Cf., Smyth, *Scandinavian Kings in the British Isles*, pp. 240 ff.

38 P. Stafford, *The East Midlands in the Early Middle Ages* (Leicester, 1985), p. 109. Smyth, *Scandinavian Kings in the British Isles*, p. 207 thinks that Ceolwulf was allocated his

share in east Mercia, but the western part of the kingdom seems a more likely area for him to have been consigned to, especially since it was in the west that Ealdorman Aethelred emerged *c.* 883; cf., Stenton, *Anglo-Saxon England*, pp. 254–5.

39 For this reconstruction, see Smyth, *Scandinavian Kings in the British Isles*, pp. 248 ff.

40 F. L. Attenborough (ed.), *The Laws of the Earliest English Kings* (Cambridge, 1922), pp. 98–101.

41 Grierson and Blackburn, *Medieval European Coinage*, Vol. I, p. 318.

42 *Hemingi Chartularium Ecclesiae Wigorniensis*, ed. T. Hearne (Oxford, 1723), Vol. I, p. 242.

43 R. H. M. Dolley and C. E. Blunt, 'The chronology of the coins of Alfred the Great', in R. H. M. Dolley (ed.), *Anglo-Saxon Coins* (London, 1961), pp. 77–95 (pp. 80–1); Grierson and Blackburn, *Medieval European Coinage*, Vol. I, p. 312.

44 Cf., Brooks, 'England in the ninth century: the crucible of defeat', pp. 1–20.

45 P. Wormald, 'Viking studies: whence and whither?', in R. T. Farrell (ed.), *The Vikings* (London, 1982), pp. 128, 53 (p. 139).

46 Cf., Brooks, 'England in the ninth century: the crucible of defeat', p. 2.

47 R. R. Darlington, 'Anglo-Saxon Wiltshire', in R. B. Pugh and E. Crittall (eds), *A History of Wiltshire*, Vol. II (The Victoria County History of England, London, 1955), p. 7.

48 Nelson, '"A king across the sea": Alfred in continental perspective', p. 55.

49 Cf., ibid., p. 53.

50 Smyth develops this aspect: *Scandinavian Kings in the British Isles*, pp. 251–5, 255 ff.

51 Brooks, 'England in the ninth century: the crucible of defeat', p. 9.

52 Cf., R. H. C. Davies, 'Alfred the Great: propaganda and truth', *History*, vol. 56 (1971), pp. 169–82 (pp. 170–3, 180–1).

53 J. Campbell, 'The Anglo-Norman state in administrative history', *Essays in Anglo-Saxon History* (London and Ronceverte, 1986), pp. 171–89 (pp. 185–6).

54 See further, now, P. Stafford, *Unification and Conquest : A Political and Social History of England in the Tenth and Eleventh Centuries* (London, 1989).

Appendix

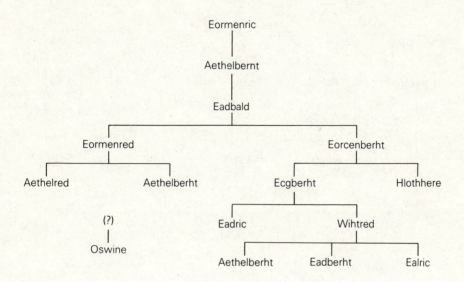

Figure 1 The descent of the kings of Kent from Eormenric

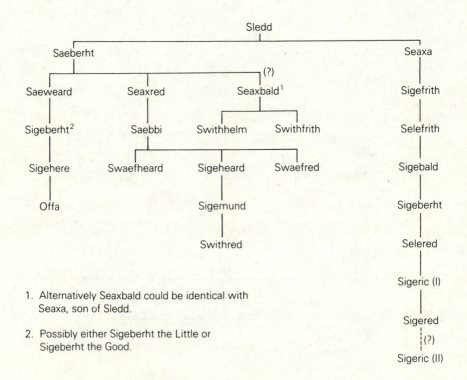

1. Alternatively Seaxbald could be identical with
   Seaxa, son of Sledd.

2. Possibly either Sigeberht the Little or
   Sigeberht the Good.

Figure 2 The descent of the kings of the East Saxons from Sledd

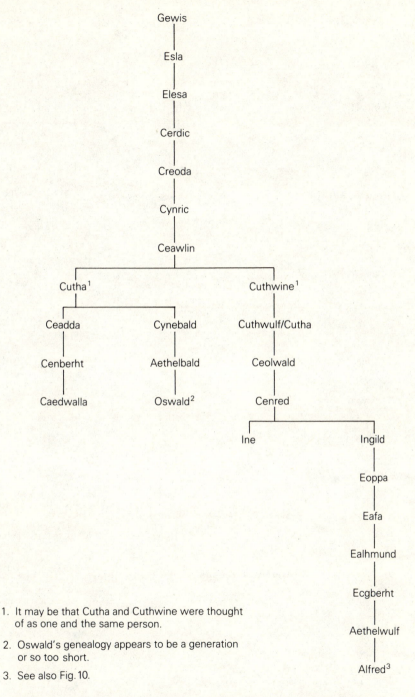

Gewis
|
Esla
|
Elesa
|
Cerdic
|
Creoda
|
Cynric
|
Ceawlin

Cutha[1]

Ceadda   Cynebald

Cenberht   Aethelbald

Caedwalla   Oswald[2]

Cuthwine[1]

Cuthwulf/Cutha
|
Ceolwald
|
Cenred

Ine   Ingild
|
Eoppa
|
Eafa
|
Ealhmund
|
Ecgberht
|
Aethelwulf
|
Alfred[3]

1. It may be that Cutha and Cuthwine were thought of as one and the same person.

2. Oswald's genealogy appears to be a generation or so too short.

3. See also Fig. 10.

Figure 3   The official genealogy of King Alfred, indicating also the alleged descent of Caedwalla, Ine and the aetheling Oswald

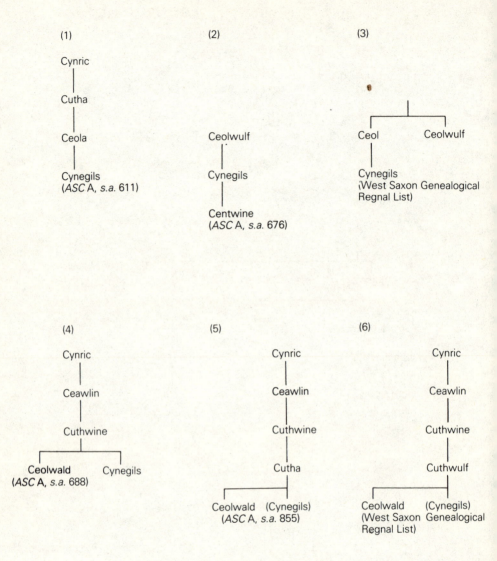

Figure 4 Cynegils in the genealogies

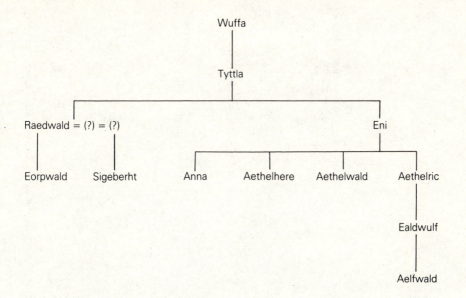

Figure 5 The descent of the kings of the eastern Angles from Wuffa

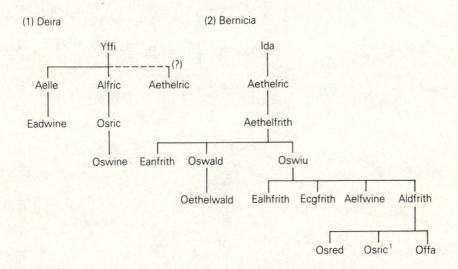

1. Alternatively, Osric could have been a son of Ealhfrith, son of Oswiu.

Figure 6 The descent of the kings of the northern Angles in the sixth and seventh centuries

(1) Deira

Aelle (569–99 or 570–600; or 571–99 or 572–600)

Aethelric (599–604 or 600–605)

Osric (633–34 or 634–35)

Oswine (642–51 or 643–52)
Oethelwald (651–55 or 652–56)
Ealhfrith (655 or 656–c.665)
Ecgfrith (c.665–70, or c.665–71)[1]
Aelfwine (?–679)[1]

[1] Sub-kings

(2) Bernicia

Ida (547–59 or 548–60)
Glappa (559–60 or 560–61)
Adda (560–68 or 561–69)
Aethelric (568–72 or 569–73)
Theodric (572–79 or 573–80)
Frithuwald (579–85 or 580–86)
Hussa (585–92 or 586–93)
Aethelfrith (592–604 or 593–605)

Eanfrith (633–34 or 634–35)

Oswiu (642–55 or 643–56)

(3) Deira and Bernicia

Aethelfrith (604–16 or 605–17)
Eadwine (616–33 or 617–34)

Oswald (634–42 or 635–43)

Oswiu (655–70 or 656–71)

Ecgfrith (670–85 or 671–85)
Aldfrith (685–704 or 685–705)
Eadwulf (704 or 705)
Osred (704–16 or 705–16).

Figure 7 Northern Anglian royalty and possible alternative regnal dates in the sixth and seventh centuries

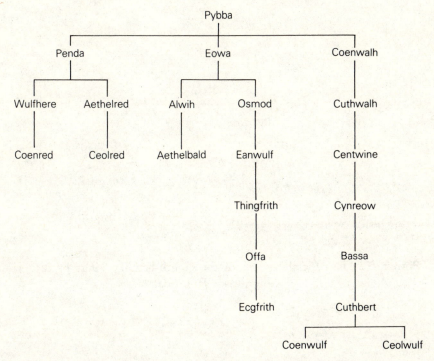

Figure 8 The official descent of the kings of the Mercians from Pybba

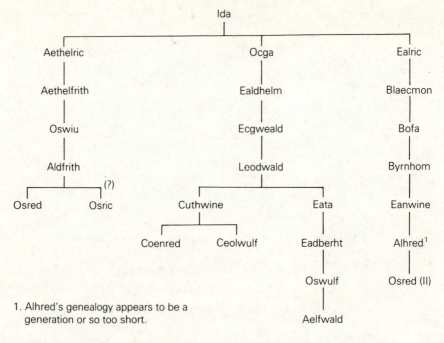

1. Alhred's genealogy appears to be a
   generation or so too short.

Figure 9 The official descent of the eighth-century kings of the
Northumbrians from Ida

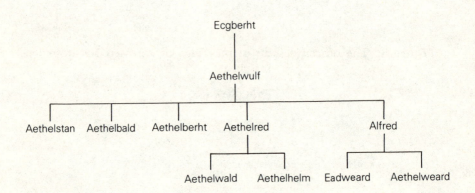

Figure 10 The relationship of the kings and princes of the West
Saxons in the ninth century

Index